W9-CBI-628

The Hidden Pope

Also by Darcy O'Brien

Power to Hurt
A Dark and Bloody Ground
Margaret in Hollywood
Murder in Little Egypt
Two of a Kind: The Hillside Stranglers
The Silver Spooner
A Way of Life, Like Any Other
Patrick Kavanagh
W. R. Rodgers
The Conscience of James Joyce

The Hidden Pope

The Untold Story of a Lifelong Friendship That Is Changing the Relationship between Catholics and Jews

•

The Personal Journey of John Paul II and Jerzy Kluger

Darcy O'Brien

Daybreak® Books
An Imprint of Rodale Books
New York, New York

Copyright © 1998 by Darcy O'Brien

All rights reserved. No part of this publication may be reproduced or transmitted in any form or by any means, electronic or mechanical, including photocopying, recording, or any other information storage and retrieval system, without the written permission of the publisher.

Printed in the United States of America on acid-free ♾, recycled paper ♲

Cover Design: Barbara de Wilde
Interior Design: Faith Hague
Cover Photograph: AP/World Wide Photos

Library of Congress Cataloging-in-Publication Data

O'Brien, Darcy.
The hidden Pope : the untold story of a lifelong friendship that is changing the relationship between Catholics and Jews / [Darcy O'Brien].
p. cm.
ISBN 0–87596–478–8 hardcover
1. John Paul II, Pope, 1920– —Friends and associates. 2. Kluger, Jerzy—Friends and associates. 3. John Paul II, Pope, 1920– —Childhood and youth. 4. Kluger, Jerzy—Childhood and youth. 5. Popes—Biography. 6. Jews—Poland—Biography. I. Title.
BX1378.5.O24 1998
282'.092—dc21
[B] 97–48680

Distributed in the book trade by St. Martin's Press

2 4 6 8 10 9 7 5 3 1 hardcover

OUR PURPOSE

"We publish books that empower people's minds and spirits."

This book is dedicated

to respect and love

between Christians and Jews

"As Christians and Jews, following the example of the faith of Abraham, we are called to be a blessing for the world. This is the common task awaiting us. It is therefore necessary for us, Christians and Jews, to be first a blessing to one another."

—John Paul II, on the fiftieth anniversary of the uprising in the Warsaw Ghetto, April 6, 1993

"To proselytize is not an attitude of love, nor is it one of knowledge."

—Johannes Cardinal Willebrands, in conversation with the author, Rome, 1996

Selected Personal and Place Names

Banas (BAHN-ahs), Stanislaw—Classmate
Beer, Regina "Ginka" (GING-kah)—Schoolmate and actress
Bernas (BHER-nahs), Zdzislaw—Classmate
Bojes (BOY-yesh), Teofil—Classmate
Czestochowa (Ches-toe-CHO-vah)—Pilgrimage site
Czuprynski (Shoo-PRIN-ski), Tadeusz—Classmate
Deskur (DES-koo), Andrzej Maria Cardinal—Informal adviser to Kluger at the Vatican
Dziwisz (DGEE-vish), Monsignor Stanislaw—Personal secretary to Pope John Paul II
Figlewicz (FEEG-le-vitch), Father Kazimierz—High school teacher, later curate of Wawel Cathedral
Kalwaria (Kahl-VAHR-ee-ah) Zebrzydowska (Zeb-rzh-ee-DOW-skah)—Pilgrimage site
Kazimierz (Kah-zhee-MEERSH)—Polish king; Jewish district of Krakow
Kesek (KESS-ek), Wiktor—Classmate
Kluger (KLU-guerre), Jerzy (YER-zee) "Jurek" (YUR-ek)
Kotlarczyk (Kot-LAR-chick), Mieczyslaw—Drama teacher and founder of Rhapsodic Theater
Krolikiewicz (Kro-lick-ee-YAY-vitch) Kwiatkowska (Kvi-at-KOV-ska), Halina—Schoolmate and actress
Kuczkowski (Kootch-KOV-ski), Monsignor Mikolaj—Violinist, lawyer, legal counsel to Archdiocese of Krakow
Kus (KOOSH), Jan—Classmate
Malinski (Mah-LEEN-ski), Father Mieczyslaw—Secret seminarian in Krakow; biographer of Pope John Paul II
Mickiewicz (Meets-kee-YAY-vitch), Adam—Poet
Norwid (NOR-vid), Cyprian—Poet
Oswiecim (Ohs-VEE-chim)—Neighboring town, renamed Auschwitz by the Germans
Pilsudski (Peel-SZOOD-ski), Marshal Jozef—World War I hero, later president of Poland
Romanski (Ro-MAHN-ski), Tomasz—Classmate
Sapieha (Sah-PEE-hah), Adam Stefan Cardinal—Archbishop of Krakow
Selinger (SEL-inger), Zygmunt—Classmate
Silkowski (Sil-KOV-ski), Zbigniew—Classmate
Slowacki (Slow-VAHK-ee), Juliusz—Poet-playwright
Szczepanska (Shep-AN-skah), Helena—Wojtyla's neighbor; Tesia's teacher
Tyranowski (Teer-an-OV-ski), Jan—Spiritual mentor
Wadowice (Vahd-oh-VEE-che)—Wojtyla's and Kluger's hometown
Wawel (VAH-vel) Cathedral—Historic Krakow cathedral where Wojtyla celebrated his first mass
Wojtyla (Vo-TEE-yah), Karol "Lolek" (LO-lek)
Zweig (Zv-eye-g), Leopold—Classmate

Chapter 1

A FEW MINUTES BEFORE SEVEN IN ROME ON THE EVENING OF MONDAY, October 16, 1978, *Ingegnere* Jerzy Kluger was lying in the dentist's chair with one of those tubes dangling from his lower lip. He half-listened to the radio that was always playing there, trying to let his mind drift.

A filling had broken off at lunch, and he drove directly from his office after the dentist agreed to fit him in. As someone who had survived a Russian slave labor camp and other inconveniences, having a tooth fixed was hardly a crisis. It was the interruption of routine that put him out of sorts.

Jerzy Kluger has the personality of a Beethoven symphony. He has a sweetness beyond words, especially in regard to his children and grandchild, but it can give way in an instant to resounding kettle drums. To him, life is a grand passion to which he clings like an obsessive lover. To keep anxiety at bay, he invents rigid schedules for himself and spends at least ten hours each weekday at his business. He is impatient with interfering trivia and apt to snap at someone who is making ado about nothing, "If that is the worst thing that's ever happened to you, you should thank God," although he never specifies the genuine tragedies that he has known. Up at dawn, in the office by eight, he lives by a maxim that he remembers hearing his grandfather say: "You are a long time dead."

On that day in the dentist's office, Jerzy was fifty-seven. He had few physical complaints other than pains in his feet and a susceptibility to pneumonia, legacies of the labor camp. Saturdays were for tennis; he still played doubles with the intensity that once took him to some of the sport's most renowned courts. At five feet ten inches, he had the tough physique of an athlete, but his soft, blue-green eyes and moderate features made him appear warm, even cuddly. Inwardly, he was wary of predators, who seemed to lurk everywhere apart from his family and a trusted friend.

In the dentist's chair, he felt trapped. The music didn't help. It sounded like Wagner or something equally oppressive.

Suddenly the music stopped in midswoon. An announcer interrupted the broadcast to take listeners to Saint Peter's Square. Jerzy heard the sounds of restless crowds of believers. A single voice exulted, "*Habemus Papam!*"

Latin had not been his strongest suit in school. He would sooner tinker with an automobile than master the ablative absolute, although he is fluent in Italian and English, competent in German and Russian, and, of course, at home in his native Polish—all tongues with a practical use. The Italian word *Ingegnere*, which customarily precedes his name as a polite form of address in the European style, means "engineer" and acknowledges his degrees. The Latin phrase from the radio, however, was plain enough.

"They have chosen a new pope at last," the dentist said, suspending operations. "The long wait is over."

With the apparatus still lodged in his mouth, Jerzy managed only a grunt. "I, too, am intensely curious about who will become the next pope," he would have added if he had been able. "You probably think that since I am a Jew, I have no interest in such things, but you are quite mistaken. All the same, I wish you would be kind enough to tend to your job so that I can get home to a glass of wine and some dinner!" He rolled up his eyes to see the dentist, idle pick in hand, eagerly turning up the volume.

This papal conclave, the second within two months, had been going on for three days, with black smoke escaping the Sistine

Chapel chimney several times to indicate a continuing lack of consensus among the cardinals. Even at the Parioli Tennis Club over the weekend, all anyone could talk about was who would be the new pope and whether he would be another Italian. Men were calculating odds, claiming to have the inside dope. Jerzy gathered that Cardinal Siri, the conservative who was going to turn back the reforms of Vatican II that had frightened some into thinking that the Church was rolling downhill like a snowball headed for hell, had entered as the three-to-one favorite. The deadlock persisted through Sunday, and interest shifted to the Florentine, Cardinal Benelli, with a longshot Frenchman and a Dutchman moving up.

Jerzy, who usually loved the gossip bubbling at his club, an elegant enclave near his apartment, had stayed uncharacteristically reserved in public about this competition. Some members might even have considered an interest in the matter inappropriate for a Jew. It was amazing how these sophisticated Romans thrived on news from the Vatican. They were worldly-wise, gold-skinned wizards at business, but when it came to rumors from behind those ancient walls, they devoured every scrap. A papal election, like the World Cup or nearly so, excited every social and economic stratum in Italy. If it had been merely the question of a new prime minister, few would have given it the time of day because it seemed that there was a new one elected nearly every month.

The irony was not lost on Jerzy that he, one of a handful of Jewish members of his club, had as close a contact within the College of Cardinals as any of the Catholics. At that moment, an old school chum of his, who happened to be the Archbishop of Krakow, was locked up in the chapel with the rest of the cardinals and had even been mentioned as a candidate. Jerzy had no idea whom his friend favored or whether he even wished so unimaginable a distinction for himself. The odds seemed to be prohibitively against any non-Italian, let alone one from behind the Iron Curtain. Nevertheless, Jerzy was rooting for his friend, not merely for personal reasons but also because he thought Karol Wojtyla was such a wonderful fellow that having him as head of the Roman Catholic Church would be a great thing for the human race.

Not that he had mentioned any of this to anyone. It was not the sort of thing one discussed. He would never do anything to compromise the friendship that he valued more than anything else in the world, except for his family. It was a bond beyond price that made him feel blessed—a precious link to the distant, happy past.

"*Ioannem Paulum Secundum!*" the radio announced. The crowd let out a swelling roar.

"Did you catch his real name?" the dentist asked. "Is he an Italian?"

Irritated, Jerzy removed the tube from his mouth. "It will be on the television later," he said. "We will learn everything so much better that way. I am sure he is Italian. Meanwhile, why don't you finish with my tooth, if you don't mind? I could grow a beard lying here. You can put the saddle on the donkey, but it takes a stick to make him move!"

"Shhh! The *Santo Padre* speaks!" the dentist admonished.

Constrained to listen, Jerzy heard a mellifluous baritone offer praise to Our Lord Jesus Christ. Slowly the voice continued, "I do not know whether I can explain myself well in your—our—Italian language. If I make a mistake, you will correct me. And so I present myself to you all to confess our common faith, our hope...."

"What kind of an accent is that?" the dentist asked.

"Polish!" Jerzy bellowed.

He struggled up from the chair, madly trying to free his arms from the smock and shouting, "It's Lolek! Lolek is the pope!"

"I beg your pardon?"

Jerzy grabbed the dentist by the shoulders. "It's Wojtyla, don't you see? I know him!"

"You know the pope?" the dentist asked skeptically.

"He is my friend! I recognized his voice immediately! He is, like me, a boy from Wadowice!" Jerzy explained excitedly.

"Congratulations, *Ingegnere* Kluger. Perhaps he will make you a cardinal." The dentist looked at him askance.

"I have to use your telephone."

"Certainly. But His Holiness may be busy just now. You could try to reach the Queen of England," the dentist said.

The receptionist had already gone home. Still in the smock, Jerzy sat at her desk and with trembling fingers dialed home. Shouting into the phone, he reeled off the news in a jumble of Italian, Polish, and English that only his wife, Renée, could have understood. He told her he would bring champagne.

"Holy Mother of God," his wife said.

Later that evening, Monsignor Stanislaw Dziwisz, who had been Cardinal Wojtyla's personal secretary for many years, telephoned the Klugers to invite them to meet His Holiness a week later at a special reception in the Vatican. Pope John Paul II, as the man christened Karol Jozef Wojtyla had named himself in honor of his short-lived predecessor, John Paul I, was calling this informal gathering "Farewell to the Motherland." He was personally inviting his closest Polish friends in Rome to join him in welcoming thousands journeying from Poland to celebrate the elevation of one of their own to the papacy. Wojtyla was the first non-Italian pontiff since Adrian VI, a Dutchman who was elected in 1522 and died the next year. And, as Jerzy knew, he was deeply attached to his homeland.

AS INSTRUCTED, THE KLUGERS ARRIVED AT THE PAUL VI AUDITORIUM, A modern structure adjacent to Saint Peter's Basilica, late the following Monday afternoon. The guests were asked to assemble there to be addressed by various members of the Polish hierarchy and, later, by the new pope himself. A few would be honored first by being summoned individually to a room backstage, where His Holiness would greet them in a succession of private audiences. In the enormous hall, which was designed for concerts, the atmosphere was a combination of religious happening and pep rally. To the pope's countrymen, this acknowledgment seemed less a farewell than a sign that they would not be forgotten.

Jerzy, Renée, their daughter Linda, and her daughter, Stephania, who was eight, mingled in the great hall with perhaps three thousand other guests. The Klugers' other daughter, Lesley, was at home, ill with the flu and frustrated at not being able to attend. Jerzy and

Renée knew a few of the other guests, mostly priests. It occurred to him that of all the people in the hall, he had undoubtedly known the new pope the longest. Even now, he thought of him in terms of his familiar old name from their school days—Lolek, the diminutive of Karol (which in English is "Charles").

Among this group of Poles, Jerzy had by far the least direct contact with the homeland. Travel to and from Communist Poland was difficult at best, but since World War II, he had never had the least desire to return there. Correspondence with Lolek, whom he often saw during the archbishop's frequent trips to Rome, and occasional phone calls were enough.

His business—importing tractors and other heavy equipment—took him all over Europe and to North and South America. He was often on business in West Germany. Yet he had not set foot in Poland since departing on a train to Russia in November of 1939, and he saw no reason why he ever would. It was not an attractive prospect to see his native land, some memories of which he held in paradoxical affection, under Russian Communist domination. But his aversion had deeper origins: he had no surviving family there.

In the auditorium, no names had yet been called. Protocol, Jerzy assumed, would dictate that Church dignitaries and Polish government officials be summoned first, according to rank. The order would place him near to last; it could take hours. Then suddenly, the words "*Ingegnere Jerzy Kluger e famiglia!*" were broadcast over a loudspeaker. He was stunned.

He turned to Renée as if for verification of their identity. She nodded toward the stage, where Monsignor Dziwisz, with that slight movement of upraised fingers to prompt the faithful that only priests seem to master, indicated that they should approach.

So it was that the last became first. Backstage, John Paul II was seated in the green room on a high-backed, white-upholstered chair. He was wearing the simple white papal garments that would be his public apparel until his death.

Monsignor Dziwisz, with a smile on his usually dour face, ushered them in. The pontiff himself was beaming as he stood to greet them with outstrectched arms. Somehow Jerzy had expected something grander—pomp, a throne, flourishes—but there was Lolek, as disarmingly unpretentious as always.

"Jurek," the pope said, addressing his friend with the familiar diminutive of his name (in English, Jerzy is "George"). "How wonderful to see all of you. How pretty Stephania looks, as always." He spoke in Polish, so the child, whose thick blond hair fell straight and shining to her shoulders, missed the compliment. But she caught her name and ran to him. He lifted her into his arms and gently patted her face. She hugged his neck as if he were her favorite uncle.

Jerzy never slept much anyway, but he certainly had not the previous night. His mind wrestled with memories, and he wondered if Lolek would already have changed and become unapproachably grand, too exalted to touch. In reality, however, his friend seemed disconcertingly normal. If Lolek had not been wearing those clothes and the white yarmulke-like cap to replace the red one that he had worn as a cardinal, Jerzy might have forgotten what had happened. How was one supposed to greet the Vicar of Christ? As His Holiness lowered Stephania gently to the floor, Jerzy also wondered whether it made any difference that he had often played table tennis with this old friend who was now the Holy Father.

Before he could decide what to say or do, he found himself enwrapped in the papal arms. Impulsively, he bent one knee and bowed his head to kiss the famous Fisherman's ring, but he failed to reach it. Instantly, he felt that strong right hand grip his elbow and lift him upright.

"You must never bow your knee to me, Jurek," John Paul II said. "Stand straight as you always have."

THE HEADLINE IN A ROMAN NEWSPAPER THE NEXT MORNING READ "POPE Grants First Audience to Hebrew Friend."

Chapter 2

JERZY KLUGER THOUGHT THAT JOHN PAUL II CHOSE HIM AS THE FIRST PERson to be granted a private audience simply because the pope had known him longer than any of the other Poles who had gathered in the auditorium. Born within a year of one another, Jerzy and the new pope had grown up together in Wadowice, a small town in southern Poland. The Holy Father believed in Providence, did he not? If a Jew was first, so be it.

From the way the media highlighted their meeting, others were bound to place great significance on this honor as well. Jerzy knew his old friend well enough to assume that he would anticipate the reaction of others and would enjoy it.

After living obscurely in Rome for twenty-five years, Jerzy suddenly found himself something of a celebrity. To interviewers he said only what he believed, that his audience with the *Santo Padre* had been purely a personal occasion. Had there been other old schoolmates present, the pope undoubtedly would have seen them first. That Jerzy happened to be Jewish showed only that John Paul II was above vulgar distinctions.

To the Jewish community of Rome, however, Jerzy's privilege evoked fond memories of another pontiff. There was a story about Pope John XXIII that circulated among the Roman Jewish community. It continues to be told today, even by bishops, but it is heard more often among the fifteen thousand Jews who live in the Eternal City, four of whose families trace their Roman roots back to the second century before Christ.

On a Saturday early in his papacy, John XXIII was being driven northward along the River Tiber. When his car was slowed by traffic along the Lungotevere Cenci, he noticed a building that he didn't recognize. Its Assyrian-Babylonian architecture may have reminded him of places that he recalled from his days as nuncio in Istanbul. Soberly dressed people approached and passed between columns to enter it. As if marking an oasis, slender palms loomed from an adjacent courtyard, adding to the Levantine effect.

"What is this *palazzo*?" Pope John asked.

"That is the great temple of the Jews," his driver said. Pope John told him to stop.

The familiar figure, large and round and with a face that radiated benevolence, emerged from the limousine. He stood there for a moment, alone in white on the busy boulevard, gazing at Hebrew characters chiseled on a gray granite slab affixed to the facade. Moving his upraised fingers, he silently blessed this place and its people. Then he sped away toward Vatican City, which lies less than a mile from the temple, across the Tiber.

Pope John XXIII encouraged democratic forces within the Church, largely on the strength of his personal goodness, to shift the emphasis of Roman Catholicism from a religion of fear and punishment to one of welcome and hope. His tangible achievement was the Second Vatican Council (Vatican II), which, among many administrative and liturgical changes, issued the single most revolutionary document in the history of the Church. It had to do with the Jews.

This document is called *Nostra Aetate* (*In Our Time*). In relation to it, previous doctrinal changes over the centuries were minor. The doctrine of the Immaculate Conception, for example, which proclaimed as dogma in 1854 that the Virgin Mary was born free from the taint of Original Sin, was the endorsement of an idea that had been debated within the Church for more than five hundred years. The idea that the Jews were responsible for the death of Christ was never seriously questioned within the Church until after World War II.

Nostra Aetate, adopted by the council in 1965, declared as false an idea that had been basic to Christian doctrine for at least seventeen hundred years of unremitting hatred and contempt. This view was that the Jews had killed Christ and that, as a people, they could never atone for that gravest of sins in any way other than by becoming Christians. John XXIII did not live to see the adoption of this monumental reversal, a radical reinterpretation of the Gospels and commentary on them. But it was he who conceived of it, approved its original text, and selected those who shepherded it on its perilous progress through the council. On the night of the pope's death, the Chief Rabbi of Rome and other leaders of the Jewish community gathered with hundreds of thousands of Catholics in Saint Peter's Square to mourn him and to pray that his benevolence had not died with him.

Fifteen years after the death of John XXIII, the memory of his spontaneous blessing of the temple and of *Nostra Aetate* revived when news reached the Roman Jewish community that a new pope had begun his papacy with a gesture that seemed reminiscent—or was it? Who was this Jerzy Kluger? A Polish Jew, a relative newcomer to Rome, he was not well-known there among his co-religionists. And it was said that he was married to a Catholic. What kind of a Jew was he? Where did his loyalties lie?

The questions persisted because not much progress had been made toward Catholic-Jewish reconciliation since John XXIII, whose papacy was as brief (1958–63) as it was decisive, and Vatican II. It was one thing for the Church, after centuries of hatred and contempt, to declare the people of Abraham innocent of Deicide. It was another for legions of the faithful to hear this message, absorb it, and accept the profound implications for Christian belief and practice.

A certain amount of interfaith dialogue had taken place since 1965, especially in America, but thirteen years later, Catholic schoolchildren were still being taught that the New Covenant had supplanted the Old Covenant. What did removing from the Jews the charge of having killed the Son of God mean in terms of the viability of Judaism itself? Weren't the Jews still expected to convert? What was contemporary Judaism but, at best, the vestige of a religion that the coming of the Messiah had rendered obsolete? Was contempt for Jews now to be supplanted by, at most, its condescending ally, pity? None of these matters had been resolved.

Politically, too, things were at a standstill. Decades after the Holocaust and thirty years after such oppositional entities as the United States and the Soviet Union had recognized the State of Israel, the Vatican was still withholding formal diplomatic recognition of the Jewish nation. This was a matter of serious offense to Jews everywhere and one with disquieting theological as well as political ramifications. No official Vatican document, not even *Nostra Aetate*, had ever mentioned the State of Israel or the centrality of the Land in Jewish identity and thought.

One of the salient aspects of Judaism is its emphasis on pride of place or *Eretz* (in Hebrew, "the Land") Israel. The Land was as important to the Jewish sense of identity as it was to the Irish, the French, the Americans, the Palestinians, or, for that matter, the Poles. "A nation is the same people living in the same place," as Leopold Bloom put it with eloquent simplicity in James Joyce's *Ulysses*. Yet not even the beloved John XXIII, amid all the proclamations of reconciliation with the Jews, had ever so much as uttered a reference to Israel or its government.

Pope Paul VI, on his personal pilgrimage to the Holy Land in 1964, had managed with pointed omission never to speak the name of Israel or to enunciate the proper title of its head of state. He referred to the president only as "Your Excellency," a form of address that placed him on a level equal to that of a bishop and below that of a cardinal, who would at least have merited "Your Eminence."

Offended by this and other aspects of Paul VI's visit, Orthodox rabbis in particular called for Jewish withdrawal from interfaith dialogue and concluded that the Church had never given up its proselytizing mission. Had it not been Christian doctrine since the second century that Jews were banished from the Promised Land as punishment for rejecting and killing Christ and that they had no right to return unless they converted? What other motive could lie behind the Church's refusal to formally acknowledge the State of Israel?

Although no Church policy toward the matter was ever publicly spelled out in detail, Vatican officials informally cited several reasons for withholding recognition. They included (1) concern about Arab reprisals against Christians in Lebanon and elsewhere—between one hundred fifty thousand and one hundred eighty thousand were living within the area known as the Holy Land, some sixty thousand in Jerusalem alone; (2) insistence on resolution of the question of a homeland for displaced Palestinians; (3) the matter of guaranteed access for Christians to holy places, especially in Jerusalem; and (4) the unsettled nature of Israel's borders.

Of these, the question of guaranteed access to holy places seemed the least contentious since Israel had controlled Jerusalem since the 1967 war. As for the matter of disputed borders, Israel was hardly the only nation with that sort of problem. The question of a Palestinian state was the most volatile and intractable issue in the region. And with the Arab boycott of Israel at its most rigorous, the issue of reprisals against Christians was a genuine concern.

From the Jewish point of view, however, the Church would surely be in a better position to mediate such issues with full diplomatic representation in place. By 1977, a full year before John Paul II's election, Israel's new prime minister, Menachem Begin, and President Anwar Sadat of Egypt had reached accommodation through the Camp David Accords, which were mediated by U.S. President Jimmy Carter.

It was difficult for the Israelis to accept Catholic rebuffs after Sadat's initiative, for which he later paid with his life. Nor were Jews convinced by the line favored by the Vatican Secretariat of State, which was that formal recognition was not a matter of such importance. Jews felt that for both political and religious reasons, recognition was extremely important.

Israel was a nation struggling to survive. Recognition by the Vatican, the oldest continuous diplomatic entity in the world, would strongly encourage that survival, in large part because Roman Catholicism was the most widespread religious denomination. Add to this the historic ties and the enmities between Christianity and Judaism—including the ancient denial of the Jews' "right of return"—and the importance of formal diplomatic recognition becomes very obvious. By denying recognition, the Church implied symbolic complicity with the Arab nations (other than Egypt) that refused to accept the existence of a Jewish state.

Jews found Catholic intransigence difficult to accept at face value. It was widely believed that within the Curia, or papal court, there existed a powerful band of anti-Semites. These Jew-haters had acquiesced to *Nostra Aetate,* but since then, they had worked to blunt its effectiveness and had largely succeeded in doing so.

For centuries, Catholic children had been taught that only their Church offered the keys to heaven: the status of Protestants was doubtful, and that of Jews was hopeless. To this powerful cadre within the Curia, it was unthinkable to accept Jews as equals. Therefore, to accept that the Jews had the right to return to the Promised Land was equally abhorrent, tantamount to surrendering a key premise of Triumphalism. In this view, heaven was an exclusive club. If Jews are admitted, the thinking went, what would be the point of belonging?

The persistence of this mind-set is illustrated by an exchange between a Catholic and a Jew that reportedly occurred in Rome in 1964 during the Vatican II debates concerning *Nostra Aetate.* At a diplomatic function, conservative Ernesto Cardinal Ruffini, Archbishop of Palermo, happened to encounter Nathan Ben-Horin, who was First Secretary at the Israeli Embassy. Ben-Horin's duties at that time related to the Italian Republic, not the Vatican, so it was on religious rather than diplomatic grounds that the cardinal greeted him.

"I understand," Cardinal Ruffini said cheerfully, "that we are about to pardon the Jews."

"Excuse me," Ben-Horin replied, "but I wasn't feeling so guilty."

Those who feared and resented such condescension or contempt within the Curia—specifically the Vatican Secretariat of State—believed that it would take a very strong pontiff to buck the diehards and progress toward the recognition of Israel. There had been a few faintly hopeful signs after the 1967 war and Israel's assumption of control over Jerusalem, although Muslims, too, claimed the city as a holy place and vowed to retake at least part of it. Paul VI, acceding to what appeared to be political realities, occasionally began to actually utter the word *Israel* and issued personal letters of greeting to its president at New Year's. John Paul I twice mentioned Israel, in praising the Camp David Accords and in stressing the need for both Jewish and Palestinian rights, but this frail pontiff lasted scarcely a month in an office he had never desired to assume. These were slender straws, however, and hardly the commitment that Jews wished from the Vatican.

And now, what could be expected from this Pole? The new pope presented serious worries. He may have granted an audience to a Jew, but Jerzy Kluger represented no Jewish organization. The papal gesture in seeing him might be construed as nothing more than a variation on the old bromide, "Some of my best friends are Jews."

Suspicions about John Paul II had everything to do with his being Polish. He had lived in Poland all his life. Poles were considered inherently anti-Semitic, and the Polish Catholic Church was known as perhaps the most conservative of any. Could the kind of leadership it would take to circumvent anti-Semites in the Vatican be expected from such a man? Was it not likely that he was one himself? There was a saying current among Jews of Polish origin, of whom Prime Minister Begin was one, that "Poles drink anti-Semitism with their mothers' milk."

Chapter 3

JERZY KLUGER WAS IN HIS OFFICE ON THE VIA NOMENTANA THE MORNING after his meeting with the pope when he received a telephone call from Dr. Meir Mendes, whom he knew as the cultural counselor to the Israeli Embassy. Dr. Mendes had heard about Jerzy's reception by John Paul II and congratulated him on the honor. There were prominent Catholics, not to mention certain heads of state, who would live a lifetime without being granted such a privilege. Would it be possible, Dr. Mendes said rather playfully, for him to be granted an audience with the pope's friend?

"Of course, Dr. Mendes," Jerzy said. "I am at your disposal. This morning everyone wants to see me. I am like the Barber of Seville!" He suggested lunch in some small restaurant "where they don't charge you an arm and a leg for a crust of bread."

Dr. Mendes said that he preferred somewhere more private. He asked to meet as soon as possible, and he said that he would be grateful if Jerzy did not mention this rendezvous to anyone. Jerzy said that he understood, but he wondered what this could possibly be about.

That afternoon, the Israeli diplomat appeared at the Klugers' apartment on the third floor of Via Francesco Denza No. 19 in the Parioli district, only a few blocks from the embassy. This was a northern section of the city outside the ancient walls on the far side of the Borghesi gardens, an area that was built up in the frenzy of construction after World War II. If it lacked the allure of old, inner Rome—a place of orange aquatints and dark green shutters, of twisty streets smelling of bread and flowers and shellac—Parioli had its own seductive elegance. The brass and marble of luxurious shops, the good cars, the restaurants filled with sleek women and manicured men—this was the enclave of upper *borghesia.* Shaded villas, dating from before the profusion of fifties-style apartment buildings shot up, remained in what had once been a suburban haven for very rich families. Some of the villas were now foreign embassies, made conspicuous by the presence of armed *carabiniere* at their gates.

The Klugers had lived at the same address since moving to Rome from England in 1954. They were among the first tenants of their buff-colored building, which was all right angles and jutting balconies. That Parioli felt mostly new suited Jerzy. He retained little from the past, although even here there were improbable echoes.

Their street, which ran up and down a hill, emptied into the Viale Maresciallo Pilsudski, named in honor of Jozef Pilsudski, the great Polish military leader who drove the Soviets back from Warsaw, captured Kiev, and became chief of state of the newly independent Polish Republic in 1918. Every year on March 19, which was the Feast of St. Joseph and thus, in accordance with Polish custom, the marshal's "name day," Jerzy placed a red and a white rose, representing Poland's colors, at the foot of the Pilsudski Monument. The offering was in memory of his father, Wilhelm, who had served as an officer with Pilsudski's Legions and had revered the marshal as the founder of Polish independence and a protector of the Jews. Jerzy performed this ritual alone, standing in silence for a few minutes as the traffic hurried on behind him.

Had he chosen the location of his apartment because of its proximity to the Viale Pilsudski? When asked the question today, he only shrugs.

At the Klugers' flat, Dr. Mendes, who was in his sixties, sat in a soft chair beside the piano, on which family pictures rested in silver frames. Across the airy room, a life-size bust of Jerzy's mother, Rozalia, sat on a low shelf. To judge from the sculpture, which was the color of unbleached linen, she must have been a woman of exceptionally refined beauty, with a clean, smooth brow, straight hair drawn back, deep-set eyes, a narrow, beveled nose, and lips at once generous and precise. An aristocrat, one would have guessed. Only the slightly bowed neck compromised her serenity.

Jerzy sat on the couch against a wall adorned with one of the several canvases in the room that had been painted by nineteenth- and early twentieth-century Polish artists. This one was a pastel portrait of a Hapsburg princess by Teodor Axentowicz. Renée served tea.

Conversation turned at first to the Klugers' daughter Lesley, who worked at the embassy as Dr. Mendes's aide and made arrangements for visiting artists and musicians. Renée spoke of how warmly Lesley referred to Dr. Mendes and his wife, who, being Italian themselves, performed so effectively as cultural ambassadors.

"Unfortunately, I am not an ambassador," Dr. Mendes said, "though I do have a rather grand-sounding title in addition to my cultural duties. I am Minister Plenipotentiary in Charge of Contacts with the Holy See. Ambassador to the Holy See would be less cumbersome, in every sense." He alluded to the difficulties inherent in the lack of formal representation between the Vatican and Israel. Dr. Mendes added that his colleagues teased him about his ambiguous position by calling him "Monsignor Mendes." He had his contacts, but there was no one with whom he could deal directly and authoritatively on matters of state. The Vatican was Byzantine, if that was the right metaphor. You could ask one question and get a hundred evasions. And he remarked that to be a Jew there, representing Israel but without proper accreditation, "one feels at times like the uninvited guest."

"Perhaps the new *Santo Padre* will rectify this matter," Jerzy suggested. "Not that I know what is on his mind."

Dr. Mendes leaned forward and stared intently at Jerzy through thick spectacles. "You didn't perhaps discuss this matter with the *Santo Padre* at your meeting? Please forgive my asking."

"You can ask me anything, Dr. Mendes, believe me. But this was purely a personal meeting. A courtesy. I know nothing about such matters," Jerzy answered.

"I understand you have known John Paul II a long time."

"Of course. I am his school friend."

"I see. You did not discuss politics then, " Dr. Mendes offered.

"Dr. Mendes, I am just a businessman. I know about tractors, if you want to ask me about that," Jerzy demurred.

"But you know him quite well?"

"We played soccer together. In recent years, we have gone skiing. Monsignor Dziwisz is a terrific skier," Jerzy said.

Dr. Mendes sipped his tea and sighed. "So, *Ingegnere* Kluger," he said at last. "What is going to happen now?"

"To happen?" Jerzy responded.

"In your estimation, as a friend of the pope. What is going to happen now, with the Vatican and the Jews?"

"Oh, that. There is nothing to worry about."

"John Paul II, is he an anti-Semite?" Dr. Mendes probed.

"Wojtyla? Absolutely not," Jerzy affirmed. "Why would you ask such a thing? Because he is Polish?"

"Exactly."

Jerzy thought for a moment. He understood too well why Dr. Mendes or anyone else would assume that because Lolek was a Polish Catholic, he must be an anti-Semite. That was the nearly universal assumption about Poles. To say that they were friends was not enough. Jerzy wanted to make the strongest possible argument on the pope's behalf without appearing either naive or defensive.

"Of course I understand why you are asking the question," he began. "Let me put it this way, Dr. Mendes. Eighty to ninety percent of the citizens of this city are more anti-Semitic than he is. He is not an anti-Semite, not a bit of one. Listen, I know a thing or two about anti-Semitism—and about Poles!"

"I am sure you do. It's something I worry about. We are all concerned about it. After all that has happened, we are concerned about what will happen now with this new pope," said Dr. Mendes.

"John Paul II is a good man. On my life, I swear it," Jerzy insisted.

Jerzy had his own ideas about the Poles and anti-Semitism, but he was not about to argue them with Dr. Mendes or anyone else. The matter was too complicated, not to mention too controversial, and while Jerzy rarely hesitated to speak his mind—he was in fact known to be exceptionally blunt, a characteristic of which his wife often reminded him—he preferred to leave politics and religion for others to dispute. He was only sorry and a bit shocked, although he supposed that he should not have been, that his dear friend Lolek could be taken for an anti-Semite simply because he was Polish. He was confident that Wojtyla's transcendent innocence of any such vulgarities would become apparent to everyone over time. Other than trying to reassure Dr. Mendes or anyone else who might ask, there was nothing Jerzy could do.

Before leaving the apartment that afternoon, Dr. Mendes asked whether Jerzy expected to see the pope again in the near future.

"I am sure he is a very busy man these days," Jerzy replied. "I wouldn't presume that he would have much time for me now. I am not exactly an important person."

TWO WEEKS LATER, JERZY WAS IN HIS OFFICE—THREE RATHER GRUNGY, DARK rooms near the Porta Pia—discussing business problems with his partner, Kurt Rosenberg. Unfortunately, Rosenberg was not listening. As usual, all he wanted to talk about was Israel.

Their current project was to import General Motors air-conditioning units and modify them for installation in city buses. Jerzy was an admirer of American technology and of General Motors in particular. That morning, just before nine o'clock, he was holding forth on the virtue of simplicity in design, illustrating his argument with drawings in colored inks. He liked to draw. He had amused friends with his caricatures all his life, and his appointment calendar was a rainbow of names, times, and grotesque faces done in swoops and curls, looking reminiscent of a medieval illustrated manuscript. He explained to Rosenberg, who knew nothing about machines, that a way would have to be found to install their units in the roofs of buses. Rosenberg, annoyingly, was staring out the window.

"You could pay attention!" Jerzy said.

"I was just thinking," Rosenberg said, "that you really ought to speak to the pope about the Vatican and Israel. I could write an article about it."

"Not again!" Jerzy thought. Rosenberg had been pestering him on the subject every day. For all of the half-century that Jerzy had known him, Rosenberg had been obsessed with politics. Even back in Poland, he had cared about nothing except Jewish nationalism. Jerzy remembered that he had even had to repeat a year in school because he neglected his studies in pursuit of his Zionist passion. Of course, neither he nor any member of his family had actually emigrated from Poland to the Promised Land. He was the sort of Jew, Jerzy's father used to say with amusement, "who would use the money of a second Jew to send the third to Palestine." Rosenberg's ambition had always been to be a political journalist, writing on behalf of the Zionist cause.

"You must speak to the pope," he repeated.

Rosenberg was a small man, no taller than five feet three-and-a-half. In the old days, his hair had been black, but now he was practically bald. Every time Jerzy saw him, which was nearly every day, he could not help but think that Rosenberg's greatest achievement in life had been to qualify for the eight-hundred-meter run in interschool competition. That was a true honor. Alas, after running in first place nearly to the finish line, he had fallen at the last moment, fifty meters from the post. A tragedy. And now, in his rather sweet, mild, earnest, and persistent way, he still had visions of fulfilling his life as a great journalist on behalf of the Jewish homeland. It was another race that he was bound to lose. How could Jerzy explain this to him?

"Who am I," Jerzy asked, "Henry Kissinger?" In exasperation, he explained for the twentieth time that just because he knew Wojtyla, it didn't mean that the pope would discuss matters of international importance with him. How did he know when and if he would talk to the Holy Father again? If he was lucky, he'd receive a Christmas card.

"You must not forget Israel," Rosenberg said.

"How could I forget with you around to remind me? Can we

talk about the air conditioner?" He called attention to his drawing of the condenser. But how could Rosenberg appreciate it, when he was nearly color blind? Maybe if it were a Jewish condenser, he would pay attention!

Just after nine o'clock, his secretary buzzed to say that Monsignor Dziwisz was on the phone. Jerzy told her to put the monsignor through. Rosenberg was all ears.

"I would of course be delighted," Jerzy said into the phone. "One o'clock. I will be there."

Jerzy waited for Rosenberg to ask before telling him of the invitation to lunch at the Vatican. "Who will be there?" Rosenberg wanted to know. "Will it be just you and the pope eating this lunch?"

"How should I know?" Jerzy said. "Maybe you think I should have inquired about what is on the menu. Something tells me it won't be kosher."

UNTIL HE TURNED FROM THE LUNGOTEVERE CASTELLO ONTO THE VIA DELLA Consolazione and Saint Peter's came into view, Jerzy didn't realize that he didn't know exactly where he was going. Monsignor Dziwisz had instructed him to give his name at the gate, but where was that? Aside from his one time at the Paul VI Auditorium the previous month, his familiarity with the Vatican was only that of a sightseer. As for where the pope took his meals, he hadn't a clue.

On the premise that one thing would surely lead to another, he followed the flow of traffic to the left around the south side of Saint Peter's Square. Glancing at his watch, he saw that he was going to be a few minutes late no matter what. It may have been a mistake to waste time running home to change his shirt. As usual, he was dressed in a smart wool suit—he had always paid close attention to his wardrobe—and his red, gold, and blue tie of the Polish First Artillery. Since he owned six identical ties with these emblems of past glories, he was never without a fresh one.

He was jammed in among the other rushing drivers, sensing himself in danger of being compelled in an arc back toward the river, when to his right he caught sight of the very thing, a big gate, complete with sentries, that appeared to guard the entrance to that mysterious place, Vatican City.

Infuriating everyone else and failing only by a miracle to ignite a chain reaction of smashups, he screeched to a stop and forced his way to the right through blasts of horns, shouts, shaking fists, and the full repertoire of obscene Italian gestures, cutting across a phalanx of cars to reach the driveway to the gate. A Swiss guard, who must have witnessed this maneuver, stepped forward to intercept him.

"I am Kluger," he announced. He could feel sweat breaking out. The guard only stared at him. Another guard, more conventionally dressed, came up.

"*Ingegnere* Kluger," Jerzy said to him. "Monsignor Dziwisz said you would have my name. I am invited to lunch with the pope."

The second guard retreated to a telephone. Jerzy looked again at his watch. Five minutes past. Had the monsignor forgotten to give his name? Was there some mix-up? Did the guards think him mad, or a terrorist? They could arrest him. That would give Rosenberg plenty to laugh about.

The guard returned to say that Signor Kluger had unfortunately come to the wrong gate. The proper entrance was on the other side of Saint Peter's, on the Via di Porta Angelica. The guards there did indeed have his name.

Before Jerzy could plead that he was late and that it would take forever to wend his way through traffic to this other gate, the guard, with a friendly salute, said that if Signor Kluger would permit it, he would be pleased to accompany him and deliver him straight to his appointment.

With the guard directing from the passenger seat, Jerzy entered at the wrong gate and circled through the forbidden city, going past the rear of the basilica, various more recent and plainer buildings that appeared to be offices or apartments, and gardens with glimpses of fountains, a cluster of columns, tombs, and statuary. It was all a blur, especially with his eyeglasses half-fogged from sweat and the unseasonable humidity. He knew that the extent of Vatican City was less than one square mile, but it seemed larger than that. And it was so quiet, an island of repose in noisy, polluted Rome. Only the cars parked here and there were reminders that this was the twentieth century. With priests, some sashed in purple or red, strolling by in their soutanes, it could have been the Renaissance.

He could not help but think, "How many other Jews before me have wandered through here during the past millennium or so? Or am I the first?" The odds were extremely good that he was the first Jew ever invited to lunch with His Holiness.

The guard instructed him to drive straight into a passageway that led beneath the high facade of what he knew must be the Vatican Palace. These enormous connected structures house the greatest library in the world, some museums, the loggias done by Raphael, and, at the end facing Saint Peter's Square, the papal apartments, where from a window the Holy Father addresses the faithful. The way was narrow and dark, paved with stones, and it wound upward; it had been built for horses, not automobiles. They climbed to a landing where light shone through and another guard, recognizing his colleague, waved them ahead to another level—or was it two? Jerzy lost count. He considered himself lucky to have gone to the wrong gate after all. He would never have been able to navigate this tortuous route on his own.

Over a final rise they drove into the light of a great cobbled expanse open to the sky, enclosed by walls set with high windows marking two stories that were higher still.

"The Courtyard of Sixtus V," Jerzy's companion announced.

With a rich patina on its ancient, rain-beaten stones, the courtyard, half in shadow but dappled by sun, seemed aware of its great age. Off to one side, a double column of perhaps twenty Franciscan friars with white surplices over their brown robes marched in sandals along a wall and disappeared two by two into the palace. What supernal business could be theirs today? In his car, Jerzy felt absurd, as if he had fallen by mistake from a time machine. A coach-and-four would have been more like it. As it was, his was the only vehicle in sight, its diesel engine making an infernal racket that reverberated off the stones.

The guard guided him across this vast, hallowed emptiness toward a doorway, where a lone figure in a black cassock and biretta stood. It was Monsignor Dziwisz, his hands clasped at his waist in his usual on-duty manner; he raised a pair of fingers slightly in welcome. The guard told Jerzy to park anywhere.

With the engine off, the silence was nearly perfect. Only a distant siren penetrated from the world outside. The guard departed with a final salute, which Jerzy, out of old army reflex, returned. The monsignor led him inside to the pope's personal elevator.

As they ascended, Jerzy remembered climbing the stairs to the flat Lolek had shared with his father in Wadowice fifty years ago. What a long and surprising journey it had been!

Jerzy's initial impression of the papal apartments was of how dark they were. A large reception room was dimly lit, and heavy brown curtains, as if retained from wartime blackouts, covered the high windows. The floor, which was marble, was mostly covered by a utilitarian carpet, also brown. A large portrait on one wall was too smoky to identify. A faint mustiness added to the impression of a grand old hotel long past its prime.

"Lolek will become depressed in this place," Jerzy thought, "if somebody doesn't brighten it up a bit. It goes against his nature."

The small dining room was equally drab, but he was immediately cheered when he saw his friend—dressed in white and wearing the thick, dark gold papal cross as he must always do now—seated at the far end of the table. They embraced. Somehow the reality of what Lolek had become had not quite sunk in until then, yet he seemed much the same.

The table was set for four. Another priest, whom Monsignor Dziwisz introduced as Monsignor John Magee, was already seated to one side. Jurek should sit where he liked, the pope said, and for a moment Jerzy hesitated between the side and the foot of the table.

"I will sit down here at the end," he said at last, "just as I always did in the army. I always made a point of sitting as far away from my commanding officer as possible, so he wouldn't be watching me and asking me too many questions!"

"Very good, Jurek," the pope said. "From now on, that place is reserved for you."

The food, Jerzy saw to his delight, was prepared and served by Polish nuns and was strictly Polish: *zurek po krakowsku*, a slightly sour soup Krakow-style, followed by *stek wieprzowy po mysliwsku*, or pork steak hunter-style. As always, Jerzy noted, his old friend ate little and only sipped at his wine while urging everyone else to take second helpings of both food and drink.

Conversation, which was mostly in Italian, centered on plans for the pope's first public appearance away from Rome, a visit to the shrine of St. Francis at Assisi scheduled for later that week. Monsignor Magee, an Irishman who had served as *segretario particolare* (personal secretary) to John Paul I, spoke no Polish. In any language, however, there was no mistaking Karol Wojtyla's enthusiasm for his new responsibilities. To Jerzy, he appeared immensely strong and eager, like a champion before a match.

The pope indicated that Assisi would be only the first of many trips beyond Vatican walls. He had already surprised everyone by making several impromptu appearances around Rome, showing an ability to inspire ordinary people that had everyone remembering John XXIII. He somehow affected Italians so personally that everyone, from shopkeepers, waiters, and laborers to businesspeople, spontaneously began to refer to him by his family name. It was Wojtyla this and Wojtyla that, as often as *Santo Padre* or the pontiff's other traditional titles. Jerzy had noticed this even at the tennis club, and now it became clear that Lolek knew exactly the effect he was having; it was what he desired. He wanted people to feel his humanity and thereby humanize the Church. And he was acutely conscious that he must reach not just the elite but also ordinary folk.

"Who can come to Rome," he asked in speaking of his plans to travel extensively, "except those who can afford to travel? And that is very few. So I must go to them. They deserve to see their pope and to see that he is just a human being who loves them and not someone remote on a throne."

"And will you go to Poland, Your Holiness?" asked Jerzy, who refrained from addressing the pope as "Lolek" when others were present. He was thinking of the outpouring of emotion, widely reported in the press, when the pope had greeted four thousand Polish pilgrims only days after his election. Although Jerzy had never for a moment doubted it, it was then clear to everyone that this man was not going to forget where he came from.

John Paul II did not reply directly to his friend's rather blunt question but only smiled that playful, almost teasing smile. His bright blue eyes spoke for him. Jerzy knew at once that the pope would visit Poland no matter what the obstacles. He obviously relished the idea and was afraid of nothing. Few understood yet how shrewdly and effectively he had undermined the Communists as Archbishop of Krakow.

To Jerzy, whose temperament inclined him toward conceiving of life in sporting or military terms, the prospect of Wojtyla's return to Poland as pope excited him in the same way as the anticipation of some great match or battle. And he was certain of who would be the winner, although he would never have expressed himself openly in those terms to Lolek. If Jerzy was a man of physical action, the pope was one of intellect and faith. Even his skiing and hiking, Jerzy had long understood, were more spiritual than sporting matters, for he thought of playing more than of winning and communed with nature almost as if he were a pantheist. In this the two men were temperamentally opposite. ("Which is why," Jerzy liked to think with amused satisfaction, "I ski better than he does and nearly always beat him at table tennis.")

In regard to Poland, the pope said that for now, he was only looking forward to greeting a delegation that was arriving the following week from the University of Lublin, where he had taught for several years as professor of ethics. His friend and former student Tadeusz Styczen, a brilliant theologian who was doing wonderful work in the area of faith and freedom, was coming with them and would bring news from the motherland.

After coffee, John Paul II took Jerzy into the kitchen to introduce him to the nuns and to thank them for the meal. Jerzy told them that he was relieved finally to have found a place in Rome that served good Polish food.

Chapter 4

FOR MANY WEEKS FOLLOWING THAT AFTERNOON AT THE VATICAN, JERZY was content to watch from a distance as his friend began to occupy the center of the world's stage. Like only John XXIII before him, who had become affectionately known as simply "Pope John," John Paul II immediately broke through the ceremony and trappings of the papacy with the strength, warmth, and accessibility of his personality. He was embraced as a man, especially during and after his triumphant trip to Mexico in January 1979. He adroitly countered the coolness of Mexico's anticlerical and authoritarian government, a corrupt oligarchy that offered him no official welcome, with some twenty-six speeches and by saying mass before adoring crowds numbering in the millions. He pointedly visited and mingled with all levels of society, from the slum-dwellers to the privileged, emphasizing the value of every individual human person.

Jerzy was not surprised by the pope's effect on crowds because he remembered well Wojtyla's theatrical talents, his ability to rivet an audience even when he was scarcely more than a boy in school productions. What was new and especially pleasing was how the intimacy of television brought his inner goodness to a world-wide audience. The hand gestures that bestowed warmth, the loving smile with its hint of mirth, those penetrating yet accepting eyes—none of these were lost on camera.

Jerzy knew that there was no disguise, that the pope was exactly as he appeared on the screen. That such a good and intelligent man could captivate the multitudes was encouraging. Earlier in the decade, John Lennon had made his infamous remark that the Beatles were more famous than Jesus Christ, meaning it not as self-praise but as a comment on people's loss of faith. Wojtyla's sudden stardom suggested that Christ did still matter in a world enthralled by mundane icons.

Not everyone was pleased by the message John Paul II brought. Some were confused by what they saw as irreconcilable contradictions in his approach to social and religious issues that had already divided Catholics since Vatican II. As a bishop and a cardinal, Wojtyla was already on record as wholly in favor of such reforms as *Nostra Aetate*, which declared the Church's opposition to coercion in matters of faith and proclaimed freedom to worship according to individual conscience as a universal civil right. Therefore, many people assumed that the new pope endorsed an entire run of liturgical, doctrinal, and administrative changes and could be expected to institute them. They assumed that the College of Cardinals had elected, in a phrase, "a Polish liberal." They did not understand that the adjective governed the noun.

On social issues, John Paul II in general sounded liberal, declaring modern society unjustly divided as to the distribution of wealth. In Mexico, a country grievously divided in this way, he deplored the imbalance of world resources between rich and poor and haves and have-nots, but without suggesting how these disparities might be redressed. At the same time, and often acerbically, he distanced himself from the so-called liberation theology that, especially in Latin America, had encouraged priests and some bishops to align the Church with leftist revolutionaries who advocated armed rebellion to overthrow oppressive regimes. Even on the papal flight to Mexico, he derided this Marxist-Leninist approach, commenting to reporters that it was a distortion of the Fourth Gospel and "not a true theology" at all. The Church, he indicated, should not stand with either right or left. How, then, was it to effect social justice? He seemed to be saying that Christianity itself, in its pure form as the gospel of love, unadulterated by appeals to class warfare, was the Church's proper mission. Faith and works inspired by faith could move the mountain of injustice.

In Mexico, he also strongly reaffirmed the Church's opposition to abortion and to artificial means of birth control, endorsing the tenets of Paul VI's encyclical *Humanae Vitae* (*Human Life*; 1965) and thereby dismaying many who had anticipated that he would at least soften Catholic doctrine in this area. And behind the scenes, he made clear to members of the hierarchy that he alone, as pope, remained the supreme authority in matters of faith and morals, confounding those who had hoped and even assumed that the papacy of John Paul II would at last encourage the evolution of the Church into a more democratically governed institution. What was desirable as a political system in society, John Paul II was saying, was not appropriate to a religion. One was based on the consent of the governed, the other on divine commandment and Scripture.

Within and without the hierarchy, many Catholics had imagined that bishops would now act as a legislature, as is the practice in Eastern Orthodoxy, to initiate policies that the executive, or pope, would then enforce. Such a structure was evidently not high on the papal agenda. On the contrary, this pope indicated that he was putting the brakes on tendencies that he regarded as less democratic than anarchic. He made plain his opposition to any drift in the direction of modern philosophy and historical and literary theory, which assumes that one person's interpretation of phenomena is as valid as another's. By doing so, he set himself apart from a relativism that was already embedded among leading academics in the United States and Western Europe, and thus he invited their hostility.

As to theologians, he put on notice those inclined to the deconstruction of doctrine rather than its elucidation. A Catholic theologian should write and teach not what seemed personally valid but rather that thing known as Roman Catholicism, as established over two thousand years. Religion was something already revealed, not made up by solitary human beings. Change, yes; tolerance of other faiths, yes; and learning from them, yes. Religion by consensus, no. The name Peter meant "rock," not "plastic."

Thus began a confusion that stemmed not from the pope but from those opposed factions who chose to view him through the prisms of their own political, social, and theological perspectives. Many saw him as a conservative or even a reactionary, determined to stop the tide of reform or to reverse it. Others, noting his obvious opposition to repressive political regimes and wide gaps between rich and poor, together with his repeated advocacy of individual liberty, saw him as progressive. Still others found him frustratingly contradictory.

In fact, he was none of these. Rather, he demonstrated a quality that the world had grown unused to: a truly spiritual leadership from someone who was of the world and entirely familiar with it. In the secularized West, intellectuals tended either to subscribe to atheistic Marxism or to separate religious beliefs entirely from social and political ones. John Paul II's true self and message were no more one thing or another, and no more contradictory, than the most fundamental idea of Christianity itself—namely, the Incarnation.

That Christ was equally human and divine was a difficult concept to grasp in the mid- or late twentieth century. Some had no wish to grasp it. Believing in it did take a leap of faith, exactly as John Paul II was saying, even as he appeared to contradict himself. The concept of incarnation was not a simple idea, even though it took a simple faith to comprehend it. And its ramifications, such as the idea that human beings cannot live by bread alone, were manifold, if elusive.

John Paul II began promulgating it at once in his first encyclical, issued on March 4, 1979, a little more than four months after his election. Entitled *Redemptoris Hominis* (*Redeemer of Humankind*), it set out the following propositions: (1) Roman Catholicism is not the sole repository of religious truth, and spiritual enlightenment may also be found in other beliefs and believers; (2) human beings cannot live without love; (3) to hold a belief is not to destroy others' beliefs; (4) truth tells us that some freedoms are illusory; (5) each human being on the planet shares in the mystery of Christ, and the

Church must minister to all of them; (6) technology is a good thing only when it serves humanity rather than destroying it; (7) materialism is the enslavement of the spirit; (8) human rights and social justice are mutually dependent and inseparable; (9) our time is hungry for spiritual renewal; (10) theology cannot be a set of personal ideas; (11) to accept God, we must be sorry for our sins and do penance; and (12) the mystery of redemption took place in the accepting womb of a woman, the Virgin Mary.

These ideas, a mixture of the progressive and the traditional, formed the core of his beliefs and appeared at once straightforward and bewildering to a world unaccustomed to a mingling of the sacred and the secular. Educated Catholics were particularly bewildered. Human rights and the Virgin Mary? Technology and penance?

Indeed, what was widely described as a crisis of belief in the Catholic Church seemed most acute in the developed West. Those regularly attending mass in France, with its history of anticlericalism since the Revolution, were mostly old women and children who could be influenced by nuns. In Catholic Ireland, church attendance had begun to fall among the young. The number of priestly vocations in America was falling, with fewer than sixty thousand priests still active in parish work. Polls showed that a majority, perhaps two-thirds, of American Roman Catholics ignored the Church's teaching on birth control. And in a country where the divorce rate was around forty percent, Catholics stayed away from mass. They were forbidden to receive the sacraments if they remarried without having obtained annulment of the previous marriage, a cumbersome and usually stressful process that often meant pain and confusion for children.

Meanwhile, in Central and Latin America, Protestant Evangelicals were making inroads into nearly four hundred years of Catholic hegemony by preaching that merely accepting Jesus Christ as a "personal savior" guaranteed salvation. They preached that the end of the world was at hand and that before that "end time" arrived, material success was what God wanted for believers. In the midst of all this, the pope's message appeared to his critics as irrelevant and woefully behind the times, like applying leeches to a cancer. It was not only the Jews who were worried about him. Many were asking, "What does this man want?"

For those willing to take the trouble to study them, Wojtyla's previous writings might have provided greater understanding of his view of life. He was the author of a profusion of poems, some plays, and two philosophical books, but very few of them had been translated from the Polish in 1979. Almost none were available in the two most widely read Western languages, English and Spanish.

His most surprising work, an examination of human sexuality that made use of the current, frank research of sexologists in America and elsewhere, was available in Polish, French, Italian, and Spanish, but not in English. It contained a key to his opposition to any but the rhythm method of family planning, a belief that was rooted in behavioral studies and physiology, not merely doctrine. It may or may not have persuaded English-speaking Catholics, but at least they would have understood that the new pontiff was anything but ignorant of human sexuality. Rather, he addressed the subject with the openness of an up-to-date clinician and showed a deep concern for women exploited by men in sexual relationships—something that would have given many of his most vociferous American critics pause.

That John Paul was Polish suggested that he wouldn't be afraid of making bold moves, nor would he fear failure or acting in defiance of majority opinion. The Polish people kept the idea of national independence alive through poetry, drama, fiction, art, and song. They adored strong leaders such as Marshal Pilsudski, who defied great odds to battle more powerful oppressors. It was useful to remember Balzac's humorous but still valid characterization, that you could show a Pole a precipice and he would hurl himself over it. He described the nation as having the mentality of a cavalry regiment "who fancy they can ride through all obstacles and come out victorious."

It was equally important to know that Karol Wojtyla was at heart and by study, talent, and preference three things: a performing artist, a poet, and a true intellectual. These were aspects of being, not merely preoccupations of youth to be sloughed off like a worn-out shirt. Like ordination to the priesthood, they left indelible marks on the soul. He had not merely dabbled in lyric, dramatic verse and acting but had mastered them. Indeed, he could have spent his life doing them, to his personal satisfaction and to public acclaim.

This artistic style persisted in his characteristic mode of expression, which is didactic but indirect, using metaphors, nuance, gesture, and parable to convey an idea. That this is also the manner of the Scriptures was hardly a coincidence. Therefore, to attempt to reduce his ideas to a formula is to miss his thoughts, which run counter to the Information Age.

Philosophically he is attracted to phenomenology, but it is his faith that impels him to intuit meaning. Although it is not his first love, he is fascinated by science and sees it as the complement of religion, not its opposite. To describe him as a mystic, as biographers persist in doing, is not so much inaccurate as seriously inadequate. This is a man who accepts Christ without rejecting Darwin, Einstein, or any other great scientific theorists.

Wojtyla's respect for the significance of observed physical phenomena extends to his personal experience of life and to the lives of those close to him—and there are many. Those who know him best, including Jerzy, understand how deeply the nightmarish German occupation of Poland during World War II—and the dreary Russian-Communist control after it—affects his beliefs, including those concerning contraception and abortion. "The stench of Auschwitz," said Styczen, the professor from Lublin who regularly visited him in Rome to continue their decades-long philosophical discussions, "was in his nostrils" and would never be forgotten. Another Polish academic, Stanislaw Grygiel, professor of philosophical anthropology at Lateran University in Rome, described Wojtyla as a man in love with life because he had seen so much death.

Who other than his intimates can know the enormous complexity of this man? The collar of the priesthood itself, while conveying authority, also deflects understanding of the human being within. The vestments of office, especially those of a pope, can be a suit of armor, discouraging penetration to the man behind it. In the instance of Wojtyla, an undiscovered universe lay within.

Chapter 5

KAROL WOJTYLA'S RETURN TO POLAND AS JOHN PAUL II, AN EVENT as dreaded in Moscow as it was eagerly awaited elsewhere, was already set for June 2, 1979. On May 17, Jerzy Kluger received another invitation to lunch at the Vatican. Since November, Jerzy and his family had visited with the Holy Father at Vatican receptions and had welcomed the personal Christmas note they had grown accustomed to receiving from Archbishop Wojtyla in the past. This invitation was the first indication to Jerzy that informal contact with the pope would continue. The initiative was, as before, a telephone call from Monsignor Dziwisz that morning asking Jerzy to appear at one o'clock.

By this time, Kurt Rosenberg was more insistent than ever that Jerzy broach with the Holy Father the subject of diplomatic recognition for Israel. Since late the previous year, Prime Minister Begin had begun approving the construction of new Jewish settlements in the West Bank and Gaza, showing that the removal of sites in Sinai, a condition of the Camp David Accords, did not preclude expansion in Judea and Samaria. This assertive policy was attracting strong criticism from the United States and Europe, not to mention Arab nations. Rosenberg suggested that Vatican support now would be most welcome.

Jerzy reminded him that the surest way to wreck their friendship was to pressure Wojtyla on behalf of Israel or any other cause. The Israelis would in all likelihood manage very well without either Jerzy's or Rosenberg's help.

Monsignor Dziwisz's instructions were for Jerzy to give his name at the gate, after which he would be shown the way to a tower where His Holiness was living while the papal apartments were being cleaned and redecorated. Although he hadn't said a word about it, Jerzy was glad of this news. At least someone would throw open a window and tear down those horrible blackout curtains. What was the point of living in a palace if your quarters were so unpleasant? Jerzy had gathered that the reason the apartments were so drab was that Paul VI, a nervous and self-effacing personality (some said a self-flagellant), had been a recluse, taking his meals alone and meeting people only in formal audiences.

Now that his friend was pope, Jerzy had become fascinated by Vatican personalities and intrigue, especially regarding Pius XII, whose silence about genocide during World War II was a matter of continuing controversy. Vatican archives of the period remained sealed, but Pius XII certainly had his vigorous defenders, including several prominent Jews such as Dr. Joseph Lichten, the representative in Rome of the Anti-Defamation League of B'nai B'rith. Dr. Lichten had published a book documenting Pius XII's efforts to save Italian Jews, pointing out that among all the occupied nations during World War II, Italy lost the smallest percentage of its Jewish population, some seventeen thousand out of a prewar total of fifty thousand.

Dr. Nahum Goldman, president of the World Jewish Congress, said of Pius XII on the occasion of the pope's death, "With special gratitude we remember all he had done for the persecuted Jews during the darkest period of their history." The pope's wartime silence about the Holocaust, however, was an issue that remained painful to most Jews and an embarrassment to many Catholics. Some charged him with pro-fascist sympathies and anti-Semitism; others sought to attribute his reluctance to publicly condemn the Axis powers to his profound antipathy to the Soviet Union and Communism.

The only European bishops to condemn Nazis as a group were

Dutch. On their part, the Dutch bishops never regretted having taken their brave stand and continued to believe, as did many Catholics, that martyrdom was preferable to equivocation. If the Church did not speak out on the most important moral issue of the century, its leader had failed the obligations of his solemn office. Again, the contrary view was that had Pius XII spoken out, the slaughter would have been worse—an argument similar to that made by the Red Cross, whose Swiss officials were certain that if they had made public their knowledge of atrocities, they would have been prevented from aiding victims and prisoners within the war zone.

This painful and controversial issue remained a divisive one between Catholics and Jews and among Catholics themselves. It was brought to a head in 1963 by a volatile play, or docudrama, *The Deputy* (*Der Stelvertreter*), written by a German Lutheran, Rolf Hochhuth, and performed all over Europe and in the United States and Canada.

The play indicted Pius XII for his silence and depicted him as a Machiavellian figure, cold and cynical, who was motivated by his view of Hitler as a crude but useful tool against Stalin. It portrayed him as a man who refused to explicitly condemn the Nazis in order to protect Catholics and not detract Hitler from his hoped-for defeat of Communism. At best, his attitude toward the fate of Jews comes across as one of indifference. (Curiously, a footnote in an annotated version of the play quotes a Jewish scholar, Pinchas Lapide, describing a meeting between Pius XII and German Foreign Minister Joachim von Ribbentrop in which the pope privately condemns Nazi atrocities by reading a list of them and dismissing the minister with a contemptuous nod.)

During the papal visit to Israel, Paul VI publicly accused Hochhuth of having "an inadequate grasp of psychological, political, and historical realities," a mild enough rebuke but one widely viewed as ill-timed, delivered as it was to Holocaust survivors who had their own grasp of historical realities.

Moral issues aside, Pius XII's silence was consistent with his withdrawn, reclusive personality. Not even His Holiness's closest relatives were permitted to sit at a table with him. Church officials, according to a memoir published by the Vatican, customarily spoke to him on their knees and exited shuffling backward. The lone exception to this formality was Francis Cardinal Spellman, who was often invited to tea. Significantly, Cardinal Spellman was one of the most vocal of all Church officials in support of Israel and the right of Jews to return to their homeland.

The American cardinal, however his views on Israel were received, knew how to please this pontiff, presenting him with a Cadillac equipped with solid gold door handles. He also gave the pope a white and gold telephone that became his preferred means of communication with Vatican department heads, to whom he would announce "Pacelli speaking," gruffly list grievances, and hang up. His only close confidante was his Bavarian housekeeper, Mother Pasqualina Lehnert, who was a tyrant by all accounts and who protected him to the extent of instructing Vatican gardeners to hide behind trees if they spotted the *Santo Padre* out for a stroll, lest they disturb his meditations.

AT THE PROPER GATE THIS TIME, JERZY RECEIVED DIRECTIONS TO THE TOWER of Saint John, built into the Vatican walls. Pope John XXIII had made this into his personal retreat, installing apartments for himself that included servants' quarters and a kitchen, removing an ugly Vatican Radio mast from the roof, and adding a seventh story. It was there, gazing down from the battlements, that he composed his great encyclical *Pacem in Terris* (*Peace on Earth*; 1963).

That document returned the Church to the center of world affairs after a long period of isolation that was painfully symbolized by the silence of Pius XII. From this tower, Pope John XXIII showed the way for John Paul II, his spiritual son, by endorsing liberty of conscience and religion, thus single-handedly demolishing the Church's unfortunate tradition of demanding liberty for itself while denying it to others. From that moment forth, the Church officially no longer saw the human race as divided into two groups, Catholics and the others.

To be fair to the problematic Pius XII, strong evidence exists that he recognized well before his death in 1958 that the Church must change direction. The outside world knows only that popes are elected by the College of Cardinals, but within the Vatican it is widely accepted that in one way or another, popes quietly choose their own successors, or at the very least make their preferences known, with nearly certain effect. Many believe that Pius XII, achieving humility, personally selected the man who would transform a Church crying out for change. However John XXIII arrived there, the view from the Tower of Saint John was a "yes" to life, although the radical change that he initiated was far from fully accepted or even understood sixteen years later.

JERZY EMERGED FROM THE ELEVATOR TO FIND THAT LOLEK HAD A SURPRISE FOR him. In a small reception room, with Michelangelo's Basilica dome visible through the leaded panes behind them, the pope was waiting beside a short, wiry fellow whom Jerzy instantly recognized. He was Tomasz Romanski, another of their Wadowice classmates. Jerzy had not seen him since the end of World War II, when they had encountered one another in Scotland. It had been thirty-four years.

As the two long-separated friends embraced and marveled at how the years had and had not changed them, the Holy Father looked on like an affectionate brother. Of the three Wadowicians, all born within a year of one another, the pope and Jerzy appeared the more youthful. Although the pope's once-blond hair was nearly white, he looked otherwise like a man in his vigorous forties. (In fact, he would turn fifty-nine the next day, so the lunch would be a birthday celebration, too.) Jerzy's hair was thinning but still dark, and his face was tan and taut from exertions on the tennis court. Romanski, grizzled and pale, had reached the point where only those who knew him could have said whether he was in his fifties or sixties.

Jerzy had remembered to buy a birthday card on his way to the Vatican, and he presented it to his friend. It was inscribed to "Holy Father." Then he displayed wallet photos of his family, and Romanski showed pictures of his wife and three sons. Since the war, Romanski had lived in Krakow, marrying in 1950 and working as a physical therapist at the Cooperative for Disabled Persons. He had come to Rome at the pope's invitation; John Paul II had insisted that Romanski be his guest at the tower. He was having a wonderful time, Romanski said, seeing Lolek and the sights. He was so proud of their friend. No one else in the class had come close to this, that was for sure.

"Listen," Jerzy said, "if Wojtyla had wanted it, he could have been president of General Motors!"

Despite having been out of touch for so long, Jerzy remembered well Romanski's heroic wartime exploits, and he recited them now, to the pope's benign approval and partly for Monsignor Dziwisz's benefit.

This tough little Pole, Jerzy said, had fought with the Twelfth Infantry during the tragic September Campaign against the Germans. Afterward, to avoid capture and death, he had fled across the Carpathians to Hungary, only to be interned there with three other schoolmates—Stanislaw Jura, Rudolf Kogler, and Zdzislaw Bernas. The four, officers all and barely twenty years of age, had escaped through Yugoslavia and Greece to Beirut, where they joined up with the Polish forces gathering there. Romanski had gone on to fight as an officer with the Kopanski Brigade in Libya, Egypt, and throughout the Italian peninsula. He had been wounded twice and received several decorations for valor. He was a true hero.

"*Dac swiadectwo prawdzie!*" the pope said, clapping Romanski on the shoulder. "Let the word go forth!"

A fourth guest arrived. He was Emery Kabongo Kanundowi, a thirty-nine-year-old priest from Zaire who was one of several papal secretaries serving under Monsignor Dziwisz. To the amazement of Jerzy and Romanski, Kabongo had managed to master the Polish language to the point of near fluency since his appointment by Wojtyla only three months before.

"I have had excellent teachers," he said when Jerzy complimented him, proclaiming his pronunciation "worthy of an aristocrat." Jerzy was equally impressed to learn that Kabongo, before concentrating on his priestly vocation, had been a boxing and cycling champion and still kept in shape by performing acrobatic stunts on wheels. He promised Jerzy that sometime he would demonstrate his daring on the Vatican garden paths where he practiced.

When the five men went in to lunch, Jerzy took his place at the foot of the table, telling Romanski how he always kept the maximum distance between himself and "our colonel." As before, the meal was the same as one that could have been enjoyed in a Polish house, with the addition of mineral water and wine and *barszcz* (beet soup) for starters.

Conversation, unimpeded by any language barrier, glided from recollection of how remarkable it had been for the Polish Army to survive to fight in the Middle East and elsewhere to what was going on now in that most volatile of regions. The Islamic revolution in Iran had deposed the shah, who with his family had fled into asylum in Panama, while his former associates seemed doomed to execution. Kabongo, who appeared to be as well-versed in foreign affairs as he was a linguist, pointed out how these events had shifted world attention for the time being away from the Arab-Israeli conflict, which could be good or bad depending on how the two sides behaved while international eyes were averted.

Jerzy was struck by the freedom of this discussion. The pope, while saying little himself, encouraged the debate, listening with total concentration, his head cocked to one side. He was like a professor thriving on stimulating students. The atmosphere encouraged Jerzy to bring up the matter that he had been keeping to himself.

"Dr. Mendes has been to see me," he finally told the pope about the meeting several months earlier. "He learned that I had seen the *Santo Padre*. I was suddenly such an important person."

"He was paying his respects to you?" the pope said with his usual touch of irony.

"Not exactly. He wanted to know what the position of the Vatican was now in regard to Israel. That was all."

The pope did not react. Jerzy felt obliged to supply a bit more but didn't mention that Dr. Mendes, like many Jews, was worried that a Polish pope must be an anti-Semite. Had he been alone with his friend, Jerzy might have added this information. But it was such a touchy, if not incendiary, issue. He presumed that the pope would already know or suspect as much anyway, since he was keenly aware of general presumptions about the Polish character. To mention it now risked offending Romanski at least. What a mine field this matter was.

"Naturally, I told Dr. Mendes that the Jews could expect absolutely fair treatment, like everyone else, from the *Santo Padre*. I told him not to worry," Jerzy said.

"You said the right thing, Jurek," the pope said, but in a manner that closed the subject. "And meanwhile, I am looking forward to my trip to the motherland."

His schedule in Poland the next month now became the focus of conversation. He had wished to arrive on May 8, the feast of Saint Stanislaus, the patron of Poland and its most revered historical figure, but the Communist government had been wary of that. Everything so far had worked out for the best. He understood that the Russians were not too pleased, but now he had a formal invitation from the state as well as from Stefan Cardinal Wyszynski, the Primate of Poland.

The date was not so important, Romanski said. Whenever John Paul II arrived, it would be the greatest event in modern Polish history. The people were ready to turn out in the millions for him. Raising his glass, Romanski quoted lines from the great early nineteenth-century poet Juliusz Slowacki, who had predicted this event more than a hundred years earlier.

In the time of quarrels God will choose
A Slavic pope, braver than the Italian
Who came before him. He will be unafraid
To take on a fight.

The little soldier had a big, resonant voice. If he had more lines in him, Jerzy urged, he should recite them now. Romanski, rising to his feet, continued.

His face shining, his power
Will stop the whirling sun;
His word will lead the nations
Into purest light.

He is coming! The blood in our veins
Will quicken! Spirit is power.
His Spirit-Power will turn the Earth.
The Folk-Pope salves our wounds.

Angels strew his throne with lilies;
He gives love where the mighty give arms.
He bestows the strength of sacrament.
A dove flies out from his song, giving hope.

The sky opens, and nations make peace.
He sweeps clean the Church,
The Slavic pope who will come
To reveal God's hand in all creation.

As he sat down to applause—except from the pope, who seemed somewhat embarrassed—Romanski wiped away a tear. He admitted that he had made sure that he had memorized these words, remembered from youth, before coming to Rome. He had meant to recite them on the pope's birthday but, with Jerzy present, this seemed the proper moment to express what all Poles felt about their beloved Wojtyla.

If this was indeed how most Poles felt about him, Jerzy thought, and he was sure it was, the pope could expect quite a welcome in June. There was no question that Romanski was about as typically Polish as a man could be and represented the best character of the nation. Hearing Romanski had been a trip backward in time to Jerzy's youth in Wadowice. He asked whether the papal itinerary in Poland would include a visit to their hometown.

He very much wanted to go there, the Holy Father answered. Arrangements were incomplete. He had been thinking a great deal about Wadowice lately. Just that morning a tender memory had entered his mind.

"Do you remember, Jurek," he said, "the story I've told you about when we were very young and I was walking through the Rynek with my father and I saw the poor, lame postman bend his knee and kiss your father's hand? I had to ask my father what this meant. Everyone stopped to watch it. It was then that I first understood what a good and respected man Lawyer Wilhelm Kluger was in Wadowice."

Of course Jerzy remembered. He explained to Monsignor Dziwisz and Kabongo that his father had been a criminal defense attorney with offices right on the Rynek Glowny, or main square of the town, and had an outstanding reputation. Everyone respected Wilhelm Kluger. He did a lot of pro bono work for the poor. In this case, he had taken on the penniless postman who spent everything he had on vodka, defended him against false accusations of crimes, and convinced a jury of his innocence. Here was this distinguished Jewish lawyer, who also had many big commercial clients, defending a Catholic postman and exonerating him. The fellow was so grateful that he humbled himself in the manner that the pope remembered.

Jerzy said that he had not remembered the incident in the Rynek until being reminded of it. It was a proud moment for the Kluger family and a good one for Catholic-Jewish relations in the town.

"Deservedly so," John Paul II said. "And a lucky one for the postman!"

Chapter 6

When Jerzy returned to his office that afternoon, he found it difficult to think about business. He telephoned Renée to tell her that it had been a pleasant lunch and that he'd remembered Lolek's birthday with a card. Although he really couldn't expect her to understand quite what a moving experience it had been to see Romanski again, she said that she did.

Jerzy absentmindedly retrieved the electric razor that he kept in the center drawer of his desk and ran it over his face. When the phone rang, he didn't answer it. Fortunately, Rosenberg was out.

As he thought about the afternoon's events, he realized that the meeting had left an indelible impression on him, partly because he felt that he would never quite get used to the idea that Lolek was now the titular head of something like a billion souls. And it was deeply meaningful that he had taken the time to arrange the surprise get-together with Romanski, whom Jerzy would otherwise never have seen again. The pope kept in touch with all the old mates. In Poland, they had had regular reunions. How many were left of the original forty or so who had sat for their final examinations together at the high school? Several had died in the war, Jerzy knew.

Jerzy was a man who rarely wept, but as he sat there assailed by voices, he felt himself possessed by emotions that he was unable to define. Joy and sadness contended in his heart. He would have thought himself drunk, except that he had had only two glasses of wine at lunch.

Impulsively, he began to rummage in a cabinet where he kept newspaper clippings about the pope, including reports and photographs of his own audience with him back in October. There was one that showed Renée, beautiful and grave, draped in a mantilla; Linda, blond and glamorous; and Stephania gazing up at the Holy Father. He would have that one framed.

He noticed a spiral notebook. It was blank except for the first page, which listed phone numbers long out of date. He tore out the used page and wrote "May 17, 1979"on the fresh page in red ink. Then, in blue, he jotted down in Polish everything he could remember of that day's events. He switched to yellow and green and back to blue as topics and his mood shifted. When he reached the moment when he had brought up Dr. Mendes's visit, he was satisfied that he'd fulfilled his obligation to the Israeli cause without offending the pope by being pushy.

It was seven when Renée called to ask when he was coming home. By then he had covered several pages in his careful, ornate script. He had accounted for just about everything except the story about his father and the postman. That Lolek had brought it up, as if to remind everyone that the Klugers had occupied a prominent place in Wadowice, was touching. He did not expect anyone else to read what he had written, but he felt better after recording it.

IT WAS IMPOSSIBLE TO SLEEP THAT NIGHT. HE KEPT THINKING ABOUT THE pope's upcoming trip to Poland and what it would be like. The papers were full of speculation about the possible political impact on the Soviet domination of Central and Eastern Europe. Those old men in the Kremlin must be sweating bullets! And would the itinerary actually include the little town of Wadowice? Hearing Romanski recite Slowacki and listening to Lolek reminisce, Jerzy had felt the slightest twinge of desire to see the town again, perhaps to be there when Lolek triumphantly returned. Now that urge had vanished, replaced by the usual aversion. No, going there was out of the question. Not after everything. Not after all that.

Still, he could not get Wadowice out of his mind. As if it were yesterday, he was walking every street, seeing every building and so many faces: his father presiding in his law offices; the Rynek thronged; his sister serving to him on the tennis courts in the park; his Grandmother Huppert in her chair watching out the window; the synagogue that he knew was gone. It was as if the Tower of Saint John had been a rocket ship, sending them all back to Wadowice.

At some point in the night, Jerzy thrashed. He felt Renée shift position and heard her groan in protest. He decided that he had better get up, or he would wake her. Throwing on his bathrobe, he groped barefoot down the hall and headed toward the sitting room. There might be an old John Wayne movie on television—the perfect way to get him through the night.

The moon and a street lamp cast their glow in the room. The marble bust of his mother looked luminous. He took a step closer to peer at her. "*Matka.*" The word formed on his lips: "Mother."

"Jurek," he heard her say.

What was she telling him? "*Matka,*" he called inaudibly. Was it time for him to be in bed? Had he played long enough? Had Grandmother learned about something he had done? He heard his mother singing for him. He let out a sigh and settled heavily into a chair, letting his head loll.

Lolek's blue eyes looked back at Poland. Half-awake, Jerzy wondered if he would ever see its men again, or its women, and a dream-vision descended on him.

LOLEK LEAPT OUT FROM BEHIND A TREE, BRANDISHING HIS MAKE-BELIEVE BOW and arrow, playing Winnetou to Jurek's Old Shatterhand.

Dropping to one knee and squinting an eye, Winnetou was

smiling as he aimed for the paleface's scalp, but he meant business this time. Shatterhand went to grab for his pistol, but seeing Winnetou's fierce visage, he thought better of it and fell to his knees, begging for mercy, scared as a kittycat confronted by a drooling Alsatian cur. Winnetou had him dead to rights. Wild breed of that ilk never made a mistake judging a man's nerve.

"Drop that gun and keep those hands in the air, man of many moons on his head. Your rampaging days are over. How do you wish to die, fried at the stake or tied down for buzzard's meat?" Winnetou demanded.

"Listen to reason, Redskin," Old Shatterhand pleaded. "Wise chief not act rash. Talk, smoke pipe of peace. Plenty wampum me give you."

"Oh, all right," Winnetou said. "Me summon braves." And Wojtyla let out a blood-curdling whoop, "Hi-i-i-i-yawp!" Old Shatterhand's sidekick Zweig surrendered, too, and from the darkness of the forest Winnetou's fearless tribesmen, played by Romanski, Kogler, Jura, and Bojes, rode up with faces painted and teeth bared.

"Powwow in teepee," Lolek said.

Except for their Polish syntax laced with make-believe frontier lingo, they could have been kids anywhere, running happily wild. The boys passed many long summer evenings that way, their thoughts free from real-life troubles. They drew their characters from Polish versions of the fantastical Western novels of the German writer Karl May and other fabulous storytellers, including Jack London, Bret Harte, and James Fenimore Cooper. The tales passed from hand to hand to transport the small-town youths to frontiers that they'd never seen. The boys acted out the stories over lush pastures and through the leafy woods of mid-July to the point of exhaustion and complete happiness.

The game would end when somebody's mother or Lolek's father called, "All in! All in!" Some, like the coal miner's son, Teofil Bojes, had to rush to catch the last train to their villages, and they would hurry back to town. Steam engines linked one place to another, Wadowice to Krakow or Andrychow, but it could have been Tombstone to Dodge City. "Goodnight, Bojes, may your train be on time tonight! It could be there's a strongbox stuffed with money for the taking! So long, God bless, take care, see you tomorrow!" they said. To the west where the sun sank was Germany, or Arizona.

Most of them, including Jurek, preferred playing Indians because instinctively their cause was the underdog's. National independence in Poland had been won scarcely a decade earlier, so while playing stouthearted pioneers with sticks for long rifles was fun, in their hearts they were the last of the Mohicans.

It was Rudek (short for Rudolf) Kogler who introduced the Wild West to them. Because he supervised the library as school marshal, he was able to order the books that the boys were most interested in, but they still had to pay the library rental fee. They contrived a scheme to raise the money. During the long winters, which often lasted from November into April, the snow piled up, and except for skiing, opportunities for outdoor play were few. So the boys chipped in to buy a Ping-Pong table. Rudek set the rules for an ongoing tournament to finance the rental of *The Call of the Wild*, *The Treasure of the Silver Lake*, *Leatherstocking Tales*, and other absorbing novels.

They rolled back the desks and stacked the chairs in the gymnasium-turned-library, and through cold, dark afternoons with snow falling, the room resounded with the "pick-pock, pick-pock" of furious play. The loser of a set had to pay five *groszy* into the book fund; the winner kept playing until he lost and someone took his place. At that rate, they could afford almost a book a week. It was a more enjoyable way of saving money than simply collecting it each week.

Lolek was a good player, steady and tireless. He had to be, because he was among the many lads to whom five *groszy*, the price of candy or a pair of shoelaces, was not a sum to be lost lightly. Yet, always the even-tempered one, he never seemed to mind when he did have to pay up. Jurek was temperamentally the opposite; he hated to lose, not because of the money but because he was so competitive. He always had spending money from his family and enjoyed the matches so much that he would sometimes quietly pay off others' debts to keep the fun going, never worrying about being reimbursed. He usually defeated all comers save one, Wiktor Kesek, who was the perennial champion.

Wiktor was another who could ill afford to lose. His mother was a schoolteacher who was raising him and his two brothers on her own. Their father had been killed fighting the Soviets in 1920, when Wiktor was a newborn. The matches between Wiktor and Jurek were marathons that attracted spectators from the girls' school, an attention that Jurek especially welcomed. There was nothing like beating Wiktor every now and then to make the girls take notice.

JERZY WAS STILL SLUMPED HALF-ASLEEP IN THE CHAIR WHEN RENÉE CAME upon him the next morning.

"Look at you," she said. "You'll be exhausted. Why don't you stay home and rest today?" Drawing her robe about her, she smoothed his forehead with her fingers, making him sigh.

"No," he said.

"Of course not. What an idiot I was to think so. You're not such a young pup, Jurek, make no mistake about that."

Still warm from the bed, her scolding voice rising and falling like a thermometer, Renée put one arm around him and chucked him under the chin.

"I beat Kesek several times," he said.

"What in the Holy Name of Jesus are you talking about?"

"Wiktor Kesek. Do you know that during the war he fought with the *Narodowy Oboz Wyzwolenia*?"

"What *are* you blathering on about?" Renée, who was Irish, had absorbed the Polish language during thirty-five years of marriage, but she could still be thrown by her husband's cryptic allusions, which seemed to be proliferating lately. "Would you speak English, if you don't mind? I'd sooner you strangled the life out of me than go on in that godforsaken tongue of yours."

"N.O.W. It was the National Liberation Front against the Krauts. Lolek told me what happened. Kesek was very brave. Lolek said a forester betrayed Kesek when he was hiding with his unit. The Germans threw him into Myslowice Prison. Later they sent him to that place. Auschwitz. They murdered him there."

She withdrew her arm and went to the window.

"He was Jewish," she said.

"Kesek? No, of course he was not Jewish," Jerzy said. "Kesek was a Catholic boy."

Chapter 7

THERE SEEMED TO BE NOTHING EXTRAORDINARY ABOUT WADOWICE other than many of the people who lived there. Neither the Catholic graveyard on Tatrzanska Street nor the Jewish one on the eastern side of the railway tracks held any tomb that drew pilgrims from afar, but both were well-tended. The grass was clipped in summer, and there were flowers everywhere. If anything, when Karol Wojtyla and Jerzy Kluger were growing up there between the great wars, the town was distinguished by being a more peaceful place than others in that part of the world.

Wadowice must have contained something extraordinary, however, to produce such an unusual result. Who can say or know why a town gives birth to someone who brings it from obscurity to homage? Neither Lolek nor Jurek was ever ashamed of Wadowice, homely though she was; they clung to the memory of her all their lives.

Wadowice lies in the foothills of the Carpathian Mountains, about thirty miles southwest of Krakow and thirty-five miles southeast of Oswiecim, which the Germans renamed Auschwitz. The Slovakian border is roughly a hundred miles to the south, with the ski resort of Zakopane an entry point. Imagine an inverted triangle with Wadowice at the apex, Krakow at the right upper angle, and Auschwitz at the left, and you get the picture. Since 1772, when the

Austro-Hungarian Empire annexed it and occupied it for the next hundred and forty-six years, this province of southern Poland has been called Galicia. This is a corruption of the name of a town, Halicz, which the Austrians preferred to the original Malopolska (smaller Poland). More precisely, Wadowice belongs to the Skawa Region, so named for the river that runs past it just to the east of town.

During the 1920s and 1930s, Wadowice had a population of some ten thousand, of whom eight thousand were Roman Catholics; the rest, with the exception of one Armenian family, were Jews.

In the unlikely event that you were a visitor from some Western metropolis, you might have thought that Wadowice had failed to notice the twentieth century or had been neglected by it. Even in the mid-1930s, there were only a half-dozen or so automobiles in or near town, the most elegant of which was a Skoda Rapide owned by a landholder who kept it at the family villa. Nor were there many bicycles. Horse-drawn buggies remained common. The open platform-truck was preferred for hauling goods, its driver balanced on spread feet and holding the reins of a sturdy draft horse. Men and women in red-and-white peasant garb—the women in long, hem-embroidered skirts—and red-faced from a life of cold, wind, and sun, kept to themselves. Shopkeepers and professional men invariably wore sober suits.

They had every reason to throng the Rynek. Just south of the church was the combined restaurant and sundries emporium owned by the mayor, Mr. Kluk, who was famous for having specially ordered two pairs of shoes made for his dog from Mr. Bat's Footwear across the way. There was Fischgrund's Stationery and Tobacco, Homme's Drugs, Foltin's Books and Printing, three watch repairers, and even a glazier. You could find almost anything in the Rynek or linger to enjoy its bustle, the clatter of hooves, and thick syllables of Slavic banter. Musicians often played old melodies for *groszy* tossed into a hat.

WEATHER PERMITTING, THE RITUAL WAS SOMETHING TO BE EXPECTED. On any given weekday afternoon in Wadowice, one could anticipate seeing the familiar figures of the middle-aged priest and the old woman strolling together through the Rynek. He was lean and tall in his cassock; she was short and bent and moved more tentatively as her eyesight weakened. Courtly, deferential toward her years and dignity, he held her gingerly by the elbow. Their free hands gesticulated as they traversed the cobblestones and talked as they made their rounds. They looked like mother and son but were not.

Except to keep a respectful distance so as not to intrude on their conversation, whatever on Earth they were talking about—someone's marriage or the price of eggs—no one paid particular attention to them. Like the open market on Thursdays or parades on Marshal Pilsudski's name day and Armistice Day, they were part of the square, nearly as permanent as the old well at the City Hall steps. Everyone saw them because everyone congregated there, either for a brief afternoon prayer at the Church of the Presentation of the Blessed Virgin Mary or to purchase imported citrus at Mr. Rzycki's superior grocery store or sweets at Mr. Hagenhuber's confectionery. Forty-five shops occupied the ground floors of the three- and four-story brick and stone buildings that lined the Rynek.

The ritual of the old priest and the woman was always the same. Canon Prochownik would appear at the door of Mrs. Huppert's house at the corner of Zatorska Street on the north side of the square, where she would be waiting for him, sporting a parasol if the sun beat down. Taking her arm, he would guide her along that side of the Rynek to Foltin's, where they paused to gaze through the window and discuss the books displayed. Uniformed girls and boys hurried in and out; students bought their schoolbooks at Foltin's. The pair inched along toward the church and passed it by, proceeding to the right, talking.

Needless to say, they never entered the church, nor did she cross herself passing that sanctuary. Mrs. Anna Huppert was Jewish. Not only that, but her son-in-law, like her father-in-law and her own husband before him, was president of the Jewish community of Wadowice. The Jews of the town, who enjoyed far better relations with Catholics than was typical in Poland, had for generations looked to her family for the forthright yet often subtle and complex leadership that enabled the two cultures to live in mutual tolerance and respect. Mrs. Huppert's friendship with Canon Prochownik was an important alliance in the interests of peace. Her son-in-law, Lawyer Wilhelm Kluger, had formed friendships with other Catholics that were equally vital—and unusual.

Maintaining this delicate balance wasn't easy, and it didn't extend to the peasantry. The peasants, or tenant farmers, often under the tutelage of priests no more enlightened than their parishioners, were unremittingly hostile to Jews. Here the religious component of anti-Semitism was crucial, although economic resentment played its part; even where most Jews were poor, notably in the *shtetls*, or Jewish villages, of the east, they were better off than the peasants.

Belief among the peasantry was rooted in the Middle Ages. It was still common for them to believe that Jews stole and murdered Christian children to mix their blood with matzo meal in Passover ritual. For centuries, Polish Jews, originally invited into Poland to help improve the country's backward agricultural economy during the fourteenth century and thereafter, had managed estates, lent money, and collected taxes for the gentry. They often dressed, as they were encouraged to do, like the nobles petty and grand for whom they became agents. Around Wadowice, as everywhere in the vicinity of Krakow, Jews were accustomed to looking to certain noble families—proprietors of vast estates who bore names like Deskur and Sapieha and Potocki—as their natural allies and referred to them among themselves as "Jewish uncles."

From the peasants' point of view, this complicity with landowners made Jews the enemy of the people as well as of the faith. In fact, Jews became more despised than the nobles they represented, since peasants dealt with Jews directly but with nobles only at a distance. At the same time, Jews, who were barred from owning land, became merchants, artisans, and professionals.

In urban settings, economic resentment was a greater factor in anti-Semitism than religious rancor, although it, too, fomented hatred. Mrs. Huppert, for instance, was thought to own more property than she actually did; her son-in-law, as Wadowice's leading attorney, was believed to be extremely rich. Were they not taking bread

L'Osservatore Romano

The first audience that the Kluger family had with Pope John Paul II in October 1978 was also the first audience granted by the new pontiff. From left are Jurek's daughter Linda, his wife, Renée, the pope, Jurek's granddaughter, Stephania, and Jurek.

Courtesy of Jurek Kluger

Jurek's mother, Rozalia, circa 1935.

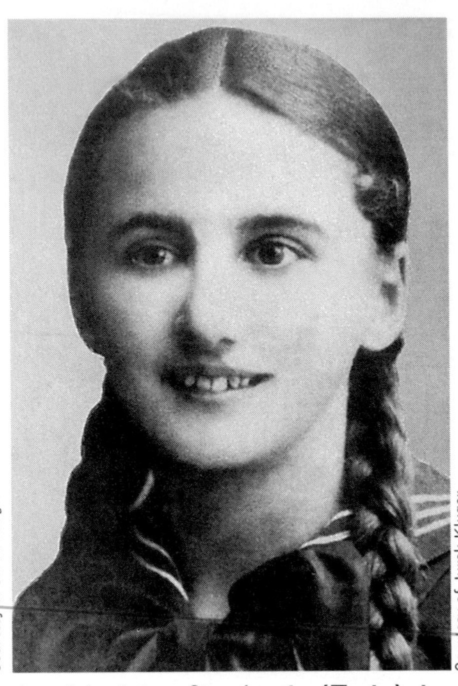
Courtesy of Jurek Kluger

Jurek's sister, Stephania (Tesia), in 1939 at age sixteen.

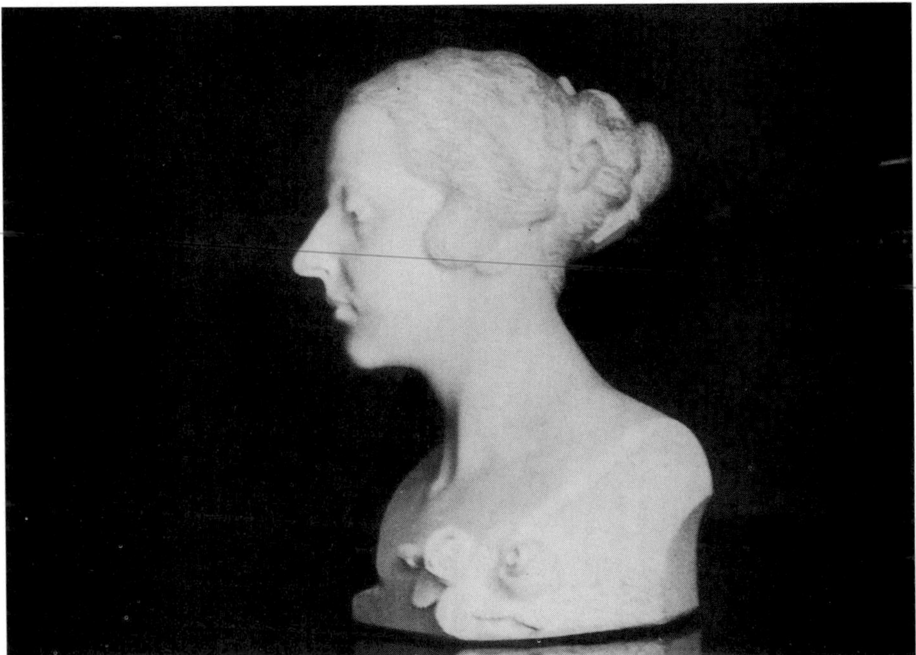
Courtesy of Jurek Kluger

Jurek's father, Wilhelm, gave this bust to his wife in honor of Jurek's birth in 1921.

Courtesy of Jurek Kluger

Jurek and Tesia play tennis in 1938 in the park that their grandfather Izrael Huppert gave to Wadowice.

Courtesy of Jurek Kluger

A family holiday on the Italian coast in the carefree days before the war, early to mid 1930s. Rozalia is in the foreground at right.

Courtesy of Jurek Kluger

Tesia, Rozalia (center), and Jurek on a climb in the hills near Wadowice, circa 1935.

Courtesy of Jurek Kluger

The Wadowice synagogue, circa 1935. Many of Wadowice's Jews and Catholics, including young Jurek and the future pope, gathered here for a performance by renowned tenor Moishe Kussawiecki in 1937.

Courtesy of Jurek Kluger

Wadowice on market day in the 1930s. The Klugers lived on the second floor of the corner house at right.

Courtesy of Jurek Kluger

Ginka Beer (right), circa 1930. Ginka, Wojtyla's neighbor and childhood friend, organized the high school theater club into a touring company. Later, she was denied admission to a university in Krakow because she was Jewish.

Courtesy of Jurek Kluger

The Wadowice boys' high school class of 1938. The future pope is at left in the second row; Jurek is fourth from left in the same row.

Courtesy of Jurek Kluger

Tesia on her way to a tennis tournament in Krakow in July 1939, only a few months before Hitler's invasion.

Courtesy of Jurek Kluger

Jurek (marked with an *X*) and Wojtyla (standing at right) at army summer camp in the countryside outside Wadowice in the late 1930s.

Courtesy of Jurek Kluger

Wojtyla (left) with fellow trainees at army summer camp, circa 1936.

Courtesy of Jurek Kluger

Karol Wojtyla's high school graduation portrait, 1938.

Courtesy of Jurek Kluger

The Wadowice synagogue after the Germans destroyed it in September 1939. The building, which dated from the turn of the century, was leveled after the war; no Jews were left in the town to worship in it.

Courtesy of Jurek Kluger

Jurek in Cairo in 1943 after he left the Russian labor camp and joined the Polish Army.

Courtesy of Jurek Kluger

Dr. Wilhelm Kluger, a captain in the Polish Army, circa 1943.

Courtesy of Jurek Kluger

Jurek (left) with his father (center) and an unidentified Polish Army companion in Palestine, 1943.

Courtesy of Jurek Kluger

Jurek in Kirkuk, Iraq, 1943.

Courtesy of Jurek Kluger

Soon after the war, Jurek pursues one of his favorite activities.

from the mouths of Catholics? Such conclusions could be expected in a town in which Jews had been forbidden to reside until 1868 but where they now comprised twenty percent of the population yet owned forty percent of the shops, not to mention several of the most desirable buildings on the Rynek.

Some Catholics felt that rich Jews looked down on them, boasting, "your streets, our houses!" No doubt some did, but the resentment surely had more to do with the inevitable conflicts between landlords and tenants of any stripe than with ethnic or religious traits. Mrs. Huppert and the Klugers did not live ostentatiously, only very comfortably. Neither owned an automobile. Nevertheless, they had more than almost anyone else. And they were that different thing, Jews. Prosperity among them had to mean to some that they were what—in many lower- and middle-class Christian imaginations—was synonymous with Jews: misers. As for the nobles, they had inherited their wealth, presumably, and were at least Christians. So it went, the irrational merry-go-round of resentment.

The steady diplomacy of Hupperts, Klugers, and others of the most prominent Jewish families, together with the goodwill of many of their Catholic counterparts, kept the envious ones at bay.

It helped that as the county seat, with its courts and administrative offices, its high schools, and its treasury and excise office, Wadowice had a high level of literacy. Concerts, plays, and films were well-attended, and people aspired to a level of gentility. It was on the whole a decorous place, and the numerous cultural attractions of Krakow were within easy reach. And people had work to do. Most were employed in businesses that required literacy—education, government, or the military. Industries that employed manual labor included an agricultural cooperative, a power plant, a paper mill, two sawmills, a tile factory, a printing shop, and a large bakery that produced Holy Communion wafers for the region. A single small hotel catered to traveling salesmen.

The illiterate were able to find employment with butchers and bakers, in retail shops, and with religious facilities, but for the most part, Wadowice was a fairly well-educated place. And its citizens remained employed, even as mines and other heavy industries in Galicia, and to the west Silesia, suffered. During the period between the wars, the people of Wadowice were too busy earning a living, raising their families, or enjoying holidays to be much concerned with the religious and ethnic differences among them.

EACH TIME CANON PROCHOWNIK ESCORTED MRS. HUPPERT AROUND THE square, it was a sign that all was well between Catholics and Jews. On his part, Dr. Kluger, whose clients beyond the town included a Catholic-owned brewery and a Jewish-owned vodka distillery, could often be observed enjoying a friendly drink or two with Catholics at Mr. Kluk's and other restaurants, or at the famous Hawelka and Wierzynek restaurants in Krakow. Because the citizenry was devoted to keeping the peace, the only killing that took place in Wadowice between the wars was the execution of the notorious murderer Nikifor Maruszeczko, who was hanged at the prison on Slowackiego Street and whose last words were reported to be "It's a beautiful life."

Mrs. Huppert did own eleven buildings with two hundred and six tenants, as young Jerzy Kluger knew from his mother, who kept the accounts. Mrs. Huppert was Jurek's maternal grandmother. Among her properties was the house on Zatorska Street where she lived with her daughter Rozalia and her husband, Wilhelm, and their children, Jurek and his younger sister Stephania, whom everyone called Tesia. Their ten-room flat, including bedrooms for a cook and a maid, occupied the entire second floor; another Jewish family lived at the rear and a third family on the floor above.

When she was not perambulating the square, Mrs. Huppert surveyed the Rynek from her favorite chair overlooking that busy field of folk. Even with her dimming eyesight, little happened in Wadowice that escaped Anna Huppert's notice, as Jurek often found out to his annoyance. How was it that she learned that he had been meeting a girl after dusk in the city park? They had only been talking, or barely touching. He might as well have been caught in adultery! That was Grandmother.

An unruly, mischievous boy, Jurek was out and about as often as he could manage. A student curfew of eight o'clock in the winter and nine on summer evenings kept him somewhat in check. Soccer, tennis, table tennis, running and jumping competitions—Jurek loved sports more than anything else. He also loved whiling away the hours playing Ferbel, an Austrian form of poker that was verboten because it involved betting.

Also forbidden was Wadowice's lone cinema, the Kino Wysoglada, where almost none of the scratchy prints that ran were approved for children under eighteen. When a notice outside announced a permissible film, it was sign enough that the film wasn't worth the bother. Jurek came close—or so he believed—to being expelled from high school when one night his Latin teacher caught him at the movies with a friend and a pair of hairdressers from the local beauty parlor. He wondered if Grandmother Huppert had tipped someone off. They were discovered only when the lights went up, revealing them like guilty lovers, which they were far from being. Rather, they were only boys on a dare. Poor Jurek was barred from a ski trip to Zakopane for that one.

A glimpse of Gloria Swanson in *Tonight or Never* supplied the boys with more romance than they could otherwise expect. In those decorous times and with schools segregated by sex, physical encounters with females usually occurred only at dances or on the skating pond during the last years of high school.

Jurek was somewhat envious of Poldek Goldberger, who was two years older, for having a girlfriend. Big and awkward though he was, Poldek had a knack for romance, writing popular songs, tangos, and waltzes for his own band that played all the dances. Poldek's sweetheart, Irka, who was almost as big as he was, used to meet him in the doorway of the house on Zatorska Street and stand holding hands with him, speechless for hours, caressing him with adoring eyes. Poldek would pretend that he was on his way upstairs to visit Jurek and just happened to run into Irka. "Ah, you're here!" Jurek used to joke as he bumped into them on his way out. "Everything's in order, all's right with the world!" Such was young love, furtive and intense, tentative and homespun, in Wadowice.

Other than what they learned from books and movies, the boys knew little about what lay beyond the town with its shops and mills. Was there a difference between what Catholic and Jewish boys dreamed of when it came to romance? If there was, no one knew or thought about it. These were just boys, dreaming of love, conquest, and whatever else, as squirmy and imaginative in southern Poland as anywhere else.

Jurek had several Jewish friends, including Kurt Rosenberg, who lived in Bielsko but often came to Wadowice because his family owned a clothing store there, just off the Rynek. But what was unusual about Jurek as a Polish Jewish boy was that he knew more Catholic boys than Jewish ones and counted several of them among his closest friends.

Many of the Jewish families sent their children to religious schools in neighboring towns or in Krakow, where the Jewish population was large and its tradition established over hundreds of years. In Poland as a whole, most Jewish children attended separate schools, with subjects taught in Yiddish and Hebrew. The figure has been estimated at sixty percent and close to a hundred percent in eastern districts. But from the first grade on, Jurek's parents entrusted their children to the state-run system, where children of all social and economic levels, Catholic and Jewish alike, intermingled. As an indication of how exceptional this choice was, there were only two other Jewish boys, Zygmunt Selinger and Leopold Zweig, in Jurek's class of about thirty-five students; at the girls' school, Tesia knew even fewer Jewish students. Their associations with other Jews came mostly from family relations and connections.

JUREK, WHO WAS NOT ESPECIALLY CLOSE TO EITHER SELINGER OR ZWEIG, WAS constantly dropping by Catholic friends' houses for a casual visit, and they likewise called on him. Among Jurek's favorites was Stanislaw Banas, the richest boy in the class, whose family owned the Skoda car. His father, a client of Wilhelm Kluger's and a former judge, had married into local nobility who owned extensive estates. Outside town, the Banases established a model agricultural village that they called Radocza, or "Place of the Joy of Living." The tenants dwelled and toiled in a self-contained world and were to all appearances happy, or at least more so than their cousins condemned to slovenly and brutal fiefdoms. The sumptuous Banas villa, which was vaguely Tuscan in effect, overlooked thousands of acres of farm and grazing land that supported cattle, hogs, goats, and various crops and had a stable for two hundred horses, including thoroughbreds and Arabians.

Jurek often took Tesia to Radocza to play tennis on the immaculate clay court bordered by white birches. Banas—tall and tanned, with blond hair and blue eyes—was always the perfect host, elegant in white flannels. Lemonade with ice was always ready in a crystal pitcher. Banas was so casual, even insouciant, that he never made Jurek or Tesia—who, slim and blond herself, might as well have been Countess Whoever—feel anything but equals. And they played so well!

"Your sister will soon be able to beat you," Banas said.

"I think she already can," Jurek admitted with a loving admiration for Tesia that he lavished on no one else.

At school in his uniform, Banas was the same as all the others, except that his style made caviar of a sausage sandwich. In warm weather, a coachman drove him and his two beautiful brothers to town in an open carriage. The carriage was drawn by a pair of sweating steeds, their manes and tails braided with red and white ribbons. En route to school, the boys never failed to halt at the house on Zatorska Street to shout and wave good morning to Jurek and Tesia, as if they were on a fantastical adventure rather than beginning another day of numbers, grammar, and history. The carriageful of rollicking rich boys catapulted Jurek into a joyful mood, and he hurried after them at a trot.

For Jurek, these were untroubled days. Other boys far less grand than Banas were equally generous within their means when Jurek dropped by their houses, and they in turn enjoyed the Klugers' hospitality. Socially and economically, they ranged from aristocracy to workers' sons and included, from one year to another, eight sons of government clerks; seven sons of teachers; four of soldiers; three of railroad workers, including the son of the local station master; three of policemen; seven of lawyers or physicians; two of shopkeepers; six of farmers or agricultural workers; and one, the poorest child, the son of a coal miner. The last boy, Teofil Bojes, who commuted by train each day from his village, was so in love with learning that his parents somehow managed to find the two hundred twenty *zlotys* (about five hundred dollars in today's currency) for his tuition. On autumn and spring mornings when heavy rains fell, he preserved his shoes by slogging barefoot through the mud to the train station.

After 1931, however, when the Great Depression hit Europe and diminished the market for Polish coal, Bojes's father was unemployed and could hardly be expected to imagine that further schooling for his child meant much when the family was scrounging to eat. To help keep Bojes in school, Father Edward Zacher, who taught Catechism at the high school, saw that his expenses were covered so that he could live at the dormitory where the handful of boarding students stayed, and several families helped out with part-time jobs and discreet gifts. Each morning, Jurek's mother packed extra food for him to share with Bojes and other hungry boys.

"Look at all this," Jurek used to say, emptying a sack packed with cheese and fruit and meat sandwiches and sweets. "My mother thinks I have the appetite of a horse! Take what you wish!" Without such acts, Bojes and others would not have been able to remain in school, which, in Poland as anywhere else, offered their best chance to rise above the precarious level of their parents.

Another boy, Karol Wojtyla, was better off than Bojes but considerably below Jurek on the economic scale. At the age of five or six, the boys learned to ski with the rest of their first-grade class, beginning to master the wooden, hand-fashioned slats in nearby foothills. Skiing in that part of Poland followed walking as surely as November gave way to December, and falling down in powder and ice was the way that Lolek and Jurek came to know one another.

Chapter 8

THEY WERE BORN NEARLY A YEAR APART—KAROL WOJTYLA ON MAY 18, 1920, and Jerzy Kluger on April 4, 1921. When Jurek asked his mother why he was so much younger than Lolek and all but one of his other classmates, she told him that she had sent him to school ahead of schedule because he was such a mischief-maker and she had to find some way to get him out of the house. Jurek rather liked that idea. Perhaps because his father was such a highly organized, disciplined, and serious fellow who committed nearly every waking moment to some larger purpose like the betterment of Poland or the welfare of the common man or the Jews of Wadowice, Jurek was quite the opposite. He admired his father's earnest endeavors, but Jurek's idea of a day well-spent was being on the playing field or the tennis court or, when he was older, in the company of a pretty girl. He thought life itself so wonderful and so full of opportunities that there didn't seem to be much point in trying to improve it.

As for being Jewish, he did not give it a great deal of thought. It was simply what he was, and in those golden days of youth, that was all right with him.

Lolek and Jurek were as different in personality as they were in religious, social, and economic backgrounds. While Jurek enjoyed the comforts of the house on Zatorska Street, Lolek from the age of nine lived alone with his father, a retired army lieutenant, in their modest apartment behind the church. Jurek attended synagogue chiefly because he was required to, especially as the son of the head of the Jewish community. Lolek served mass every morning, was the leader of the altar boys, and was president of the Sodality of the Blessed Virgin, founding the local chapter of that international society that encouraged piety in adolescent boys.

In school, Jurek often got himself into hot water for the pranks he pulled. If a teacher discovered his galoshes nailed to the floor or the sleeves of his overcoat sticky with glue, Jurek was among the usual suspects; Lolek never was. Nor did Lolek join in the clandestine poker games at the library, since he had no interest in cards or gambling. Although no one ever discovered who stole a certain teacher's grade book after a fiendishly difficult test, many believed that Jurek was the culprit, but not because he worried about his own grades. Though not quite at Lolek's superior level, Jurek was a fine student without working at it. He simply could not resist subversive jokes.

For all his good behavior, it must be emphasized that Lolek was no priss or prig; had he been, he and Jurek could never have been such good friends. He took his own quiet amusement in Jurek's and others' shenanigans; he was simply more mature than they. Those who knew Wojtyla well cherished a humor that was so subtle that it was difficult to define—an affectionate sort of irony that endeared him to others less studious and religious than he. He had a philosophical cast to him, as if he were observing everyone from a bright, steadfast star. There was a reserve about him that commanded respect, yet he was also curious about others. This was shown not so much by his asking questions as by an intense ability to listen, as if something important were hidden within the most common banter. Talking to him gave the impression that he knew what you were saying better than you did yourself. Jerzy puts it this way: around Wojtyla, it was impossible to lie, because he saw right through you, even if he seemed to be enjoying your fabrications.

For all that, he was very much a physical presence. He was a handsome blond with large-boned Slavic features, stronger and taller than most. Like his father, he would have made a fine soldier. In class and on the playing field, he was one of the boys. And yet he wasn't.

His habitual mood was cheerful, but during the times that he experienced first one and then another death in his already small family, friends could sense his melancholy. His mother, Emilia, died of kidney and heart disease in 1929, when he was barely nine years old. Three years later, in 1932, his beloved and only brother, Ed mund, who was fourteen years his senior and had just completed medical studies in Krakow, succumbed to scarlet fever contracted from a patient. A sister had died in infancy before Lolek's birth.

By all accounts, Lolek adored his brother, who even in death remained a model for him. Edmund had been as vigorously athletic as he had been studious, and he had been devoted to his family, especially his little brother. As John Paul II, Wojtyla confided to a writer, "My brother's death probably affected me more deeply than my mother's because of the peculiar circumstances, which were certainly tragic, and because I was more grown up." His mother had been ill for at least two years before her death; Lieutenant Wojtyla had retired from active duty to care for her and Lolek. Edmund was carried away at the age of twenty-six, on the cusp of achievement and promise, after four days of excruciating sickness.

These tragedies intensified Lolek's attachment to his father, who, until their roles were reversed, devoted his life to caring for Lolek and to his religion. They also caused Lolek to cherish his friendships with an unusual and understandable intensity that made at least a few of the boys, Jurek included, feel as if they had become members of his family and he of theirs.

What Lolek innately possessed was the virtue of hope, which gave him the kind of joyful expectation that we all are born with but that most of us gradually lose as disappointments take their toll. He had a serious playfulness about him—an aspect of personality perhaps better expressed through parable than by the accumulation of facts.

About thirteen hundred years ago, an Irish monk, inspired by apocryphal sources that contained luminous truths, wrote a poem capturing what Jesus must have been like as a boy. The poem, only as long as a pair of sonnets, describes what happens when Jesus at the age of five is caught violating the Sabbath by playing in mud puddles on the Lord's day. Worse yet, this imagined verbal snapshot from antiquity shows us, Jesus is breaking a proscription of the Second Commandment, "Thou shalt not make unto thee any graven image" (Exodus 20:3–4), as he is modeling the wet clay into birdlike shapes. Strict interpretation forbade making representations of any beings, for to do so was to assume creative tasks properly reserved to God. Jesus, of course, is only behaving naturally, as a child.

Reproached by an elder for this impious frivolity, the boy claps his hands and immediately performs a miracle, changing his mud pies into actual sparrows, which fly off twittering toward the heavens. And the birds hear Jesus call out to them (in a translation by Seamus Heaney):

> *"So that you may know who made you*
> *Fly home now. Away! Be off!"*
> *A witness spread the news: a story*
> *Everybody marveled at.*
> *They listened and could hear distinctly*
> *The little cries of birds in flight.*

No one thought of young Wojtyla in Christ-like terms, least of all Lolek himself, who came late to the idea of a religious vocation. He performed no miracles—at least not any of this sort—was anything but preachy, and his sturdy athleticism contrasted with conventional images of the Redeemer. But in other ways, Lolek resembled this portrait of Christ as a child, and the resemblance continued through adolescence and beyond. The joyful, playful delight in common things, the instinctive love of nature as of God, the impulse toward artistic transformation, the sense of the hand of the divine in the ordinary, the unconscious assumption of purpose and order in the universe, the sheer joy in creativity, the lightness of touch, the happiness in mere being and doing, awareness of the transcendent—

all of these were apparent in Lolek's personality, in the very way he carried himself, and in his personal style. There was something about him that caused everyone around him to think, if only for a moment, that life might be marvelous after all.

His religion teacher, Father Zacher, said just after Wojtyla's election to the papacy that Lolek was "the nearest thing to a genius that I ever had the good fortune to teach." But it was his genius for ordinary life, as for friendship, that touched Jurek Kluger and others.

THIS PLAYFULNESS ABOUT HIM—WHAT WERE ITS SIGNS? IT WAS SIGNALED BY the half-smile that was his usual expression under all but tragic circumstances, as if some joyful melody were playing in his head. Always a voracious reader of everything from classical and religious texts to popular historical literature, he wore his learning lightly. He could turn a table tennis game into mock-heroic grandeur by comparing it to some epic victory or defeat, quoting a line from Homer, say, or from a novel by the Polish Nobel Prize winner Henryk Sienkiewicz. A win by Jurek might evoke from Lolek praise of King Kazimierz the Great for welcoming Jews into Poland six hundred years earlier, when other European nations had expelled them.

Lolek's delight in historical parody was complemented by his great talent for mimicry, often in tandem with Jurek's gift for caricature. They found the same people funny, notably their teacher of Greek, Professor Tadeusz Szeliski, whom they nicknamed "Krupa" (a vile kind of barley soup). While Jurek drew bluntly two-dimensional portraits, Lolek's mimicry had a subtlety that managed to convey the humanity of the target as well as his absurdity. Another difference between them was that Jurek was recklessly prolific, and his pictures had a way of turning up in unwelcome places, such as on a teacher's desk. Lolek , on the other hand, performed his hilarious impressions only when prompted by trusted friends and never in the presence of the subjects. In this way, no one's feelings were hurt, and Lolek could keep his irreverence concealed from all but a happy few.

The rigid formality of Polish schooling, as ceremonious as it was rigorous, was irresistible to this pair of satirists. High school teachers, all of whom held master's degrees and a few of whom had doctorates, were invariably addressed as professor or doctor. When they retired, their names were added to the list of distinguished pedagogues and graduates that adorned a wall at the school.

When a professor entered the classroom, students rose in respectful greeting. Krupa, with spectacles, a mustache, and his big, bald head crowned by two bumps, was the ideal mark for Jurek's wicked pen. On his part, Lolek mimicked the professor's relentless diatribes against the evils of tobacco and the way he furiously threw open the windows when he caught a whiff of the noxious weed that Jurek and others (but not Lolek) had been puffing in the bathroom between classes. In Lolek's version, Krupa was somehow as endearing as he was ridiculous, a man defending his absurd but touching dignity against barbarians.

It was the same with Professor Zygmunt Damasiewicz, who wore English suits and mirror-polished shoes and enforced the strictest discipline in his Latin and Greek classes. His pair of unfortunate sons trailed him about town like puppy dogs, carrying his briefcase and bundles for him as he braved all weather to perform his daily constitutional. Damazy, as the students called him among themselves, had a horror of perfume equal to Krupa's aversion to tobacco. The smell, Jurek joked, must have reminded him of degradations of the boudoir. Jurek drew him recoiling in horror from a bottle of scent, while Lolek impersonated the way the professor seized a student by the ear and with violent imprecations threw him out the door after some unknown jester—could it have been Jurek?—had doused the unfortunate victim with perfume before class. Lolek's version magically transformed the enraged Damazy into an object as much of affection as of ridicule.

And then there was the winsome Dr. Sabina Rottenberg. Whatever age she was, maybe thirty, their German teacher must have been aware of the tumult she caused in adolescent hearts, as she was beautiful and, it appeared, flirtatious. Why else did she begin every class by taking a seat in the first row, twisting around to stare at them in painful silence, and pursing her lips into a pout? For what felt like minutes, she would let her big, dark eyes fall on them, a delicious torture, as she seemed to wait for a reaction.

Lolek invariably remained silent throughout these overtures, sitting absolutely still with his hands folded on his desk. Jurek, however—perhaps because Dr. Rottenberg was Jewish and therefore provoked in him the same degree of rebelliousness that he felt against his family—would begin to cough, fidget, moan softly, or make a rude noise by blowing air into his fist, inspiring others to a general restlessness. And everyone knew what he was up to when he dropped wads of paper on the floor, fell to his hands and knees to pick them up, and pretended to look up the professor's skirt. Some could not control their laughter. At last Dr. Rottenberg would rise and say, "*Ruhe*" ("Hush" in German), drawing out the two soft syllables, and commence the grammar lesson.

Jurek's drawings of the divine Sabina became keepsakes; he failed to goad Lolek into doing a full impersonation of Dr. Rottenberg, however, beyond a perfect imitation of her contralto, cooing "*Ruhe, ruhe*!"

By that time, Lolek had discovered the drama club as a more elevated circumstance for the exercise of his acting talents. The club, a joint venture with the girls' high school, performed at community festivals that featured parades, music, speeches, and dramatic recitations. These occasions were numerous, such as May 3, which commemorated the Constitution of 1791 and honored the Blessed Virgin as Queen of Poland; Armistice Day; and the Feast of Saint Joseph on March 19, which also honored the Polish hero Marshal Pilsudski.

The inextricable union of Catholicism with nationalism at these events would appear to have the effect of marginalizing Jews, but in Wadowice they actively participated. Jurek's father, wearing his legionnaire's uniform, regularly spoke in tribute to Pilsudski or to bolster the fragile harmony between religions. But by 1933, when young Wojtyla's voice began to mature, the highlight was his performance of stunning recitations from Slowacki, Adam Mickiewicz, or other great romantic-nationalist Polish poets. Lolek's poise before an audience and his talent for verbal expression, first recognized by his teachers and through the drama club, became treasured by his fellow townspeople. He struck patriotic and religious chords in every heart.

For these official appearances, Lolek needed no prodding, taking to the platform like the born Demosthenes he was. He had the romantic, musical style of recitation, the rhythmic transformation of poetry into song—rhapsodic and Homeric, a manly and enchanting loveliness of speech. He had a mastery of language and cadence and knew just the right dramatic gesture to mesmerize a crowd and make them feel that the soul of this youth was unfurling in beautiful words and that his soul was Poland's, too.

Lolek's Polish language, literature, and drama teacher, Mieczyslaw Kotlarczyk, who was only a few years older than his students, introduced him to this style of reverence for words and singled him out as the most talented. Lolek at once displayed an instinct for performance that transcended acting in the usual sense. Somehow, one got the feeling that he was also projecting his inner life, being, and sensitivity to feelings and ideas far beyond conventional description. What the German Romantics called *Geist*, or whatever it was that the Apostles were able to convey after the Holy Ghost descended on them in tongues of flame—that was what Lolek was able to express. Another age would have found him chanting verses to the accompaniment of a lyre. His talent was epic; it captured the deepest, most pervasive character and experience of Poland and its people—the longing for freedom, the reckless bravery, the colors and configurations of the Polish landscape, and the sting or softness of northern seasons. He was able to master a page in a single reading or two and, with a precision that was vital to enchantment, never missed a syllable.

I hear a Polish army marching on the land!
Above the French our white eagles soar.
At Napoleon's signal they will cross
The Niemen—our Homeland's Resurrection!

These were lines from one of his favorite poems, Mickiewicz's epic *Pan Tadeusz* (1834), in context spoken by a patriotic priest. To the Poles, Napoleon was the quintessential romantic hero and France the great ally and exemplar of liberty—before World War II, that is. And the co-mingling of religion and nationalism, the idea of Poland as the Risen Christ, was standard. Paradoxically, Mickiewicz, like other Polish Romantics, included Jews within the pantheon of Polish heroics, not least of all because of their alliance with nobility. And why not, since Christ was one. This was among the reasons that a family like the Klugers, although they were not typical, felt no contradiction in being Jewish and Polish, too. Hearing young Wojtyla recite to the crowd gathered in the Rynek put everyone into a joyous, proud mood, as if the Polish nation were itself one, holy, catholic, and apostolic—or, like the Jews, chosen.

Wojtyla also performed in patriotic plays (as virtually all Polish dramas were). One year, Lolek directed and played the lead in Slowacki's *Kordian*, which was revolutionary scheming in verse. It took place at the Sokol, a gymnastics building that also served as the town concert hall and theater. He was so authoritative and so much at ease in his performance that people began to talk in terms of his future on the stage.

It wasn't the lines Lolek delivered that affected people, it was his uncanny ability to project some inner, invisible life. At this time, only a few observers would have described that hidden spirit as specifically religious. He discovered that the sound and color of words induced in him an awe of language itself, as if words were gemstones polished on the tongue. Remembering this period of his life more than a half-century later, he recalled that in high school he had no thoughts whatever of the priesthood because "I was completely absorbed by a passion for literature, especially for dramatic literature, and for the theater." It proved to be a passion too powerful ever to leave him; it was not a passing phase but a portal.

When the Metropolitan Archbishop of Krakow visited Wadowice to bestow the sacrament of confirmation on boys and girls of age, Father Zacher chose Lolek to deliver the welcoming address. Prince Adam Stefan Sapieha was the most revered prelate in Poland, and his bearing was equal to his title and aristocratic family name. Afterward, he inquired what course of study this prodigy would undertake at the university in Krakow. Father Zacher replied that the young man would probably study Polish language and letters.

"A pity it is not theology," His Excellency said.

Others who knew Lolek also advised him to consider the seminary. In later years, he was known to joke at his own expense that perhaps some of these people were looking out for his economic security, thinking that as a priest he would be "set for life." What other practical course was there for this romantic dreamer, unless it was the stage? It was true that in addition to his other interests and talents, Lolek was an intensely religious young man. To him, however, religion was neither something consciously chosen nor a renunciation of life but rather the most natural form of celebration of God's creation as well as of his identity as a Pole. Language, nationality, and religion—these were the hallmarks of Polish pride.

Foreigners often make the mistake of considering Poles a people caught between Germanic cultures on the west and south and Russian-dominated ones on the east, a hodgepodge of the Slavic and the Teutonic. There is some truth to this, but Poland has a distinct culture, even after its long status as an occupied nation in which invaders made efforts to discourage native identity by changing placenames, removing indigenous subjects from school curricula, and all the other usual methods of conquerors. As has happened repeatedly throughout modern history, the national identity proved stronger than was thought, and it re-emerged after independence, when exiles returned. In some ways, that reborn nation had changed less than the European powers that had oppressed it.

Poland emerged far less secularized than Western Europe. Nothing in its culture urged religious rejection in the pursuit of art or science. At the great Jagiellonian University in Krakow, which, like Prague, Oxford and Cambridge, and all of the other oldest and greatest institutions of learning in Europe, was founded by monarchs and sponsored by the state, theology was among the most revered courses of study. Nicolaus Copernicus (1473–1543), the astronomer who altered forever our understanding of the Earth's place in the solar system, was among the institution's most distinguished students, and a statue of him stands not far from the university church, Saint Anne's.

The idea of secular education—that is, learning devoid of religion—is as alien to Polish sensibilities as life itself would be without the Church, which was something that Nazis and, later, Communists would discover. Should anyone be impertinent enough to ask a Catholic-born Pole whether he or she is devout or has left the Church, the probable response would be, "That is for the Church to decide."

To be sure, young Wojtyla's faith, like everything else about him, was particularly intense, even in a land of believers. It was marked, especially after the death of his mother, by special devotion to the Blessed Mother. In Poland, she had many visages—the familiar Virgin Mary, Queen of Heaven and Earth, Virgin Bride, Sorrowful Mother, Refuge of Sinners, Comforter of the Afflicted, and most poignantly, Queen of Poland. Mary, Mother of God, was the very image and essence of the motherland.

It is a curious thing that nations and empires tend to identify themselves as either masculine or feminine, with clearer identifications in some instances than in others. The Roman Empire—with its legendary founders, either Romulus and Remus or Aeneas—saw itself as distinctly masculine. So did the British Empire, which cast aside the image of Britannia in favor of John Bull. The United States has long been personified as Uncle Sam, and *Vaterland*—Fatherland—means Germany. But France is forever *La Belle France,* and Ireland identified with Kathleen ni Houlihan or the Poor Old Woman, who, to the Catholic majority, probably brings to mind the Virgin Mary. In Poland, however, the Lady of Heaven and the motherland are synonymous as nowhere else.

Perhaps these territorial associations with one sex or the other all have to do with the relative presence or absence of Catholicism. Predominantly Catholic nations believe in the powerful presence of the Virgin as the central intercessor between the faithful and the Lord. Certainly this appears true in Poland, where in his devotion to the Blessed Mother, young Wojtyla was celebrating love for the motherland, too.

The Blessed Virgin provided special solace and comfort to Lolek and his father after the death of his mother, Emilia. Lolek would wake up in the middle of the night to find his father—widowed at fifty—on his knees, praying to the image of the Black Madonna of Czestochowa. Every day his father prayed in the church across the street from their apartment, often in a side-chapel dedicated to Our Lady of Perpetual Help. This is where Lolek also served mass and prayed with his classmates before school, sometimes returning after school for brief devotions.

Three times a day, the bells rang out from that church to sound the Angelus in celebration of the Annunciation. Then father and son recited the rosary together, each decade of its fifty Hail Marys in honor of one of the five joyful, sorrowful, or glorious mysteries, followed by the *Salve Regina*: "To thee do we cry, poor banished children of Eve; to thee do we send up our sighs, mourning and weeping in this valley of tears." The presence of the Virgin was constant.

Their devotion to the Virgin was so great that they made pilgrimages together to Czestochowa, about a three-hour journey by train to the north. Here, veneration of the Virgin mingles with reverence for the cause of Poland. It is one of the three most visited religious places in Europe, exceeded only by Rome and Lourdes. For Poles, Czestochowa has unique significance. The miraculous icon of the Black Madonna is housed behind a screen and revealed each day with fanfare. It was crowned Queen of Poland by priests in 1717 as an act of defiance against forces of the czar and Eastern Orthodoxy. Before that and since, it has been associated with the rescue of Poland from her enemies. By legend, it was painted by Saint Luke on a beam from the house of the Holy Family in Nazareth. Its powerful hold on the imagination of Poles is unequaled by any other religious image. Reproductions of it may be found in every church in Poland and in virtually every home.

MANY PEOPLE FROM WADOWICE ALSO REGULARLY VISITED THE CARMELITE monastery situated on a hilltop just outside of town and had their confessions heard by the monks, whose order is also associated with the Virgin. From them, Lolek, at the age of about ten, received the scapular of Our Lady of Mount Carmel—two cloth holy pictures joined by strings and worn next to the skin. He continued to wear it throughout his life.

Another place of pilgrimage, Kalwaria Zebrzydowska, is situated in the hills around a neighboring town, only ten miles from Wadowice on the main road and railway line to Krakow and thus close enough for frequent visitation by father and son. They often made impromptu journeys or reserved two or three days to take part in the religious spectacles held there twice a year. An eccentric replica of the biblical Jerusalem that was unique not only in Europe but also the world, Kalwaria Zebrzydowska made such a deep and joyful impression on the young Wojtyla that he continued to visit it throughout his life. Any understanding of the way his sensibilities developed must include it.

Wojtyla's artistic disposition meant that facts and theories held little importance unless he could make them part of human experience. To a mathematician or a physicist, a line can exist as an idea and be no less real than a broomstick or anything else. But to an artist, a line must have powerful metphysical meaning. For Wojtyla, Kalwaria Zebrzydowska made religious abstractions real in a distinctively Roman Catholic way, like the smell of flowers and incense or the taste of the Eucharist.

Kalwaria is the name of the little town, whose inhabitants are famous for centuries of furniture-making. Dominating a hilltop at the end of a broad, curving drive is the sprawling Bernadine monastery. Its church and cloisters, completed in 1609 in the Polish Baroque style, express Poland's place as the northern- and easternmost stronghold of the Church of Rome. Twisting pathways stretch out from the monastery through the surrounding hills, leading to forty-one holy stations that commemorate Christ's Passion and the Blessed Mother's life.

This complex is laid out so that a wandering pilgrim may relive and visualize Christ's last days and Resurrection. The

Blessed Virgin's place in these events as well as her existence before and after her Son's life, death, and Ascension is also well-established here. To a cultural relativist, Kalwaria Zebrzydowska may appear as a prototype of Disneyland, with religion as its theme and Christ and the Virgin the stars for an age of believers. Kalwaria Zebrzydowska has never been a commercial enterprise, however; admission is free, and donations go only to maintain the grounds.

The original circuit of buildings, beginning with Pontius Pilate's Roman villa, traces Christ's Passion, following the Stations of the Cross. Later, a Cenacle, a two-story house where the Last Supper took place, was added. The sequence ends with Golgotha, a hill where the Church of the Crucifixion, the Chapel of Unction, and the Tomb of Our Lord stand. In the 1630s, no doubt in recognition of her powerful place in Polish Catholicism, a second circuit honoring the Virgin was completed.

The scale of all of the buildings is small enough to seem welcoming to a child. One building, the Chapel of Saint Mary's Heart, is no more than a hut, with a single round peephole or window at child's height, edged like the low doorway in pinkish stone. In the centuries of commentary on this place, no one has remarked that Mary's circuit surely must have been designed primarily for children, but this is obvious when one walks through it. Every child's desire to build a playhouse and a secret garden is here fulfilled in the form of little buildings, except that as each is keyed to the Holy Mother's life, the idea of a supreme, embracing maternal presence also settles on the mind of child and adult alike.

Each structure conveys love, security, forgiveness, and hope in approachable, human terms. One imagines an orphan who comes here discovering that he or she has a mother after all. A boy like Lolek, without a mother, may find that Mary is not only the Queen of Poland but also a kindly creature who has provided shelter for lonely children's souls. No wonder his father chose this place to bring his sons to pray after their mother's funeral. It seems reasonable to say that young Wojtyla's concept of the Church as a refuge and a source of hope rather than a body of accusation took shape along these pathways through Galician hills.

From August 13 to 15 each year, when throngs crowded in from all over Poland to celebrate the Feast of the Assumption, the experience was of a different kind, although it was one that Lolek and his father also enjoyed and regularly attended. People milled about, reassured that the Virgin's reign in heaven and in Poland continued. On the days before Easter, however, during Holy Week, Kalwaria Zebrzydowska presented a different story, one that invariably, until recently, produced feelings less joyful than mixed.

Chapter 9

In those days, Lolek and Jurek did not discuss the matter specifically, but Kalwaria Zebrzydowska naturally meant different things to the Wojtyla and Kluger families. Celebrations surrounding the Feast of the Assumption hardly registered with the Klugers, who were often away on holiday during August. The annual Easter pageant, however, which attracted bigger crowds and was the principal reason for the place's popularity among visitors from neighboring countries, was followed every year by violent outbreaks of anti-Semitism. While no attacks directly related to Kalwaria occurred within the town limits of Wadowice, Jews in surrounding villages and towns dreaded Holy Week as a time that was sure to bring out the latent contempt and hostility among some members of the Catholic majority.

Both Easter and Christmas were times for Jews in Poland, especially in rural or semi-rural areas, to be wary. They were times that threatened the common sense of Polish identity and defined citizens, at least in the minds of many, as being either for or against Christ. Not in cosmopolitan Krakow itself but elsewhere throughout Galicia, Jews habitually and prudently stocked up on food and fuel so they could remain safely in their houses; if they ventured out, they tried not to do so alone.

The danger only increased in years when Passover—which begins on the fifteenth day of April and lasts eight days—overlapped with Easter week. The two faiths appeared to be juxtaposed in opposition, as if, however contrary to historical fact the idea was, the Jews were celebrating their rejection of Christ rather than deliverance from bondage in Egypt and the coming of spring. Without doubt, Catholic ritual itself incited ill-will. At the time, a Good Friday devotional prayer referred to the Jews as "that pernicious race," in the course of appealing for their conversion. "I propose now and ever to adore Thee...in the stead of and for the conversion of all heretics, schismatics, impious, atheists, blasphemers, sorcerers, Turks, Jews, and idolaters," declared the prayer known as an "Act of Reparation" for crimes committed against Jesus.

Good Friday was the only day of the year in which the Church prayed publicly for the entire human race, including non-Catholics. Presumably, Jews were not pleased at their inclusion in the above-listed collection of miscreants, and the recitation of this list of unappealing types did nothing to encourage love of one's neighbor.

Another prayer recited on this day and known as "Good Friday Reproaches" was cast in the imagined words, not found in any Scripture, of Christ himself and consisted of several accusations against the Jews.

> Because I brought thee out of the Land of Egypt, thou hast prepared a cross for thy Saviour.... Because I led thee through the desert forty years and fed thee with manna and brought thee into an excellent land, thou has prepared a cross for thy Saviour.... I have planted for thee My most beautiful vineyard: and thou hast proved very bitter to Me: for in My thirst thou gavest Me vinegar to drink; and with a spear thou hast pierced the side of thy Saviour.... For thy sake, I scourged Egypt with her first-born; and thou has delivered me to be scourged.... My people! What have I done to thee? Or in what have I grieved thee? Answer me.

Typical of the strongly anti-Jewish character of Good Friday observances, the "Reproaches" attributed acts that, according to the Gospels, were committed by Roman soldiers—such as the offering of the sponge of vinegar and the thrusting of the spear—to the Jews, or conflated Romans and Jews, thus placing full blame on the children of Abraham and Moses. The words of Christ quoted during the Stations of the Cross, which are an integral part of Good Friday observances, went still further in the attribution of guilt, plainly indicating that it will be inherited from generation to generation. At the Eighth Station, "Jesus Speaks to the Daughters of Jerusalem," the Savior, "streaming with blood," says to the women, "Weep not for me but for your children."

Although these and other aspects of Good Friday traditions were hostile enough, they were mild compared to the negative emotional effects of a gruesome ritual common on that day throughout Europe since the thirteenth century. The Passion Play was the principal attraction at Kalwaria Zebrzydowska, where the drama has been an annual event since the completion of Christ's circuit.

As with all melodrama, the touchstone of audience reaction is the loathsome villain. In this instance, it was not only Judas but an entire people whose descendants were some three-and-a-half million strong in Poland. This Polish version had the ability to move some among the audience into a dangerous frenzy against those featured as Christ's killers and their children.

Passion Plays traditionally focused on the Jews as villains, inculcating the idea of the Hebrew as scapegoat for all of humankind's sins. That Christ himself died to redeem everyone's failings, not just those of the Jews, was a truth central to Christianity that Passion Plays obscured wherever they were performed.

The play at Kalwaria Zebrzydowska was particularly reversionary because of the large concentration of Jews in Poland and the realism of the setting. As to the latter, pilgrims did not sit as an audience before a stage, where they would sense the make-believe quality of a theatrical production. They became part of the drama, following along Christ's circuit at the shrine in the wake of the bleeding, scourged Savior. The often inclement weather at that season added to the realism; the days and nights might be fine or laced with snow or rain, turning the grounds to mud. By the time the pilgrims followed Christ to Golgotha to see him not actually nailed but tied to the cross, the agony was everyone's. The actors, moreover, were people like themselves, local peasants and monks, adding to the sense that this was less a play than everyone's experience.

In the main church of the Bernadine monastery, a large, anonymous, seventeenth-century painting was another Holy Week attraction. Thousands filed past it each year to be affected by its grotesque imagery. It showed Christ falling under his cross as a throng of Jews, made to look like animals—with claws for hands, stained, jagged teeth, and evil eyes—tore, kicked, and spat at him. What was mimicked in the play was here permanently framed, given honor and validity by its prominent position on a wall of the sanctuary. Its image burned in the minds of pilgrims as they took their journeys homeward. That was when the trouble always started.

Some of the peasants, with their economic resentments now mixing with hatred of demonic Christ-killers, indulged in physical attacks on Jews. The young peasant men who did most of the damage to Jewish persons and property were traveling on foot through villages and across the countryside, their religious ire likely fueled by vodka after days of fasting and prayer at Kalwaria. It was easy for them to identify the Jews, who, with their uncut beards and hair and their distinctive clothing, were imprudent enough to stray from their houses. Unlike the Klugers and their relations, eighty percent of Polish Jews were Orthodox or members of the distinctive Hassidic movement. If challenged, they would respond, if at all, in heavily accented Polish laced with Yiddish—ripe targets for beatings.

Such violence had been a common feature in the aftermath of Passion Plays throughout Europe for hundreds of years. The cause was not the Poles but the plays and the religious anti-Semitism that such crude dramas encouraged.

KAROL WOJTYLA'S LATER WRITINGS, SPEECHES, AND CONVERSATION SHOW that he favored the Feast of the Assumption and private prayer and meditation at Kalwaria Zebrzydowska over the Easter pageant. He and his father did attend the Passion Play—in fact, his grandfather and great-grandfather on his father's side had worked as volunteer guides for pilgrims. The soldiers and craftspeople (tailors and saddlers) probably would not have shared in the peasants' specific idea of Jews. That Wojtyla's friendship with one Jew actually flourished inside a Roman Catholic church in Wadowice is a significant factor in understanding his character. As with all of his ideas, his understanding of Jews and Judaism came not from received opinion or doctrine but out of personal experience that was later shaped by religious and philosophical tradition.

An incident involving Jerzy Kluger occurred in 1930 and shows that Wojtyla's concept of the place of the Jews in relation to Christianity was already formed by the age of ten.

THAT JUNE, LOLEK AND JUREK HAD JUST COMPLETED ELEMENTARY SCHOOL together, the last four years in rooms set aside at City Hall. To qualify for high school, they had to pass an examination that measured literacy and competence in arithmetic through long division. As was the case in most of Europe then, the age of ten or eleven was the time to determine who would continue their education and who would be better off leaving school to pursue manual labor or some kind of trade. Fortunately, in Poland, students had the opportunity to repeat grades or retake examinations.

There was little doubt that boys as bright as Lolek and Jurek would pass, but Jurek was a born worrier and fretted about the possibility that he might not be able to join Lolek and others in high school that fall. The high school, founded in 1866, was a three-story rectangular building that had stood on Mickiewicz Street since 1874. In the days of Austrian rule, Jurek's father graduated from it before entering the University of Vienna for his legal studies. He certainly expected Jurek to finish his secondary education at least. For him to have to repeat a grade would embarrass the family.

Jurek hurried from his house, across the Rynek and three blocks west along Mickiewicz Street to the school, which seemed an immense edifice to a nine-year-old. In the foyer, a few of his pals were already gathered around a woman who was just posting the list of the lucky ones. Stanislaw Banas whooped when he saw his name at the top. Bojes...Kesek...and there it was, J. Kluger! Kus and others followed, down to Wojtyla, Zweig, and Zmuda. Hooray! They had made it!

But where was Lolek this morning? As usual, he was serving mass. Jurek was bursting to tell him the news. Imagine, in a few weeks they would all be wearing that handsome uniform—a dark blue jacket with a light blue stripe on one sleeve, long Zouave-like striped trousers, and, of course, the jaunty *maciejowka*, a blue beret popularized by Marshal Pilsudski, with a golden torch symbolizing knowledge pinned to the front. Everyone would know who they were!

Jurek wanted so much to tell Lolek how happy he was that they would be sticking together. He simply had to tell him and be the one to see Lolek's face light up. He could not contain himself. Confiding in no one about his mission, he took off for the church.

Out the door, down the street, dodging vegetable carts and horses through the Rynek, he ran all the way to the entrance of the church and paused to catch his breath. He hesitated. He had never been inside this or any other Catholic church in his life, but he knew that Lolek surely would want him to go ahead. He pushed open the huge door to enter the sanctuary.

Jurek marveled at the enormous vaulted chamber with its marble and gold handiwork and statues all around. It was so much grander than the synagogue, he thought. Except for scattered figures kneeling among the pews, it was practically empty, which made Jurek feel more conspicuous. At the end of the wide aisle, he recognized the back of Lolek's blond head as he knelt in costume beside a priest who turned to face the people, opened his hands, and spoke in Latin. Jurek recognized Canon Prochownik, his grandmother's walking companion in the Rynek.

He decided not to walk straight down the center aisle. Instead he tiptoed to the side and made his way to the far left of the altar rail. He leaned over and waved, trying to catch Lolek's attention. Everyone else was kneeling, so he did, too, on the cushion at the rail, and waved again. Lolek had his eyes closed and head bowed as Canon Prochownik read aloud from a big book.

"Psst! Lolek!" Jurek called in a stage whisper. Canon Prochownik paused. *"Lolek!"* Lolek twisted around to catch sight of him. "He is very surprised to see me," Jurek thought happily.

"Lolek! I have to tell you something!"

Lolek pointed toward the pews and mouthed, "Wait for me! Sit down!"

Jurek picked a spot in the first pew. An old lady was kneeling and praying near him, but she soon sat back on the bench, so Jurek did, too, and took in his surroundings. The altar had a little house of gold at its center that reminded him of the *aron* where the Torah was kept at the synagogue. The big red prayer book had silky ribbons of green, purple, and white dangling from it. At the left front, he saw a rostrum like a *bimah,* and to the rear, there was a light burning inside red-colored glass hanging from a chain. Jurek was pleased to see that except for the big cross, everything was much the same as in the synagogue. It was mainly the statues and the language that made the church much different. He felt rather pleased with himself and excited to be there. If only Lolek could get Canon Prochownik to hurry up.

The mass ended with everyone except Jurek saying several prayers aloud in Polish and asking Saint Michael to thrust into hell Satan and the other evil spirits who roam through the world seeking the destruction of souls. Jurek thought that it sounded like a good idea. Now, he reasoned, Lolek would come down to see him—but instead he followed Canon Prochownik through a side door. He needed to change clothes first, Jurek reasoned.

The woman had to squeeze past him to get out and as she did, she gave him a hard look.

"Why, you're Lawyer Kluger's son," she said. "Your father is the head of the Jewish community, isn't he?"

Jurek said nothing, looking into her rheumy eyes. She arched her brows, crossed herself, and left.

Just then Lolek reappeared, still in cassock and surplice, and came down from the altar and through a gate in the rail. He was grinning. "What's up?" he asked.

Jurek spluttered out the great news. They would be together! They hugged and gave each other manly claps on the back, and Jurek recited the names of all who had made it and the unfortunate two or three who hadn't. It would be a great class, they agreed.

"By the way," Lolek said, "what was that old woman saying to you just now?"

"She asked me if I was the son of the president of the Jewish community," Jurek answered. "I don't think she thought I belonged here. Maybe she was surprised to see a Jew in church."

"Why?" Lolek laughed. "Aren't we all God's children?"

Chapter 10

WHILE LOLEK'S ATTITUDE TOWARD JEWS IN GENERAL AND TOWARD Jurek in particular was unique in the uncompromising nature of its embrace, Jurek himself had little direct experience with virulent anti-Semitism when he was young. Lolek was the only one among his Catholic classmates who actually declared an acceptance of Jews as equal in the eyes of God and expressed in other ways his instinctive rejection of religious and other forms of anti-Jewish sentiment. Among his classmates, however, Jurek could identify only two as openly anti-Semitic, initially by their occasional remarks and later by their actions.

Of course, even in Wadowice, there were incidents. In 1933, a shoving match between one of his Jewish classmates, Zygmunt Selinger, and an older boy who had been taunting Selinger about being a kike or a Yid, ended in tragedy. Selinger, who grew up carrying heavy sacks of flour at his father's mill, was an ill-chosen target for abuse. When Selinger reacted by giving his taunter a good push, the other boy fell backward, hit his head on the ground, and was killed. It says something about the relative security of Jews in Wadowice at the time that Selinger was not charged with any crime.

The physical strength of both of Jurek's Jewish classmates, along with his own athleticism, helped them gain acceptance. One of the boys, Leopold Zweig, was four years older than his classmates because he had failed entrance examinations that many times. He was also the best footballer (soccer player) in the school. With his short, powerful physique and age advantage, he was probably the toughest as well. Popular with the girls, who favored older fellows, he was also unanimously elected president of the sports club, a position that carried even more prestige than that of school marshal. Even the anti-Semites voted for him because, it was said, they could expect a beating from Zweig's fellow athletes, Jewish and Christian alike, if they didn't.

As for the two open anti-Semites in Jurek's class, one was the son of a doctor who had died. He was a good student who played no sports because of what he said was a heart condition. Jurek believed, however, that he used his supposedly poor health to avoid being hit when he provoked an argument. A badgerer, he was always accusing Jews of being Communists.

The other boy, who was the son of a schoolmaster, seemed to hate Jews simply on principle and used them as targets of his aggressive and hostile personality. He had the face of a ruffian, was often on the verge of being expelled for "hooliganism," and was often suspected of stealing and destroying property. The two, who did not care much for each other, either, posed no threat to their three Jewish classmates. If there were other serious anti-Semites in the class, they kept their animosity quiet.

AND THEN THERE WAS WOJTYLA. AS THE MOST RESPECTED BOY IN THE CLASS, he set an example by being such close friends with Jurek. Lolek did not get into fights, although when playing goalie, he was no pushover on the soccer field. His dignity and kindness, which nearly all of the students and faculty appreciated, were themselves powerful deterrents against ugly behavior. As any teacher knows, one student like that can counteract much malevolence.

Soccer was not an official school sport. Technically, it was banned because it tended to excite uncontrollable degrees of partisanship. But no one interfered when the boys organized casual pickup matches in a field, piling up jackets and school bags as goal posts and choosing up sides. Here ethnic divisions came to the fore, which was another reason for school officials to wisely discourage the game: elsewhere in Poland, Jewish soccer teams frequently encountered violence from Gentiles, especially when playing away from home. In Wadowice, the boys usually separated into Catholic versus Jewish teams, giving vent to oppositions deeper than sporting ones. Even with players drawn from various school grades, however, there were sometimes not enough Jews to fill a side. When this happened, Lolek often played goalie for the Jews, especially if the enormous Poldek Goldberger, whose bulk made scoring against him difficult, was absent.

In the heat of these matches, even with Lolek and perhaps another Catholic boy or two on the Jewish side, hostilities came to the surface. The Jews gave as good as they got, to be sure, but they could expect to hear "Crack the Jew's skull!" and the like. The best response to this was to score another goal. At these moments, it gave Jurek satisfaction to watch Lolek, who was very good, defending the Jewish goal—especially when, with Zweig's strength and Jurek's speed, the Jews won.

As for official competitions, whether intramural against the nearby Zywiec or Bielsko-Biala high school or annually in the national high school championships, Catholics and Jews competed side by side or individually without regard to religious distinction. In these games, held in Wadowice at the Blonie, a big field by the river near the army grounds, Jurek was often the winner in the hundred meters, the long jump, and table tennis. Lolek participated in these competitions, but only locally, and not with Jurek's dedication and determination. The drama club was Lolek's passion, and there he had no peer.

At tennis, Jurek usually beat everyone in his age group in Wadowice, where matches were played on the courts in the park. He also did well enough in national competitions to travel to other towns and cities, falling short of the finals but winning his share and proudly having the satisfaction of representing his hometown. After reaching the semifinals in Lodz, the second largest city in Poland, he came home and told everyone that they should be glad to live in Wadowice, modest town though it was, and not in some industrial nightmare. He described Lodz as the filthiest, most depressing place he had ever seen, with nothing but smoke and soot and a terrible stink from the textile factories. Grandmother Huppert admonished him that some of Poland's most prominent Jewish families, such as the Poznanskis, lived there, and his father reminded him that Lodz was the birthplace of Artur Rubinstein, the most magnificent of all Chopin interpreters. It may have money and music, was Jurek's response, but it's not fit to live in.

He already had his own ideas of the good life. If he could improve his tennis a bit, he might tour the world like a true gentleman sportsman. He might put Wadowice on the map. His family wondered, however, why he couldn't be more like Tesia. For her age and sex, Tesia was at least as good a tennis player as he was, or even better. At fourteen, she was already on the national team, representing Poland in Prague and elsewhere—a young champion. But Tesia also paid more attention to her studies. No one loved or admired Tesia more than he did, Jurek thought, but he had more fun.

SO IT WAS THAT JUREK FELT LIKE ANYTHING BUT AN OUTSIDER IN WADOWICE. At the beginning of each lesson every schoolday, two hundred twenty days a year, the fearsome Damasiewicz and the other professors monitored attendance by reciting the roll of between thirty and forty students. Everyone knew the list by heart and sometimes amused each other by reciting it like a comical mantra. It was his class at the Old Shed or the Doghouse, as Polish students traditionally called their school, that gave Jurek his sense of identity as much as being Jewish did, and it mitigated if not entirely obliterated the sense of separateness that was felt, maintained by, and to an extent imposed on most Polish Jews.

Only a few hours each week were spent apart from the Catholic majority. Every Sunday, the Catholic students attended mass together at the parish church, girls on one side of the aisle, boys on the other, singing hymns together, with Father Zacher the celebrant. On

Friday evenings, when his mother lit the *Shabbath* candles, and on Saturdays in the synagogue, Jurek was with his own and other families for religious observance. Three hours a week in school, Jewish and Catholic students went to different classrooms for religious instruction; one class was taught by Professor Chaim Reiter and the other by Father Zacher or Father Kazimierz Figlewicz. Thus the Polish state accommodated both faiths within the prescribed curriculum. Other than that, in class or out, it was to his classmates that Jurek belonged, as Lolek did, studying or playing, through most of the waking hours of the week.

On Thursday afternoons, officers of the Twelfth Infantry drilled and lectured them on military tactics and plans for national defense; in the summer they attended compulsory army camp together at Ustron Slaski on the Vistula River, living in tents and learning how to survive in the woods. A ski camp in Zakopane, sponsored by the school, was a regular feature as long as snow still clung to the Tatras. And throughout the year, there were numerous school excursions, each cued to some aspect of the national culture and life—a visit to a hydroelectric project on the Sola River, to the castle of the Prince of Zator, to the salt mine at Wieliczka (in operation since medieval times), and to the various attractions of Krakow. So it was that they grew into manhood with a stronger and stronger sense of what it meant to bear the common name of "Poles."

While a few boys came and went as family circumstances dictated, the core remained through graduation. In 1934, Stanislaw Jura, a boy from Kety whose parents preferred the superior Wadowice school, joined them, living at the dormitory for boarders and quickly becoming friends with Lolek and Jurek. Also in that year, Zbigniew Silkowski, who lived over the train station where his father was master, failed a grade and became a new member of the class. Lolek, with a pastoral impulse that was already a marked feature of his personality, always went out of his way to welcome newcomers. Silkowski, a tall, blond youth who was no doubt shamed by his failure, was very shy at first. But Lolek saw inhibited qualities. He helped the boy with his studies, especially Latin and Greek, and invited him to share a double desk in class; Jurek sat directly behind them.

Silkowski soon became one of the better students and, again at Lolek's urging, joined the drama club and the Sodality of the Blessed Virgin, where his professed agnosticism melted under what must have been a powerful influence. Silkowski was a skier and was good at handball and volleyball: he and Lolek, who were alike in temperament, became the best of friends.

Lolek, Jurek, and their pals had such a wealth of pastimes to choose from that it was as if God had made that world for the young. In summer, there was swimming in the Skawa and maybe a walk to Grandmother Huppert's farm to pick cherries and gorge on them until their stomachs ached. In winter, any break in the weather meant a brisk hike into the hills for a few hours of skiing. A mile or so from town, the military had rigged up a kind of trampoline to practice ski-jumping. Often Lolek and Jurek wandered alone, with skis on their shoulders, far enough to worry about wolves, then raced each other home as darkness fell (as early as three o'clock in January). Any frozen pond invited a makeshift hockey game, with sticks snapped from trees and a stone or a block of wood for a puck.

On the far bank of the river was Venezia, a restaurant that was Italian in name only and was rather romantic, with a beautiful garden in summer and its own tennis court. It was a popular family gathering spot. On icy winter evenings, the court was flooded to make a rink and strung with colored lights, and patrons skated to waltzes from a gramophone.

Wadowicians of all ages mingled there, but Jurek tried to skate with Lolek and other boys and girls away from his mother's watchful eye. She was likely to embarrass him by warning him to stop roughhousing or risking his neck with reckless leaps. She was a good skater herself, unlike his father, who would venture out, fall down, and return to his glass of brandy, much to Jurek's amusement. Tesia, with her pirouettes and back-bending twirls, her pale hair sweeping the ice, was best of all. People stopped to admire her and applaud.

As close as they were, Lolek and Jurek diverged along certain lines. On school expeditions to Krakow, for instance, Lolek was enthralled by performances at the Teatr Slowackiego, a magnificent place modeled on the Paris Opera, and he intensely studied Junosza Stepowski and other renowned actors. Jurek managed to get himself thrown out for making too much noise with other boys. On one trip, while Lolek was at the theater, Jurek was drinking wine in a cellar on Florianska Street with Teofil Bojes and another boy; on another, Jurek was ejected by the police from under a reviewing stand, where he was trying to get a close-up view of Marshal Pilsudski.

In his love of pranks and general rebelliousness, Jurek's usual cohort was Tadeusz Czuprynski, nicknamed Don Giovanni. Tadeusz's talent for landing in trouble so exasperated his mother that she enrolled him in a strict private school run by the Pallottine Fathers. In an escape attempt, Tadeusz fell off the wall, broke a leg, and succeeded in getting himself expelled. Welcomed back to the high school like a wounded veteran, he and Jurek resumed their favorite diversion, lurking in the *Aleja Milosci,* or lovers' lane, a secluded pathway in the park about which the joke was that the trees there were more sinned against than sinning. Girls from their school nearby would enter the lane from one end, boys from the other, and they would meet to pair off for furtive hugging and kissing—until they were caught, nearly always, it seemed, by one of Grandmother Huppert's ubiquitous informants.

Professor Jan Gebhardt, who taught history, was another menace. He liked to walk his red setter through the park, and Jurek complained that if only Gebhardt would encourage his dog to sniff out birds instead of lovers, the professor could feed his family for nothing. The consequences of being discovered—although the *delicto* fell well short of *flagrante*—were dire but more threatened than administered.

It was not that Lolek shunned the company of girls, however. He encountered them almost daily at drama club rehearsals. He was closest to Regina Beer, a Jewish girl who was two years older than he and was assistant coach to Professor Kotlarczyk, and to Halina Krolikiewicz, whose father, Jan, was principal at the boys' high school and also tutored Lolek in Greek. A third was Kazia Zak, a tall, slender beauty whose aura of mystery and vagueness suited perfectly the abstract, poetic quality of much of the Polish-Romantic repertoire.

Halina, a regal blond who, like Lolek, projected a precocious dignity in what were primarily aristocratic parts, most often played opposite him in leading roles. On one memorable occasion, a performance of Slowacki's *Balladyna*, she found herself playing alongside two very different Loleks—one the hero, who dies early, and the other the villain, who dominates the last act. It happened because Halina's father suspended the boy who was to play the dastardly Kostryn; it seems that the actor had threatened a teacher with violence at the prospect of a failing grade. Lolek, with forty-eight hours' notice, changed from noble Kirkor's costume to play Kostryn and managed both parts without a hitch. He had all the parts memorized, he told Halina, as if that were any actor's normal preparation. "So it may be," she told him, "for you!"

Halina was not intimidated by Lolek's memory or formidable presence. The two developed the kind of competition that brings a performance alive, with each trying to upstage the other. It was a friendly rivalry, to be sure, but both openly acknowledged it. And it came to a head when Kazimiera Rychter, one of Poland's greatest actresses, sponsored a recitation contest in Krakow. Lolek chose a difficult passage from Cyprian Norwid's *Promethidion*, a highly philosophical dialogue tied to Polish history. Halina elected to recite something more directly human and emotional, a fable from Polish folklore. Lolek placed second to Halina's first. "You beat me this time," he said, and somehow found the money to present her with flowers.

Regina Beer, whom everyone called Ginka, was so lively and versatile, with a natural talent for comedy and satire, that she lit up the stage with her vivacity, a perfect foil to Lolek's and Halina's gravity. And it was Ginka who organized what had been only a school club into a truly regional theater, which she named the Wadowice Theater Circle. Had the title existed, she would have been called their producer. It was she who made arrangements for performances in neighboring towns, raising funds for transportation, cajoling local carpenters into building sets for free, and encouraging patrons to search their attics for costumes.

With all of this and her acting, Ginka was also the top scholar at the girls' school, where she excelled in science. She seemed equally well suited for a career in the theater or in a laboratory. Some, including Jurek, were of the opinion that she had even more acting talent than Lolek and Halina. All of them, including Kazia, could conceivably one day perform amidst the Hapsburg opulence of the Teatr Slowackiego. But Ginka might just as plausibly emulate her heroine Marie Curie, winner of two Nobel Prizes for her discoveries of polonium and radium. Although usually presumed to be French, Madame Curie, as Ginka was fond of pointing out, had been born Manya Sklodowska in Warsaw; her death in 1934 was an occasion of national mourning in Poland.

Little seemed to be beyond Ginka or, for that matter, any of the stars of the Wadowice Theater Circle.

AH, GINKA! JUREK WAS SELDOM ENVIOUS OF ANYONE, BUT IF THERE WAS ANYthing he coveted, it was Lolek's good fortune, not only in being around Ginka so often but also in living right next door to her. Ginka, with her pixie freckle-face, her alabaster skin and dark hair, and her irrepressible energy, was adorable. Her wit, her laughter that bubbled like a pot on the boil, the tiny space between her teeth—everything about her was entrancing. It was probably a good thing, Jurek thought, that she was nearly three years older than he, or he might have made a fool of himself for love, although that was hardly his style. Being inaccessible, Ginka was the most delightful of dreams. He always hoped to catch a glimpse of her when he visited the building where both the Wojtylas and the Beers lived.

Nothing in Wadowice was very far from anything else, but Jurek and Lolek were practically neighbors. All Jurek had to do to call at the Wojtylas' was to turn right behind the church, walk into Rynek Street (later changed to Koscielna Street) and climb the iron stairs at No. 2, where Lolek was born and where he and his father remained after Mrs. Wojtyla's death. From the first landing, a walkway led through an open court past the apartment where Ginka lived with her parents; the next door, at the end of the walkway and facing the street and the rear of the church, was the Wojtylas'.

Jurek knew everyone in this building, with its mixed tenancy of

Catholics and Jews; it was a modest place but comfortable enough for a decent life. On the ground floor, the Jewish landlord, Chaim Balamuth, lived with his family behind their glass and crystal shop. They also repaired and sold bicycles and motorcycles to the few who could afford them. Upstairs, across from the Wojtylas and the Beers, Mrs. Helena Szczepanska lived with her husband. In her forties, the kindly woman helped Lieutenant Wojtyla care for his son. She was also one of Tesia's teachers. His sister was such a good girl, Mrs. Szczepanska liked to tease Jurek. Why didn't he make has parents happy by staying out of trouble and studying as hard as Tesia did?

"An excellent suggestion, Mrs. Szczepanska," Jurek would reply, doffing his *maciejowka* and displaying his school bag. "As a matter of fact, I'm here to do homework with Lolek. I am sure I'll benefit from his good influence."

"What a rascal you are, Jurek Kluger," she'd say, and pinch his cheek.

Yet he was telling the truth. Nothing was more pleasant on a wintry afternoon than to study with Lolek in that simple but cozy apartment, which consisted of the bedroom where father and son slept, a sitting room that was hardly used since Mrs. Wojtyla's death, and a small kitchen, where the coal-fired stove provided heat. Lolek studied at the round kitchen table; in a corner was his father's desk, always piled with books and papers. Lieutenant Wojtyla was usually seated there when Jurek came in.

There was a *prie-dieu* and a holy-water font near the front door; along with the holy pictures, including the Black Madonna, they identified it as a Catholic house. Jurek scarcely noticed these emblems of faith, which were familiar to any Catholic dwelling, including the Banas villa. Since he felt entirely welcome, the religious symbols were simply part of the decor. Nor would he have dreamed of refusing a snack of sausage or a ham sandwich when it was offered, especially here, where such a gesture meant more than it would have in an affluent house. At home, his mother kept a kosher kitchen; her husband, after all, was president of the Jewish community, however liberal his views, and Grandmother Huppert required it. But that did not mean that Jurek should refuse Gentile hospitality.

Physical grace and courage, the avoidance of affectation, loyalty, adaptability, and, above all, courtesy—these were the marks of a gentleman, Wilhelm Kluger had instructed his son. Good manners apart, Jurek would never have had the willpower to resist an offering of the local, highly spiced *kielbasa.*

Lolek's father, who had apprenticed as a tailor, his father's trade, was drafted into the Austrian Army in 1900 and stayed in to make soldiering his career. His service during World War I merited him the Iron Cross of Merit. After the war, the new Polish Army promoted him to first lieutenant, and he remained stationed in Wadowice until his retirement. Of medium height, with a full mustache and somewhat bald by the time Jurek knew him, he was accurately described in his military file: "Extraordinarily well-developed with a righteous character, serious, well-mannered, with a strongly developed sense of responsibility, very gentle, and tireless."

If "very gentle" seems a peculiar virtue for a military officer, it should be remembered that Karol Senior spent most of his career in an accountant's capacity, overseeing supplies, rather than engaging in specifically military activities. This experience no doubt served him well after retirement, when his pension was his family's only income. He had also retained his tailoring skills and cut expenses by stitching handsome suits for Lolek from old uniforms. He did the same out of kindness for other needy boys. Consequently, Lolek, when not in school uniform, was always well-dressed.

Jurek, visiting the Wojtylas from his own comparatively luxurious surroundings, was impressed by how decently Lolek and his father managed to live. The lieutenant's absolute commitment to his son's education was also touching. There was never the slightest suggestion that Lolek should neglect his studies by working even part-time. Lieutenant Wojtyla was the opposite of those parents who lived for the day when their sons would start bringing home a paycheck. It was clear also that Lieutenant Wojtyla thought of Lolek's education, which would doubtless continue through university, not as primarily the ticket to a job but as something valuable for its own sake. Whatever Lolek wished to study, and for however many years, was fine with the lieutenant. Indeed, it was his principal point of pride. The longer he knew them, the more Jurek understood how Lolek was indeed his father's son. It was little wonder that the two were so close and never seemed to quarrel.

The lieutenant, for all his military bearing, Spartan sense of duty, and intense piety, was also a learned man, with prodigious knowledge in the fields of history, mythology, and legend. To see his busy desk and hear him discuss his latest readings in German as well as Polish authors, one might have mistaken him for a professor. Jurek never knew how the nickname came about, but perhaps it was because of his learning that everyone usually addressed him not formally but affectionately as "Captain," as if he deserved the promotion whether or not he had actually received it.

It was easy to see how Lolek had acquired his fascination with Polish culture from his father, whose own formal education had ended after only three years of high school. At that time, under Austrian rule, Polish history, language, and literature were barred from the school curricula as vestigial remnants of a conquered people. The official language was German, and the glories of the Hapsburgs were the focus of study. Like other nationalists, Lolek's father studied Polish subjects on his own or in the company of fellow patriots, with the result that everything Polish was all the more precious to him.

"What are you learning in history today?" the captain would ask the boys as they settled down at the table with their books. "Ah, the wars against the Swedes! Have you read Sienkiewicz? Do you want to hear about how we survived the Thirty Years War?"

Tales of Polish bravery unfurled, martyrdom and resurrection rambling out from the hoard of his reading. A true raconteur, Lolek's father set scene after scene. He brought to life the saintly Queen Jadwiga, who, in the fourteenth century, united Poland with Europe's last un-Christianized nation, Lithuania, and made her country into a bulwark against the Turks and, for a while, a European power. The captain reminded the boys that the tombs of these great Poles were close by, at the Wawel Cathedral in Krakow, and that they should visit. Lolek's father had several books in the house, but his true library was in his head.

His mellifluous baritone rising and falling with dramatic incident, he told the boys stories of ancient Greece and Rome—how Aeneas carried his father, Anchises, piggyback through the burning ruins of Troy on their way to an escape by sea that led him to found Rome. Every story conveyed some character isolated by a deed.

When the Angelus rang out and it was time for Jurek to go home to his dinner, the captain and the boys sometimes played a pretend game of soccer in the sitting room for a minute or two, using a knot of rags for a ball.

Chapter 11

JUREK MAY HAVE RESENTED PROFESSOR GEBHARDT'S NOSY DOG, BUT HE respected the history teacher, just as Lolek and the other good students did. Gebhardt had gone to high school with Wilhelm Kluger, and they remained good friends.

For the most part, politics and current events were rarely discussed in class. After Marshal Pilsudski's death in 1935, when Poland plunged into political crisis, the issues of the day become more and more controversial. Teachers were anxious to keep politics out of the classroom, but Gebhardt was different.

The professor reserved time each week for students to express their views on current affairs—a novel idea in an educational system that stresses rote learning and where students are supposed to know their place. Participation in the discussion was not required but merited extra credit. Jurek saw a chance to gain favor when he began reading a Krakow Jewish newspaper to which his father subscribed. Called *Nowy Dziennik* (*New Gazette*), it alerted readers to threats against civil liberties in Poland and, increasingly, in Germany, where Hitler had been in power since 1933. The paper was aimed at supplying an antidote to such virulently nationalist and anti-Semitic rags as *Oredownik* and *Polska Karta*, whose motto, "*Jak lep na muchy, tak* Polska Karta *na Zydow*" ("As flypaper kills flies, so *Polska Karta* kills Jews"), was proclaimed atop the front page.

Each week Jurek condensed and slightly rephrased an article from *Nowy Dziennik* and read it aloud as if it were his own essay. Usually he cribbed from columns by the highly respected David Singer, the most eloquent Polish Jewish journalist of his time. As he was confident that no one else was reading this or any other Jewish paper, he figured that there was little chance of being caught plagiarizing, and because this paper, although written by Jews for Jews, was worldly rather than parochial in outlook, its stories and opinions were suitable for a general audience. Jurek received highest marks for his efforts, and Professor Gebhardt began treating him with a certain deference as the class's messenger from the world beyond Wadowice.

Jurek eventually realized that what may have started as a bit of a ruse on his part was causing him to be better informed than anyone else on issues of the day. He also concluded that Professor Gebhardt knew very well what he was up to, since a boy of fifteen or sixteen could hardly have formed such sophisticated opinions out of thin air. As he grew more confident, he advanced from parroting the original to shaping it into his own style. His spirited defense when challenged made his failure to credit sources a trivial enough offense, although, being Jurek, he continued to enjoy the idea that he was getting away with something.

What Jurek conveyed about events in Poland itself was news to most of his classmates, who like all adolescents were consumed with their own interests. In the days before mass electronic communications, a place like Wadowice could go on about its business relatively unaware of the outside world, with a local sporting event being bigger news than a national election.

In bits and pieces, Jurek, who now referred to himself as "the specialist," told his classmates how the political structure in Poland, held together for a decade by Marshal Pilsudski, was disintegrating. It had taken a benevolent dictator to prevent chaos in a nation that, having aspired to independence for nearly one hundred fifty years, found itself with internal factions as divisive as Partition had been. Fully a third of Poland's thirty million citizens belonged to minorities, of which the largest was four-and-a-half million Ukrainians in the east; Jews were scattered throughout in cities, towns, and *shtetls* and heavily concentrated in Galicia. In the northeast were a million Belorussians (White Russians); to the west were some seven hundred fifty thousand *Volksdeutsche*, or ethnic Germans. Adding to this mix was the propensity to cling to class distinctions. In a country that had lagged behind its Western neighbors in industrialization, adhering to gradations in social rank conflicted with the democratic principles supposedly enshrined in the new constitution.

Some ninety-two officially registered political parties represented every conceivable social, economic, ethnic, and ideological position. Between 1918 and 1925, Poland had been ruled by fourteen separate governments, until Pilsudski in a coup d'etat brought a rather liberal dictatorship to bear on the chaos, with parliament retaining some powers and the opposition blocs as vociferous as ever. Several socialist groups and a small Communist party occupied the left; the right was dominated by the National Democratic Movement, which stigmatized Jews as the most dangerous minority, a "foreign" element, and advocated repressive anti-Semitic measures. Until his death opened the way for the National Democrats to seize power, Pilsudski, who had always been pledged to equality for Jews and whose army included many Jewish officers such as Jurek's father, had kept extremists under control.

By 1936, "the colonels," as those who took over the government in Pilsudski's wake were known, were on the verge of establishing a military dictatorship, with nationalism, Catholicism, and virulent anti-Semitism as the sinews of their policy and propaganda. They received support from powerful elements within the Church. Poland's largest Catholic publishing house, located at the Franciscan monastery at Niepokalanow, in 1935 launched a newspaper, *Maly Dziennik* (*Little Gazette*), whose name belied its considerable influence. With a weekday circulation of nearly one hundred forty thousand and more than two hundred thousand on Sundays, the paper portrayed Jews as interlopers who could never become truly Polish without converting to Catholicism. Although less venomous than sheets like *Polska Karta*, *Maly Dziennik*'s Church sponsorship gave it special authority and weight in contributing to an increasingly poisonous atmosphere that threatened Jews.

IN 1936, AUGUST CARDINAL HLOND, PRIMATE OF POLAND, WENT FURTHER, advocating a boycott of Jewish businesses. In a pastoral letter, the cardinal argued that:

> [T]here will be the Jewish problem as long as Jews remain.... [I]t is a fact that the Jews are fighting against the Catholic Church, persisting in free thinking, and are the vanguard of godlessness, Bolshevism, subversion.... It is a fact that the Jews deceive, levy interest, and are pimps. It is a fact that the religious and ethical influence of the Jewish young people on Polish people is a negative one.

With such sentiments being expressed by the head of the Catholic Church in Poland, anti-Semites hardly needed to look across the border to Germany or eastward for encouragement, but as anti-Jewish sentiment was on the rise all over Europe, literature from the outside was complementary to the native variety. The *Protocols of the Elders of Zion*, a document forged in czarist Russia that purported to be the master plan for an international Jewish conspiracy, was widely distributed and read. This was the work that Adolph Hitler praised in *Mein Kampf* for revealing "the nature and activity of the Jewish people and expos[ing] their inner contexts as well as their final aims," namely, control of world finance and culture by "the Jewish menace."

On the whole, Polish anti-Semitism manifested itself in far more parochial terms. It was directed not against the specter of international Jewry but against Jewish-owned retail businesses that were far out of proportion (as in Wadowice) to the number of Jews in the general population. Jewish ownership of manufacturing facilities such as mills, textile factories, and metal workshops also became a target of resentment. The irony was that Jews were now being berated for exactly those energies and skills that had caused a succession of Polish nobles and monarchs, beginning with Kazimierz the Great in the fourteenth century, to invite them into Poland.

Kazimierz was revered equally by Catholics and Jews. The former, however, tended to forget or deny that the consort and only great love of this first great king of Poland was Jewish, and a powerful influence on him. She was Esterka (Esther), a tailor's daughter who bore him four children—two raised as Jews and two as Catholics. No wonder Kazimierz, who was the first to codify the nation's laws, issued an edict protecting Jews from persecution. And no wonder the Jews of Krakow adopted the name Kazimierz for the district, originally a separate town, in which they settled.

The anti-Semitic leaflets and posters that began to proliferate in 1936 displayed a singular ignorance of the Catholic-Jewish union, love, and respect that marked the beginning of the modern Polish state. So did, of course, Catholic Nationalist rhetoric, with its undertone of Jews as immoral, materialistic Christ-killers. The following message, printed under a drawing of a rapacious, bald-headed Jew—complete with enormous nose, claws for hands, and the striped trousers and swallow-tailed coat of a banker—who was about to pounce on an obviously Gentile family evicted from their house into a muddy ditch, was typical.

> Fellow countrymen! We are being murdered by Jews and yet we keep supporting them. We give them money to fight us. This is a shame and a disgrace. Polish consciousness awake! Let the innocent blood of our comrades stand before you when you are about to commit a deed calling for God's revenge, when you are about to carry money to a Jew. You, our countrymen and our Polish mothers, remember: Avoid your enemy the Jew. Support only your own kind!

Another characteristic poster depicted two shops, one labeled "Polish" and the other "Jewish," with respectable middle-class and virtuous peasant customers entering the former and a pig, a donkey, and a sheep entering the latter. "Note who buys from Jews!" the caption read. "Which side are you?"

The source of these posters was right-wing nationalist, but the idea that because one group prospers, others must suffer may as well have been Marxist nonsense, too. That business enterprise creates wealth rather than depriving the poor of it was an economic truth not accepted by extremists on the left or the right. Unlike Cardinal Hlond, some Catholic spokesmen, such as Father Maximillian Kolbe, suggested that it would be better to build up Polish Catholic enterprises rather than to try to exclude Jewish ones, while praying for Jewish conversions. But by now Jews were looking back to the period under Kazimierz and his successors as their *Goldene Medine* (Yiddish for "Golden Age"). It had been hoped that Pilsudski was ushering in a new golden era. By the mid-1930s, the wisdom of the past was being subsumed by the foolish and pernicious idea that every Jewish *zloty* earned was a *zloty* taken from Catholic Poles.

How many Poles actually believed this is another matter. It is vital to remember how fragmented the Polish population was and how divided its opinions were on all economic and political matters. There was no Polish consensus, no powerful center of moderation. A rather widespread anti-Semitism of various kinds existed for demagogues to exploit during a period of economic hardship. The Jews became scapegoats for the ignorant to seize upon. The educational level toward which those crude posters were directed is obvious enough. It was no audience of sophisticates.

Of the educated segment of the population, Lolek, Jurek, and their classmates represented the variances in Polish attitudes. Students who expressed political views, no doubt reflecting those of their parents, ranged from nationalists to socialists, with no Communists among them. While most of them were greatly influenced by the Church, they didn't necessarily endorse or have awareness of Cardinal Hlond's anti-Semitic views. There is no evidence that Canon Prochownik or any local priests shared the cardinal's sentiments or conveyed them to parishioners, as would have been customary but not required. As Mrs. Huppert had reason to know and as Jurek understood, the clergy of Wadowice were liberal men, and they could not have been unique. Likewise, within the classrooms at the high school, with its easy accommodation of Jewish religious instruction, it was tolerance, not bigotry, that was the dominant note. In Germany during those years, the books assigned to students from the first grade on were replete with anti-Semitic pictures and text. Such material never entered Polish classrooms. Nor was Hitlerian racialist theory, which denigrated Slavs nearly as vehemently as Jews, a factor.

Significantly, Jurek was not only permitted but encouraged to enlighten his classmates about threats to personal liberties as he educated himself from the pages of that Jewish newspaper. Professor Gebhardt, who proclaimed his own socialist politics by wearing a red tie on May 1 each year, did not promote his personal views but rather was astute enough to realize that his students would pay more attention when listening to one of their own.

Tall, thin, and unsmiling, the professor would stand to one side of the room, his seriousness inspiring order rather than imposing it; when irritated, he expressed no more emotion than to take his glasses off to clean them. His lectures were orderly and precise and not open to question; but during these political discussions, he played the role of the silent protector of his students' right to say what they wished. That he permitted Jurek to take the floor so regularly was his way of indicating that what this Jewish boy had to say was something the class ought to hear. Presumably, since Jurek nearly always discussed anti-Semitism, Professor Gebhardt believed that this was a subject well worth the students' attention. He would have been more aware than Jurek, for a while at least, of the susceptibility of Poles to anti-Jewish attitudes. That few openly expressed contempt for or resentment of Jews did not mean that some did not harbor such feelings.

Jurek frequently spoke of the situation in Germany after the proclamation of the Nuremberg Laws in September of 1935. These abolished German citizenship for Jews, reducing them to the status of "subjects," and forbade marriage and sexual contact between Aryans and Jews—a Jew being defined as anyone having three Jewish grandparents. Jews had already been excluded from public office, the civil service, journalism, radio, farming, teaching, the theater, films, and the stock exchanges. As Jurek reported, German Jews were also being systematically excluded from the practices of law and medicine and from engaging in most businesses. This was what the policies of the National Democrats would lead to, Jurek warned, if permitted to continue. Was it for this, he asked his classmates, that patriots had fought and died, or for this that Pilsudski had defeated the Bolsheviks?

In the debates, Jurek found himself confronting the two openly anti-Semitic boys in his class, whose familiar line was that Jews were Communists. Was it not true that most of the leaders of the Polish Communist Party were Jews?

Jurek's reading and discussion with his father had prepared him for this canard. The total membership of the Polish Communist Party numbered only twenty thousand, of whom far from a majority were Jewish. With three-and-a-half million Polish Jews, what did this say about the percentage of them who were Communists? His own family was an example. He could assure everyone that among the Klugers and the Hupperts, a Communist was about as welcome as the plague. Anyone who knew his grandmother could imagine what she thought of Communists. As for his father, this was a grave and deeply offensive charge, about which Jurek expressed the most vehement resentment. To call someone a Bolshevik was to accuse them of treason.

"There is an international conspiracy of world Jewry," one of the anti-Semites would say again and again. "Jews are foreigners. All you have to do is look at them or hear them talk!" The boy was repeating the line adhered to by Roman Dmowski, head of the National Democratic Movement, who, with other right-wing politicians, was expressing interest in a German scheme to remove Jews to Madagascar. His cohort always nodded in agreement but said nothing much himself; he was the sort of fellow who would sooner hit someone than speak.

"Who is a foreigner?" Jurek would snap back. "We are all Poles."

"Jews speak Yiddish. They have no nation."

"Do you hear me speaking Yiddish? My Polish is every bit as good as yours! And by the way, what was your grade in Greek?"

Jurek would have found these exchanges more troubling had he not had the support of Catholics such as Romanski, Jura, Kogler, Kus, and Kesek, who always came to his defense. And above all, there was Lolek, who had a way of entering the debate at just the right moment. He had the ability to silence everyone, usually with a quotation from some unassailable figure of Polish literature such as Mickiewicz or Norwid, who revered Poland's Catholics and Jews as equally ennobling. It was Norwid who wrote that a true nation was "the internal alliance of related races" and that "a nation has an existence to the extent that it is capable of respecting the human individual." Lolek was also quick to appeal to faith in the brotherhood of man and the love of God for all creatures.

Occasionally, a professor opposed to the rights of Jews would drop an anti-Semitic remark. There were two such men. The offhand, snide comments from one about rich, greedy Hebrews had nothing to do with the subject being studied (physics), but the other professor taught geography, which gave him ample opportunities to discuss concentrations of wealth, demographics, and so on, encouraging the two hostile students to chime in. When Jurek responded, one of them would make physical threats. The support of Lolek and the others was not only gratifying but a guarantee that Jurek would not be assaulted after class. Outside Wadowice, sporadic attacks on Jews were becoming more frequent, as with the pogrom at Przytyk in 1936, when rioting left two Jews and one Catholic dead and Jewish shops were wrecked.

Ginka Beer, who graduated in 1936, decided to study medicine at the Jagiellonian University. That summer, word reached her and her parents from Krakow that her admission to the university was denied. The government had imposed a quota for Jewish students, with the percentage unspecified. Whatever it was, Ginka was refused admission.

Government policy now dictated that, except under the most extraordinary of circumstances, no Jews at all were to be admitted to the major Polish universities in Warsaw and Krakow. Only a handful of Jews, those with special connections of one kind or another, were permitted to matriculate. Ginka had applied strictly on her merits. Before the decree, Jews made up nearly a quarter of the university student population; after it, the numbers rapidly declined to eight percent and were falling.

The injustice done to Ginka was particularly alarming to Jurek, whose father had received his first law degree at the Jagiellonian in

1906 before going on to Vienna to become a doctor of laws. Was life to be worse for the Jews in an independent Poland than it had been under the Austrians? If Ginka could not get in, what chance had Jurek, who was hardly the superb scholar she was?

Professor Szybalska, the headmistress at the girls' school, could not sit back and let her best student be passed over. She traveled to Krakow to lobby on Ginka's behalf and enlisted a network of allies to write letters of support. But the problem was less with the university itself than with the state that controlled it. The headmistress, however, was equipped to confront that adversary. She happened to be one of the few women who had actually fought with Pilsudski's Legion, attaining the rank of captain, and she had been a close associate of the marshal's. He had personally bestowed on her the nation's highest military decoration, the *Virtuti Militari*. A formidable woman physically as well as intellectually, and strongly opposed to anti-Semitism, she won this battle. Ginka was at last admitted.

But the circumstances were dispiriting. What kind of welcome could the girl expect? Lolek, Jurek, Halina, Kazia, Professor Szybalska, and others accompanied Ginka and her parents to the train station. True to form, she was undaunted, or was a good enough actress to appear so. Several other Wadowice graduates boarded the train to Krakow with her. With final hugs and kisses, she told everyone to stop worrying, that she would be fine. And besides, things were bound to improve.

BEFORE THE ACADEMIC YEAR WAS OUT, GINKA WAS BACK IN WADOWICE, returning to her parents' apartment without telling anyone and holing up there for a few days. Not even her next-door neighbor Lolek knew that she was there. She told her parents that anti-Semitism among the students was rampant, but she could deal with that, and she had. Her professors had been, with a couple of exceptions, quite decent to her. But her roommate had a boyfriend who was a Communist and who was being followed by the police. When Ginka's roommate tried to hide the boy in their room, the police broke in, arrested him, and reported the two girls to university authorities.

Guilty by association, Ginka felt that she had no choice but to withdraw from the university. She had gone to study medicine and had been stigmatized by politics and anti-Semitism. She concluded that she ought to have known not to go where she was not welcome, but what other choice did she have?

It was a turn of events for which her parents were prepared, or partly so. Her father, who was the manager of a local bank, had already weighed the options for leaving Poland. Open immigration to the United States had ended in 1924; fewer than seven thousand Poles, a figure that included both Catholics and Jews, succeeded in obtaining visas to emigrate there during the late 1930s. Severe economic conditions caused many South American countries to tighten immigration restrictions, although several thousand Polish Jews did reach Argentina and other Latin nations with already established Jewish communities. And there was Palestine. Under British mandate at the time, Palestine was experiencing a severe political and economic crisis because of the increasing numbers of German and other European Jews who were in a near panic to reach its shores.

Ginka's father had not been a committed Zionist. Like the Klugers, the Beers had believed that Poland was their home and that Ginka's future would be bright there. But no longer. In Palestine, the British had resorted to enlisting Jewish partisans to help put down the Arab Revolt. But after her humiliations in Krakow, Ginka believed that things could only get worse for Jews in Poland. The Zionist argument that Jews had no future in Europe and should seize any opportunity to reclaim *Eretz* Israel was finally making sense. There was a strong religious component in Zionism that believed that the Jews were destined to return after two thousand years to their ancestral homeland, that it was a necessary prelude to the coming of the Messiah. For the Beers, however, as for so many Jews at this perilous time, the allure of Palestine was more a matter of survival.

Emigration was not simply a matter of deciding to go. There were now some four hundred thousand Jews in Palestine and about twice as many Arabs. With the rise of Hitler, Jewish immigration had rapidly increased; more than sixty thousand arrived in 1935 alone. The British, to allay Arab fears of becoming overwhelmed, tightened restrictions just as the situation for German Jews had reached the panic stage. Jews with capital were still permitted to come in freely, on the premise that their investments would benefit economic development for Jews and Arabs alike—a premise about which the Arabs were understandably skeptical. Jews without money could be admitted only with labor certificates showing that their work would benefit the region, and only then under a quota, which averaged under ten thousand a year. With an estimated half of German Jews without any means of livelihood by 1936, and with American immigration now so tightly restricted, the pressure for these certificates was enormous. Fewer than a third of the applications for them were being granted. With no capital of their own, Ginka and her parents had to get labor certification if they were to get in, but the odds were against it.

Fortunately, Ginka and her parents managed to obtain labor certification for her to emigrate to Palestine. She would go ahead alone, while her mother and father tried to wind up their affairs and waited, or hoped, to obtain permission to join her.

Years later, Ginka recalled the pain of this decision and how she broke the news to the boy next door.

> I knew I was very popular with Polish boys and girls, but there was anti-Semitism, too. There was only one family who never showed any racial hostility toward us, and that was Lolek and his dad....[When I was about] to leave Poland for Palestine because...disaster faced the Jews...I went to say goodbye to Lolek and his father. Mr. Wojtyla was upset about my departure, and when he asked me why, I told him. Again and again he said to me, "Not all Poles are anti-Semitic. You know I am not!" I spoke to him frankly and said that very few Poles were like him. He was very upset. But Lolek was even more upset than his father. He did not say a word, but his face went very red. I said farewell to him as kindly as I could, but he was so moved that he could not find a single word in reply. So I just shook the father's hand and left.

Chapter 12

On the Friday evening after Ginka left, Jurek and his family observed as always the *Shabbath* ritual, with Rozalia lighting the candles and Wilhelm reading the familiar words, "And there was evening, and there was morning." When the cook had retired and while the maid was clearing the dishes, Jurek wanted to talk about Ginka.

"She will be a brilliant doctor in Palestine," he said, "and we will be left here with drunken quacks."

"If you would eat your cabbage," Grandmother Huppert said, "you wouldn't need a doctor." She was almost completely blind now but still saw everything. And she held to the view that as with all times of suffering for the Jews, this one, too, would pass.

"Where is the justice of trying to keep us out of the university?" Jurek asked his father. "What about laws?"

" '*Legibus sumptis desinentibus, lege naturae utendum est,*' " his father said. " 'When laws of the state fail, we must act by the law of nature.' "

"The law of the jungle," Jurek said.

"Not exactly. '*Jus naturale est quod apud omnes homines eandem habet potentiam.*' 'Natural right has the same force in all men.' When natural rights are denied, the citizenry must respond, one way or another."

"There is going to be a fight," Jurek said.

"Men of goodwill stand together to fight the forces of oppression. What is happening in Poland now is unfortunate, but eventually we will be one people, standing for freedom."

That was the way his father always talked, the same as he did in court. It was inspiring, although the formality of it did sometimes make Jurek a bit impatient, just as he was with a very long novel in which the characters were always making speeches. But he appreciated the orderliness of his father's life and the steadiness with which he held to his principles. Governments came and went; laws were passed and rescinded. Through it all the family remained as always, in that house, where everything was in order and was kept so, like the polished parquet that Grandmother Huppert, with her family connections to a sawmill, had installed years ago.

As for following Ginka's example and departing for Palestine, the idea was inconceivable to the Klugers. For Dr. Kluger to get out would have been to question every reason for his and the family's existence. Poland was his country, as it had been his father's and his ancestors' as far back as was worth remembering. They were Poles first, Jews second. Wilhelm was not anti-Zionist, but he was no Zionist himself. For some Jews, the Holy Land was a good idea, but not for one whose roots in Polish life, history, and culture ran as deep as any Catholic's. To deny that would be to deny the messianic vision of Judaism that he, like most of his assimilated co-religionists, embraced.

Most Polish Jews were different from Dr. Kluger. Orthodox believers put faith in Hebraic law and the written word as passed down from the Hebrew Bible through centuries of scholarship and commentary. The other principal group of Polish Jews, Hassidim, followed the example of the eighteenth-century rabbi Israel Baal Shem Tov, who had taught, rather like the Protestant Christian preachers of his era known as Enthusiasts, that the human heart was the true guide to God. Judaism, like Christianity, was split between those who adhered to a received order and those who preached intuition, self-scrutiny, patience, forbearance, the rejection of worldly conceits, and, above all, love as the avenue to a self-contained life. For Jews in either camp, the Zionist idea became increasingly attractive during the late nineteenth and early twentieth centuries—the notion of a separate, distinct place, ordained by Scripture, where Jews might flourish as a people unto themselves. In this urge toward separate territory, Zionism found its mirror image in Christian separatist movements such as Mormonism, whose founders, like the Zionists, sought religious community in surroundings isolated from the conflicts besetting the wider world.

Dr. Kluger believed in a very different, cosmopolitan and yet nationalistic kind of Judaism. It was a faith that in his mind was consistent with Polish patriotism. In his view, the Polish people had, out of ignorance, succumbed to a kind of economic and spiritual complacency. The average workers preferred to live off the public payroll or under the thumb of landowners and exploitative factory owners rather than assert themselves in a country devoted to personal initiative. In his view, the Poles—Catholic and Jewish alike—had failed to accept the changes sweeping Western Europe that would lift them from miserable poverty. The Jews themselves, contrary to anti-Semitic propaganda, were examples of this lethargy. Most were very poor, but unlike the peasant population, they were literate and able to count.

To Dr. Kluger, both Jewish Orthodoxy and Hassidic beliefs were backward tendencies within Judaism, as much barriers to advancement as the most medieval, retrograde aspects of Polish Catholicism. It was all very well to talk, as the Hassidic rabbis did, of spirituality and the sanctity of Jewish life and to confine commercial activities to handicrafts and internalized trade. But what about the dynamic Jewish youths, such as his own son, who rejected the idea of Jewish separatism as well as the curse of Jewish misfortune? Dr. Kluger identified with the concept of Judaism as a march toward emancipation, as from Pharaoh's bondage, and to political and economic freedom.

Jurek's father was among those Western-oriented, Enlightenment-influenced Jews. They were children of a philosophical reasoning for an end to servitude, whether to man or God, and were not attracted by Hassidic miracles or Orthodoxy. Dr. Kluger was one of those whose idea of Judaism was to transform the learning of the

Orthodox and the fervor of the Hassidim into a new kind of redemption—manifested in a reborn Polish state. He hoped that the new Poland would be a place as encouraging to the rise of the common man as was America. (As for women, strong ones were accommodated, but their general advancement was not yet on this agenda.) No Leninist, Dr. Kluger and his like had no wish to cast aside religion. In his own earnest and sometimes pedantic way, Dr. Kluger conceived of himself as a Jewish Polish officer on the march toward a Promised Land under a red and white flag, not a blue and white one.

Should David Ben-Gurion, who was from Plonsk, near Warsaw, and Chaim Weizmann and their colleagues succeed in establishing a Jewish state, Dr. Kluger would welcome it. At the same time, he would feel torn by a conflict of emotional and political interest. He told Jurek as much during his preferred time to expound, on Friday evenings, in a kind of ad hoc school of philosophy. As he expatiated, the ash from his cigarette would lengthen and, to his wife's exasperation, drop and burn a hole in his trousers. If he would be less the absent-minded professor, she remonstrated, he might reach the New Jerusalem wearing a decent pair of pants.

As the son of the president of the Jewish community, Jurek had to sit at the right hand of Rabbi Seltenreich every Saturday in synagogue, which meant that he got away with nothing. The rabbi, who had been in office since 1913, knew all the prayers by heart and was constantly looking over to make sure that Jurek had his book open to the correct page. When he did not, because he was dreaming of being outside playing soccer on the lawn with his friends, the rabbi gave him a knock in the ribs with his elbow.

Dr. Kluger's duties as president included accounting for a tax that was levied to support the Jewish poor; making sure that the poorhouse and all the religious facilities, including the ritual bath, were maintained properly; and looking out for the Jewish soldiers who were stationed in Wadowice, usually more than fifty of them, who had to be supplied with kosher food daily and with locally baked matzos on the holidays. He also had to promote goodwill between Jews and Catholics, a responsibility that he readily assumed, since he counted several Catholics among his closest friends.

Clean-shaven, fit from the fifty pullups he did every morning, his precise Polish laced with Latin maxims and Polish proverbs having to do with a donkey's stubbornness or the stupidity of geese, he was about as assimilated as any Jew could be. He made sure that his children were, too. He forbade Yiddish to be spoken in the house; Jurek and Tesia knew no more than a few phrases in that language anyway, and he carefully monitored their Polish to ensure its perfection. There were certain Yiddish songs that everyone knew, but that was the extent of the presence in the Kluger household of the tongue of most Polish Jews. In the census of 1931, seventy-nine percent of Polish Jews listed Yiddish as their native language, while nine percent named Hebrew and only twelve percent Polish. With its Old German root and its admixture of Polish, Russian, and other Balto-Slavic expressions, Yiddish, Dr. Kluger believed, was not a "true" language. He felt that it invited Gentile mockery and even encouraged discrimination—a point of view at odds with that of most Jews, who celebrated the closeness and separateness that Yiddish preserved as essential to spiritual intensity.

For the majority, Judaism was not merely a set of beliefs but a complete way of life dedicated to God. To Dr. Kluger, anything that served to exclude Jews from the mainstream of Polish life, including even characteristic gestures, clothing, and uncut hair, was asking for trouble. Dr. Kluger himself spoke Yiddish fluently and as a graduate student in Vienna had delivered fiery speeches in the language. He was then an active member of the Bund, or Jewish Socialist Workers' Party, which believed that socialism, rather than Zionism, was the answer to Jewish problems. As his politics became more centrist, he felt that Yiddish had become an encumbrance to Jewish progress. He saw no reason why Jews could not preserve their religious identity through Hebrew, even as the Catholics did theirs through Latin, without isolating themselves from general society. He was also enthusiastic about Esperanto, an artificial language whose advocates at that time imagined that it might replace European tongues and promote universal brotherhood. In his own way, Jurek's father was representative of many observant but somewhat secularized Jews, who reshaped the messianic zeal of traditional Judaism into visions for the betterment of humankind.

Of course, had the Klugers actually considered leaving for Palestine, they would have been admitted at once under the quotaless category of Jews with capital. The Hupperts had been among the first Jews to settle in Wadowice and had husbanded their resources prudently and with an eye to neighborliness. Until 1868, Jews in the Skawa region were confined to surrounding villages; in that year, Emperor Franz Joseph declared equal rights for all religious denominations and nationalities living within the Austro-Hungarian Empire, including the right to live and own property anywhere. And in that year Baruch Thieberg appeared at the town gate with his horse and cart and, brandishing a blunderbuss, demanded his rights as a Jew to take up residence. He received the support of a local nobleman, who arrived with fifteen armed men to protect Thieberg as he built his house on the Rynek.

The second Jew to arrive was Anna Huppert's husband, Izrael, who moved from Kalwaria and soon obtained the exclusive license to manufacture and distribute alcoholic beverages within the district. Buying up properties, Huppert became president of the growing Jewish community in 1907, the first Jewish member of the town council, and vice-mayor. His numerous charitable acts, which assured Catholic goodwill, included donating land for the park. His grandchildren played tennis on courts built with a trust fund that Huppert established to improve and maintain the park grounds.

Anna bore Izrael nine children and saw to it that most of them married into prominent families—the Haberfelds, Joseferts, Tellers, Gronners, and Aleksandrowiczes, all names to be reckoned with among Polish Jewry. She was less pleased by her youngest daughter's alliance with Wilhelm Kluger, who, although his father Zachariasz had a prosperous clothing store in Wadowice, was merely a young attorney and far from grand. Worse, Dr. Kluger was a member of the Polish Socialist Party and was prone to make disturbing comments about the low wages and ghastly working conditions of Polish laborers. His politics were mild enough, however, and as his practice flourished, he dropped his party allegiance. He proved to be so learned and cultured that Mrs. Huppert, after about ten years of scrutiny, came to like him so much that she generally took his side in family disputes.

It was in the course of informing himself about family background that Jurek, at dinner one Friday after prayers, asked his father why the Klugers and most of their relatives had German names rather than Polish ones. It had been some Austrian emperor's idea a hundred years or more ago, his father told him, for all the Jews of Galicia to take on German-language surnames. Some adopted the names of their trades; others paid a fee for a good name such as Kluger, which meant "clever," or "the clever one."

"Kluger must have cost a lot of money," Jurek said.

"For a lot less, you could have been called manure," his father said, and added that Huppert had been pricier, since it meant nothing.

Dr. Kluger owned the building where he had his offices, across the Rynek from Zatorska Street and adjacent to the county courthouse. Five or six attorneys worked under him in several rooms hung with paintings by recent or contemporary Polish artists. The paintings represented a mixture of conventional subject matter, but one very striking canvas in his own office depicted a Cossack on horseback riding past a Jew killed in a pogrom, who lay dead in the street. The canvas was by a prominent Catholic painter and was a highly unusual if not unique choice of theme for a Christian. Anyone who saw the painting and took the time to think about its significance would know how Dr. Kluger felt about anti-Semitism.

Among his business clients, his relatives the Haberfelds were the most important. In Oswiecim, then a nondescript town near a coal mine, the Haberfelds lived on the main street in a crenelated mansion known locally as the castle. Since 1806, their business had been the distilling, bottling, and distribution of Gdanska, a vodka prized by czars, lords of the Kremlin, or anyone willing to pay top price to watch flecks of gold leaf float through the smoothest of liquors and catch the light. Napoleon retreated from Moscow, the saying went, when he ran short of Gdanska; murders had been committed over the precious elixir. The profits generated by the vodka provided the

Haberfelds with a very grand lifestyle indeed, and one that was truly Continental. One of the heirs spent most of his time in France, Italy, and England racing motorcars, playing polo, and attracting exquisite women. When the family wished to travel together, they had their own private railroad car as grand as any Vanderbilt's, and they were generous with their wealth, especially to relatives. Jurek, Tesia, and their parents spent six weeks or more during two summers with the Haberfelds traveling in the private car through Prague and south to the Italian seaside resort of Viareggio and to the Dalmation coast for swimming and tennis.

SUCH GAIETIES WERE SOMEWHAT CURTAILED BY THE TIME ADOLPH HITLER began making noises about *Volksdeutsche* in the Sudetenland. Even an optimist like Dr. Kluger began to worry; there were bad signs very close to home, too. A new colonel, a pistol champion with the demeanor of an Erich von Stroheim, took over the local regiment. Previous commandants had always made a point of calling on the president of the Jewish community as a courtesy; this one did not. Word came to Dr. Kluger that in line with new government policy, the colonel planned to support a boycott of Jewish shops. Such a posture on the part of the local military establishment would spell serious trouble, not least of all for the Jewish soldiers stationed in Wadowice. Dr. Kluger wondered how to approach this man, to reason with him, without appearing to beg. Perhaps if he went accompanied by Catholic friends—or would this be asking too much of them?

There was a terrific snow and ice storm that winter of 1937, with telephone lines down and even train service interrupted by the huge drifts. Dr. Kluger nevertheless had to get to Krakow on business and was among the few passengers waiting for the train to arrive. He noticed that the new colonel was also waiting in the station for the same express, stamping his boots and cursing the inconvenience. Dr. Kluger knew that the colonel must have recognized him, too, but as they had never been introduced, and as he might well have been hostile, Dr. Kluger made no move to approach him. For a good hour they stood around, each pretending that the other did not exist.

At last the colonel's adjutant came running up and announced that a car was ready to take them to Krakow. The colonel started to leave, then suddenly turned toward Dr. Kluger, hesitated, and walked up to him, extending a hand.

"We are going by automobile. I understand the road is passable. May I offer you a ride in my car, Dr. Kluger?" he asked.

"I would be delighted, Colonel Stawarz," Dr. Kluger replied.

Jurek was still up after midnight when his father, obviously rather tipsy, returned. Of course this Colonel Stawarz was a bit of an anti-Semite, Jurek's father said, but not the worst, and they had a delightful time together, meeting for dinner at Hawelka. He was open enough to the Jewish point of view, especially after a vodka or two. Yes, he was actually a delightful fellow. They had exchanged war stories. This was just the way to keep the peace, meeting on a human level. You could catch more flies with honey, and so on.

"The colonel and I have experienced *assensio mentium*—a meeting of minds. Stawarz turns out to be a rather cultivated gentleman. He appreciates music. We had a fine discussion about Chopin," Dr. Kluger elaborated.

AMONG ALL OF DR. KLUGER'S EFFORTS AT INTERFAITH COMMUNICATION, HIS promotion of dialogue through music stood out. For as long as Jurek could remember, the string quartet his father had organized and led met every week for rehearsal at the house on Zatorska Street, practicing behind closed doors in the dining room. Besides Dr. Kluger, who played first violin, the musicians included one other Jew, the very stout, bald dentist, Goldberger, who lived in the apartment upstairs. Goldberger alternated on the cello with the engineer Gorecki, who was from an aristocratic family and was always elegantly dressed. He liked to drop French phrases, such as "*C'est mon violon d'Ingres*," which meant that like the French painter's violin, his music was only a hobby—a stylish way of explaining frequent mistakes. Engineer Zagorski, whose wife had to give piano lessons because his business was failing and whose playing was as mournful as he looked, was second violin. Lawyer Kaminski played the viola; his daughter was Tesia's classmate and best friend. (Jurek liked to say that the girls complemented each other perfectly because they were both blond, but Tesia's nose sloped downward while her friend's pointed toward the stars.) Mikolaj Kuczkowski, another Catholic lawyer, who had only just received his degree, sometimes substituted on violin.

Lolek gradually became practically a member of the ensemble himself, although he played no instrument. His love of music, which actively expressed itself in his singing in the choir at school and in church, was so intense that he would come to the house nearly every evening when the quartet practiced, sitting quietly and listening outside the dining room door while Jurek, who would have preferred being at the movies, crouched in the next room with his ear to the radio or sprawled on the floor constructing model airplanes. By 1937, Dr. Kluger permitted Lolek to sit in a corner within the inner sanctum, absorbing Beethoven or Mendelssohn with a concentration so absolute that Jurek teased him about becoming part of the furnishings, like Grandmother Huppert's chair or the marble bust of Mrs. Kluger that rested atop the piano.

Sometimes, if the piece called for a piano, Mrs. Kluger played, but she usually did not last long because her execution fell too far short of her husband's standards, and he would grow exasperated with her. Through it all, Lolek remained still and rapt in a straight chair beside the sideboard that held the family plates, silver, and the menorah.

After rehearsal the atmosphere lightened as the men took a few measures from a bottle of slivovitz that Dr. Kluger brought up from Grandmother Huppert's well-stocked cellar. They smoked, joked, and sometimes offered the boys a sip of the hundred-year-old plum brandy.

Lolek also came over to listen to the Klugers' big radio, always the latest and most powerful model. When he wasn't turning the dial to find some musical or other broadcasts from Warsaw, Leipzig, or even Paris or London on clear nights, he would persuade Jurek to put classical music on the gramophone, to which Jurek acceded but which he alternated with dance tunes. And it was Lolek's love of music that led to his visit to the synagogue.

This occasion was another and the boldest of Dr. Kluger's efforts to find common ground between the religions through music. In 1937, Moishe Kussawiecki, the youngest in a great line of cantors and opera singers, who at eighteen was already renowned for his soaring tenor voice, was posted to Wadowice to fulfill his military service. By then, with anti-Semitic hysteria rising, there was already talk of excluding Jews from the army, which would have been an extremely disruptive move since there were already well over a hundred thousand Jews serving in the active military and, like Dr. Kluger, in the reserves.

Making a political as well as a cultural point, Dr. Kluger arranged for Kussawiecki to substitute for the regular cantor and invited several Catholics to attend, including the members of the quartet and Lolek and his father. This was a highly unusual and dramatic gesture for its time and place, and its significance was not lost on anyone. To begin with, Catholics were actively discouraged by their clergy from participating in non-Catholic religious services, other than attendance at weddings or funerals. In addition, for a singer of Kussawiecki's caliber (he was already being compared to Caruso and John McCormack) to perform in a provincial town like Wadowice was an event of unprecedented magnitude. It was hoped that he might give a public concert, but none had been scheduled, making this appearance at the synagogue all the more exciting and eagerly anticipated.

All of the Catholics whom Dr. Kluger invited accepted. For once, it was a privilege for Christians to be included among Jews, rather than the reverse. None of the Catholics had ever set foot inside a synagogue before.

Kussawiecki, with the permission of Colonel Stawarz, arrived at the synagogue in full uniform that Saturday afternoon. He was accompanied by the fifty or so Jewish soldiers, who as usual marched from Twelfth Infantry barracks up Pierackiego Street to the sanctuary, with its tall, arched side windows and copper-sheathed dome.

Inside, instead of donning a yarmulke, Kussawiecki proudly wore his military cap. He faced this mixed audience with a confident smile.

Jurek sat between Lolek and his father and, for once, kept absolutely still. From the first pure note of the sacred songs, which included "*Yismach Moshe*" ("Moses Shall Rejoice"), "*Brich Shme*" ("Blessed Be His Name") in Aramaic, and "*Tikantah Shabbath*" ("Thou Hast Created the Sabbath," a prayer to celebrate the Sabbath one day in Jerusalem), Kussawiecki was sensational. He enthralled his audience, some of whom, of course, had never heard these mournful melodies that were familiar to every Jew. Jurek kept glancing over at his friend, who looked as if he were hearing an angel sing.

Afterward, Lolek was his usual curious self, peppering Jurek with questions about the origin and meaning of the songs, which Jurek did his best to answer. The idea that several were derived from biblical times and that one was in Aramaic, the language Jesus spoke, seemed to fill Lolek with particular pleasure and fascination. And Jurek was glad of all those Saturdays that he had spent in temple learning something! The Catholic guests were profuse in their thanks to Dr. Kluger and to Rabbi Seltenreich for inviting them to attend this marvelous event. For the Jews, it was a unique moment. For once, at least some Christians had experienced the beauty and dignity of an older faith, a religion better lived than explained, a faith that at its core was, like music, beyond words.

In the ensuing weeks, Kussawiecki also gave public performances at the Sokol that included Italian arias and Polish songs. Wadowice had its share of music-lovers; the concerts were fully attended by people of both religions, and everyone seemed to agree that they constituted the major and most enjoyable cultural events within memory for the town. But Lolek and Jurek both felt that nothing could quite equal that Saturday in the synagogue.

Chapter 13

THAT SHOW OF JEWISH-CATHOLIC SOLIDARITY AT THE SYNAGOGUE STOOD out at a time when anti-Semitism was intensifying. During Lolek's and Jurek's last year in high school together, 1937–38, members of the National Democratic Movement sporadically picketed Jewish shops, including the Balamuth business in the building where Lolek and his father lived and where Ginka's parents were still awaiting permission to join their daughter in Palestine. On two or three occasions, small bands of "ND" youths—Jurek assumed that one of his anti-Semitic classmates must have been among them—smashed Jewish shop windows and looted in nocturnal raids.

Although it continued to support boycotting, the national government actively discouraged such violence, no doubt fearing the international condemnation of such activity in Germany. "*Owszem!*" became the policy, that is, "yes," or "certainly," you may go this far, but no farther. It was not a distinction that gave Jews much reassurance.

Other manifestations of hatred touched the Klugers directly. Urged on by an anti-Semitic lawyer named Rayman, bullies appeared at the railway station to try to prevent farmers and other business visitors from hiring Jewish lawyers. Most distressing of all to Dr. Kluger and his family, the National Association of Lawyers passed a resolution requiring every Jewish attorney to add the Hebrew version of his name to his office and stationery. So for several months, the law offices of Wilhelm Kluger became those of Wilhelm Zev Kluger. That the order was eventually rescinded did not lessen its sting.

Dr. Kluger could take some satisfaction in knowing that things might have been worse had he not managed to maintain such good relations with town officials, including Colonel Stawarz, who made it clear that Jewish property was to be protected by his soldiers like any other and that physical attacks on Jews would not be tolerated.

Relative to other towns and cities, Wadowice remained a tolerant place. In the midst of the general unease, Dr. Kluger retained enough faith in the ordinary citizens of his town to take on a highly controversial lawsuit that risked either exacerbating interfaith tensions or calming them, depending on whether his client won or lost.

In the nearby town of Zywiec, a factory called Solali, which produced cigarette papers, was owned by a Jew who employed another Jew, Goldberg, as manager. It was precisely the sort of situation to which anti-Semites pointed as an example of how Jews controlled wealth while Catholics did the work. When Goldberg caught a Catholic worker, Skrzypek, stealing, he sacked him on the spot—and thereby precipitated allegations against himself and, by extension, Jews in general. Skrzypek, urged on by agitators, publicly denounced Goldberg as a murderous traitor, spreading the story, which was repeated in newspapers, that Goldberg had connived with the *Cheka* (the Soviet secret police) during the Russian Revolution to betray Poles, resulting in numerous deaths of patriots.

Dr. Kluger, who represented the Solali factory, advised Goldberg to sue for defamation. Far from being a Communist, Goldberg had been fighting with the Polish Army on the far eastern front near China, when Pilsudski's forces were allied with Austria during World War I. His commander was General Jozef Czuma, who could confirm Goldberg's loyalty—if, that is, the general would be willing to testify on behalf of a Jew. Fortunately, General Czuma was still alive.

The case quickly became a national sensation when Dr. Kluger listed General Czuma, who even in old age retained great prestige as a war hero, as a witness for the plaintiff. Whether the general would actually travel from Warsaw to assize court in Wadowice on behalf of Goldberg was a matter of intense speculation before the trial. If he did, it would be an act of far greater social and political significance than the case itself. After all, calling a Jew a Communist was nothing out of the ordinary.

The case of *Goldberg v. Skrzypek* became an exciting adventure shared between Lolek and Jurek. Lolek's respect for Jurek's father, beginning from the day when he saw the grateful postman kiss Dr. Kluger's hand in the square, was very great. When Lolek said that he would dearly love to be present at the Goldberg-Skrzypek trial, Jurek vowed to somehow get both of them into the courtroom. They petitioned and received permission from Headmaster Krolikiewicz to skip school on the day that General Czuma was scheduled to appear.

With all the journalists in town for the event and the intense interest from all quarters, the boys could not find seats for themselves. With the permission of Jurek's father, they huddled together in a doorway to the rear of the bench. Dr. Kluger, who had engaged a prominent Jewish lawyer from Krakow as co-counsel, led General Czuma through a series of questions that brought out his distinguished army service. Then, with all of his oratorical power and flourish, Dr. Kluger recited Skrzypek's allegations against Goldberg and inquired if, to the general's knowledge, any of these charges could be true.

"They are all lies!" the general said with vehemence, a phrase that became headlines the next day. He went on to attest to Goldberg's valor as a soldier under him. As was the custom in Polish law, there was no jury in this, a civil case. Instead the tribunal, a panel of three judges—all of them Catholics—lost little time in deciding unequivocally for Goldberg, awarding him costs, restoring his reputation, and most important of all, providing a highly public lesson in the dangers of anti-Semitism.

Parallels with the Dreyfus Affair were widely noted and became the focus of Jurek's report, with Lolek adding his own praise for Dr. Kluger's skills, when they discussed the Goldberg case in Dr. Gebhardt's class. As Dr. Kluger explained to the boys, Dreyfus was a Jewish officer who in 1894 was, like Goldberg, accused of treason. Unlike Goldberg, however, Dreyfus had no General Czuma to exonerate him but rather had the entire French military establishment, along with powerful anti-Semites in government and intellectual circles, against him. He was convicted on forged evidence and sentenced to solitary confinement for life on Devil's Island, where he remained for twelve years until he was pardoned.

In France, this loyal Jew had never received justice in court, even with a second trial, which also returned a scandalous verdict of guilty. The case so shocked a Viennese Jewish journalist named Theodor Herzl that he became the founder of the international Zionist movement. He had concluded that Jews could never receive justice or full equality in a Christian Europe that despised them, and so they must find their own country in which to survive. If such a thing could happen to a patriotic Jewish soldier in France, the supposed cradle of liberty and equality, one could only imagine what was in store for Jews elsewhere.

Yet, in Poland more than forty years later, another loyal Jewish soldier was cleared by the brave testimony of an unimpeachable Catholic general. This was a moment to be proud of Poland and of Polish justice, Jurek told the class. There was reason to hope that one day Catholics and Jews would again live in harmony, as under Kazimierz the Great. At least one could hope for a return to the policies of Marshal Pilsudski.

Lolek led the applause for Jurek's speech, and Jurek was so moved by this and by the pride he felt in his heart for his father that he nearly lost his composure. For once, his two Jew-hating classmates were silenced.

UNFORTUNATELY, JUREK SOON RECEIVED A DIFFERENT MESSAGE FROM THE Polish military. During their last term in high school, all the boys were required to take a physical examination certifying them for military service. Like Lolek, Jurek received an "A," or full qualification. Unlike the others who passed, however, Jurek and the other Jews in the class did not immediately receive notification of their assignment during the following summer to an army *obóz pracy*, or work camp, which was a required preliminary to entering a university. Jurek had heard of a movement to eliminate Jews from officers' candidate school, as from universities, but this was the first indication he had that such a policy was actually being phased into effect. His father began to look into the matter.

Whether he would actually be admitted to a university in any case would also depend on how well he did on his *Matura*, or leaving examination. Lolek, as had long been expected, would be going to study literature and language at the Jagiellonian. Jurek and his family agreed that his own talents and interests made the Warsaw Polytechnic University an appropriate choice for him.

In 1938, the economic situation in Poland had improved somewhat, but with money and jobs still very scarce, paying university tuition and supporting a youth through higher education was not an option for many of the students' families. Lolek would undoubtedly qualify for one of the very few full scholarships available; others, no matter how good their marks, would have to seek employment. Under these circumstances, only ten boys hoped to enter the Jagiellonian to study in various fields, including literature, theology, law, medicine, agriculture, and chemistry. Another student chose the teachers' college in Krakow; two planned to enroll at the Polytechnic in Lvov, and Jurek in Warsaw. Of the rest, nineteen, many for lack of knowing what else to do, chose various branches of the army, two decided on the air force, and the other seven elected to join the labor force as farmers and various kinds of workers.

To no one's surprise, Lolek scored the highest marks on the *Matura*. As it turned out, none of the boys hoping to go on to universities failed to qualify. The only real shock was how well Jurek Kluger did in the Latin examination. Everyone had expected him to excel in such areas as physics, chemistry, and history, as he had always done. But Latin? Perhaps the most amazed of all that Jurek nearly equaled Lolek in his Latin grade was Dr. Kluger, whom Jurek regularly disappointed when asked to translate one of his father's countless maxims.

At the time he took the exam, Jurek himself was not so sure that he would do well. In fact, confronted with what seemed like a nearly impenetrable Horatian ode, which apparently had something to do with an angry bull, he began to panic. He had the gist, but one line in particular made no sense whatever to him. He knew enough to pass, but that line would make the difference between an excellent grade and an ordinary one.

Lolek was sitting directly in front of him, scribbling away, no doubt producing the finest translation ever of Horace into Polish. If only Lolek might move those broad shoulders of his aside, just a few inches. Jurek stared at Lolek's back as hard as he could, hoping to convey his desperation through mental telepathy. As helpful as he was otherwise, Lolek was disinclined to make it easy for someone else to crib from him—unlike another fine student, Jan Kus, who practically offered his work to anyone in a position to look at it. Unfortunately, Kus's desk was on the other side of the room.

Lolek stopped writing, leaned back, and stretched his arms. He was finished, ahead of everyone else. Couldn't he allow just a peek? Then, as if in answer to Jurek's prayer, Lolek did move to one side, and he stayed there long enough for Jurek to read just what he needed.

Jurek was sure that Lolek knew exactly what he was doing, since Jurek had been confiding to him for days how worried he was about the Latin, especially Horace. But he decided it was better not to bring the matter up.

FOR MORE THAN A YEAR, LOLEK, JUREK, AND MOST OF THEIR CLASSMATES HAD been taking dancing lessons at a class taught at the girls' school. This was part of their education as gentlemen, but it was also in preparation for *Komers*, or the graduation ball, the culmination of their twelve years together. The classes were quite formal. Boys and girls sat on opposite sides of the room while the teacher, an old but very vigorous and stern woman, demonstrated the steps to the music from a gramophone. One by one, the boys then asked the girls, "May I have this dance? It would be a great honor." The couples tried mazurkas, Viennese waltzes, English waltzes, or, in triple time, that most essential dance of all—the polonaise, without which one can scarcely call oneself a Pole.

Lolek, with his tremendous musicality, was perhaps the best, most graceful dancer among the boys, especially with Halina Krolikiewicz as his partner. The two knew each other so well, and after playing so many roles on the stage together, they had not a bit of self-consciousness between them. For Jurek, dancing was something of a struggle, but he was willing to endure the embarrassment of being out of step just for the chance to get close to a girl. He could always make a joke about his lack of rhythm.

When the boys arrived together at *Komers*, however, after all this preparation, they were distressed to see that most of the girls had selected older boys from town, many of them officers from the Twelfth Infantry, as escorts. Lolek and Jurek clustered with other boys on one side of the great salon at the *Kasyno Urzednicze*, or State Administrator's Club, consoling themselves with a few vodkas and commenting on how awkward the girls were on the floor with those big, clumsy soldiers. Eventually, Jurek and Tadeusz Czuprynski got up nerve to cut in. Lolek saw that Halina had arrived with another girl. Many of the boys never left the vodka table for the dance floor. But when Poldek Goldberger's band struck up the final polonaise, Jurek was swirling about with a girl he had dreamed about, and Lolek was still dancing with Halina, who, like him, would be off to the Jagiellonian in the fall.

NOTHING IN THE HISTORICAL RECORD OR IN THE REMINISCENCES OF LOLEK, Jurek, or any of their friends suggests that in Poland in 1938 there was general fear or a sense that Europe was heading for catastrophe. On March 11 that year, Hitler had marched into Vienna to cheering mobs of Austrians. In a plebiscite that shortly followed, the Austrians voted overwhelmingly in favor of annexation to the Third Reich. In Poland, certainly, there was no Winston Churchill in the wings warning that Hitler would stop at nothing before gobbling up most of Europe and that he had to be stopped. And when, at the end of

September, the British and French governments finally capitulated to Hitler's demands for the Sudetenland, and Czechoslovakia, which had been carved out of the old Austro-Hungarian Empire in 1918, ceased to exist, most Poles seemed to believe that was the end of it. The Fuehrer was now satisfied, or would be, surely, with some Polish compromises over his demands to seize Gdansk, the city Germans called Danzig.

Not even Lolek's and Jurek's fathers, with their military experience and memories, believed that Poland was in any immediate danger of invasion by the Germans. But not even most Germans guessed at what the Fuehrer had in store for them.

That summer, with no intention whatever of emigrating, Jurek's relatives the Haberfelds were already making plans to visit the World's Fair in New York the following year. They were to display their unique vodka and their valuable stamp collections as part of the Polish national exhibit. They were aware, of course, that more than three hundred thousand German Jews had already left Germany and that thousands more would already have departed if they had been able to find some country to let them in. But that was Germany—and, of course, Austria, and yes, what had been Czechoslovakia, too. Poland, they would never have dreamed otherwise, was another story altogether. The anti-Semitism was a crisis, to be sure, but a temporary one that would solve itself as the slowly recovering economy righted itself. That was where the World's Fair came in. In another year, Poland would be displaying itself as an emerging, modern, mercantile nation.

THERE WAS NO REASON FOR LOLEK'S FATHER, WHO WAS NOT IN THE BEST OF health, to stay in Wadowice with his son gone, and it would also have been beyond his means to support himself and his son separately, as Lolek's scholarship covered tuition but not room and board. The two moved into a basement flat at No. 10 Tyniecka Street, which borders the west bank of the Vistula in the Debniki district of Krakow, with the city center and the university only about a mile's walk across a bridge over the river. Krakow at that time was a city of about a quarter-million inhabitants. Debniki itself was a pretty suburb of mixed working- and middle-class families. Their house was owned by Lolek's unmarried maternal uncle, a master leather craftsman, who had built the house himself and who lived in the two upper floors with his two unmarried sisters. They were the Wojtylas' only relatives in Krakow.

Tanned and fit after his work-camp experience building a road in the mountains south of Wadowice, Lolek at the time looked very much the part of an arts student. His rather long hair touched the open collar he favored over neckties; a black jacket, a long tweed overcoat as winter arrived, and a black short-visor cap that he wore jauntily at an angle all added to the bohemian look. Polish students called it the Slowacki look, after the romantic poet. Today in New York, Paris, London, or, for that matter, Krakow, it remains the style of literary or film students with or without money. Lolek linked up quickly with those, including his friend Halina, who shared his passions for poetry and theater. They attended poetry readings where he recited his earliest compositions, although his own writing did not begin to flow until that first year at university had passed. Like any first-year student, albeit an unusually serious and hard-working one, he was initially consumed by his studies.

The courses, lectures, and tutorials he attended indicated how literature and language dominated his mind and emotions. At the Jagiellonian, literature was studied within what was called the faculty of philosophy rather than being divided into separate departments. For Lolek's first year, that meant study of Principles of Polish Etymology; Elements of Polish Phonetics; Grammar of Old Church Slavonic; Theater and Drama in Poland since the Middle Ages; Theory of Drama; Novels, Memoirs, and Letters of Stanislaw Brzozowski; Literature of the Polish Middle Ages; Exercises in Old Polish Literature; Dramatic Interpretation of Stanislaw Wyspianski; Interpretation of Contemporary Lyricism; Humor, Comicality, and Irony and Their Role in Literary Work; Exercises in the History of Polish Literature; Character of Literary Antiquities; Beginning Russian; and Introduction to Russian Literature.

Two aspects of this rather daunting list were its almost exclusively Polish focus and the absence, other than in recurrent themes in Polish literature, of specifically religious subjects. With the preparation that his high school education and his own studies had afforded him, he was ready, like all of those admitted to the Jagiellonian, to specialize. At that university, as in all the major centers of higher learning in Europe, one does not spend the first year or two exploring various fields. Even this formidable array of Polish studies was not enough for him, as he also found a private tutor in French, attended plays regularly at the Slowacki and other theaters, and gravitated toward kindred spirits, including Halina, for discussions of drama and literature in various houses and in the numerous literary cafés in and around the Rynek Glowny and the university district. Krakow was an artistic and intellectual feast and one in which Jews remained participants in spite of pressures at the university.

Not that he neglected his religion. Father Kazimierz Figlewicz, who had been transferred from Wadowice to the Wawel Cathedral in Krakow, became Lolek's confessor. This cathedral, which is as significant to Poland as Westminster Abbey is to England, holds the tombs of Saint Stanislaw, Queen Jadwiga, and Kazimierz the Great and other monarchs as well those of Adam Mickiewicz and Juliusz Slowacki. Far more than the Abbey, the Wawel Cathedral embodies the inextricable bonds between literature and religion, symbolizing how in the Polish sensibility, patriotism, piety, and poetry—along with music and art—intermingle as a single phenomenon. No one has expressed the significance of this church or what its effects were on young Wojtyla better than John Paul II himself: "The sanctuary of the nation," he has termed the cathedral, which "cannot be entered without an inner trembling, without an awe, for here—as in few cathedrals of the world—is contained a vast greatness which speaks to us of the history of Poland, of all our past." Although Lolek was also active in his local parish in Debniki, where Salesian fathers presided, and joined a group called the Living Rosary there, the Wawel was transcendent for him.

Just inside the entrance to the cathedral is a collection of prehistoric bones, including the skull of a hairy rhinoceros and the shinbone of a mammoth. While their presence may seem rather incongruous to the uninitiated, they provide a link to the pre-Christian Slavic past, and the legend surrounding them suggests that as long as they remain there, the cathedral will stand. The Polonian Slavs inhabiting the great plain that became Poland did not convert to Christianity until the tenth century. It is not within the Polish way of looking at Poland's history to reject the pre-Christian past as benighted but rather to see in it prefigurations of greatness, as continuity rather than disjunction, rather in the way that Christians often interpret the Hebrew Bible as predictive of the New Testament.

Lolek was so animated by his readings in language and literature and so moved by his own artistic expression that he used this theme of Polish cultural continuity in his first sustained effort to write poetry. From spring through summer, he produced a manuscript that he entitled *Renesansowy psalterz: Ksiega slowianska* (*The Renaissance Psalter: A Slav Book*), which consisted of a series of poems of varying length that celebrated exactly this—the continuity between pre-Christian and Christian Polish life, literature, and belief. The book was never published as a bound volume, but it has all the coherence as well as the artistic skill of a fine poet's first collection. The title expresses this theme, linking the word *renaissance* with the medieval word *psalter*, meaning an ancient stringed instrument or lyre, a book of psalms, or devotions to the Blessed Virgin in the form of the rosary. When followed by the phrase *A Slav Book*, the idea of a renaissance of the medieval, or the medieval as redefined through the renaissance, becomes joined to the primitive, tribal origins of Polish civilization.

One of the most accomplished of these early poems is "Magnificat," inspired by the canticle and ascribed traditionally to the Virgin Mary herself, who is supposed to have recited it in praise of the Lord upon learning that she would give birth to Jesus. Wojtyla's poem is also a hymn of praise to God but spoken in the voice of the spirit of Poland, both ancient and modern, pagan and Christian, combining the nature worship of tribal days with Christian revelation. Reflecting Wojtyla's intense study of ancient Slavic languages and poetry, "Magnificat" unites through diction as well as imagery the pagan, the medieval, the renaissance, and the modern. The ancient worship of the oak tree, for instance, becomes transformed into Christian belief without leaving behind the pagan symbolism; rather, it incorporates it, somewhat in the way that those ancient bones hang in the cathedral. God was present in the ancient soil, in the rocks of the Tatras, and in the oaks, but now the mystery becomes incarnate in Christ:

and in this melody You came as Christ, a vision.
Look ahead, young Slav, look, the solstice fires!
The sacred oak is still in leaf, your king has not
withered, but become for the people a lord and priest.

The "solstice fires" refers to that pagan festival celebrating fire and water, now reborn in Christ, but as the sacred oak still thrives, kings have not died but are metamorphosed through Jesus. And the poet sings of his part in this:

A Slav troubadour, I walk Your roads and play
to maidens at the solstice, to shepherds with their
flock, but, wide as this vale, my song of prayer
I throw for You only, before your throne of oak.

If the language of this poem, even in translation, comes across as rather antiquated, it was surely deliberately contrived to be so, given the poet's intentions, which may be compared to attempts by other poets early in this century to revive the past in order to invigorate the present. But young Wojtyla was not imprisoned by this sort of diction. When he wished to express himself on a more personal level, as he also did during his first year at the university, he accomplished this in the simplest, most colloquial and direct way, as in this memory of his mother, written in Krakow during the spring of 1939.

Over this your white grave
the flowers of life in white—
so many years without you—
how many have passed out of sight?...

Coming straight from his heart without claptrap, "Over This Your White Grave" needs no comment. The ebullient scholar, the Slav troubadour, as he gaily called himself in "Magnificat," singing to maidens, could also write with the unadorned sadness of the boy who had lost his mother. He had already mastered the most elusive aspect of the poet's craft, the ability to put feeling into words. He had all the words, and all the feelings, too, and joined them with a simplicity that only his intense aesthetic sense and spirituality could have taught him. He had, by his twentieth year, become an artist, of a certain and ancient kind. He sang not only of himself but also of the glories of creation, past and present and to come.

LOLEK WAS ONE OF THOSE FORTUNATE SOULS WHO TAKE WELL TO UNIVERSITY life and to a city. Krakow just happened to be the spiritual and cultural heart of the nation at the time, and he got as much enjoyment and productivity out of it as can be imagined. One thinks of Dante in Florence, Joyce in Dublin, Byron in Rome. Wojtyla's mood at the conclusion of that first academic year—truly his coming of age given his productivity and his flowering—may be gauged from reports of his performance in June 1939 in a musical comedy skit. Studio 39, a university drama club, staged a sort of farce called *Moon Cavalier* through eight evening performances outdoors in the courtyard of the Collegium Maius. Lolek, along with Halina and ten other student actors, played characters meant to represent signs of the zodiac. The event was a celebration of the end of classes and the coming of summer holidays.

To appreciate the atmosphere that prevailed in Krakow that May or June, one has only to remember youth as spent on any university campus during intervals of peace. As his birth sign was Taurus and he was a strong and virile young fellow, Lolek played the Bull—and did so roaring and frolicking around behind a huge, horned, papier-mâché mask.

He allowed himself to get so much into character that, as Halina and others remembered forever after, he continued on after the performance, running about, doffing his mask, saying, "I am Taurus! I am the Bull!" He was only pretending to scare everyone, but Halina, who was never scared by anyone, reminded him that Taurus's characteristics include stubbornness to the point of obstinacy. He did not appear to mind that a bit, delighting in it as if to say, "So I am."

IN RETROSPECT, THIS FRIVOLITY AMONG POLISH STUDENTS IN THE SUMMER OF 1939 takes on a certain poignancy. It was not as if in their delightful silliness they were entirely oblivious to the dangers manifesting themselves in Europe at that moment. Fantastic self-deceptions were at work, to be sure, but the approach of death always encourages dancing and lovemaking. Realities did intrude on the university. Jagiellonian students hanged and burned Adolph Hitler in effigy at anti-Nazi rallies—which were not about Germany's treatment of the Jews so much as Hitler's threats against Poland and the derogatory Nazi characterizations of all Slavic peoples.

By exalting the Aryan race, whatever that was supposed to be, the Germans intensified racial consciousness everywhere, although it must be said that the racialist idea, a product of distorted Darwinism, had been in vogue long before anyone had ever heard of Hitler. Even young Wojtyla's enthusiasm for Slavs, for instance, exhibited innocently enough in "Magnificat" with its celebration of Slavic tribal customs and traditions, had parallels within every European ethnic group. Distress over dreary industrialization inspired reverence for acorns and fantasies concerning whose hides made better thongs in the old days. The difference between young Wojtyla's ethnic pride and Hitlerism was as vast as the difference between love and hate, or as wide as the gap between Christ and Nietzsche. One had to do with love, the other with racial superiority and the hate that results from it. To love the little platoon into which one is born, as Edmund Burke phrased it, is the first germ of public, or human, affections. Trouble begins when that platoon vilifies others and takes up the gun.

Within the Circle of Polish Philology at the Jagiellonian, a group to which Lolek belonged, discussions about what was truly Polish in literature turned into arguments about who was a Pole and who was not, and whether Jews were Poles. What is a national literature, the argument went, if not written in the national language? If Hebrew- or Yiddish-speaking Jews were not Slavs, or Poles, did they belong in a university supported by the Polish state? Some students in the group, although they were in the minority, supported the anti-Semitic policies of the government in power and advocated barring Jews altogether from the university. Lolek vehemently opposed this view, citing as always the words of Norwid, Mickiewicz, and other Polish writers who embraced Jewish contributions to Polish life and culture. He was also able to argue, from his personal experience of Jews and Jewish life, that anti-Semitism had less to do with differences between Jews and Christians than with resentment.

Lolek had not forgotten Ginka Beer and her parents or the Klugers. In Warsaw, meanwhile, Jurek had experienced his own introduction to university life, one that was quite different from Lolek's.

Chapter 14

Like Lolek and his father in Krakow, Jurek arrived in Warsaw before the university term began. He took up residence with a relative, Uncle Wiktor Huppert, who lived in an elegant apartment on one of Warsaw's most fashionable streets. The Aleje Jerozolimskie had nothing to do with Jerusalem or Jews except that Uncle Wiktor lived there, at No. 11.

A lawyer and unmarried, Wiktor was one of Jurek's favorite relatives. A dashing, witty fellow, he had been a member of the government until he resigned over anti-Semitic policies. He continued to move among the highest levels of Warsaw society, however. Grandmother Huppert had often talked about how this son of hers, who was the only one of her offspring to have no spouse, ought to find a good wife, preferably from a prominent family, and become a father. She did not know, and would have been horrified to learn, that Wiktor had a lover who had substantial means but was a countess from one of Poland's most exalted noble families. It was perhaps the only secret unknown to Grandmother Huppert—that Wiktor and the countess planned to marry as soon as he could get up the nerve to ask for Mrs. Huppert's permission or to endure what were sure to be her vehement objections. He could only hope that they would not include financial ostracism.

Like virtually any Jewish matriarch, Grandmother Huppert regarded marrying a Gentile as being among the gravest sins one of her children, or any Jew, could commit. To do so threatened the survival of the Jewish family and, by extension, the Jewish people. For a son to marry a Christian was even worse than for a daughter to do so, since Jewish identity passes through the female line, regardless of who the father may be.

The countess's family, as typical of the Polish aristocracy, had no objection to her marrying a Jew, or at least not one of Wiktor Huppert's style, sophistication, and political astuteness. His French was as perfect as his Polish. Wiktor and the countess did not live together; that would have been by aristocratic lights more a vulgar than a sinful arrangement. Her family found nothing untoward, however, about their traveling together for holidays in Paris or on the Côte d'Azure. They often visited Krakow, with Wiktor stopping off alone on the way to call on his mother and listen to her nattering on about how he should get married. Jurek knew that when his uncle alighted at the station, the countess remained on the train, then met him in a few days' time for a romantic rendezvous in Krakow at the Hotel Francuski.

This alliance, and particularly its subterfuge, delighted Jurek, who for himself could imagine nothing more thrilling than the affections of a countess. She lived up to his idea of her when they met in Warsaw. At dinner, he watched her drink champagne and could hardly speak. He, too, must have such a life, he thought, and he might never return to Wadowice if this was what life was like in Warsaw.

Uncle Wiktor, with his connections, had secured Jurek's place at the Polytechnic. Wiktor had warned him that he might encounter some disagreeable persons among the students, but he also said that Jurek shouldn't worry, he would be all right. Through registration and various preliminaries, he encountered nothing unusual. Nothing in the forms that he had to fill out questioned his religion, for such formal identification remained illegal in Poland even amid the increasingly hostile atmosphere for Jews. It occurred to him that he might blend in with the other students without anyone's knowing whether or not he was Jewish, as some Gentiles had German names, too, and while he was not blond like Tesia, neither were his features very obviously Semitic.

At the Polytechnic, all new students attended introductory lectures together in a big hall. He had his initial encounter with what was to be a common experience on his first day. As he entered the hall among four hundred to five hundred young men and a handful of women, he was immediately confronted by several boys who asked him his name. When he said "Kluger," one of them, in a loud voice, said, "Jew! You sit over there!" and pointed to a nearly empty section of benches on the left at the rear.

Normally, his instinct would have been to fight, but in this strange place, shocked and confused, he walked over and sat down where he was told with the rest of the Jews, perhaps twenty-five or thirty of them.

The Jews, with empty places surrounding them, were an obviously separated bunch in that corner of the huge room. When the professor came in, Jurek thought that he might notice them, say something, and stop this nonsense, but he did not. Instead, he labored over his lecture without looking up from his notes.

Jurek felt himself flush with anger as he sat there, not even trying to hear what the professor was saying. He looked around and saw several of the bullies staring at him, smirking. As for his fellow Jews, most of them were taking notes, or pretending to; others held their heads in their hands or stared at the nearest wall. "Surely we are not going to take this," Jurek thought, but he let the hour pass.

He spoke to no one on the way out, and no one spoke to him. Rather than risk further humiliation that day, he hurried home on foot to Uncle Wiktor's. His uncle was out, so Jurek had the entire day to think about what had happened. The bullies had not known him on sight, but they had known from his name that he was Jewish. It was obvious that because the only Jews admitted to the Polytechnic in 1938 had accomplished this through connections of some kind, word had been passed about who they were.

He decided to say nothing to Uncle Wiktor, who, if he protested to the authorities, might cause even more trouble. The best way to handle this, Jurek decided, was on his own.

The next day, he made sure that he arrived at the lecture hall early. He took a seat right in the middle, and as other Jews whom he recognized entered, he motioned to them to join him. There were no Jewish girls that he noticed. A few of the boys nervously sat down near him, but others ignored him and went resignedly to the section on the left.

"They want to sit in the ghetto, let them!" Jurek said to the fellow next to him, who managed a slight smile.

The hall filled up. A student came to sit in the empty place on Jurek's other side, recognized that he was one of *them*, and sat elsewhere. "Once the professor comes in," Jurek thought, "it will be all right. I have stood my ground, and I have won. Tomorrow, the other Jews will see how foolish they are to give in."

But even as he was thinking that, he felt hands on his shoulders, and someone gave him a shove so violent that he fell forward and hit his head on the bench in front of him. The next thing he knew, several boys were on him, punching him and dragging him and his companion out of their seats.

"Get the Jews!" he heard. "Throw the Jews out!"

He and the other fellow managed to fight back, and a couple of other Jews came to help them. But they were so outnumbered, with more than a dozen thugs against them, that they were getting much the worst of it. They were on the floor being kicked when the professor entered, and the attackers let up after a few more licks.

From his position on the floor in the aisle, Jurek looked up to see the professor, who reminded him of Damasiewicz, with his eyes lowered, shuffling through his papers. There was no way, unless he had kept his eyes closed while walking to the lectern, that he could not have noticed or heard what was going on. But he said and did nothing and soon began droning ahead in a monotone. Jurek dragged himself back to his seat and heard a voice behind him saying, "Next time, we won't be so easy on you, dirty Jew."

It was the same in all the lecture rooms. In the next several days,

Jurek alternated between sitting in the center and acquiescing by sitting in the so-called Jewish section and hating himself for it. He continued to get attacked, usually after class and once during it, when several boys simply lifted him out of his seat at the center and threw him over to the left side of the hall. None of the professors ever said or did anything about it. Either they were anti-Semites themselves or they were afraid like many of the Jews who went meekly to their seats on the left each day. What was even more discouraging to him than the inaction of the professors was the way that the Catholics who were not actually beating him just sat there, turning their heads. This was nothing like Wadowice, where he had always had far more allies than he even needed. There was no Lolek to remind everyone about the children of God.

Jurek did not want to be a crybaby or to disappoint his uncle and his father, but he soon had to tell Wiktor about what was going on. He could not explain away the bruises; he was beginning to look as if he were studying prize-fighting, not engineering. And of course, he was studying nothing. It was all he could do to get up the courage to attend class, let alone do any work. And he noticed that, after a week or two, the number of Jews had dropped by at least half, then more. So, they were being driven out. He would stay on, no matter what, he vowed. Nothing was going to intimidate him—not even the gangs of Jew-hating ruffians who were roaming through the streets of Warsaw with clubs augmented with razor blades. Sometimes they lay in wait as the few Jews that were left went home from the Polytechnic. Jurek saw them several times but eluded or outran them, thinking that he must have broken his personal record in doing so.

When Jurek finally told Uncle Wiktor the full truth of what was going on, Wiktor protested to the authorities but received a runaround. He was afraid it was no use, Wiktor said, and the countess agreed with him. Jurek should accept that these were impossible times, in Warsaw at any rate, and that he would have to go to university somewhere else, perhaps in France or England. It could be arranged, but not at once. Jurek refused and made Wiktor promise not to tell Dr. Kluger what was going on.

But when Jurek's father visited Warsaw on business about a

month into the school term, Uncle Wiktor did tell him and advised that he take Jurek home. The situation was too dangerous, and it might get worse. Dr. Kluger immediately agreed.

As bad as things were, Jurek was not happy to go. He felt like a quitter. He had never given up on a fight before. On the train, he went into the lavatory to cry so that his father wouldn't see him. He worried what his friends would think—and then he remembered that nearly all of them were gone. He would be alone at home with nothing to do. What a rotten turn of events!

THERE WAS NO POSSIBILITY OF RETURNING TO SCHOOL IN WARSAW. AFTER THE New Year in 1939, Jurek went to work at the Czeczowiczka textile factory, which was owned by Czech Jews and employed three thousand in the town of Andrychow, about eight miles from Wadowice. He traveled there by bicycle in good weather and by train in bad. As the months passed, he moved from department to department, learning the business, particularly its technical aspects. The experience was not exactly enjoyable, but it was better than being beaten up, and it gave him a different kind of education.

He had already learned brutally what it meant to be a member of a minority despised by some and unloved by most during economic hard times. He now came to better understand the gap between him and the working classes of any religion, and he appreciated the social and economic position his family had achieved. Most of the factory workers were Catholic, but some were poor Jews who were faring little better, if at all, than their Christian counterparts. Jurek soon came to sympathize more with his father's politics, which by this time could hardly be called even socialist. Dr. Kluger did not advocate state ownership of industry, for instance, but he still felt sympathy and support for common laborers, whose tedious, arduous lives left no energy or time for pleasure of any sort other than alcoholic oblivion at the end of the day. Jurek himself was exhausted by the time he returned to Wadowice each evening.

Enough to eat, freedom from the terror of unemployment, heat, and a roof without leaks—the workers did not need much, but few had any of these, even though the Czeczowiczka brothers paid more than the prevailing wage. Watching them at their tasks every day filled Jurek with a dread of falling to their level. Fortunately, to assure that he would not, his parents were making plans to send him to pursue a degree in textile engineering in Nottingham, England, that fall. By midsummer, everything was set; he had his railway ticket that would take him across the continent and the channel and his acceptance at the college in hand. He did not have a very clear idea of what England would be like, other than that it remained the center of the greatest empire in the history of the world and was a true parliamentary democracy but with a powerful aristocracy—all quite confusing. At the moment, his father told him, the important thing was that it would be a wonderful place to learn about manufacturing and that anti-Semitism there was nothing like the problem it had become in Central Europe. And England was Poland's ally.

Jurek rarely ran into any of his old classmates in Wadowice, and most of his time was spent at the factory. He had Lolek's address in Krakow, but somehow he could not find the words to write. He was humiliated by having to quit his studies, but he was also angry and perhaps indignant at the injustice that his Catholic friends were able to go on as if life were normal, while he was not. He did not want to sound bitter.

Twice that summer, Jurek accompanied Tesia to Krakow to watch her play in tennis tournaments. Among her opponents was the second-ranked woman in the world, the Polish champion Jadwiga Jedrzejowska, against whom Tesia, who was only sixteen, did commendably well. She was also giving Tesia lessons. The atmosphere was perfectly proper, dignified as tennis matches always were, a sport for gentlemen and ladies. Several people congratulated Jurek on his sister's performance and predicted that Tesia would soon be internationally ranked herself. No one questioned her right to compete. But what would happen when she applied for admission to the Jagiellonian? From what Jurek had heard, the Jewish students there—however they had gained entrance—faced incidents of hostility, although not to the same degree as in Warsaw. Nor did he see bands of thugs roaming the streets of Krakow wielding clubs. Could

Warsaw, whose population was one-third Jewish, be that much more anti-Semitic than Krakow, where about one in four citizens was a Jew? The situation was peculiar. It unnerved him, less because it was threatening than because it made no sense. When he brought it up with Tesia, however, she only shrugged.

He envied Tesia's equilibrium, her ability to concentrate on the task at hand, whether it was tennis or her studies. She was rather like Lolek in that way, more than anyone else he knew. When you brought up some problem with Lolek, he would listen intently, think about it, and say something sensible, always unperturbed; Tesia would simply smile and go on with whatever she had to do, and do it well.

With his journey to an unknown land before him, Jurek decided that seeing Lolek before he left would be important. It would reassure him that nothing had changed between them and that they would remain friends forever, no matter what else was going on. In the past year, Jurek had begun to miss Lolek's company more than that of any of his other classmates. There was something invigorating about his presence that was all the more apparent in its absence.

The Wojtylas had no telephone. One day soon, he would simply show up at their house, he thought, or find Lolek at the university. What a surprise that would be.

MEANWHILE, NEWSPAPERS WERE REPORTING THAT THE POLISH GOVERNMENT, both privately and publicly, was continuing to reject Hitler's demands to cede territory to Germany. The Fuehrer now wanted not only Danzig, which was Poland's only seaport, but the right to build an autobahn along a corridor through Polish territory to East Prussia, which had been divided from Germany proper by the Treaty of Versailles. If they were not conceded this much or more, the Germans threatened to take the areas by force. It was the view of the Polish government that Hitler was bluffing.

For the past six years, Poland had been spending half its national budget on defense and had great confidence in its military, which included an air force. If Pilsudski had managed to defeat the armies of Lenin in 1920, surely now, with every able-bodied youth over eighteen having had at least some military training, the Polish forces could repulse any attack by Hitler until assistance from the British and French arrived. By August, the signals from London and Paris were definite that this time there would be no capitulation to the Fuehrer.

At the same time, the Poles were so confident in their own military capabilities that they flatly rejected British and French pressure to permit Russian troops on Polish soil as a further deterrent to the Germans. They had no military pact with the Soviets, the Poles said, and they did not want one. They were disinclined to believe that welcoming one hereditary enemy for the sake of discouraging another was a wise idea. The British and French found the Poles' stubbornness on this issue exasperating, if not downright foolish or even stupid.

The Poles, however, except for the small cadre of actual Moscow-directed Communists, did not share in the illusions concerning Stalin, or Lenin before him, that were prevalent in the West. Their historical experience with Russian barbarism and their geographical proximity to the Soviet Union informed them about the actual state of affairs across the border to the east. They knew that millions of farmers in the Ukraine and central Russia were being thrown off their land, deported to a wasteland in Kazakhstan, and left to die. They knew that in the Soviet Union, millions were dying from state-induced famine, a form of population control made possible by the centralized tyranny of the Communist state.

They also knew that millions more were being arrested as enemies of the state, made to confess to absurdities in sham trials, and sent to perish in labor camps. Informed Poles did not know the exact number of victims, but research almost a half-century later would reveal it to be something like fourteen-and-a-half million "premature" deaths—higher than the total of the deaths for all countries in World War I. But any Pole with contacts in Russia, obviously including those working within the foreign ministry, knew that life within the Soviet Union was a nightmare of starvation, murder, and fear. Imprecise though their information was, only Poles oblivious to neighboring realities could have reached the level of fatuous delusion common in the West. (Renowned American journalist Lincoln

Steffens, after visiting the Soviet Union and evaluating the results of the Russian Revolution, concluded, "I have seen the future, and it works.") No, inviting the Russians into Poland did not seem like a good idea.

It was the general Polish view, which is now the common interpretation of the events of 1936 to 1939, that Hitler had succeeded in militarizing the Rhineland and taking over Austria and Czechoslovakia only because of Allied indecision as well as the unfortunate acquiescence of the Austrians and the Czechs. Now, the Poles believed, the combined weight of the French Army, the British Navy, and Polish forces would deter Hitler from further adventures. The Poles were also reassured by the widely shared assumption that the Soviet Union, although no friend to Poland, was an implacable enemy of German fascism. Surely not even Herr Hitler would be reckless enough to provoke the Soviets by invading Poland and approaching the Soviet border, thus assuring that Germany would be attacked from both east and west. The logic of this analysis seemed persuasive, at least to the Poles.

IN THIS ATMOSPHERE, WHICH IF NOT QUITE ONE OF CONFIDENCE WAS AT LEAST one of faith in the immediate European future, Jurek readied himself for England. His relatives, the Haberfelds, set sail for New York and the World's Fair in July of 1939 with cases of golden vodka and their stamp collections. Alfons and Lucia Haberfeld, with not a thought of emigrating, considered this a business and pleasure trip. Their children were amusing themselves for the summer in Italy and elsewhere, leaving behind only a grandmother to watch over the family castle in Oswiecim. Wiktor Huppert accompanied them, intending only a short visit to the United States. His return ticket placed him back in Warsaw by the end of August to resume his law practice and his liaison with the countess.

While the Haberfelds were still in New York and Uncle Wiktor was on his return voyage, a momentous change occurred in the European political and military situation.

In Moscow on the evening of August 23, Foreign Minister

Joachim von Ribbentrop of Germany and his counterpart, Vyacheslav Molotov of the Soviet Union, signed, in the presence of Joseph Stalin, a nonaggression pact between their two countries. The published provisions of this Russo-German treaty, which had been under secret negotiation for weeks, came as a complete shock to the Allies as well as to sincere Communists everywhere, who were hard put to rationalize it. The signators guaranteed that neither power would attack the other. In the event that either Germany or the Soviet Union became "the object of belligerent action" by a third country, the other party to the treaty would "in no manner lend its support to this third party." Nor would either Germany or the Soviet Union "join any grouping of powers whatsoever which is aimed directly or indirectly at the other party."

Of all the countries affected, Poland may have been the least surprised by this agreement, which proved false the general assumption that Hitler would never come to agreement with Boshe-viks any more than Stalin would betray all ideological principle (or pretense) by signing a treaty with fascist Germany. The Poles, who trusted the Russians less than the Germans, could only think that Stalin was acting true to Russian form, as perfidious as any czar and just as contemptuous of Poland. The British and the French blamed the Poles for not having accepted Russian intervention while it was still a possibility. Only the Poles themselves believed that they could repulse a German invasion for any length of time. How long it would take the British and French to come to their rescue was anyone's guess, as no concrete plans for such a contingency had been laid.

Typical of informed, non-Polish opinion, and no doubt shared by Hitler's generals, was the view of Robin Campbell, the British Reuters correspondent in Warsaw. When the Russo-German pact was announced, Campbell had already dispatched his children to England. Although his written reports presented a somewhat ambiguous impression of the Polish situation, he believed it to be hopeless. He and his wife at once packed their bags and were back in London by August 29, certain that Warsaw was doomed and that to remain there unprotected was suicide. The Campbells, who had been stationed in Berlin before taking the Polish assignment early in 1939, knew, without needing to wait for it to be tested in action, what the Nazi war machine had become. They also had observed Polish troops in training, with their horse-drawn artillery and their officers on horseback with gleaming swords. The Poles looked glamorous and brave, but they were equipped only for warfare in a past era.

Even with their bravery and self-confidence, the Poles would have been shaken by the unpublished "Secret Additional Protocol" of the Russo-German pact. Its consequences would become known soon enough. As it was, the public provisions of the treaty caused both Poland and France to place their active troops on alert and to call up all reserves.

FORTY-EIGHT HOURS AFTER THE ANNOUNCEMENT OF THE RUSSO-GERMAN pact, Wilhelm Kluger received notice to report to his army regiment by September 3. He took the view, as did nearly all of his fellow Polish soldiers, that this was the best way to show the Germans that the Poles meant business. Dr. Kluger, who was then fifty-four years old, had scrupulously maintained his reserve status as an army captain, and he was pleased to be able to serve his country again. And like most of his comrades in arms, he did not expect this deployment to last beyond a couple of weeks, once Hitler understood that the Poles and their allies would fight. After all, the British had already reaffirmed their intention to come to Poland's aid, if necessary, and had fully mobilized their navy, army, and most of their air force. On August 31, the French published a communique stating that they would "firmly fulfill" their treaty obligations to Poland in the event of an attack on her.

Dr. Kluger was not unaware of the unfortunate irony in his being called up while his able-bodied, eighteen-year-old son was being ignored by the military. Apparently, a middle-aged Jewish officer was acceptable, but a strong Jewish youth was not. It was part of the present, lamentable confusion, which perhaps the present crisis would help to resolve. All Poles would now realize, Dr. Kluger reasoned, that they must unite against common enemies, against intolerance. He retained faith in the ultimate reasonableness of the Polish people, even if some were temporarily misled. He also took some comfort in noting that if this were truly a national emergency, with the actual survival of the nation at stake, Poles would stand united as they always had—Catholics and Jews together—and the generals would not care if a fit young man was a Jew or, for that matter, a Turk or a Hottentot. As it was, there was no reason to think that Jurek should not go on to England as planned.

The headquarters of the division to which Dr. Kluger's regiment belonged had been moved strategically out of Krakow, its normal base, east to the town of Rzeszow. His wife was not so sanguine as he about his leaving. As August ended and the day of his departure drew close, she tried to console herself with the thought that Rzeszow was not very far away—only a couple of hours by train from Krakow. Dr. Kluger sensed her anxiety as she resewed the buttons on his old uniform, and Jurek told her not to be afraid, since his father was not.

"No one should worry," Dr. Kluger told them. "We just have to show this Hitler that we're not Czechs!"

"I WILL NEVER FORGET THE DAY OF 1 SEPTEMBER 1939," POPE JOHN PAUL II has written, adding that "it was the First Friday of the month." It happened also to be the day on which World War II began.

At dawn, Lolek and his father awoke to the sound of squadrons of planes and exploding bombs. On that first raid, the Germans hit the railroad yards and other industrial targets around Krakow, then sped away. Soon word spread through the city that the Germans had attacked, but few understood this as an unquestionable act of war. It could reasonably be presumed, however, that if the Luftwaffe had come once, they would soon return. Perhaps this was Hitler's way of coercing territorial concessions from Poland? In those first hours the atmosphere was one of uncertainty and apprehension.

To Lolek, however, any First Friday, which devout Catholics observe as a kind of mini-Good Friday, meant making confession, attending mass, and receiving Holy Communion, rituals that he had been performing regularly during the past year at the Wawel Cathedral. That a few bombs had fallen did not seem to him sufficient reason to alter this routine. No young man believes that he will die, but his decision that morning to take his customary walk to the cathedral does suggest an unusual indifference to mortality—or perhaps a reasonable conclusion that if a bomb was going to fall on him, better that it should do so on his way to church. Not many thought as he did. When he left the house, the streets were mostly deserted.

After crossing the Vistula, Lolek turned right at the end of Debniki Bridge and proceeded perhaps a half-mile to climb the steep, cobbled lane up Wawel Hill, which dominates Krakow the way the Temple Mount must once have crowned Jerusalem. Here stands the magnificent, flamboyantly Italianate Royal Palace, designed in the early sixteenth century by a Florentine. Here also is the elaborate compound of the great cathedral, truly Poland's national sanctuary, with its gothic nave and its three towers in different yet strangely complementary styles. Nearly every king and queen of Poland was crowned in this place, where on this clear morning, as always, the golden dome of Sigismund's Chapel shone with early light. Today, however, the panoramic view of the city afforded by Wawel Hill showed columns of smoke rising here and there in the distance, and from far away came the clanging and whooping of ambulances and fire engines.

Usually by that hour, the stony expanse of courtyard was coming alive with hurrying priests, nuns, and other early massgoers. On this day that had dawned unlike any other, Lolek found himself alone. He pushed open the cathedral's great bronze door, embossed with a profusion of K's honoring King Kazimierz, and entered into that cool gloom to find no one. Even the confessional boxes were empty of priests. Father Figlewicz had not arrived to dispense absolution at his usual First Friday post.

Lolek heard his own footsteps echoing as he walked toward the main altar at the center of the building and knelt to pray. The altar holds what is certainly, after the Black Madonna, the most revered object in Poland—the solid silver sarcophagus of Saint Stanislaw. The saint was martyred by King Boleslaw the Generous in 1079, but the sarcophagus—for that is what it is called despite being fashioned of precious metal instead of stone—expresses well the continuity of Polish beliefs through centuries. It was not made until six hundred years later, at the height of the Polish Baroque period, and it is as extravagant in design as the medieval saint himself was austere. Ornate cherubim with hands joined in prayer adorn the sides of the coffin; a pair of cherubs kneeling atop the lid hold up the miter, also solid silver, of the archbishop; and four silver seraphim at the corners bear its weight between their wings.

Faintly gleaming in perpetual candlelight, this perhaps excessively ornate tomb would seem out of place in any other gothic cathedral, but not here. For reasons beyond any conventional aesthetic measure, its excesses themselves seem appropriate because they embody the idea of a glorious martyrdom, that of Poland's patron saint. Seeing the tomb, it is difficult to resist the urge to sneak up to touch it.

It was after seven, the hour when mass was to begin, but no bells had tolled, and there was no priest. Lolek was so deep in prayer that he did not hear anyone approach but, at some minutes past the hour, he felt a hand on his shoulder and looked up to see Father Figlewicz in his vestments. He would go ahead with the mass, the priest said. Would Lolek be good enough to serve?

Wordlessly, Lolek followed his old teacher, who was now curate of the cathedral, to the altar. So it was to be just the two of them, the celebrant and his former altar boy from Wadowice, alone without a congregation in the vast cathedral, among only the ghosts of saints, kings and queens, and poets.

Their voices alternated in the Latin. Father Figlewicz had not yet reached the canon of the mass when sirens sounded across the city; then came the drone of planes and the dull thuds of bombs, one after another, soon overlapping in awful sequence. Father Figlewicz raised his voice above the roar and shriek of dive-bombers and explosions to pray for God's mercy on Poland and for the intercession of Mary, Queen of Poland. He continued with the familiar words, through the breaking of the bread and the eating of Christ's body and the drinking of the precious blood.

Again the cathedral was not hit, and it never was. The Germans had other plans for the Wawel, and this would be the last time for many years that Lolek or any other Pole would freely enter the cathedral.

In those first chaotic hours, military intelligence was fragmentary on the Polish side. No one could put all the pieces together; the onslaught was unimaginable. The Poles were woefully unprepared for anything like it. Then again, in the history of the world, nothing like this had ever befallen any country. Far to the north of Krakow, near the East Prussian border, a Polish officer watched through binoculars as a group of small children was led by their teacher into the shelter of a wood; bombers rumbled in formation overhead. "Suddenly, there was the roar of an aeroplane," the officer later wrote. "The pilot circled round, descending to a height of fifty metres. As he dropped his bombs and fired his machine guns, the children scattered like sparrows. The aeroplane disappeared as quickly as it had come, but on the field some crumpled and lifeless bundles of bright clothing remained. The nature of the new war was already clear."

And on the ground came the tanks and other armored vehicles. Although some in the Polish Army had suspected, based on reports from Poles fleeing across the border from East Prussia and Germany proper, that massive tank formations and infantry had been lining up on the German side in the days immediately before September 1, most did not take these reports seriously enough. Not until late August had the Poles begun to lay out barbed-wire entanglements and dig in. A full mobilization was ordered and then canceled on August 28. No thorough radio communications network had been established from the high command in Warsaw to the rest of the country, or not one that could function properly when every line of defense was breached almost simultaneously.

So it was that the military in and around Krakow had no idea that when the Germans started bombing them, Stukas and Heinkel 111s were also hitting Warsaw, with far greater intensity. Certainly no one other than the Germans knew that at the dawning of that clear and balmy Friday, the word *Blitzkrieg* had entered the world's vocabulary. Lightning-war was Hitler's new strategy to avoid the prolonged trench warfare that had assured Germany's defeat in

World War I, because the Fatherland lacked the natural resources to sustain a drawn-out conflict. He had built up an air force, army, and navy of more than two million men. As for the industry to sustain this force, it would come from conquered territory—first Czechoslovakia and now Poland.

Blitzkrieg meant hurling Germany's four fully mobilized divisions, led by the Luftwaffe, against Poland's defenses, which Germany knew consisted largely of horse-drawn artillery and a cavalry on horseback. As the bombing and the strafing began that dawn, German tanks and troops accompanied by light, quick armor poured across the Polish border at fourteen widely separated points—four from the north along the East Prussian border, seven from the west, and three from what had been Czechoslovakia in the south. The plan was to strike everywhere at once before the Poles had any idea of what was coming.

As for the British and French response on which the Poles relied, the idea was that the invasion would be a fait accompli before the Allies could do anything about it. Beyond that, Hitler was gambling that, based on their policy of appeasement during the past four years, the British and the French would do nothing. He was so confident of French inertia that he left Germany's entire western front without tanks or airplanes in order to throw everything against Poland. He had good reason to believe that German propaganda, together with prominent Western appeasers—including Communists who were now parroting Stalin's line that England, not Germany, was the true imperialist enemy—had convinced the West that the Nazis had even more tanks and airplanes than they actually did.

The Fuehrer had decided on the September 1 raid the previous April, and the Russo-German pact, more than any other factor, sealed Poland's fate. This was the latest possible date for a highly mechanized offensive because by mid-September, heavy rains nearly always turned Poland into a sea of mud. Now, with Poland's abundant natural resources (coal, copper, lead, salt, sulfur, zinc, and even small deposits of oil and gas), Germany would have what it needed to dominate the Continent.

The Germans had an elaborate communications network

among their divisions and precise intelligence on the locations of all Polish military emplacements, from high priority targets to relatively minor ones. Thus the Polish Air Force, consisting of about five hundred planes, was eliminated at once—bombed at its various fields, mostly around Warsaw, before a single fighter could leave the ground. And at the same moment that bombers were hitting Warsaw and Krakow, others struck at what was hardly a significant target—the Fifth Horse Artillery, situated along with a cavalry brigade near Oswiecim. The bombs hit there at exactly five minutes past five on the morning of September 1.

It required only a couple of Stukas to do a job on the barracks and stables, which were wood and plaster structures dating from Austro-Hungarian days, when war was still an equestrian pursuit; alas, for the Poles, it still largely was. The horses that were not killed or disabled ran in panic through the camp and into the town. Without the animals to haul it, the artillery, including anti-aircraft guns, was useless. It sat silent as Heinkels swooped in to drop bombs that finished off the camp. With no plans in hand for evacuation, the officers organized their scattered men into ranks and marched them into Oswiecim. They could not remain defenseless in the burnt-out shell of their base; perhaps they could board a train.

Oswiecim was a town of about twelve thousand then, some five thousand of whom were Jews and a large proportion of the rest *Volksdeutsche*. Many of these ethnic Germans, taking the opportunity to display their allegiance to the Fatherland, aimed pistols and rifles through the windows of their houses and fired on the lines of bewildered Polish troops. Officers had to restrain their men from torching Oswiecim and marched them on the double to the outskirts, where they were ordered to repair damaged tracks so that they could get to safety. By the next morning, the freight train they had finally managed to commandeer hadn't even reached Krakow, a distance of only fifty miles, when Heinkel 111s spotted the moving target and struck. Trapped in boxcars, hundreds of soldiers died. Those who survived joined knots of refugees walking eastward, away from the Germans and toward what they hoped would be the protection of the Polish army—but where, they weren't sure.

Meanwhile, on the main street of Oswiecim, an old Jewish woman remained in her castle with her granddaughter and their servants. Alfons and Lucia Haberfeld, the old woman's son and daughter-in-law, were still in New York. On news that Poland had been invaded, they tried to book passage home, so little could they imagine what was actually happening there. The Haberfelds boarded a ship sailing for England, but at Newcastle they were refused permission to disembark because Britain, like France, was now in a state of war against Germany, even though neither country was doing anything to help Poland. The French, of course, could have invaded Germany and would easily have overrun it, since most of the German army and all of its tanks and planes were in Poland. This was the start of the period known as the Phony War, or in Germany *Sitzkrieg*, when Britain and France sat and did nothing.

At this time, it was an accepted convention of maritime law that if a ship was refused permission to land at its port of destination, it must be allowed to return to its port of origin and be accepted there. So it was that the Haberfelds found themselves back in New York by the end of September. They were naturally concerned for the fate of the grandmother and child who had been left behind in Oswiecim, but they did not yet comprehend how much danger Jews in Poland really were in or what a peculiar thing it was that this ship landed again in New York, while others could not. (In contrast, only that May, a German ship carrying nine hundred Jewish refugees to Cuba had been refused entry at Havana and at Miami and other U.S. ports. Forced to return to Europe, the *Saint Louis* discharged its passengers in England, France, and Holland. Only those Jews lucky enough to be accepted by the British survived.)

The Haberfelds were still in New York when the Gestapo took over their castle and removed the grandmother and all the other Jews of Oswiecim to a ghetto in nearby Chrzanow, where they could await further developments. At that time, the Germans changed the name of Oswiecim to Auschwitz.

Uncle Wiktor Huppert, however, did make it home to Warsaw from the World's Fair. He had returned on schedule and was sleeping in his apartment on the Aleje Jerozolimskie when the bombs began to drop. He was there to learn of the fall of Krakow and also when the Polish government fled the city to take refuge in Lublin. He remained there on September 8, as the Fourth Panzer Division reached Warsaw. Citizens fought back as they could, overturning tram cars as barricades and firing small arms against automatic weapons and tanks as their beautiful capital collapsed into rubble. Wiktor was with the people, firing his revolver, wearing the uniform of a second lieutenant.

He was in Warsaw to hear the news when the battle to the north, for Gdansk/Danzig and the so-called Polish Corridor, ended in defeat. Poles on horseback charged German tanks and were slaughtered by the thousands, breaking their long lances against oncoming steel killing machines. Don Quixote tilted with windmills, the Poles with Panzers. The world noticed, and did nothing. It was Poland's finest hour, maybe the bravest display of any army in world history as well as the most futile and tragic.

Wiktor was also in Warsaw on September 15, when the Polish government, thoroughly discredited because of its misreading of German strengths and intentions, fled to Romania and was interned there. And he was there on September 28, when at last the city succumbed and was no longer the capital of anything.

The Germans immediately issued orders establishing themselves as masters over Polish slaves, with Jews lowest on the scale. All at once, Poland became not merely an occupied country but a nation of servants. In the face of this situation, Wiktor reached a decision.

He understood what was certain to happen to him and to the woman he loved. Because they were lovers, he and the countess were criminals under the law of the Reich. Both would be found guilty of violating the edict against interracial intercourse, a proscription that was perfectly expressive of the perversion that inspired it and one that, like the rattle of a snake, signaled death. Wiktor did not wish to live without his love, but if he stayed with her, he would be her ruin.

The servants found his body, a pistol in his hand. When the countess learned that her Wiktor was dead, she hurled herself from a fifth-floor window.

Chapter 15

No bombs fell on Wadowice, but on September 1, everyone heard the planes and saw formations coming from the southwest and the northwest, headed toward Krakow. Wadowice was in the line of flight and—although the townspeople didn't know this yet—in the line of march between Krakow and a corner of the former Czechoslovakia, a staging point for German infantry.

Dr. Kluger was briefed by the few officers of the Twelfth Infantry who were not already at the front; the radio brought more news, most of it confusing and none of it good. He decided that he had better join his regiment immediately, rather than waiting until September 3 as ordered. He also decided that Jurek should accompany him to Rzeszow. Certainly, the anti-Semites would understand who the real enemy of Poland was, and they would be quite happy to muster all the strong Jewish boys they could. As for Jurek, he was glad to be able to go with his father and fight the Germans, if that was what it was coming to. He had spent the past year feeling rather useless and rejected by his country. If Poland needed him now, he was ready.

A few Jewish families in Wadowice, terrified at the prospect of the town's being occupied by Nazis, prepared to head east. But it was the collective judgment of the Klugers—most strongly influenced, of course, by Wilhelm—that Rozalia, Tesia, and Grandmother Huppert would be safest staying at home. Where would they go otherwise, and how would they get there? They had no car; the trains had suddenly become uncertain and would become more so as the bombing continued. As for the frightening prospect of occupation, surely it would be a mistake to confuse ordinary German soldiers with madmen like Hitler and his cohorts. Left to do his job, the German soldier would behave decently. Germany was not Russia but a civilized country, the heart of European civilization, was it not? There was no reason to think that German soldiers would wish to harm women and children. And as there was nothing worth bombing in Wadowice now that all but a small contingent of the Twelfth Infantry had left, it appeared to be a relatively safe place for the women.

In the end, there was not much to discuss, since Grandmother Huppert was too blind and feeble to go anywhere. Rozalia packed three handsome leather suitcases, souvenirs of Italian holidays with the Haberfelds, for her husband and son. Dr. Kluger, who had never learned to drive an automobile, managed to secure a military car and driver for Jurek and himself, put on his uniform, and prepared to depart.

During those last moments with the family, there was some talk of how long it would take the British and the French to honor their pledge to defend Poland. Radio reports spoke of rumors that a deal was being cooked up that would betray Poland, but Dr. Kluger did not believe them. Then the car pulled up in Zatorska Street, and everyone exchanged tearful goodbyes and mutual reassurances.

Goldberger, the cello-playing dentist from upstairs, and cousins who occupied the apartment at the rear came to see them off. For Jurek and his father, it was reassuring to think that the women would not be left alone but would have friends and relatives in the same building to keep them company and help out if there was trouble. At any rate, no one expected this war to last very long.

Outside, the Rynek was nearly full of people talking quietly and taking courage from their numbers and their warm familiarity with one another in this, their town. Many waved goodbye as Dr. Kluger and his son drove off. The last face Jurek saw was Tesia's, which was tear-streaked as she stood at Grandmother Huppert's favorite window.

TO REACH THE ROAD TO THE EAST, THEY HAD TO DRIVE THROUGH HILLY countryside past Kalwaria and into Krakow. By the time they entered the city, the bombing had stopped for the day. They could see damage here and there, but the surest sign of what was going on was the chaos in the streets. Half the population, it seemed, was trying to get out—on foot, in wagons, on trucks, and some in automobiles crammed with belongings. Everyone was headed in the same direction, so progress was inch by inch.

As they crawled along the Vistula embankment and passed Debniki Bridge, Jurek thought fleetingly of Lolek and his father. To think that he had been planning to visit the Wojtylas this weekend or next! Near the Wawel, Dr. Kluger ordered the driver to detour into the adjacent Kazimierz district, to the house of Engineer Zilz, a railroad official who was married to Dr. Kluger's sister. If their neighborhood had been bombed, they might need help. They found the Zilzes unscathed but preparing to leave, loading up two automobiles. The Zilzes, along with their two daughters and their husbands, had decided that getting as far away from the Germans as possible was more important than clinging to houses and possessions. As the chief administrator for Polish railroads in Krakow, Zilz was informed better than most about the astonishingly rapid movement of armor and troops toward Krakow; they were approaching at a rate of twenty or thirty miles an hour, reports said. Enemy occupation of the city seemed inevitable, and he had little doubt of how the Germans would regard a Jew in his position.

Zilz invited Captain Kluger and Jurek to accompany them to the east. As a high-ranking officer, the captain could perhaps speed their way and protect them, if necessary, with his revolver. Dismissing their driver, the Klugers transferred their baggage to the bigger car, a Skoda Rapide, and climbed into the rear seat. The others followed in the coupe, through the city toward the road to Rzeszow.

THE BOMBING OF KRAKOW STARTED AGAIN PROMPTLY AT FIRST LIGHT THE next morning. In their apartment on Tyniecka Street, Lolek and his father discussed whether to flee. Anti-aircraft fire was scoring some hits, but the waves of German planes continued their assault, and Debniki itself came under heavy bombardment because of the powerful radio transmitter located there. But to leave was a difficult choice, because Karol Senior, who had turned sixty in July, suffered from a weak heart and had scarcely had the strength to leave the apartment in recent weeks. He insisted, however, that he was up to a journey and preferred not to wait passively for the Germans to take over. Like so many others who could not believe that the Poles would be left in the lurch, he imagined that he and Lolek could find safe refuge behind Polish lines and return home before too long. There was also a possibility that Lolek would be needed to fight in the east. Neither of them would be doing Poland any good by staying at home.

With Lolek carrying a single valise for the two of them, father and son left their apartment on foot to join what had become a river of refugees flowing east and swelling with every mile. Their pace was extremely slow; it took all of the old lieutenant's strength and will to keep up, and when a family offered them space on a platform truck, they gratefully accepted the ride.

By the time the Wojtylas left Krakow that Saturday, Jurek and his father, although they had driven all night, were only a few miles ahead of them and still short of Tarnow, a distance from Krakow of only fifty miles. Beyond Krakow, country people joined the march, driving their cattle before them.

The sun came up in their faces along this old road, which for hundreds of years had been the trade route from Kiev, Budapest, and even Byzantium to Krakow. It cut a nearly straight line through the rich, alluvial plain, paralleling the Vistula to the north, crossed by many smaller streams, and with a line of forested hills just to the south. In another September, hunters would have been cleaning their rifles in anticipation of shooting wild boar and deer in those hills, instead of Germans. Dust from the procession of refugees powdered the leaves of trees and blackberry brambles. In the dark green fields, crops remained. The Klugers and the Zilzes inched along in their cars. Peasants either stood in the doorways of red-roofed houses watching them, tended to their geese and sheep, or decided to join the march.

At midmorning they crossed the small Raba River and entered Bochnia, where many more Jews were leaving their houses. At the center of that small town, miners stood around at the entrance to a salt-mine shaft, leaning on their picks, staring, not knowing whether to go down to work or to leave. One of them waved, and Jurek waved back.

They were between Bochnia and Brzesko that afternoon when the Stukas struck, diving in from the south with that terrible screaming sound, bombing and strafing the road. The attack was so sudden and unexpected that even Captain Kluger, who had been to war but not to one like this, sat paralyzed as the planes passed overhead at a height of maybe two to three hundred feet. Around them, people hit the ground and crawled into the ditches. There was nowhere to run. Jurek saw a bomb slam into a house and explode as pigs in the yard fell over dead or tore about. Through the windshield he watched the planes, one after another, raking the people with machine-gun fire.

The raid lasted less than a minute. Their cars were not hit, but carnage was all around them. In the immediate aftermath, Jurek saw a bloody-headed horse collapse between wagon-shafts and empty its bowels. Beside the car, a woman was screaming, holding a bloody baby. Jurek started to get out to help, but his father grabbed his arm.

"You must drive on," Captain Kluger said to Zilz, who was trying to comfort his wife.

They zigzagged through the dead and wounded and around bomb craters. If the planes came again, they agreed, they should leave the cars and lie in the ditches. One bullet could turn a car into a bomb.

Brzesko, a heavily Jewish town, looked practically deserted. All the Jewish houses, distinguishable by their arched windows and doors, unlike the square ones built by Catholics, appeared to have been abandoned. "Where will all these people go, and who will feed them?" Jurek wanted to know, but no one had an answer. He was beginning to think that they had made a mistake by leaving Wadowice. They were lucky to have the cars, of course—unless they blew up.

That afternoon, the Stukas struck again. Jurek rolled into a ditch with the others, his hands over his head. If we are going to die, he prayed, please spare Mother and Tesia. But again, they were lucky, and the cars remained intact, unlike many people around them. On the road ahead, the ditches were lined with bodies.

Twin church spires, one on either side of the road a mile or two in the distance, marked Tarnow on the morning of the third day. There, exhausted, they stopped to rest at the house of another of Jurek's uncles. From this house on Zydowska (Jewish) Street, one could look across a small square to a Baroque synagogue that had stood there since the days when Shakespeare was writing *The Merchant of Venice*. Tarnow, a city of about a hundred thousand inhabitants, was at least half Jewish. Jurek's uncle, a doctor, told him that many Jews had panicked and taken to the road eastward but that he was staying put, and so were most of his neighbors. Every family on this street had lived there for as long as anyone could remember and were not about to be driven out by the fear of another occupation. If the Germans came, so be it. Was this anything new in the history of Poland and its Jews? What was there in the east for the Jews, except Cossacks?

LOLEK AND HIS FATHER, TRAVELING AS BEST AS THEY COULD ON FOOT OR hitching rides, followed the same route eastward as the Klugers in search of the Polish Army, only to be told in every town that soldiers had been seen retreating farther and farther along the road. In five days, the Wojtylas covered perhaps a hundred miles, dodging bombs and bullets, sleeping in fields or in barns. Past Rzeszow, it became too much for the old man, and they gave up. Lolek tried to carry him, but it was no good. Like many of the other discouraged refugees, they turned back.

In Krakow again, they found that their apartment had survived the bombing, and they moved back in. They learned that the city had fallen to the Germans on September 6. There was nothing to do now but survive while the Germans established their domination.

The little caravan of Klugers and Zilzes did not find the tattered remnants of the Polish Army until, on September 10, they reached Tarnopol, in the far southeastern corner of what was then still Poland. The last few miles had been quick because few other refugees made it that far. After Lvov, the ranks had thinned and the Stukas no longer pursued them, so the road was no longer lined with corpses. Along the way, they had heard of Krakow's fall. As for Wadowice, they knew nothing of what might be happening there. Whatever, it could be no worse than what Jurek and his father had witnessed during their journey. This war was less a clash of armies than the mass murder of ordinary people: the slaughter of refugees; peasants machine-gunned in their fields; and in town after town, hospitals, sanitariums, schools, houses, and apartment blocks bombed. Even the dead did not escape, as they were machine-gunned from the air in the ditches where they lay putrefying.

In Tarnopol, Captain Kluger entered immediately into service, but there was little for him to do. He had experience with artillery in the last war; here all the Poles really needed were doctors. Kluger's regiment and the others straggling into the city were an army in bandages. As for Jurek, he joined up, but this amounted to little more than signing his name. For him, the army had neither a uniform nor a gun. Polish forces did have use for the big Skoda, which they quickly requisitioned.

Jurek and his father had to wonder why they had come this far, to this place. Polish soldiers converged on Tarnopol after making their way from as far north as the East Prussian border; they were driven into retreat at town after town, from the outskirts of Warsaw, south along the Vistula, through hopeless skirmishes at Lublin, on down to their present, desperate attempt to regroup and make a last stand.

With them they brought stories of bewilderment and brutality, of civilians lined up and shot, of entire towns and villages bombed and burnt out. It was not so much a war, they said, as a massacre.

Perhaps the Poles could hold Tarnopol and a few other outposts, Polish commanders thought, until the British and the French at last fulfilled their pledges to intervene. There was no longer a unified Polish command. By late September, some units tried to make a run for the Romanian or Hungarian borders with the idea of fighting again from foreign soil. The Russians had other plans for them.

On September 17, a phalanx of Soviet T-26 tanks, trailed by thousands of Russian soldiers, reached Tarnopol from the east. The Poles had already learned from radio reports that Russians were crossing the border in great numbers and advancing into eastern Poland. What could this mean? Although Poland had no mutual defense pact with the Soviet Union, the two countries did share a treaty guaranteeing that neither would invade the other. At the same time, there was now the Russo-German pact, stipulating that the Russians would stay out of any Polish-German conflict. Remarkably, many sophisticated statesmen actually believed that such treaties carried weight even when circumstances favored violation of them by one party or the other. It was as if people imagined that a piece of paper signed by nations was more valid than an agreement between a gangster and his mark. In this instance, no one beyond Stalin, Molotov, Hitler, and von Ribbentrop knew about the secret clauses of the August Russo-German agreement.

On that day in September, loudspeakers attached to the Russian tanks broadcast this message in Russian-accented Polish.

> Valiant comrades of the Polish Army! We have crossed the border to join with you in the struggle against the Germans, the deadly enemies of the Slavs and of the entire human race! You must join with us immediately, after surrendering your arms, which will be returned to you later!

The Poles were too stunned, exhausted, and confused to react. Resisting the Russians while also being routed by the Germans was not an option. Russian soldiers entered Tarnopol without firing a shot. Jurek and his father stood on the margins of the central square as it filled up with Soviet troops.

The Russian soldiers were gaunt, with rifles slung from their necks on string; their tattered uniforms hung on them. They were well-drilled, however, and gave every appearance of being happy warriors. They formed ranks and, on cue from a major, began to sing Russian folk songs with that alarming lustiness that only a male Russian chorus can project.

That night, the soldiers pitched their tents in the square, lit fires, and sang on and on for hours, songs of the steppes and of the Volga and the Don, songs of Mother Russia, of arctic nights and ice castles and summers filled with honey and wildflowers and kisses. Always the lead singer, the *zapiewajlo*, led the chorus. It was as if they were less an army than a traveling choir. Local Ukrainians cheered and sang along and rushed up to embrace their comrades. Jurek and his father retreated into shadows. Four centuries of Polish rule were ending.

IN THE FOLLOWING DAYS, THE FULL EXTENT OF UKRAINIAN ENTHUSIASM REGistered as the Russians took over. Many proclaimed themselves Communists and formed a citizens' militia, displaying red armbands and firing Russian-supplied rifles into the air in jubilation.

Jurek and his father were sorry to see that there were many Jews among those welcoming the Russians. It shamed and angered them to see Jews in such great numbers pledging allegiance to Bolshevism, although the Klugers knew that this would be far less the case among Jews farther to the west in Poland. "Let them see how they like living under the Ukrainians and the Russians for a while," Jurek's father said. "They'll be praying for the Poles to return soon enough."

Elsewhere in eastern Poland, the Russians took over less smoothly. They dropped leaflets urging Poles to welcome "the brotherly help of the Red Army," whose soldiers came "not as enemies but as your brothers in class solidarity, as your liberators from the oppression of landlords and capitalists." When citizens failed to embrace this rhetoric, the Russians opened fire, in one instance dragging a Polish officer from his car and killing him in front of his wife and troops; in another, executing thirty Polish policemen; and in another, executing one hundred thirty schoolboys. In this way, Poland was partitioned for the fourth time since 1772, taken over again by the same imperial powers as of old. Everything went according to plan, this one being the "Secret Protocol" attached to the Russo-German agreement of August 23.

The unexpected rapidity of the German advance did require some improvisation on the part of the aggressors. By September 8, Foreign Minister von Ribbentrop in Berlin was frantically cabling Foreign Commissar Molotov in Moscow that it was time for the Russians to enter eastern Poland. Stalin was not ready; he had not yet concocted the excuse for the invasion, which was that the Russians had to rescue their Slav brothers—a pretense that infuriated Hitler but that he had to swallow. The Germans had already advanced beyond the agreed-upon line of demarcation, which was supposed to have been north-south along the course of the rivers Pissa, Narew, Vistula, and San. Stalin suggested that Hitler could keep what he had gained of Poland in return for ceding Lithuania and the other Baltic states to Russia. The Fuehrer accepted this division of the spoils, and Poland once again disappeared from the map. Pockets of troops held out until October 5; after that, their fate depended on whether they ended up in the Russian- or the German-occupied zones.

Quixotic and bloody, the September Campaign was an honorable defeat. Alone at that hour, Poland forcefully resisted the Germans, setting an example to shame appeasers and collaborationists in other nations. The Poles suffered two hundred thousand soldiers and uncounted civilians killed in four weeks, yet they also managed to kill forty-five thousand German troops, to shoot down seven hundred enemy planes, and to destroy nearly a thousand tanks and other armored vehicles. Outnumbered four to one, they would have held out longer had the Russians not swarmed in from the east and blocked their escape to neutral territory.

While the Poles' courage did attract world attention (photographs published in *Life* magazine conveyed indelible images of soldiers on horseback charging Panzers), the Jewish contribution to the September Campaign drew little or no attention. Yet one hundred twenty thousand Polish Jewish soldiers fought, and thirty thousand died in battle. Polish Jewish soldiers accounted for fifteen percent of deaths on the battlefield, far in excess of their proportion in the population. Had the army not resisted their enlistment during the year or so before the war, more would have fought and died for Poland that month.

Chapter 16

Now that they had conquered Poland once again, the Russians and the Germans had to decide what to do with its people. Other than imposing the Communist political and economic structure at once, the Russians took their time in divulging their plans. The Germans were less ambiguous; they immediately annexed western provinces, including Silesia, to the Reich. The border west of Krakow was drawn at the River Skawa, which put Wadowice in Germany. The great central expanse of the country, including Warsaw, Krakow, and Lublin, became a kind of colony, which was called the General Government and had Krakow as its capital. Hitler appointed his chief legal adviser, Dr. Hans Frank, as governor general; Frank, who was president of the German Legal Academy and a top Nazi, installed himself in the Royal Castle on Wawel Hill.

Very much aware of the symbolism, Frank immediately closed the Wawel Cathedral, permitting Father Figlewicz and one other priest to say mass there once a month, but with no one other than German guards in attendance. "It is essential that the great German people should consider as its major task to destroy all Poles," proclaimed Reich Minister for the Interior and S.S. Chief Heinrich Himmler. Governor General Frank knew that there was no more visible way of beginning this process than to shut down or desecrate the principal sites of Polish history, culture, and religion.

For Polish Jews, the oppression was even worse. Before the invasion, in a speech on January 30, 1939, Hitler proclaimed that European Jews would be annihilated in the event of war. (The word he used then was *Vernichtung*, which is literally "the condition of becoming nothing.") In the meantime, the Reich and the General Government ordered Polish Jews into sealed-off, heavily guarded ghettos, the principal ones being at Lodz, Warsaw, and Lublin. If the Germans at first regarded them as way stations or holding pens, as it were, on the route to deportation, the ghettos quickly became a method of eradication in their own right.

Never a politically or socially coherent population group, Poland's Jews were now isolated and completely dependent on the outside world, packed into tiny areas of such density that it was not possible to survive there for more than a limited period of time. In Warsaw, for example, where the ghetto was established between October and November of 1940, four hundred fifty thousand people were crammed into an area measuring 1.3 square miles and containing just under sixty-one thousand three hundred rooms. That meant that an average of 7.2 people had to live in each room—a space the size of a typical bedroom. Under these conditions, and with a food allocation of one-and-a-half loaves of bread per person per week, epidemics of intestinal typhus, tuberculosis, and influenza rapidly decimated the inhabitants, who had practically no access to serum or other medical supplies.

On March 21, 1942, the Propaganda Division of the Warsaw district reported:

> The death figure in the ghetto still hovers around five thousand per month. A few days ago, the first case of hunger cannibalism was recorded. In a Jewish family, the man and his three children died within a few days. From the flesh of the child who died last—a twelve-year-old boy—the mother ate a piece. To be sure, this could not save her either, and she herself died two days later.

By September, the Warsaw ghetto had buried eighty-three thousand people, some of whom were finished off by soldiers who enjoyed entering the ghetto to take target practice on the inhabitants. Well before the machinery of the "final solution" was in place at Auschwitz and other camps, the Jews of Poland were disappearing at a rapid rate.

For many months, Jews in some remote small towns, including Wadowice, were spared the ghetto. Some took the opportunity to hide, and perhaps a hundred thousand found refuge with Christian neighbors and passed as Catholics, with children receiving baptism or forged baptismal certificates from sympathetic priests. (The figures have never been certain and could be greater or smaller.) But only relatively assimilated Jews, who spoke unaccented Polish and did not have distinctly Semitic features, could blend into the Catholic population. This meant that most had no chance of passing as Christians, even if they could find Christians willing to help them. The penalty for hiding or assisting Jews in any way was death.

Krakow, which the conquerors envisioned as one day becoming a truly "German" city, with Germans as the masters and Slavs as their slaves, was an exception within the General Government. There the idea was to make the capital of this colony *judenrein* (clean of Jews) as quickly as possible. This policy illustrates more vividly than anything else the distinction that the Germans made between Jews and Slavs: both were considered drastically inferior to Aryan peoples, but Slavs could be tolerated as workers as long as they understood their low biological and cultural status; for Jews there was no place at all.

To "Germanize" Krakow, Governor General Frank himself devised a special racial cleansing policy for the city's more than sixty thousand Jews. Up to August 15, 1940, Frank gave them the opportunity to move to any ghetto of their choice within the General Government. By the deadline, twenty-three thousand had left, and by mid-September, another nine thousand had been forcibly expelled. By the end of the year, the total number of Jewish evacuees reached forty-three thousand. The remaining Krakow Jews were then evicted from their houses in Kazimierz and elsewhere and driven into a congested ghetto in the Podgorce district.

Frank had accomplished his goal, if not of making Krakow completely *judenrein* then at least making it a place that was no longer "crawling" with Jews, where a "decent person" could step into the street without having to encounter one. The Jews' houses were taken over by German nationals, many of whom were connected to industrial concerns such as I. G. Farben, which was constructing a vast chemical plant at Auschwitz, and were lured by tax incentives and the slave labor provided by the prisoners at Auschwitz. Soon Krakow's German population, minuscule before the war, reached twenty percent.

Even as the removal of Jews was being carried out, Governor General Frank reiterated more comprehensive intentions: "The German Reich has a special mission to fulfill: to finish off the Poles at all cost." What he, like Himmler and Hitler in their identical declarations, meant by this required some explaining. Toward non-Jewish Poles, the policy was not complete annihilation but exploitation. "Constantly," Frank explained with characteristic drollery, "the necessity arises to recall the proverb: 'You must not kill the cow you want to milk.' However, the Reich wants to kill the cow...and milk it."

Through such methods as starvation, imprisonment, random executions, and brutal working conditions, the Germans set about trying to break the Polish spirit and to weed out those too biologically weak for slavery. To adopt Frank's bovine analogy, it was like culling the herd. Weekly rations were set at fifty grams of marmalade, one hundred grams of peas, two hundred fifty grams of artificial honey, one gram of lemon, and sixty-two-and-a-half grams each of butter and margarine. More than a million Poles were routed from their homes and shipped off in unheated boxcars to work as slaves within the Reich; many of them arrived dead. Another two million were forcibly removed from the annexed territories and simply dropped off at random country stations within the General Government, where they had to fend for themselves and depend on the charity of locals. *Volksdeutsche* transported from the Balkans took over vacated homes in Silesia, Pomerania, and the other western provinces.

Within the Reich, displaced Polish workers were required to display a white patch with a violet letter P sewn to their clothing, just as Jews had to wear the Star of David. Polish women faced the additional horror of being rounded up and conscripted into service in brothels for German officers within the General Government or the Reich. The following incident, from an affidavit sworn in 1940 by an eyewitness and smuggled out to the Polish government-in-exile, shows the consequences of resistance to slave status and how the Germans sometimes used Jews to remind other Poles that they were little better than Jews and could easily end up beneath them.

> At Warsaw on February 14, 1940, on the place used for executions in the Sejm Gardens in Wiejska Street, I saw Germans in the uniform of the Gestapo herding about a dozen Jews with spades in their hands. They were made to dig nine holes in the ground, after which they were beaten and driven off. When they had gone, I saw nine condemned persons arrive. One was in the uniform of a Polish customs official, two others were in the uniform of the Polish police without caps or belts, the others were civilians without hats or coats.... Six German policemen placed themselves in front of the first three, placing their revolvers against the condemned men's chests. There was no command to fire. Then I saw the three victims fall. I saw the Jewish gravediggers reappear and fill in the first three tombs. They were driven away again, ill-treated as before. The [remaining] Polish policeman knelt; one of the civilians tried to make the sign of the cross. He received a bullet in his stomach. The first was finished off with a revolver as he knelt; the other was doubled in two holding his stomach. I did not have the courage to watch any longer. It was the most inhuman, the most atrocious spectacle I ever saw. I hurried away.

HAVING RETURNED TO THEIR APARTMENT ON TYNIECKA STREET, THE WOJtylas at first had no idea how or to what extent ordinary life might continue under the occupation. Karol Senior's army pension, like all others, stopped; they had enough money for a few weeks' food at most. Sooner or later, Lolek would have to find work, but it was dangerous to apply for it. An able-bodied youth like him was a prime candidate for forced labor in the Reich, meaning that his father would be left to die. Naively, perhaps, Lolek anticipated continuing his studies at the university, or at least trying to do so, and finding a job as well.

On November 6, 1939, the day on which the new academic year was scheduled to start, Governor General Frank issued an invitation to all the professors at the Jagiellonian to discuss relations between Polish educational authorities and the Reich. The stated purpose of the occasion reveals in retrospect another example of Hans Frank's sense of humor, but at the time few professors saw through to the joke.

One hundred seventy-nine of them showed up for the meeting; none left a free man. They were arrested and detained in Krakow, then at Breslau; from there they were shipped to the Sachsenhausen-Oranienburg concentration camp near Berlin. Fourteen died there as a result of brutal treatment (which included being doused with cold water outdoors in freezing temperatures) during their three months' detention; three others died shortly after their release. It suited the Germans to have some of the professors back in Krakow as visible examples of the consequences of defying the regime; after all, they had done nothing other than be Polish teachers, which was now a targeted offense. Sixty-two of them remained at Sachsenhausen or were sent on to Dachau, which Frank knew well from his tenure as Minister of Justice for Bavaria.

The closing of the Jagiellonian, along with all other Polish institutions of higher learning, was only one aspect of a comprehensive assault on Polish culture. In October 1939, the Germans also shut down all high schools. Primary schools were allowed to remain open, but with a drastically revised curriculum. High school teachers, men and women alike, were routinely imprisoned and were among the first prisoners at Auschwitz when it began functioning as a concentration camp in the summer of 1940.

With his knack for specious legalisms, Frank declared a "general public art patrimony" for the "*Sicherung*" (protection) of Polish artifacts, which in practice meant the seizure of all publicly and privately held works of art, including religious objects, paintings, books, and rare manuscripts. Items of great value—a Leonardo da Vinci, an Andrea del Sarto, and a Rembrandt among them—disappeared into Germany. The impact of their loss, however, was not so much a matter of their material value as of their significance to Polish culture.

Private libraries were confiscated and their owners imprisoned and tortured (to death, in many instances). Theaters, including the Slowacki in Krakow, were closed, along with concert halls. Performances of works by Chopin and other Polish composers were forbidden, with only the coarsest sort of music-hall entertainment tolerated. Soldiers destroyed the Chopin monument in Warsaw and pulled down the statue of Mickiewicz in the Rynek in Krakow. Governor General Frank pillaged treasures from the Wawel Castle and, with Bavarian flair, installed drinking halls in former royal apartments and turned the Loggia of Queen Jadwiga into a capacious lavatory. These were some of the most visible aspects of the culture war, or *Kulturkampf.* The Germans were intent on destroying the part of Poland that they could not subdue by military means alone—the national identity and spirit.

The Poles responded to the military occupation at once by forming what became the largest and most effective resistance force in Europe, the AK (*Armia Krajowa*, or Home Army), which operated in bands throughout the country and had underground headquarters in Warsaw. The Germans could not set up a pro-German Polish state, similar to what they were able to do with Vichy, France, because the governing body would have to consist of Pro-German Poles, and there were virtually none to be found.

Parallel to the AK, the culture war created *Unia*, an underground cultural resistance whose members, like those in the AK, took an oath to risk death to keep the Polish spirit alive. They believed that if Polish culture lived, the people would retain a belief in the motherland, its language, and its traditions—an essential and appropriate task for a nation that had always defined itself in terms of its poetry, drama, music, learning, and religion, the hallmarks of the Polish soul.

Most of the young people associated with the university and the theater, including Karol Wojtyla, took the *Unia* oath immediately after the closing of the Jagiellonian and entered into numerous activities subversive of the *Kulturkampf.* Discovery of Lolek's work would have had the certain consequence of imprisonment. By mid-1940, that meant Auschwitz, from which, as one of his friends later remarked, there was no exit except through the chimney.

Although its infamy worldwide stems primarily from its unequaled role in the extermination of Jews, Auschwitz was originally built to contain the large numbers of resistance fighters uncovered in southwestern Galicia. It soon also became the principal concentration camp for members of the Polish intelligentsia as part of the German campaign to eliminate Poland's leadership class, including army officers, teachers, intellectuals, and priests.

The first transport, carrying non-Jewish Polish prisoners—seven hundred twenty-eight inmates who had been held at Tarnow—arrived at Auschwitz on June 14, 1940. Three hundred Jews from Oswiecim had been used to level the terrain and lay foundations for the initial eleven blocks. By the time Heinrich Himmler made his first visit in March 1941, Auschwitz held ten thousand nine hundred prisoners, a few of them German criminals but nearly all the rest Polish Catholics who by virtue of their professions and known sympathies fit the targeted profile of cultural leaders. Simply being a high school teacher was enough reason for a man or woman to merit arrest and incarceration without trial.

Although the gas chambers and crematoria were not operating until 1942, they were originally intended as a practical solution to the unmanageable levels of sickness and death among prisoners held in intolerably harsh conditions—a technological answer to the question of how to get rid of the sick and dispose of the bodies. From the beginning, the life expectancy for women prisoners, who from 1940 through early 1942 were mostly teachers in their twenties and thirties, was from two to three months. Men, especially because many were fed slightly better so that they could be used as slave labor in adjacent mines and factories, lasted somewhat longer. The most conservative, current estimates of non-Jewish Poles sent to the camp between 1940 and its liberation by Soviet troops on January 18, 1945, place the numbers at between one hundred forty thousand and one hundred fifty thousand.

Many of these were priests, who shared the fate of other patriots. From the beginning of the occupation, priests suffered outrages at the hands of German soldiers who, in numerous documented instances, tortured, beat, and shot them in front of their parishioners in spectacles of contempt. In the ghettos, rabbis were prodded with rifle butts, made to dance in the streets in their ritual robes, and publicly murdered. In Poznan in 1940, eight Catholic priests and eight Jews were made to clean latrines with their hands; Jesuits were lined up in rows and forced to beat each other. More than three thousand priests were sent to Dachau, but once Auschwitz become operational, it was a favored destination for them. Many who had been interned elsewhere were transferred to Auschwitz along with the newly arrested.

As Hitler instructed Hans Frank on October 2, 1940, Polish priests "will preach what we want them to preach. If any priest acts differently, we shall make short work of him. The task of the priest is to keep the Poles quiet, stupid, and dull-witted.... There should be one master only for the Poles, the German. Therefore all representatives of the Polish intelligentsia are to be exterminated. This sounds cruel, but such is the law of life."

Lolek was acutely aware that the Germans included priests among the condemned intelligentsia. At the beginning of the occupation, seven Salesian fathers from Lolek's local parish in Debniki were deported to Dachau, leaving only an old parish priest and the provincial inspector. Obviously, the imprisoned seven had not conformed to the Fuehrer's job description for them. Their sacrifice, which in effect decapitated the parish, and Lolek's lifelong spiritual commitment led him to entertain the possibility of a priestly vocation for himself. But that decision came later; for now, he remained immersed in the clandestine cultural struggle.

HIS UNDERGROUND ACTIVITIES INCLUDED ORGANIZING AN ALTERNATIVE secret university. Students and some professors who had been released from the camps began meeting in small groups to continue their studies, making use of one another's houses and those of sympathizers as classrooms. They took great precautions. To avoid having to communicate between meetings, they decided on the date, time, and site of the next rendezvous at the end of each session and arrived at staggered intervals so that they would not attract the attention of patrolling soldiers and police. The most dangerous time for them was during curfew hours, which extended from eight P.M. till five A.M., when they had to rely on their intimate knowledge of Krakow's back streets to avoid arrest or being shot on sight.

Because they never doubted that their university would reopen one day in a free Poland, they kept careful records of their readings and discussions, gave each other examinations and grades, and hid the documentation away for future credit toward degrees. Lolek's group of about a dozen also held poetry readings and recitations and gave informal presentations of their own works, all expressive of patriotic themes and commonly interwoven with religious ones in traditional Polish fashion.

There was tremendous excitement in this defiance of the enemy, the thrill not merely of surviving but of risking one's life in a network of cultural solidarity. In this heady atmosphere—so much more inspiring than any merely personal artistic effort could ever be—Lolek began an outpouring of literary composition, using his pen as a weapon of resistance. For solace and inspiration, he turned to the Hebrew Bible, struck by analogies between the plight of the Poles and the captivities and other tribulations of the ancient Children of Israel. By Christmas 1940, Lolek had completed *David*, a verse drama inspired by the figure of the boy who slew Goliath, became king and defeated the Philistines, and composed the Psalms to the accompaniment of his lyre. "How long shall I take counsel in my soul, having sorrow in my heart daily? How long shall mine enemy be exalted over me?" David lamented in Psalm 13: 1–2.

David expressed exactly the questions that were burdening Lolek: the question of the hidden God whose face is obscured by suffering; the question of how long the poet, unable to understand God's purpose in permitting horrors, must search within himself for answers; and the question of how long the present Philistine tyranny would last. It was characteristic of Lolek's verse not to present answers based on dogma and unquestioning faith but to pour forth agonies of doubt while never losing hope. This quality would remain consistent in the pope's writings and would make his words always affectingly human.

Lolek followed *David* rapidly with two other verse dramas whose titles indicate their similar themes: *Job* and *Jeremiah*. The latter explicitly connects the thundering prophet with two eighteenth- and nineteenth-century Polish priests, one an actual person and the other a character from Mickiewicz, who combined both patriotic and religious exhortations. In keeping with biblical sources, *Job* suggests that Poland's suffering is not merely an affliction but a test from God, and *Jeremiah* implies that the nation's plight must in some way be understood as punishment for past transgressions against the Lord, defined as injustices tolerated within Polish society.

This last theme would appear to have arisen inevitably, not only from Jeremiah's original prophecies but also because Lolek was writing about Poland in terms of Jewish history. And while he composed these plays, the forced exodus of Jews from Krakow was taking place, as Governor General Frank made certain everyone was aware. Like the biblical Jeremiah, however, the play anticipates a day of regeneration when, like Israel, Poland will see deliverance and restoration.

"Our liberation must be the gateway of Christ," Lolek wrote to his old drama teacher and friend Miecyzslaw Kotlarczyk, who remained in Wadowice. "I think of an Athenian Poland, but of an Athens immensely perfected by the greatness of Christianity. Bards and prophets of the Babylonian slavery thought of such an Athens...." He told Kotlarczyk that the play embodying this vision "was born like lightning, like a revelation during a reading of Jeremiah's prophecy."

HALINA KROLIKIEWICZ ACTED AS THE COURIER FOR THIS HIGHLY INCRIMINATING correspondence. She sometimes received permission from authorities to visit her parents in Wadowice; more often, she sneaked across the Skawa carrying letters. She brought back news from their hometown, which had its own contingent of German soldiers and where conditions were much the same as in Krakow, except that food was slightly more plentiful because of the surrounding farms. She was usually able to gather a few eggs to share with friends in Krakow.

These were small peasant farms. Large-scale farmers had been removed from their estates. Stanislaw Banas and his family were living with relatives somewhere around Kalwaria, Halina learned, needless to say without their automobile and carriages. Lolek was always anxious for news about his old neighbors, teachers, and classmates. At least two classmates, he knew, were already dead: Jozef Wasik was publicly executed in Krakow in 1939 for his underground activities, and Tadeusz Galuszka had been killed during the September Campaign. Many had been in the army; some had disappeared. Romanski, Jura, Kogler, and Zdzislaw Bernas, who had joined the Twelfth Infantry together, were listed as missing in action. Zbigniew Silkowski, wounded at Tomaszow, had escaped from a POW camp and was back in Wadowice and active in the AK.

Two who had been students at the Jagiellonian, Jan Kus in medicine and Wiktor Kesek in law, were also with the resistance. Late in 1940, Halina learned from Silkowski that Kesek, while hiding out in a forest, had been betrayed and was a prisoner at Auschwitz. Teofil Bojes, caught in Russian-held territory with the Twelfth, had escaped from Lvov and made his way home on foot. According to Father Zacher, Bojes had found work as a coal miner in Sosnowiec but was soon deported as a slave laborer to the Reich, probably to the coal mines of Westphalia, although no one knew for sure.

And Jurek Kluger had last been seen leaving for the front with his father in an army car. Neither Jurek nor Dr. Kluger had been heard from since. Within Wadowice, Halina reported, the Jews, with their businesses shut down, kept to their houses. As of early 1941, there had been no expulsions, but it seemed only a matter of time until they were evicted to ghettos. The Germans had ordered Jurek's mother and sister to work in a paper mill; the Kluger women remained with the grandmother in the house on Zatorska Street. In the Wojtylas' old building, the Balamuths and Ginka Beer's parents, who had never managed to join their daughter in Palestine, also stayed on. Halina visited them and Mrs. Szczepanska, Lolek's other neighbor there. They told her what many others were saying: all the Jews who could do so should go into hiding. Some had, but not many.

Mrs. Szczepanska had urged Jurek's mother to flee with her daughter. Forged papers could be arranged through the AK. With her blond looks and perfect Polish, Tesia especially could easily pass for a Catholic girl. She had grown up with Catholics. Several people had offered to help Tesia and her mother, but Mrs. Kluger and her daughter were unwilling to leave the grandmother, who was too blind and feeble to go anywhere, and who at any rate would never be mistaken for a Christian. Their loyalty to the old woman was a moving thing, but eventually this would be a matter that only God could judge.

The Jews of Wadowice had lost their rabbi, who was trapped in the Krakow ghetto after trying to visit family in the city. And they had lost their synagogue, which the Germans blew up soon after the occupation. The blast shattered windows up and down Pierackiego Street and even over at the girls' high school. There was nothing left of it now but a roofless shell.

STILL IN TARNOPOL AT THE BEGINNING OF OCTOBER 1939, JUREK, HIS FATHER, and the Zilzes debated what to do. There was some sentiment to try and flee to Romania, but the Klugers did not want to put still more distance between themselves and the women stuck in Wadowice. When some train service resumed under the Russians, they all decided to travel as far toward home as they could. The end of the line turned out to be Lvov, some thirty miles short of the border that now separated Russian from German territory. At least Lvov was a big city and, unlike Tarnopol, predominantly Polish. Surely there they could find something to do. They were nearly out of money.

At the time, Lvov had a population of over three hundred thousand and was perhaps thirty-five percent Jewish, or possibly more than that considering the refugees who had poured in to escape the Germans. People camped in parks and slept in the streets, but Engineer Zilz found lodgings with a Jewish family, and through army contacts, Dr. Kluger located shelter for himself and Jurek with a Catholic officer and his family. Like Dr. Kluger, who had disposed of his uniform, military identification, and revolver, this man was not advertising his officer status to the Russians. The men agreed that it would be imprudent to cooperate more than necessary with a country that had never endorsed the Geneva Convention's rules on the treatment of prisoners of war. In Tarnopol, Dr. Kluger had seen the Russians dividing commissioned from noncommissioned Polish officers and directing them to trains heading in uncertain directions. That was when he had gotten rid of his uniform, declining the free ride. Technically, one supposed, Poland was not at war with Russia, but what did one term those who moved tanks and troops into one's country without being asked?

Although the railroad was now in Russian control, Engineer Zilz secured a position and was able to earn enough to feed his family. As November came and the weather turned bitter, neither Jurek nor his father had luck finding work; to their frustration and embarrassment, they relied on their host family, eating as little as possible and keeping an account of what they did eat. Jurek sometimes ran into friends from home, but they were in no position to help. Kurt Rosenberg, who was a student at the Lvov Polytechnic, had been joined by his refugee parents, younger brother, and sister; they were barely surviving themselves. Jurek's Jewish classmates, Selinger and Zweig, had also fled on their own to Lvov and were staying wherever they could from day to day.

One day, as Jurek was going from shop to shop offering to sweep up or run errands, he spotted another familiar figure across the street. It was his cousin Adas Josefert from Krakow—walking with a woman who was wearing a Russian uniform! Yes, that was Adas, all right.

Jurek raced across the street. A dark and dashing fellow of about thirty, Adas was wearing his coat in that insouciant way of his, thrown about his shoulders in the manner of a boulevardier. He greeted Jurek with an embrace and kisses and introduced him to the blond Russian lady, who was an officer. Looking uneasy, she made some excuse and departed, but not without a fond glance back at Adas.

He had only been in the city a few days, Adas said, and this charming creature—she was really quite cultivated, a truly sympathetic soul, and very efficient—from Petrograd, or rather Leningrad, had managed to secure Adas a room in the best hotel. It turned out that she was high up in the administration of Lvov these days—a stroke of good fortune in desperate times.

Ah, Adas! He was already Jurek's idol in certain respects. His mother was a Huppert, one of Jurek's mother's sisters; his father was an international businessman and president of the Krakow Chamber of Commerce—or had been. His parents remained in Krakow, Adas said, but he was determined to smuggle them out. Life under German occupation was worse than Jurek could imagine. Unfortunately, Adas had no news from Wadowice. He had gone underground in the first days of the invasion and had been lucky to make it into the Russian zone.

If anything was possible, Jurek believed, Adas would accomplish it. A boxing champion and doctor of economics from the Jagiellonian, he managed much of the family's international trading but had never let anything interfere with his enjoyment of life. When he came to Wadowice to visit Grandmother Huppert, he used to tear around the Rynek on his 800cc BMW motorcycle and give Jurek rides. A year or so earlier—the memory flashed back to him now—when he had done so well on his Latin *Matura*, Jurek's parents had told him that he deserved a present. He wanted nothing, Jurek said, except to visit Adas Josefert in Italy, where his cousin was operating as vice-president of a Polish coal consortium. He could study finance with Adas, Jurek told his parents, although that was not precisely what he had in mind. That July of 1938 with Adas...speeding into Portofino in the Lancia Astura...the Italian girls—Jurek had never stopped thinking about it. So much had happened since!

Now Adas took him into a café for coffee. He would be leaving Lvov soon, Adas said, to fight the Germans with the AK. Some factions in the Home Army were against allowing Jews to join the secret organization. It had to be admitted that too many Jews in the east were known to be either cooperating with the Communists or Communists themselves, but he had contacts who knew him and were glad to have a fighter such as he. Eventually, everyone would understand that this was every Pole's fight to the death.

Jurek wanted to go with him. No, he had better stay with his father for now, Adas said. Later, perhaps, the AK would contact him and send for him. Where was he staying?

Jurek explained the situation and how desperate he and his friends were for work. He would take care of that, Adas said. His Russian friend would be glad to help. She had nothing against Jews, he laughed, that he had noticed.

By the next day, Jurek, Selinger, and Zweig were employed by the Russians. As all buildings had been nationalized, every block in Lvov, including apartments, required a sign displaying its name, number, and the name of its local commissar. Jurek received the exclusive license to paint the signs and install them with his crew of classmates. Cousin Adas, Jurek told his father, knew just how to deal with Communists.

As the weeks in Lvov dragged on past the New Year, Dr. Kluger never did find work. He spent his days sitting in a café drinking coffee, worrying about the women in Wadowice and studying the Russian language, which by spring he had mastered. If they were going to have to live under the Russians, he said, it would be better to be able to communicate with them. He was already fluent in German, but he hoped that he would never have to use it. One day soon, he predicted, these Russians and Germans would be at each other's throats. You could hear it in what the Russians said.

IN APRIL 1940, A DIFFERENT RUSSIAN SCHEME BEGAN TO SHOW ITSELF. ON the tenth of that month, the entire Rosenberg family was arrested, put on a train, and transported somewhere to the east. Jurek did not learn what had happened until, about two weeks later, Kurt Rosenberg reappeared in the city, on the run and looking as if he had narrowly escaped death. The Russians had discovered that his father was an army officer, Rosenberg said, and had deported him with other Polish officers and their families to the Soviet Union. At a certain point, the officers were separated from their wives and children, if they had any, and marched onto another train. It was then that he decided to run. He urged his mother, sister, and brother to come with him, but they were too frightened. He was so certain that only disaster could lie to the east that he jumped off before the train ever left the Lvov station. He did not dare go near the Polytechnic for fear of being arrested again. He did not know what he was going to do. He was thinking of Romania.

Dr. Kluger was not especially worried about being found out. How would the Russians know his officer status? It must have been Kurt Rosenberg's registration at the Polytechnic that had somehow tipped them off about his father.

Dr. Kluger's optimism or, if not that, his equilibrium, was buoyed because at last one of the countless letters and postcards that he and Jurek had been sending to Wadowice had gotten through, and Rozalia and Tesia had written back. They were all right, they said, on a card clearly composed with an eye to the censorship; only cards got through, with sealed letters being strictly verboten. They did manage to send a package of warm clothing, however, with a few *zlotys* concealed inside. Things were not so bad, they said. They were working under the Germans, but they did not say at what or where. Grandmother Huppert was weak but enduring.

It was infuriating and unjust, Dr. Kluger said, that his dear wife and daughter were being forced to work under Nazis, and certainly for unjust wages. "*Inter arma leges silent*," he lamented—"In war the laws remain inactive." But this was better news than he had anticipated and the best that one could hope for under these conditions.

He and Jurek spent some of the money on tickets to a performance of *Madama Butterfly* at Lvov's gloriously ornate Ivan Franko Opera House—a monument to Polish cultural influence. It was one of the few artistic programs still available to the public. Unfortunately, they were not properly dressed, but very few were. The music made them both cry profusely.

THE KNOCK ON THE DOOR CAME AT FOUR O'CLOCK ONE MORNING IN THAT early May of 1940. Jurek and his father, asleep in the sitting room of the apartment where they were still guests, awakened and heard a man's voice shouting in a Russian accent, "Wilhelm Kluger, Jerzy

Kluger, Zygmunt Selinger, Leopold Zweig!"

Jurek opened the door to a quartet of Russian soldiers.

"Your name?" one of them asked.

Jurek identified himself and his father and unearthed their papers. He was employed by the Soviet government, Jurek said, displaying his sign-painting license and dropping the name of Cousin Adas's ladyfriend.

"You have no residence here," the soldier said.

Dr. Kluger admitted that they were staying at the apartment through the kindness of the family that lived there. It was a matter of circumstances. He spoke in his newly acquired Russian, which seemed to please the soldiers, and added that he and his son were in Lvov owing to the barbaric invasion of Poland by right-wing reactionary-fascist-imperialist German beasts, who were exploiting the people for the sake of capitalist warmongers.

"Put your things together," the Russian said. "You're going somewhere else."

They were polite enough, these Russians, Jurek thought, with their rifles and backpacks, although the fellow standing next to him smelled like a badger. Their spokesman explained only that it had been decided that all Poles without permanent residence in Lvov would be relocated. To where, he said, he did not know. But one could be sure that this was a very well conceived plan that would be executed in the interest of the common good.

After saying goodbye to their hosts during these past eight months of exile, Jurek and his father carried their beautiful suitcases downstairs and assembled in the dark street, where Selinger and Zweig, who had only tied-up bundles of clothes under their arms, stood crowded together with several others who had been routed from their beds. From what Jurek could tell, these dozen or so other Poles were about equally divided between Jews and Christians. He couldn't see much, but he could feel the apprehension. There were women and two children among the group.

Two Russian army trucks stood with engines running.

"Wilhelm Kluger and Jerzy Kluger, you are father and son?" a higher-ranking Russian officer addressed them. "Family, into that truck," he pointed, and directed Selinger, Zweig, and some of the others, all men, to the second truck. Jurek held up his hand in farewell to his classmates.

The truck took them to the railway station, where they boarded a train. Later, when the strong summer sun finally broke over the trees that were visible through the train window, Jurek saw that they were heading east. He asked his father where he thought they were going, but Dr. Kluger only reached into a suitcase and handed him a Russian grammar. "You'd better start learning this," Dr. Kluger said.

Whatever their destination, this train was no express. Two weeks later, they were still on it.

Chapter 17

"THE STORY OF MY PRIESTLY VOCATION? IT IS KNOWN ABOVE ALL TO GOD," Pope John Paul II begins a lyrical memoir, *Gift and Mystery*, published in 1996. "At its deepest level, every vocation to the priesthood is *a great mystery*; it is a gift which infinitely transcends the individual.... Faced with the greatness of the gift, we sense our own inadequacy." Despite this sense of mystery, however, the pope manages in a few succinct paragraphs to isolate certain events, people, and circumstances that affected his decision to begin studies toward his ordination. This decision was not made definite until late 1942, under the most trying and dangerous of conditions.

Although he does not say it directly, the determining and all-encompassing factor among many was the war and the particularly ghastly form that it took in Poland under the German occupation. Faced with the loss of companions and loved ones and, soon enough, the unimaginable horrors of mass exterminations, he confronted what he would later come to term the affliction of the twentieth century—"the culture of death." In the midst of unspeakable *Vernichtung* (annihilation), to use Hitler's word, he asked himself, "What is to be done?" How best to affirm life, against the apparent triumph of death? Becoming a priest seemed at least the beginning of an answer or, as he would say it, God's answer.

Other than the paramount and cumulative effects of the war itself, there were seven subsidiary factors that may be considered as strong influences on his choice of vocation. Alone, none of these would have been sufficient to convince him to redirect his focus from literature and drama to the priesthood. A point must be emphasized, however, and it is something that has often been misunderstood about Wojtyla: he never wholly abandoned those first two loves but rather continued them as serious avocations within a larger purpose. Whatever else it meant giving up, for him the priesthood never required renunciation of poetry, drama, or, indeed, performance.

The first wartime influence on his vocation included his experiences as a common laborer. He worked among people whom, as a university-centered intellectual, he would otherwise never have intimately encountered. After holding various odd jobs, including running errands for a restaurant, to support himself and his father, Lolek was vulnerable to the fate of Teofil Bojes and tens of thousands of other Polish men and women who were deported to the Reich as slave laborers. The only safeguard was to obtain an identity card, or *Ausweiss*, which stated that the holder was employed in an industry essential to the German war effort.

As with Jurek's good fortune under the Russians, Lolek was able to enlist the help of a sympathetic official who was in a position to be of assistance. Because of the expertise of the Polish manager of the Solway bicarbonate plant, the Germans left him in place, although the name of the plant was changed to the East German Chemical Works. Located west of Debniki in the Borek Falecki industrial district, the plant produced limestone-derived products, including caustic soda, an ingredient in explosives. It also produced numerous other chemicals that were of no specific military use. The patriotic manager, who was a friend of Lolek's French tutor, was eager to help protect the cultural underground and hired Lolek and several of his friends, while another Solway official quietly bribed members of the Gestapo to dull their curiosity.

One of Lolek's companions was Juliusz Kydrynski, whom Lolek described to Mieczyslaw Kotlarczyk, his Wadowice drama teacher, as "a wild man of the theater" and who had introduced Lolek to Krakow's artistic circles. Another was the writer-actor Tadeusz Kwiatkowski, who later married Halina Krolikiewicz. Much in the manner of Jews saved from Auschwitz by Oskar Schindler, these young Poles were now protected from slavery or worse by their *Ausweiss* cards.

Beginning in September 1940, Lolek worked in the limestone quarry; a year later he transferred to the less arduous water-purification facility. The experience, which lasted nearly four years, meant far more to him than just escaping deportation, as he reflects in *Gift and Mystery*.

> For me, at that point in my life, the plant was a true seminary, albeit a secret one.... At the time I did not realize how important the experience would be for me. Only later...did I realize how important contact with the world of work had become for the Church and the priesthood in the West. This contact was already a part of my life experience.... Having worked with my hands, I knew quite well the meaning of physical labor. Every day I had been with people who did heavy work. I came to know their living situations, their families, their interests, their human worth, and their dignity. They knew that I was a student and they knew that, when circumstances permitted, I would return to my studies. I never encountered hostility on this account. It did not bother them that I brought books to work. They would say: "We'll keep watch; you go ahead and read." This happened especially during the night shifts. They would often say: "You go and take a break, we'll keep an eye open."
>
> I made friends with the workers. Sometimes they invited me to their homes. Later, as a priest and bishop, I baptized their children and grandchildren, blessed their marriages, and officiated at many of their funerals. I was able to observe their deep but quiet religiosity and their great wisdom about life....

The pope's words are eloquent enough, but it is important to clarify that it was by becoming a laborer that young Wojtyla gradually came to understand how as a priest he might bridge the world of complex thought with the wisdom and example of ordinary people. He learned how such people could teach him the virtues of simple faith and release him from the isolation from common life that is characteristic of intellectuals. It was among workers that he discovered how physical labor itself may embody and reveal truths as valid and profound as any expressed through higher art and thought.

These revelations soon found eloquent expression in his poetry, which had already assumed a simpler, more colloquial style and now, under the influence of his new companions, took on an almost conversational aspect. Clarity and the use of the personal voice became hallmarks of his poetic approach, and concrete simplicity of expression enabled him to deal with a subject that was unusual although not unprecedented in poetry in any language: the physical realities of labor and its inherent nobility.

In a four-part poem entitled *Material*, for instance, he discerns how a man becomes one with the very substance of his work. He neither preaches nor explains this but rather, in the sinews of his lines, shows the actual material and action of the work: how the specific qualities of limestone, which can be cut in any direction without splitting, embody the integrity of the laborer. He implies that like the stone that retains its wholeness even when blasted and split, these men cannot be altered even by totalitarian enemies. In bondage, they endure.

Bound are the blocks of stone, the low-voltage wire
cuts deep in their flesh, an invisible whip—
stones know this violence.
When an elusive blast rips their compactness
and tears them from their eternal simplicity,
the stones know this violence.
Yet can the current unbind their full strength?
It is he who carries that strength in his hands:
the worker.

In the original Polish, the sounds and rhythms of these lines powerfully mimic the act of quarrying. Later, Wojtyla was present when a dynamite charge sent rocks at a worker and killed him.

And a stone smashed his temples
and cut through his heart's chamber.
They took his body, and walked in a silent line.
Toil still lingered about him, a sense of wrong.

Wojtyla called this section "In Memory of a Fellow Worker," expressing his personal solidarity with the fallen one and the injustice of his life and death. At the same time, he did not forget that when the occupation was over, he could resume a privileged existence and would not have to spend the rest of his life in backbreaking or heartbreaking toil. As he recalls in *Gift and Mystery*:

> The managers of the quarry, who were Poles, tried to spare us students from the heaviest work. In my case, they made me assistant to the rock-blaster: his name was Franciszek Labus. I remember him because he would occasionally say things like: "Karol, you should be a priest. You have a good voice and will sing well; then you'll be all set...."
>
> He said this in all simplicity, expressing a view then widely held in society about how priests lived. These words of the old workman have stuck in my memory.

As it happened, it was the heroism of many priests in the cause of Poland that became a second great influence on Lolek's priestly vocation. Writing of these priests—as well as of "the great sacrifice of countless men and women of my generation"—the pope explains that "by their sacrifice they showed me the most profound and essential truth about the priesthood of Christ," that under the greatest of human challenges, it should be not a profession or a career but a humble reflection of the Savior's own sacrifice. There were thousands of such examples, some personally known to him, but one stands out.

On February 17, 1941, all Poland was dismayed, although not surprised, by the arrest of Father Maximillian Maria Kolbe, a Franciscan who through his writings was one of the most known and admired clerics in the country. In the final edition of his magazine *Knight of the Immaculate*, he urged Poles to retain inner virtue and a sense of truth despite "armies of occupation and the hecatombs of extermination camps," with a frankness that the Gestapo did not ignore. On May 26, Father Kolbe was interned at Auschwitz, tattooed with the number 16670, and put to work building a crematorium.

The circumstances of Father Kolbe's death were leaked out in detail through the AK, which had contacts within Auschwitz through workers delivering supplies to the camp, prisoners who worked outside the camp itself, bribes to S.S. personnel, and other means. The story quickly became the stuff of legend, although an entirely factual one.

One day in July, it was thought that a prisoner had escaped. He was later found drowned in a camp latrine, but in the meantime authorities began the usual reprisal, which was to kill ten or fifteen prisoners for every escapee. In this instance, one of the ten selected at random for execution, Franciszek Gajowniczek, cried out, "My wife, my children, I shall never see them again!"

Father Kolbe, identifying himself as a Catholic priest, stepped forward and volunteered to take Gajowniczek's place, a bargain that was accepted by the condemned man as well as the guards. With the other nine, Father Kolbe was marched down into the windowless basement cells of Block 11, known as the Execution Block, which featured underground torture chambers and some cells so small that a single prisoner could not stand up or extend his arms in them. The outer yard had a steel-faced wall to deflect the errant bullets of firing squads and was paved with loose gravel to catch the blood. No prisoner ever emerged alive from Block 11.

Stripped naked so that their filthy uniforms could be supplied to fresh arrivals, the men were thrown together in a subterranean cell just large enough to contain them. They were given no food or water and were kicked or shot to death if they complained. When the S.S. men were out of earshot, Father Kolbe led the condemned in saying the rosary and singing hymns to "The Holy Mother of the Unhappy," as Bruno Burgowiec, a prisoner who was a janitor and interpreter in the bunker, reported. "I had the impression of being in a church," was the way he phrased it. (In the summer of 1941, nearly all

Auschwitz prisoners were Catholic Poles; they were soon joined by Soviet POWs.)

After two weeks, only Father Kolbe and three others remained alive. As Burgowiec witnessed (and S.S. guards confirmed after the war), the authorities concluded that the dying was taking too long.

> [T]he cell was needed for new victims. So one day, they brought in the head of the sick-quarters, a German, a common criminal called Bock, who gave each in his turn an injection of carbolic acid in the vein of his left hand. Father Kolbe with a prayer on his lips gave his arm to the executioner.

Father Kolbe was murdered on August 14, 1941; the fortunate Gajowniczek survived to rejoin his wife and children. It was at this time (July or August, according to postwar testimony at Nuremberg) that Auschwitz Commandant Rudolph Hoess was summoned to Berlin and informed personally by Heinrich Himmler that Auschwitz would now assume a broader function.

> The Fuehrer [Hoess recalled Himmler's instructing him] has ordered the final solution of the Jewish question and we, the S.S., were assigned this mission. The existing liquidation sites in the East cannot cope with the large operations expected in the future. I have therefore chosen Auschwitz for this purpose, first because of its convenient location in terms of transportation, and, second, because the site can be easily isolated and concealed.

While for the time being, these plans remained known to only a few, word of Father's Kolbe's martyrdom quickly reached underground circles in nearby Krakow. Within a few weeks, it was common knowledge throughout Poland. Had another priest acted with comparable selflessness and valor, as no doubt others had, the heroism might not have attracted such interest. But Father Kolbe had been such a prominent figure that for Catholic Poland, his Christlike sacrifice at once became the epitome of the union between patriotism and religion. The subsequent sacrifice of more than a million Jews at Auschwitz-Birkenau (according to the most conservative current estimates) was far beyond human understanding, but the single instance of Father Kolbe's passion invited inspiration and challenged believers to imitation.

FOR LOLEK, FATHER KOLBE'S FATE WAS DOUBLY AFFECTING BECAUSE IT COINcided with the death of his father. On February 18, the day after Father Kolbe's arrest, Lolek stopped by the house of his friend and quarry-mate Kydrynski. Kydrynski's mother, whom Lolek had taken to calling Mama or Grandmama, fixed a meal and set aside something for the old lieutenant. Karol Senior, who was then sixty-two, had been in failing health since Christmas and was bedridden. Kydrynski's sister, Maria, decided to keep Lolek company on his way home and help him heat the food. She was at the stove in the Wojtylas' apartment when Lolek came in from the bedroom to say that his father had died—of a heart attack, it was later determined.

Kydrynski came over to comfort Lolek, pray with him, and keep watch over the body through the night. Three days later, Father Figlewicz presided as Karol Senior was laid to rest in Krakow's military cemetery. Lolek himself, although he had known for weeks that his father probably was near death, was extremely distraught. He remonstrated with himself for not having been present when his father died and regretted that he had not received the last rites. Lolek had not been in attendance at the moment of his mother's death, either, and he felt guilty about this—or perhaps stricken, as if his parents had left him without a final farewell.

The acuteness of his sense of loss, however, is understandable and moving for the simple reason that he and his father were so close. His situation was made all the more difficult by his father's kindly, warm, and loving nature. He was a man who wanted nothing other than to be a father to his son and to share life with him—a strong man who was also maternal in his selflessness. One could easily deduce as much, and the pope tells us about his father, "We never spoke about a vocation to the priesthood, but *his example was in a way my first seminary*, a kind of domestic seminary."

Many of Lolek's friends thought that his loneliness following his father's death influenced his decision to enter the priesthood, as if the Church offered the family he no longer had. Perhaps there is truth in this, but his own analysis—that his father's living example was a model—counts as much or more. He did find the Tyniecka Street apartment unbearable in his father's absence, though, and he moved in with the Kydrynskis for the next six months.

A fourth and doubtless the most direct influence on his decision appeared in the person of an eccentric tailor named Jan Tyranowski, who was about forty when Lolek met him toward the beginning of the occupation. Had Lolek been a novelist, he would surely have based a character on this remarkable figure, whose quiet but messianic zeal might have sprung from the pages of Dostoyevsky. A kind of Holy Fool, Tyranowski was a layman who, after the arrest of the Debniki Salesian priests, assumed leadership of a parish group called the Living Rosary. It was made up of young men and boys divided into five "decades" to pray together, read theology, and discuss how to nourish spirituality during arduous times. Tyranowski would stand on the church steps after mass, looking rather like a spy in his trench coat, and intercept a likely candidate for the association. "Good morning, may I talk to you?" he would say. "I have noticed you at mass. Would you care to join our Living Rosary circle?"

One of Lolek's friends, an engineering student named Mieczyslaw Malinski, who forty years later wrote a biography of John Paul II, met Lolek in Tyranowski's book-strewn apartment after having been importuned in this way. At first he thought Tyranowski was rather irritating, pompous, obsessive, and likely a little mad, as the pious tailor urged daily meditation and a rigorous schedule of devotions, with every hour of one's life accounted for in a notebook. He also said that he liked being a tailor because he could pray while cutting and sewing.

Malinski joined the Living Rosary more because he was impressed with Lolek than because of Tyranowski, whom he tolerated more than believed in. But soon he came to agree with Lolek that, although Tyranowski was peculiar, he had a holy quality about him, and his rigorous methods brought participants great peace and personal conviction. Under him, the Living Rosary attracted more members than could be absorbed and became in its own way part of the cultural underground, fostering patriotic as well as religious fervor in meetings. Wojtyla and Malinski found themselves acting as unordained ministers to youths looking for guidance under tyranny.

Perhaps Tyranowski's being a tailor also led Lolek, in his bereavement, to embrace him as a surrogate father. Certainly the man had great insight into what young Wojtyla spiritually sought when he suggested that he read the Spanish mystic Juan de la Cruz (Saint John of the Cross). His poetry and other meditations impressed Lolek so deeply that he learned Spanish to read them in the original. For him, the beauty of Juan de la Cruz lay not so much in his rejection of worldly goods, for Lolek had none anyway, as in his idea that, as T. S. Eliot translated it (in "Little Gidding"):

What we call the beginning is often the end
And to make an end is to make a beginning.

This is the *via negativa*, or the knowledge that in its opposite, truth may be manifest. For Lolek at that crucial moment, it meant that in his father's death, in the death of countrymen, in the dark night of Poland's soul, life and truth and regeneration might be discovered. This was the answer to the questions of the hidden God and the problem of suffering that he had been asking in his poetry and plays. Suddenly, acts of sacrifice such as Father Kolbe's had even clearer and transcendent meaning. In this darkness, the greater implications of the sacrifice of the mass itself became brilliantly illuminated through Juan de la Cruz's meditations. Or (as Seamus Heaney translates one of the saint's poems):

This eternal fountain hides and splashes
within this living bread that is life to us
although it is the night....

I am repining for this living fountain.
Within this bread of life I see it plain
although it is the night.

When Lolek's drama teacher, Kotlarczyk, managed to cross the Skawa with his wife and two children and move to Krakow, the fifth—and least obvious—influence toward the priesthood came into play. The Kotlarczyks accepted Lolek's invitation to live with him back at the two-room apartment on Tyniecka Street. Proximity to Kotlarczyk resulted in their co-founding the underground Rhapsodic Theater, which became one of the most important activities of the cultural resistance. On November 1, 1941, they staged their first performance, with Lolek and Halina Krolikiewicz in the lead roles of Slowacki's *The King-Spirit*, before an audience of about twenty in the house of friends whose daughter accompanied them, playing Chopin on the piano. Lolek and Halina were electrifying in their roles, and thus began a clandestine dramatic tradition whose inspiring, patriotic effect extended far beyond the small number of people who risked arrest to attend.

The term *Rhapsodic* derived from the ancient Greek Rhapsodists, a school of poet-reciters and musicians who performed Homer in ecstatic celebration of the bard's heroic stories. This style of performance placed emphasis on each word and on precise rhythmic rendering of passages rather than on dramatic stage movement. Sets and costumes were minimal or nonexistent, both of necessity and so as not to detract from the language. Thus, out of circumstantial difficulty, brilliant expression of the national spirit emerged.

Halina, whose memory of those performances remains vivid, recalls that Lolek was the most talented and persuasive of all, in any role he played. "He scarcely moved a muscle when reciting," she says, "but with that voice and his feeling for the words and a way he had of tilting his head slightly so that every eye was on him, he had everyone transfixed. I was so moved by him, I had to keep reminding myself that I was in the play, too." But the pope himself has lately revealed that the Rhapsodic, as everyone affectionately called the movement, was also having an unexpected effect on him personally.

Intensified by his study of language and literature, his performances with the Rhapsodic (for which he gives full credit to Kotlarczyk, whose theory of "the drama of the living word" was the rationale for the troupe's acting style) also brought him closer to the priesthood. His acting—really a form of dramatic recitation—was, as he understood it, a natural extension of his fascination with language and his studies in philology, including etymology.

> The word, before it is ever spoken on the stage, is already present in human history as a fundamental dimension of man's spiritual experience. Ultimately, the mystery of language brings us back to *the inscrutable mystery of God himself.* As I came to appreciate the power of the word in my literary and linguistic studies, I inevitably drew closer to the mystery of the Word—that Word of which we speak every day and the Angelus: "And the Word became flesh and dwelt among us...."

Thus the Rhapsodic, the in-dwelling spirit incarnate in the sound and etymology of its name, was for him an inherently spiritual entity. Performance was an ecstatic affirmation of the divine in human utterance, and the reciting actor was a priest not only of dramatic art but of God-in-language. It is entirely characteristic of Wojtyla that for him, revelation never begins in the abstract, in any philosophical or theological statement, but in the physical. In this case, it was in the sense that the human voice makes in uttering words, which sound and resound as they are formed and breathed out.

A half-century after he came to these understandings, Pope John Paul II takes a long time to say mass because he loves the words so much. He cherishes every syllable of whatever language he chooses for this or that occasion. Because of this, one can observe a performance very much like what his Rhapsodic roles must have been. This sense of the miraculous as present in physical phenomena also affected the maturation of his devotion to the Virgin Mary, especially after he had read, at Tyranowski's suggestion, *Treatise of True Devotion to the Blessed Virgin*, by Saint Louis Marie Gringion de Monfort. This work shows how the *human* quality of the Holy Mother, even more than her innocence, leads toward Christ, and how Christ leads us back to her. A mother's sacrifice of her child is the most sorrowful and powerful sacrifice a human being can make, as God knew when asking the same of Abraham. In Mary and through Mary, the Word is made flesh, and the abstract becomes concrete. Through her, the divine life begins, but it begins as a human life in her actual womb; the seed is the Word, the *Annunciation* (from the Latin, "to announce").

All at once, the fragments of young Wojtyla's various interests, passions, and activities coalesced and became a unity—rather like the Trinitarian unity, in which the whole is greater than its parts. With these kinds of insights, how could he fail to choose to serve Mother Church?

Under Tyranowski's guidance, Wojtyla made long intervals of silent prayer and meditation part of his stringent daily routine. But he also came to these realizations in happy association with friends and colleagues, the larger family into which he moved seamlessly as his own family diminished and died out. One kind of ending gave way to many beginnings, strengthening his sense of spiritual bond with a community of people who believed not only in Catholicism but also in the value and hope of life and what he later repeatedly termed *the human person*. This sense of community, which so suited his basically gregarious nature, may be understood cumulatively as the sixth impetus toward the most significant beginning of all, for him as for the world.

ONE DAY IN THE AUTUMN OF 1942, WHEN THE RHAPSODIC WAS GOING strong and many of his friends assumed that Lolek was on his way toward a major career as an actor after the war, he told Malinski that he was going to make a visit to the Wawel. He asked if Malinski would care to accompany him. Without inquiring what this journey was about, Malinski tagged along. Years later, he recalled:

> We entered the precincts of the castle, which, being the residence of the Nazi governor general, was guarded by German police. Father Figlewicz lived in a building opposite the main entrance to the cathedral. We walked up a flight of broad, highly polished wooden stairs and were greeted by a cheerful-looking priest with pleasant manners who gave us tea in a small parlour. He then went off with Karol to another room, and they did not come back for some time. I wondered

> what could be going on—it seemed too long for confession or for an ordinary chat. Eventually, they came back and exchanged a few words of farewell, after which Karol and I set off for home.
>
> "Why were you there so long?" I asked.
>
> Karol did not seem to hear my question, but simply said: "I wanted to tell you that I've decided to become a priest."
>
> I said nothing, but reflected: "Just as I thought."
>
> "That's what I was talking to him about."

Later, Malinski, who was thinking about a vocation himself, learned that Father Figlewicz took Karol to see Archbishop Adam Stefan Sapieha, who had shunned contact with Governor General Frank and, in defiance of German prohibitions, had quietly organized an underground seminary. Lolek became one of the original seven secret seminarians, who met clandestinely one on one with their tutors in secret locations throughout Krakow.

Lolek, who was still working mostly night shifts at the Solway plant, also continued with his roles for the Rhapsodic—after Kotlarczyk and the others got over the shock that their star and co-founder would eventually abandon the stage for the altar.

For the time being, however, his participation in the Rhapsodic, which was for him a spiritual as well as a political activity, complemented his theological studies rather than being in conflict with them. His perspective had enlarged to the point where each daily activity comprised a unity in the service of God, humanity, and the motherland. In that sense, he had already entered into his vocation as a priest, lacking only Holy Orders and the power to administer the sacraments.

In proceeding toward actual ordination, he was aware of many examples of priests who, far from renouncing the world, devoted their lives to improving it. Historically prominent among these was the Polish patriot Adam Chmielowski, who lost a leg fighting in the January Uprising of 1864 and was a talented painter. At a certain point in his life, Chmielowski, known to all Poles as Brother Saint Albert, chose to become a priest and devote his life to helping Krakow's poor. "For me [Brother Albert] was particularly important," the pope explains in his book, "because I found in him a real *spiritual support and example* in leaving behind the world of art, literature and the theater, and *in making the radical choice of vocation to the priesthood.*"

His principal mentor now became Archbishop Sapieha, who was the most revered prelate in Poland. Sapieha's titular superior, Cardinal Hlond, had fled to Rome at the beginning of the occupation. It was difficult for many of the faithful to understand or accept how it was appropriate for the Primate of Poland to reside in the safety of exile while at home, priests risked ultimate sacrifice. Other members of the hierarchy, including the bishops of Lodz and Lublin, were imprisoned.

Why the Germans left Sapieha alone in the Archbishop's Palace in Franciszkanska Street, with a Gestapo office directly across the way, may be explained in two ways. First, Sapieha's aristocratic mien confronted the enemy with the silence not of compliance but of contempt, as if they were creatures too far below decency to merit any sign of recognition. And second, the archbishop was too cunning to permit the Germans to know what he was doing behind the scenes, including encouraging priests to grant Jews baptismal certificates—with or without instruction in the faith—and establishing the secret seminary.

Archbishop Sapieha, or the Prince Metropolitan, as Krakowians liked to refer to him, became the seventh determinant influence on Lolek's vocation. As long as he remained in his palace, the archbishop was the symbol of Poland's spiritual vitality. He was also the man who had singled Lolek out years before in Wadowice as a worthy candidate for theological studies, in effect already anointing him. Perhaps the archbishop was not only the final influence toward his vocation but also the progenitor of it.

LOLEK BECAME A SECRET SEMINARIAN DURING THE OCCUPATION'S DARKEST hours, when the four powerful crematoria at Auschwitz-Birkenau were incinerating as many as two thousand bodies a day, nearly all of them Jews evacuated from Polish ghettos and shipped in from all parts of occupied Europe. The sickly sweet smell of burning human flesh and bones drifted for miles through the countryside surrounding the camp.

The AK, thoroughly informed about what was going on, possessed smuggled diagrams of the crematoria and gas chambers and passed the drawings by courier to the Polish government-in-exile in London. The government-in-exile lobbied with fellow Allied governments to have the crematoria bombed, an action that was entirely feasible and morally acceptable, since the prisoners were doomed anyway. Bombing would have halted the killing, at least for several months. But the British and Americans declined to act, on the grounds that such a mission would detract from the overall war effort. The Polish government went to the extent of sending a Catholic army officer and foreign office official as an emissary to confront Prime Minister Winston Churchill and President Franklin D. Roosevelt with documentation of the horrors.

This man, whose name was Jan Karski, had escaped from Poland after being captured and tortured by the Gestapo and had been an eyewitness to the situation in the Warsaw ghetto and the death camps. In Washington in July 1943, Karski also met with Roosevelt's confidant, Justice Felix Frankfurter, to inform him in detail about what was happening to the Jews of Poland. Frankfurter responded enigmatically that, while he was not accusing Karski of lying, he was "unable" to believe him. The government-in-exile had already been issuing what it called Polish White Books, published openly for general audiences in London and New York, since early 1942, documenting the realities of German atrocities against Christian and Jewish Poles. It was not as if the world knew nothing or did not have every opportunity to know. As early as December 13, 1942, Edward R. Murrow was advising his American radio listeners:

> It seems that the Germans hope to escape retribution by the sheer magnitude of their crimes. They are exterminating the Jews and the potential leaders of the subject people [Poles] with ruthless efficiency. That is why newspapers, individuals, and spokesmen of the Church in this country [Britain] are demanding that the government make a solemn statement that retribution will be dealt out to those responsible for the cold-blooded massacre of Jews in Poland.

Even within Auschwitz, as survivors later testified, prisoners were praying for the bombing that never came.

Some of the killing went on not behind the fences of death camps but openly in cities. On April 19, 1943, the Germans decided to evacuate the sixty thousand Jews still surviving in the Warsaw ghetto to death camps (primarily Treblinka), thus precipitating the Warsaw Ghetto Uprising. Willing to die fighting, the Jews held out with the few weapons they had until May 16; in the process, they lost about half their number, and Treblinka received the rest. In Krakow, the clearing of the ghetto on March 13 became a public spectacle when the Germans mowed down scores of Jews in a massacre in Zgoda Square.

Among the victims in the square was Aszer Anszil Icchak Seltenreich, whom Wojtyla knew as the rabbi from the Wadowice synagogue. In Wadowice, the Jews had by then been confined to a makeshift ghetto just off the Rynek. How long would it be before the Germans came for Jurek Kluger's grandmother, mother, and sister, and the rest? Poland was becoming a vast graveyard. What was a young man in Krakow to do? For Lolek, the Word alone was certain good. He contemplated Juan de la Cruz and placed his faith in:

That eternal fountain, hidden away,
I know its haven and its secrecy
although it is the night.

Chapter 18

JUREK AND HIS FATHER HAD SCARCELY A CLUE AS TO WHAT WAS GOING ON inside German-occupied Poland during those years. On that June morning in 1940, the Russian train shunted them to Tarnopol, where more displaced Poles boarded. Then it jerked and rattled slowly—painfully slowly—past Kiev and northeast through Russia to places with unfamiliar names that Dr. Kluger sounded out, practicing his Russian diction: Suhinici, Aleksin, Arzamas. They had no idea where they were going, except deeper into the Soviet Union and farther away from home.

When asked the destination, the Russian soldiers only shrugged. Jurek said that he was beginning to think that not even the engineer knew where he was going. He wondered what had happened to Selinger and Zweig and the Zilzes, who must be on other trains, headed somewhere. But why? What was the point of this? Dr. Kluger said that under the circumstances, they could only be alert and hope for the best. This much was apparent, however: Russia was clearing out Poles from the eastern third of what had been Poland.

In the name of people's democracy and so-called autonomous republics and all of that, the Russians had seized seventy-seven thousand five hundred square miles, from the border of what had been East Prussia in the north, including Brest-Litovsk, along the River

San and down to the Slovakian and Hungarian borders. The abolition of private property, the nationalization of industry and commerce, and steps toward the collectivization of farms followed at once, along with an election of the usual Communist type.

Eastern Poland consisted of about fifty percent Poles (Catholic and Jewish combined) and roughly thirty percent Ukrainians, with the remaining twenty percent divided among Belorussians and other minorities. Supplied with a single list of candidates, the voters elected an assembly that petitioned to be admitted to the Soviet Union as part of the Ukrainian or Belorussian Socialist Republics, a request that Moscow granted. The Red Army issued leaflets (with phrases such as "For Poles, masters and dogs—a dog's death" and other colorful exhortations) urging Ukrainians and others to attack the remaining Poles. The Russians then proceeded to "cleanse" the territory of Poles, shipping between one-and-a-half and two million Catholics and Jews, most of whom were refugees from the Germans, to various points within the Soviet Union.

The Klugers, the Zilzes, Selinger, and Zweig were among those displaced. They had been preceded by between forty-five thousand and sixty thousand Polish officers. (In April 1943, German troops disinterred four thousand corpses in the Katyn Forest near Smolensk and identified them as Polish officers murdered by the Russians. At the time, this was widely discredited as Nazi propaganda, but in 1989, Soviet authorities finally admitted responsibility for fifteen thousand killings; the number was actually triple that, and it was only a tiny portion of the Polish losses under the Russians. Wilhelm Kluger had been wiser than he knew in concealing his officer status.)

On the train, of course, Jurek and his father had no idea of the magnitude of the expulsions of which they were a tiny part. They knew only that if the train kept going in this generally northeasterly direction, even at this pace, they would eventually cross the Urals and enter Siberia.

A WEEK PASSED, THEN TWO. CONDITIONS COULD HAVE BEEN WORSE, JUREK and his father told themselves. This was a freight train whose extra-long, wooden cars had been fitted with three tiers of wooden bunks that were actually shelves strewn with straw. It was quite a bit below the Haberfelds' private carriage of yore, but...well, at least there were bunks. The soldiers provided soup, tea, and bread. Although passengers were free to wander through the six or seven cars, guards prevented any possibility of jumping off, as Kurt Rosenberg had.

With his father, Jurek passed the time studying Russian. By the second week, he was trying to read his father's copy of *War and Peace* and had reached the point where Natasha falls in love. He also spent hours each day talking to a Jewish girl named Anna, who was with her mother three cars ahead. Her Polish was excellent, but she also spoke Yiddish and teased Jurek for not knowing much of the language beyond the words to "Yiddische Mama." On some nights, when her mother was asleep, Jurek managed to sneak into an empty seat with Anna to hold hands and steal some kisses. Anna was hoping to meet up with her father, a Polish officer. She had not heard from him since May, when his almost daily letters had suddenly stopped coming.

On the seventeenth day, the train stopped in the middle of a dense forest beside a compound of crudely built wooden buildings with steeply sloped tin roofs. Men traveling without women were ordered to gather their belongings, get off, and form ranks beside the tracks. Jurek watched the train pull out again. He saw Anna's face at a window and waved to her, and she waved back. He thought he could see that she was crying.

They had arrived at a work camp somewhere within the Soviet Socialist Republic of Maryjskaja. That was all they were told. Dr. Kluger estimated that it was about four hundred miles due east of Moscow as the crow flies, but it was in the middle of nowhere for all they could tell of their surroundings. Except for the faint sounds of saws against wood and the wind in the pines and birches, it was dead quiet in the forest as they stood for what seemed like an hour beside the tracks.

THERE WERE SIX HUNDRED POLISH MEN INTERNED AT THIS CAMP, ALONG WITH many Tatars who had been there for years after being displaced from the Crimea. The Klugers and the other Poles—no distinction was made between Catholics and Jews—were classified as "socially dangerous," a category that made them subject to slave labor but which, as Jurek and his father eventually learned, placed them above the level of "criminals," meaning anyone who had been accused, tried, and (always) found guilty of anti-Soviet activity. Had they been caught trying to cross the border into Romania or Hungary, for instance, they would have earned a ten-year sentence to an actual *gulag*, or prison camp, in the far north near Arkangel or in Siberia.

Members of a broad category of Poles were sentenced under the Soviet Code for counterrevolutionary activity simply because they had served the capitalist system as factory owners, landowners, and managers. Civil servants, schoolteachers, small landowners, shopkeepers, and the heads of communal and professional organizations also ranked as enemies of the proletariat. And some army officers, perhaps ten thousand of them, ended up in the gold and lead mines of far-eastern Kolyma. At most, five hundred survived. The rest died of malnutrition, the cold, or exhaustion; some expired while pushing carts with the stumps of hands and feet that had been amputated because of frostbite. Compared to them, the Klugers were fortunate: theirs was classified as a "family" camp.

From dawn to dusk, they cut timber with hand saws and dragged it to the railroad or the nearby Volga River for transport downstream. As winter came, their working hours shrank from ten to eleven a day to as few as seven to eight, since they could not saw in the dark, but the hardship of working in the cold made up for the shorter days. The rule was that they did not have to work when the temperature dropped below –30° centigrade. This was determined by spitting: if the spit froze before it hit the ground, the workers merited a holiday. They got a few days off that way, but for most of that winter of 1940–41, the thermometer stayed just above the cutoff point.

Worse than the work itself was the food and the system that was in place to earn it. To gain a full portion of the standard ration—a bowl of *kasza* (soup made from groats), a portion of *kilki* (tiny fish), and dark bread that had to be squeezed to remove the water—a laborer had to fulfill his daily norm of cut wood. If he exceeded the norm, he received a "Stakhanov premium," which was perhaps a little more food, *machorka* (tobacco roots smoked in rolled newspaper), or sugarless tea. Failure to fulfill the norm, however, meant less food. In this way, the weak were soon weeded out as they grew sick and died.

Jurek always managed to fulfill his norm. He made friends with the most efficient of all the workers, a Catholic Pole named Szafran who was a warrant officer with Polish aviation. Szafran showed Jurek how to saw and stack the wood so quickly that on some days they fulfilled their norms early and could go back to the barracks to rest. When the camp received a tractor and a man was needed to drive it, Jurek volunteered at once. He had learned to operate this sort of machine from one of his Haberfeld cousins, who had owned the distributorship for American tractors in southern Poland. Driving it was not only less arduous but automatically earned him the fulfilled norm each day. For this, he experienced some resentment from other prisoners.

"Why does that Jew have a tractor and we don't?" one exploded. "I'm going to finish off this dirty Jew!" He shoved Jurek, who responded with a good right straight to the mouth, knocking out a tooth and ending the dispute. Jurek's torn knuckles, however, developed an infection, which he cured by wrapping his hand in *machorka*.

Bad feelings among the prisoners surfaced mostly when they lined up at six in the morning or at the end of the day for food. The Tatar guards, whose dialect few could understand, kept them in rank depending on how much wood they had cut. The Stakhanovites—so-called after Alexei Stakhanov, a Donetz coal miner who in 1935 exceeded his norm by fourteen times and thereby became officially a Hero of the Soviet Union—were naturally resented, but Jurek was not about to give up his tractor to solicit the approval of the starving.

Lack of vitamins in the diet soon caused scurvy, influenza, and other fatal ailments. Jurek broke out with boils on his neck and by winter's end had lost five teeth from bleeding gums. A little citrus, dispensed by what was euphemistically called the infirmary, helped somewhat, along with a surprise: two packages from his mother and sister containing a few onions hidden among warm clothing.

These packages, which miraculously arrived unopened, came via the Red Cross, which also managed to deliver one or two cards from Jurek and his father to Wadowice. As this was still during the period prior to the establishment of the Wadowice ghetto, Rozalia and Tesia continued to report that they were being treated acceptably by the Germans. Worrying about the women back home was the worst of the hardships in the camp.

About ten of the men in Jurek's barracks died that winter, but he tried not to keep count. He made sure that he retained his right to the tractor by keeping it in good repair and learning how to fashion makeshift parts. His main concern was frostbite. Twice he was careless about drying out the felt boots that the Russians issued, which were fine in the snow but turned soggy from the heat of the tractor's engine and could then freeze up from the inside. He lost feeling in his toes, which turned bluish black, but at least they did not fall off.

In a way, idle hours were worse than ones spent in labor because leisure, such as it was, encouraged thought. People told stories from their lives and talked about their families, the jobs they had done in the past, and how pretty their homes had been. Some sang, and a few musical instruments turned up, so the prisoners formed a sort of orchestra and played Polish melodies to break the heart. There was no violin, so Dr. Kluger learned the balalaika. It was a good instrument, he said, but not like the Guarneri he had left behind.

Except for having boils and some other relatively minor afflictions, Dr. Kluger was not a worry to his son. He took every opportunity to converse with the camp commandant, Colonel Boris Anatolievitch Smyrnov, and soon ingratiated himself. The commandant confided to him that he had once been a fairly high-ranking Communist Party member, but he had fallen into disgrace for reasons he had never been able to fathom. He assumed that someone had stabbed him in the back. Although he avoided being put on trial, he was banished to this lonely outpost, far from his family and with his promising career at an end. While still a fervent Communist, he was bitter and resentful of Party bosses, and he eventually ventured criticisms of Stalin himself to Dr. Kluger, saying things that he would never have dared to utter to another Russian.

In a sense, Dr. Kluger became Smyrnov's confessor, someone who was psychologically so necessary to him that the commandant created a special job for Jurek's father just so he would be able to talk to him. The title was night watchman; what it really meant was watching and listening to Smyrnov—and being released from any hard labor.

Their talks, which took place in the commandant's office and often lasted from late in the evening until dawn, covered all manner of personal, political, philosophical, and literary matters and were lubricated by the vodka that Smyrnov kept in his desk. When Smyrnov fell asleep, Dr. Kluger passed the time by reading one of the many books the commandant supplied him, which he then gave to Jurek. Because of his tractor, Jurek was not as exhausted as the others and was able to read after they were asleep.

Smyrnov was in charge of the entire complex of camps, which held about two thousand prisoners. Through his father, Jurek learned the whereabouts of the women's camp, or *posiolek*, and secretly began visiting Anna there. He would stash his tractor in the woods and jump aboard the little train that ran back and forth, concealing himself down among the logs. At least he thought he was hidden.

"Your son has a weakness," Colonel Smyrnov said to Dr. Kluger one night.

"And what is that, Boris Anatolievitch?" Dr. Kluger asked.

"My dear Wilhelm, your boy, Jurek, likes the women. He's been seeing a girl at the *posiolek*. He thinks no one knows he is a rascal, but I myself have seen him trying to pretend he is a tree!"

"Girls have always been my son's weakness," Dr. Kluger admitted with a sigh.

Instead of excoriating him, however, Smyrnov offered a toast to Jurek. "This fellow is a true romantic!" he said, slamming down his glass and refilling it.

"He loves Pushkin," Dr. Kluger offered. "He has been reading *Eugene Onegin* and the entire volume of Pushkin that you loaned us."

"You see?" Smyrnov said. "He is like I was when I was young. But what am I now, stuck in this horrible place watching over poor wretches day and night? I love this boy of yours, *tovaritch*! May he find all the beautiful women he wants in life!"

THE ROMANCE OF JUREK AND ANNA, HOWEVER, ENDED THAT SUMMER. ON June 22, 1941, exactly a year after the fall of France, Hitler's mechanized and other divisions crossed the River Nieman and quickly penetrated into Russia. Within three weeks, along a thousand-mile front, the Germans made astonishingly rapid advances. They had driven the Russians from eastern Poland, occupied Lvov, and were threatening Kiev. Elsewhere, forty-five divisions had pushed four hundred fifty miles from Bialystok to Smolensk. Moscow, which soon came under Luftwaffe attack, was only two hundred miles ahead.

As the Wehrmacht rolled on, special *Einsatzgruppen*, or killing squads, followed with a specific mission. The task of these mobile assassins, which numbered in all about three thousand men, was to finish off the Jews of eastern Poland and the western USSR. This they accomplished efficiently with mass shootings and burials, their work made easier by the cooperation of local Ukrainians and other citizens and by the dense concentration of these Jews in urban areas. By the next year, when the murder machinery at Auschwitz-Birkenau and other death camps became fully operational, thousands of eastern Polish and western Russian Jews had already been eliminated. Eventually, conservative estimates would place the number of Soviet Jews killed—most of them shot—at more than half a million.

At the labor camp in Maryjskaya, Jurek first heard hints of the German invasion in static-filled broadcasts that he picked up on a crystal set that he had managed to construct. Since these were Soviet broadcasts, however, they were heavily censored and, of course, minimized German advances and Russian defeats. Still, by mid-July he had concluded that Germany must have declared war on Russia, although Commandant Smyrnov denied this when Dr. Kluger asked him about it. By August, however, rumors were flying around the camp, and Jurek noticed that discipline was being allowed to slacken.

Finally, on or about August 15, several high-ranking Russian officers arrived at the camp to announce the news, previously inconceivable, that all the Polish prisoners were being freed. But to what? Where were they to go? An agreement had been signed, an officer said, between the Polish government-in-exile in London and the Soviet Union for the formation of a Polish Army to fight alongside the glorious Red Army to defeat their common enemy, the Germans. Polish General Wladyslaw Anders, who was conferring at this moment with Soviet leaders in Moscow, had agreed to command this force, which would fight under the rules of the Sovereign Polish State and was even now being organized somewhere to the south.

"SO WHO WILL BE GOING TO JOIN THE POLISH ARMY?" THE OFFICER ASKED the assembled prisoners, or former prisoners.

"We will!" Jurek and his father shouted. "Where is it?"

"We have not been given certain information as yet," the officer said. "We suggest you travel south along the Volga. Surely you will find it."

Jurek and his father needed no further encouragement to set off, even without knowing where they were going. It was enough that they would be in search of the Polish Army or that such an entity might actually exist. They were among the first to leave the camp, but they were not by themselves. Dr. Kluger selected a pair of traveling companions, two distinguished gentlemen who went by the names of Tadeusz and Jozef and were good Catholic boys who also happened to be crooks. Dr. Kluger had defended them years earlier against charges of thievery. How they had ended up together in the "family" camp was a good question; they may have pretended to be brothers when they fell into the hands of the Russians in Lvov. One of Dr. Kluger's many qualities, not always characteristic of a lawyer, was his ability to distinguish honest crooks from dishonest ones. There would be nothing better than to have a pair of honest crooks along on an uncertain journey.

Their first step was to reach Joskar-Ola, the capital of Maryjskaja and a railroad center. On the edge of the camp, they hopped a logging train, sprawling atop the logs on the open cars. As they passed the *posiolek*, they waved and shouted at the women who were packing up there; Jurek looked for Anna, in vain.

Arriving at Joskar-Ola was one thing; getting out of it was another. Other camps must have been freed before theirs, because the train station was pandemonium, with thousands of refugees—Poles, Tatars, Russians, Mongols, and what looked like Gypsies and Arabs or who-knew-what—thronging the place, shouting, crying, and pushing. Tadeusz and Jozef pointed out thieves with knives and razors slashing suitcases and clothes and advised Jurek and his father to hold tightly to their lone valise and guard themselves. None of the four had any money, but the Russians had provided them with *Udostovierienie licrnosti*, documents that were beyond anything an ordinary Soviet citizen could dream of and certainly would be desirable to steal. These were passes that granted them free passage to anywhere in the Soviet Union by train or boat, with the right to two pounds of bread each day per person and Turkish baths at train depots to kill lice.

Beyond the station, more refugees were camped in fields, waiting for trains to somewhere, anywhere. The next train to the west and Ceboksary was scheduled to leave in two hours, but the departure time passed with no train in sight. Another two hours passed, then three. Tadeusz and Jozef scurried about; at one point, Jurek noticed that Jozef was suddenly wearing an expensive gold watch. Finally, after eight hours, the train pulled in. "Follow us," Tadeusz and

Jozef said, and they forced their way ahead, knocking people aside and pulling Jurek and his father aboard.

It was after dark when the train left. Jurek found himself jammed against the window, with eight people crowded into the compartment. One of the others, a Tatar, held a big sack between his knees. Jurek was exhausted and dozed off. In the middle of the night, he found that he had more room than he thought and stretched out, trying not to think of home.

When it was light, he awoke to discover that although the train had not stopped anywhere that he had noticed, only the four of them occupied the compartment. Tadeusz now held the sack in his lap. He grinned at Jurek and said that the sack was full of sugar, maybe thirty pounds of the precious stuff.

At the port city of Ceboksary, they alighted and made their way through beggars to the docks. Wretched, scabrous children in rags pulled at Jurek, asking for anything—an orange rind, soup bones—that he might be carrying, only because he seemed to be going somewhere, although he looked as ragged and starved as they did. At the pier, Tadeusz grabbed a deckhand by the shirt and pressed the bag of sugar on him, and they climbed aboard a rusty steamer that was pulling out, whistling as if it were headed for some important place. They found a niche against the rail on the crowded deck, chockablock with people and three or four sheep.

At night, Tadeusz and Jozef guarded them against the thieves. No one had anything that would be worth stealing in ordinary times, just filthy clothes wadded up in the suitcase, but the thieves were after anything. They sneaked around, using straight razors to slice boot soles from dozing officials. Here and there, people had sex under the moon. On the second night, some tough-looking fellows, Armenians by the prayers they shouted, butchered a sheep, tossed the entrails into the river, and cooked it over an open fire of wood scraps and dung. Pieces of meat passed from hand to hand; Jurek and his father and their friends got some, along with a sip or two from a bottle of vodka. It was freedom, of a kind—and a sense of community.

At Kazan—whose university, Dr. Kluger said, had the distinction of having expelled V. I. Lenin for troublesome behavior during his freshman year—and at Ulyanovsk, they looked for signs of the army and inquired if anyone had seen Polish troops. No soldiers, they were told, but many Poles in desperate condition had been observed heading downriver for several days running. People had given them food. Some of them looked wild and like death.

At last, at Kuybyshev, which lies about a third of the way between Kazan and what once was Stalingrad, they spotted something that moved the four of them to great emotion. Fluttering above a small building near the pier was the White Eagle of the red-and-white Polish flag.

Chapter 19

THE BUILDING WITH THE FLAG WAS A POLISH MILITARY POLICE OUTPOST. Here Dr. Kluger proudly announced his captain's rank and his experience with the artillery and the military courts years earlier. He was given command of an enlistment post in Kuybyshev, while Jurek traveled farther south to Saratov to enroll at the infantry officers' school being established there. Dr. Kluger advised Tadeusz and Jozef not to give their real names when enlisting, on the chance that they would end up going from a Russian prison to a Polish military one.

They were pleased to note that they were welcomed to this army-in-exile, the II Polish Corps, strictly as fellow Poles, with no inquiry as to their religion. They soon learned that Commanding General Anders, who had recently been released from Moscow's notorious Lubianka prison, where he was beaten and tortured regularly for eighteen months, had issued strict orders against discrimination of any kind.

Some Polish Jewish leaders suggested to him that separate Jewish units should be formed to protect Jewish soldiers from the potential backlash of Polish anti-Semitism and the resentment against the Jews who had welcomed the Soviet invasion of Poland. Anders countered that if he allowed this, he would also have to create separate Ukrainian, White Russian, and other units for minorities, which would only encourage disunity. Accepting his reasoning, Jewish representatives sent an open letter, dated October 31, 1941, to the Polish Embassy in Kuybyshev, which Anders made sure received prominent notice and which stated in part:

> 1. We entirely agree with the principle formulated by General Anders, which means that the Polish Army should be created as a unified organization based on the equal treatment of all Polish citizens without distinction of religion or nationality, and that the main aim of this army should be the struggle for a free democratic Poland, the common mother country of all her citizens.
>
> 2. It was with satisfaction that we heard General Anders declare that he had issued very definite instructions that, in the Polish Army in the USSR, all propaganda aimed at the creating of dissension among people of different nationalities should be suppressed, and above all any manifestation of anti-Semitism, and that he intended to enforce these instructions.

That winter of 1941–42, Jurek's father strongly advised him to apply for entrance to the artillery officers' school being formed in conjunction with the Russians at Karasu, about four hundred fifty miles to the southeast in the Kazakh Republic. If he was going to fight with the Russians, Dr. Kluger said, Jurek would be much better off in the artillery, behind the front lines, rather than with the infantry. Russian military tradition was notorious for having a less-than-scrupulous regard for the number of losses within its own ranks.

With his aptitude for mathematics and with a good reason to succeed, Jurek passed the entrance examination. With five hundred other Poles, he arrived by train at the valley of Fergana, a warm, beautiful place. It is by legend the location of the Garden of Eden and is nestled in the Kazakh Hills, which form foothills of the Himalayas. There, on the site of what had been a tuberculosis sanatorium, the Poles joined four thousand Russian cadets in the highly specialized training, which took advantage of the mountainous surroundings to teach students how to calculate the trajectory of artillery fire. Jurek was among the one hundred fifty-six Poles who qualified after the first seven months of instruction.

It was in Karasu that Jurek learned from another Polish cadet the fate of Selinger and Zweig. After his classmates' release from a prison camp in 1941, they were traveling in a barge pulled by a tug along the River Ob. One night, a fierce current overturned the barge, drowning everyone aboard. Jurek also learned that Engineer Zilz, who had been put to work on a railroad by the Russians, had died of a heart attack. His family survived, however, and his sons-in-law were now with the Polish Army.

In September 1942, Jurek and his fellow cadets waited to find out where they would be sent. In remote Karasu, they had only sketchy information about the course of the war, which seemed to be going very much Hitler's way.

FOR MANY MONTHS, THE ROLE OF THE POLISH ARMY HAD BECOME A MATTER of dispute and a test of nerves between General Anders and the Russians. The general had become aware of the brutality with which most of his countrymen had been treated. Very few officers were showing up, and Anders already suspected what was later confirmed, that the Russians had murdered thousands of them.

When General Wladyslaw Sikorski, head of the government-in-exile, flew to Moscow to confer with Stalin and Molotov, he and General Anders argued that the Polish Army could be of greatest use in Persia to help protect the oil fields for the Allies. Stalin had seemed to agree and then, through most of 1942, refused to confirm this. The Russians had promised to supply the Polish Army, but for months, the only uniforms had been sent by the British. Rations were also in short supply, and no weapons were forthcoming. General Anders now believed that if he did not soon succeed in evacuating his army and hundreds of thousands of Polish civilians from the USSR, they would all perish.

In the summer of 1942, using a Soviet plane detailed for him, Anders flew to the Middle East and to London to confer with

British generals, U.S. Ambassador Averill Harriman, and Prime Minister Churchill. Churchill agreed to pressure Stalin to permit the Poles to leave Russia. Anders returned to Kuybyshev to face further Russian recalcitrance and double-talk. At last, on August 14, Churchill flew to Moscow, where Anders met with him at three in the morning at Stalin's villa outside the city. Churchill assured him that the evacuation of the Poles to Persia would begin at once and should be completed within two weeks. Anders would have the direct assistance of Marshal Grigori Zhukhov in completing this task.

To the end, however, the Soviets broke their word. By September, General Anders had succeeded in evacuating about one hundred fifteen thousand Polish troops and approximately one hundred thirty-five thousand civilians, mostly the wives and children of soldiers. At the last minute, however, Stalin issued an order forbidding any Poles of Jewish origin—other than families of those on active service with the Polish Army—to leave. Anders was incensed by this. There were thousands of Polish Jews trapped in the Soviet Union who had no attachment to the army. From his long meeting with Stalin and from what was by then a thorough acquaintance with the Bolshevik mentality, Anders understood that he was dealing with a criminal phenomenon that was no different from thugs on a waterfront.

Anders comprehended hatred of the Jews as an excuse for sadism. Bolsheviks imputed anti-Semitism to the Poles while killing Jews themselves. He could imagine no other reason for the Russians to prevent Jews, or for that matter, any Poles, from leaving the USSR, except to watch them die in captivity; the motive was as crude as that. It was a matter not of the Russian Communists' deep paranoia, of which Western theorists loved to prate, but of something more sinister: a morbid impulse, a love of killing. It was the same with the Nazis, under a different ideological camouflage. What was Stalin but a nobody from the back country who was taking his revenge on his origins by killing Poles?

If he did not get his people out now, Anders knew, most of them would die during the next winter. His task, more than forming an army, was to try to prevent mass murder. And yet he could save only a few Poles, as he later reflected in his autobiography. Of his million-and-a-half countrymen trapped in the Soviet Union, he remembered:

> We considered that half of them had already died, their bones scattered over the vast spaces of the Soviet Republics. We who had survived, had survived by a miracle. For us the summer of 1942 was the dawn of freedom. But we left behind in Russia hundreds of thousands, and our hearts were heavy.

Among those saved by General Anders was Jurek Kluger, who was one of the last of the Poles to escape from Russia that September. On notice of evacuation, he managed to obtain a five-day leave to rescue five cousins, the Aleksandrowiczes, who were trapped in a camp at Kizyl-Orda, and put them on a train for Persia. He found that his British uniform was useful in persuading the guards to do his bidding.

Then, with thirty-five Polish companions, he traveled by train to Krasnovodsk and by ship across the Caspian Sea to Pahlevi, Persia, where he talked to some of the other Polish escapees and asked them how they felt. As if they had escaped from a long nightmare, they said, and they looked it.

From there, he and his colleagues took an unnerving journey by truck over mountain passes to Habanija. Jurek has said that the trip was far more threatening than his stay in a Russian labor camp. The Persian drivers were stoned on opium and had no idea what they were doing. He was happy to board a rattletrap British bomber and land safely in Cairo.

The British put him and his fellow Poles to work plotting diversionary artillery fire in preparation for the battle of El Alamein, which began on October 23, 1942, lasted about two weeks, and led to the eventual expulsion of the Germans from North Africa by May of the next year.

AFTER THE NEW YEAR, JUREK WAS TRANSFERRED TO A PLACE THAT, FROM what he could tell, was near Kirkuk, in the deserts of Iraq. There his old classmates Romanski, Kogler, and Bernas appeared; they told him how they had escaped to Hungary after the September Campaign. With the help of anti-Nazi partisans, they broke out of the Hungarian internment camp and hid in Budapest. When they received word that the Polish Army was regrouping in the Middle East under Anders, they made their way to Beirut. Stanislaw Jura, who had been with them on these adventures, was now stationed in England as the pilot of a Wellington bomber and was flying missions over Germany with the Royal Air Force.

Jura had always wanted to be a pilot. He had taken lessons in Poland and had even flown a glider. Now he was among those Polish pilots who were impressing the British and Americans with their daring. The 303 Polish Spitfire Squadron was the talk of the RAF. The Russians had been spreading the word that the Poles did not want to fight the Germans, but now the world would find out who the real fighters were.

Another classmate, Jurek's old cohort in amorous pursuits, Tadeusz Czuprynski, also turned up in Iraq; he had escaped from the Russians through Romania. It was like a class reunion held in the desert. Unfortunately, no one knew what was going on in Wadowice itself. Jurek sensed an uneasiness in his friends when he brought up the subject of his family.

They were standing beside a tent in the middle of nowhere swatting bugs and looking out for snakes when the discussion about home took place. His father was in Palestine with the military courts, and Jurek knew that he would be safe. It was the women back in Wadowice who filled his thoughts with worry. The words *Mother*, *Tesia*, and *Grandmother* on Jurek's lips sent a shaft of feeling through his brain. He could not draw a breath. A summons to home hit him. The caressing appeal of his mother's and sister's voices wafted over him and tugged at him with small, invisible hands. The house on Zatorska Street rose up just across the way, in the middle of hummocks of sand and dirt. He had to struggle to maintain his composure.

For the balance of that year and into the next, Jurek was posted back to Cairo, where he taught artillery surveying and rapidly improved his English. He spent his free hours mostly at the Ghezirah

Club, an enclave of colonial rule. On the verandah, Nubian males in white skirts and green turbans brought iced drinks. The aristocratic English environment of the Ghezirah, with its racecourse, polo fields, and tennis courts, brought out the old sportsman and bon vivant in Jurek. As a cadet lieutenant, looking smart in British tropicals with Polish insignia, he was welcome.

It was one morning on the swept clay courts of the Ghezirah that Jurek was overcome by the strongest wave he had ever felt of what Commandant Smyrnov called his weakness. In a mixed-doubles match, she was on the opposite side of the net, slender, with very dark hair and blue eyes. At the sight of her, he thought for a split second that he was twelve again and had sneaked into the cinema. She was nearly as tall as he and looked as if she had never been subjected to severe weather. He lost his concentration at the net.

As they sat together later on the verandah, she told him that she had driven ambulances in Southampton and Liverpool when the Jerries were bombing hell out of the docks. Every girl had to do her bit. She had been eighteen then. When she saw a chance to ship out and become a driver for generals in Egypt, she grabbed it. Listening to her and looking at her close up, he thought that God had sent him to Maryjskaja and down the Volga just so that he would arrive at the Ghezirah to see those pretty teeth and hear that rising and falling voice that covered a great range, from soprano to contralto. She had some sort of accent.

"I'm Irish," she said, "or I was born there." She was born in Cork. The family had lived there until she was seven. Something had driven them out, houses burning down, politics—Jurek paid no attention to that. What mattered to him was that they were alone together.

"Renée?" He pronounced it "REN-knee." She said her actual name was Irene White. Her mother was a Doyle from Cork.

"A nice Irish Catholic girl," she said, "fresh from the convent. Kluger sounds awfully Kraut."

"I'm a Jew. It's not that I look Jewish, it's just that a lot of other Jews happen to look like me."

"You're a good tennis player," she said.

"My sister is a champion."

"Shall we have another drink?"

They spent all the time they could together. They hardly noticed Cairo or the Sphinx or the Nile, which Jurek said was nothing compared to the Vistula. He told her, without going into details, how he and his father had passed the time in Russia reading. She carried around a book of stories by an Irish writer the way other people did a newspaper, and she read him a passage about snow and death that he thought was beautiful. When word came down that the II Polish Corps was going to fight somewhere, and soon, they dreaded being apart and decided that the best possible thing was to get married at once.

"My mother won't like it, me marrying a Jew," she said. "My father will adore you. What will your family think?"

Jurek had seen much death during the past three years, on the road to Tarnopol, at the prison camp, and lately at the battle of El Alamein. Now he faced the prospect of combat with a certain equilibrium, knowing that his death was about as likely as his survival. As an artillery officer, he would either have an enemy shell dropped on him or not; there would be very little he could do about it one way or another.

Under these circumstances, his identity as a Jew and Renée's as a Catholic receded. Why should religion keep them apart? Should not faith in God be something to bring people together rather than separate them? He tried to imagine what Grandmother Huppert would think. Was she even still alive? Was any of his family? He had no idea. If Grandmother Huppert should suddenly appear in Egypt like an avenging angel, maybe perched atop a pyramid, to condemn his marriage to a Christian, he would have to say to her, "I'm sorry, but I have to do this. Remember the proverb, 'You are a long time dead.' " Marrying Renée was at least a wager on the future. He was betting everything, the only thing he had, on it—his life.

They were married August 26, 1943, in a military ceremony. Catholic and Jewish rites, to honor their families and their faiths, would have to come with the peace, if both of them lived to see it.

He liked to talk about what his family was like when he was growing up and about his friends and the games they played and the little town they lived in, and he spoke with great affection about his father. But he avoided saying much of anything about what the women in his family might think or do after the war, so she stopped asking about them.

BY APRIL 1944, JUREK WAS WITH HIS REGIMENT JUST ABOVE NAPLES ON THE southern Italian coast. The Allied advance up the peninsula had stalled in the valley of the rivers Rapido and Liri, where the Germans occupied the broad top of a mountain that rose to seventeen hundred feet and provided them with a three-hundred-sixty-degree perspective from which to blast Allied troops at will. To achieve the Allied objective—opening the road to Rome—the German position on the mountain had to be eliminated. But the enemy had dug in and around sacred ground, a monastery that was founded by Saint Benedict in 529. It was the mother church of the Benedictine Order and a treasure-trove of medieval and Renaissance art and architecture. To attack it was to put at risk a sublime monument of Western civilization—just what the Allies were fighting to preserve. This was Monte Cassino.

Since January, successive American, New Zealander, and Indian assaults on the mountain and the monastery had failed to dislodge the Germans. Nor had four hundred forty-two tons of bombs dropped directly onto the abbey had any discernible effect, except to reduce the venerable structure to rubble. The Allied loss of life was horrendous. And the Germans, by removing many of the abbey's portable treasures to Rome before the attack, secured a major propaganda victory at what they were terming the impregnable Gate to Rome. At the height of weeks of Allied frustration and in the wake of the failure of all the other Allied nations' combined efforts to do so, General Anders accepted the invitation for his II Polish Corps to take Monte Cassino.

Jurek felt as all of his comrades in arms did. However formidable the challenge, it was the greatest opportunity imaginable for the Poles to show the world what they could do. It would also redeem their national honor and, not to put too fine a point on it, exact revenge against the Germans.

Jurek and his surveying unit arrived in the valley to take measurements for the artillery bombardment that would precede the assault. His first sight of the monastery, or what was left of it, was shocking. Nothing but a stark, bombed-out jumble of broken walls and parapets remained of what had been a thousand years of beauty. Just as shocking, however, was the barrier that the mountain presented, with its sheer face rising up from the valley as if in mockery of any idea that it could be conquered. And skeptics about the bombing had been correct: the ruins now provided even better defense for the Germans than the untouched, enormous building had done.

He did not know how the Poles were supposed to accomplish what others had failed to do, but if it was humanly possible, they would. The morale was fantastic. "We Poles have a completely different attitude toward fighting," one of Jurek's colleagues commented. "We are heroic; the British are methodical. Without our unplanned, spontaneous uprisings, the Polish nation would never have existed." They laughed, joked, and seemed to find it annoying to have to stay hidden to preserve an element of surprise. And, as many of the British observed, they seemed consumed by hatred of those who occupied their motherland.

Climbing adjacent Mount Cairo to observe topographical points, Jurek completed his surveys for positioning twelve hundred six heavy guns. He had made a dangerous ascent with five subordinate officers; they had only their revolvers to defend them in the dark. The measurements had to be taken precisely at sunrise, when the atmosphere was at its stillest. When he returned to base camp with his figures completed, his colonel informed him that his bravery on this mission had earned him the Polish Cross of Valor.

With thrilled satisfaction, Jurek read the message that General Anders sent to the troops on the afternoon of May 11, the eve of battle.

Soldiers!

The moment for battle has arrived! We have long awaited the moment for revenge and retribution over our hereditary enemy.... The task assigned to us will cover with glory the name of the Polish soldier all over the world. At this moment, the thoughts and hearts of our whole nation will be with us. Trusting in the Justice of Divine Providence, we go forward with the sacred slogan in our hearts: God, Honour, Country.

Wladyslaw Anders, Lt.-General Commander, II Polish Army Corps

At eleven that night, hidden among rocks with only a camouflaged tin roof overhead, Jurek was playing poker with a handful of his fellow surveyors when suddenly the heavy guns thundered into action.

"What a pity!" Jurek shouted. "Just when I was winning!"

The maddening noise continued for forty minutes. Around him, German shells burst in response. Partially obscured by a smoke screen, the first Polish troops began their assault.

The losses were very heavy. The first wave fell back, unable to hold position. On May 18, a fresh wave of Polish troops began another attack. At twenty minutes past ten the next morning, they hoisted the White Eagle over the one wall still standing in the monastery. An hour later, Jurek joined the troops making their way up the steep road, and General Anders ordered the Union Jack raised alongside the Polish flag. Jurek saw corpses of Polish and British soldiers everywhere, some still locked in fighting poses after hand-to-hand struggles. The air was thick with the smell of death.

Jurek's assignment was to assess the accuracy of the artillery fire he had directed. It had been on target, all right, but what effect it had actually had on the Germans was impossible to determine. The monastery itself was a wasteland, but its lower crypts and passageways remained untouched. No wonder the Germans had been able to hold out so long.

A battle at nearby Piedimonte immediately followed. As there had been no time in which to do accurate firing calculations, Jurek "volunteered" to ride in a tank and radio back instructions to the artillery. Unfortunately, the tank's driver-commander wanted everyone, apparently including the Germans, to know that he had been a member of a certain aristocratic Polish cavalry regiment. He insisted on flying the bright yellow flag of this elite group from atop the tank's turret, making it an easy target. An enemy shell soon hit the side of the machine, putting it out of action. Jurek and the five other men inside managed to scramble out and take shelter underneath the crippled tank as the battle raged around them. "You are as stupid as your horse!" Jurek informed the driver.

There were other close calls for him as the Poles fought their way up the Adriatic coast to Ancona and inland. But nothing came close to equaling the horror and glory of Cassino, which did accomplish for the Polish cause everything that General Anders had hoped, if not in practical results for the Polish nation at least for the pride of its soldiers and people. At the time, there was due recognition from the Allies. On May 25, Jurek stood at attention in an olive grove on the slopes of Monte Cassino as General Anders accepted investiture in the Companionship of the Order of the Bath from General Harold Alexander, who represented King George VI. Anders called the honor "a possession of all the soldiers of the II Polish Corps," who had suffered more than three thousand casualties at Cassino and Piedimonte alone. At Cassino, Jurek and his companions left behind more than a thousand Polish dead, with nineteen Jewish soldiers among them, in graves lining a hill to the west of the ruined abbey. Not long afterward, a white obelisk was raised there, bearing these words:

We Polish soldiers
For our freedom and yours
Have given our souls to God
Our bodies to the soil of Italy
And our hearts to Poland.

Chapter 20

UNTIL LATE IN THE SUMMER OF 1944, LOLEK CONTINUED WORKING AT the chemical plant at night while studying secretly to become a priest during the day. His friend Malinski also became an underground seminarian. On Sunday, August 6, of that year, however, the Germans launched a house-to-house search through Krakow to round up all young men, netting at least eight thousand in the first twenty-four hours and sending them to concentration camps. Lolek and Malinski had to go into hiding.

The roundup was an attempt to forestall an armed rebellion such as the explosive one that had burst out in Warsaw on August 1. Some one hundred fifty thousand Warsaw citizens, only a quarter of whom had arms, rose up against the Germans in a well-planned attack that in the first few days captured many strategically important buildings and other sites in the city, although, unfortunately, not the airport and some key bridges. They were aided by most of the population, not by the Communist underground army, which was taking orders from Moscow and which by then was bitterly opposed by the AK.

The timing of the Warsaw Uprising was because of the advance of the Red Army, which by then had routed the Wehrmacht from eastern Poland and had reached the Vistula. The insurgents assumed that the Russians would continue their march, bomb German troop concentrations ahead, and reach Warsaw by mid-August at the latest.

This plan was a perfectly sound, if very courageous, one, but it depended on the assumption that the Allies actually wanted to help Poland regain its freedom. In perhaps the most cynical and shameful Allied action (or inaction) of the war, however, the Russians halted their advance at the Vistula and sat there as the Germans gradually slaughtered the rebels and razed Warsaw. Churchill and Roosevelt, to their credit, did plead with Stalin to go to the aid of the insurgents and asked for landing facilities so that British and American planes could drop arms for the rebels; Stalin refused.

"Sooner or later," Stalin replied, as Churchill later revealed, "the truth about the group of criminals who have embarked on the Warsaw adventure in order to seize power will become known to everybody." Stalin had already formulated Soviet plans for Poland after the war; Polish troops of the Soviet-created "People's Army" were among those waiting across the Vistula. He was now pleased to sit back and watch the Germans eliminate just those young men who would otherwise have been obstacles to the Russian domination of their homeland, while the Polish Communist underground survived.

The fighters held out for an astonishing two months; the AK losses, some twenty-five thousand, were staggering enough, but two hundred twenty-five thousand civilians were also killed. Perhaps fifty thousand died in mass executions, while others perished as the Germans obliterated residential blocks, hospitals, and business districts. When the firing ceased, the Germans sent a half-million of the survivors to concentration camps. Another one hundred fifty thousand were forced into labor in the Reich. When the Russians finally walked into Warsaw three months later, they found not a single person still living within the limits of a city that in 1939 had been home to more than a million-and-a-quarter Catholic and Jewish Poles. Except for the two cities hit by atomic bombs, no others in Europe or Asia suffered devastation equal to that of Warsaw, caught between German wrath and Allied perfidy.

As the Germans carried out the preemptive arrests in Krakow during the first days of the Warsaw Uprising, Archbishop Sapieha acted quickly to try to protect his secret seminarians. On August 7, he dispatched messengers to summon the young men, who now numbered sixteen, to take refuge in the Archbishop's Palace. The problem was how to get Wojtyla, Malinski, and the others safely away from where they were living or working to Franciszkanska Street and inside the archbishop's residence.

The archbishop arranged for women to act as escorts to divert attention. On the morning of August 7, Mrs. Irena Szkocka, in whose house the Rhapsodic held performances and whom Lolek affectionately called *Babcia* (Granny), led him and a priest across the Debniki Bridge and through alleyways, peeking around corners to see if the coast was clear. They would have been a curious sight to the Gestapo—the old woman, the priest in his cassock, and Lolek in his worker's overalls—but they made it to the palace without incident. A few hours later, Malinski, who had been hiding in his sisters' house, also arrived safely.

The secret seminarians joined three others who had been hiding in the palace since their own seminary had been shut down in 1939. They lived in a dormitory that Archbishop Sapieha had prepared for them on the second floor next to the chapel, with metal beds and desks for each. The archbishop, who was in close touch with the AK, shared the assumption that the Russians would soon cross the Vistula and reach Krakow after liberating Warsaw. Unless the Gestapo across the street noticed the new residents during the next few days, they'd be safe.

When Lolek was absent from work at the Solway plant, the Germans began searching for him. Malinski's sisters arrived at the palace in tears to report that the Gestapo were looking for him, too. The Germans had already taken hostages, and they warned that they would shoot ten for every man caught hiding. Fearing that the palace would soon be raided, the archbishop obtained forged identity papers for the seminarians and dressed them in borrowed cassocks so that they might pass as priests retreating from the conflict.

Six months later, Lolek and the others were still hiding in the palace, engaged in a regular program of study and prayer. The great actor Juliusz Osterwa came to give the young men instruction in elocution, but other than that, they had little contact with the outside. The archbishop himself was mostly involved in relief work for refugees from Warsaw who reached the city. When the Germans finally left, the Polish Church would have at least a few good young men to send into a shattered civilization.

For Lolek and his companions, the war ended on January 16, 1945, to the sounds of gunfire outside the Archbishop's Palace and an explosion that blew out all the windows facing Franciszkanska Street. At that moment, he and the others were on their knees at evening chapel. Archbishop Sapieha halted the service and told everyone to go down to the cellars, where they heard the sounds of tanks and guns of all calibers throughout the night. The Russians had arrived.

The big boom was the Debniki Bridge blowing up, one of the Germans' last acts of destruction as they abandoned the city. Krakow was spared the obliteration that Warsaw experienced, although the Wehrmacht did not go quietly.

Before dawn on the morning of January 17, the first Russian soldiers were outside the palace, and the seminarians opened the gates to welcome them and give them tea and bread. In the morning, Lolek and Malinski ventured outside for the first time in six months to see the remains of the bridge. They crossed the ice on the frozen Vistula, which was strewn with the bodies of dead soldiers, to visit family and friends.

Later that day, as the seminarians worked to clean up and repair the damaged palace, three Russian generals arrived to pay their respects to Archbishop Sapieha for his anti-Nazi activities during the past long years. Two days later, a Polish general, dressed in a prewar uniform complete with jodhpurs and a saber, drew up in a Jeep and strode into the palace on a similar mission of tribute.

He was Marshal Rola-Zymierski, commander of the army of the so-called Polish Provisional Government of National Unity, a Moscow-directed, Communist puppet state that was established with the formal approval of Britain and the United States. Having permitted the Germans to decimate the non-Communist resistance during the Warsaw Uprising, Stalin was now free to place compliant Communist Polish leaders over their war-weary countrymen. A period of internecine skirmishing followed, but its outcome was never in doubt. For Poland there was no VE Day.

IN ITALY, WHERE JUREK KLUGER HAD BEEN MADE COMMANDER OF HIS artillery surveying platoon and was decorated for bravery, the II Polish Corps had become an army without a country. General Anders, indignant and disheartened by what he could only see as betrayal by the very allies with whom his troops had fought so valiantly, attempted to withdraw the II Polish Corps from further combat. He relented when General Alexander told him that there were no other units to replace the Poles. They fought on for the idea of a freedom already lost.

The Russians liberated Wadowice on January 20. There were no Jews living there. At midafternoon a week later, the Russians entered Auschwitz-Birkenau, finding heaps of bodies and about seven thousand inmates still alive. No one named Kluger was among them.

JUREK'S FIRST SPECIFIC KNOWLEDGE OF WHAT HAD HAPPENED TO HIS FAMILY came from a distant cousin, Captain David Kupferman of the II Polish Corps. Late in April 1945, just after the Poles had taken Bologna, Jurek ran into him at Castelbolognese. At first, Kupferman could only say that Jurek's mother, sister, and grandmother had been killed by the Germans, but he was unable to supply details. Later, however, after visiting the Bergen-Belsen death camp and making further contact with the Red Cross and with Adas Josefert, Kupferman learned what had happened to Jurek's family and others from Wadowice.

In July of 1942, the Germans evicted Grandmother Huppert, the Kluger women, and the other residents from the house on Zatorska Street and sent them to a ghetto created on the site of a former vegetable market. The house was turned into the local Gestapo headquarters. Jurek realized that from the shack where they were confined, his family could easily see their former home. Jurek's uncle, the lawyer Dr. Bronislaw Huppert, who had lived in the rear apartment on Zatorska, organized an elementary school in the ghetto, while his wife and twenty-year-old daughter, Wanda, ran a soup kitchen. A Catholic classmate of Jurek's, Tadeusz Luty, was in love with Wanda and tried to rescue her, but he was shot by a German sentry and barely escaped to Krakow. Jurek also heard about how several Christian friends had tried to help his mother and sister with forged papers, before and after the establishment of the ghetto, but Rozalia and Tesia had refused to abandon Grandmother Huppert. Several other Jewish families from Wadowice had survived because of this sort of help.

In July 1943, soldiers began clearing the ghetto. They removed Grandmother Huppert first, putting her on a train to the Belzec camp far to the east. It was not known, given her advanced age and weak condition, whether she perished on the way or was shot or gassed there. At Belzec, the sick and the old were typically separated from the rest on the train platform, placed face-down near a pit, shot, and dumped in.

In August, Rozalia and Tesia, together with Lawyer Huppert and his wife and daughter, were put on a train to Auschwitz, just a short journey away. Their names did not appear on any lists of survivors; they were probably gassed and cremated at once, as was the policy with deportees from nearby places, who knew what was in store for them. Others arrived from distant parts of Europe under the illusion that they were being resettled, so it was possible to take the time to relieve them of their valuables or put them to work. Jurek tried to think that at least his mother and Tesia had died quickly, without additional suffering, but that was hardly a comfort.

AFTER THE ARMISTICE WAS DECLARED ON MAY 7, JUREK OBTAINED LEAVE TO travel to Palestine to grieve with his father, who had already heard about their family's fate. They pondered the mystery and injustice in having survived while others more deserving of survival had been murdered. Nearly as disturbing was why Jurek had come through the savage Italian campaign unscathed, while his classmate Romanski had been seriously wounded and Czuprynski had been killed at the battle of Loreto.

Jurek was unable to bring himself to write in detail about his family to Renée, who had been transferred to England for the duration of the war. He told her only that they had been lost somehow. The entire subject was too painful to talk about, and he tried to bury it within himself. As a family, or what was left of one, he and Dr. Kluger could hardly comprehend even how many relatives had been lost to them personally, let alone absorb the enormity of the entire tragedy. And here the two of them were, still in Polish uniform.

In Palestine, Dr. Kluger had encountered Zionists committed to Theodor Herzl's belief that the worst catastrophe would occur in those countries where Jews believed that they were most assimilated. After what had happened to their family, and, paradoxically, after what Jurek had been through in Italy in the Polish cause, what were he and his father to think? "Perhaps," Dr. Kluger admitted, "we would have been better off if we had come to Palestine sooner."

Jurek knew that despite the circumstances, his father did not regret his Polish patriotism or renounce it. The Poland that General Anders represented remained worth fighting for. Had not Anders, a kind of Moses, led them and their Christian fellow citizens out of bondage in Russia, which was now gobbling up the homeland? Jurek and his father continued to believe in the nobility of General Anders's lost cause even after word leaked out of Poland that a year after the war's end, some forty Jewish survivors in the town of Kielce had been murdered by Catholic Poles in a pogrom. It was the ancient blood slander again: rumors had circulated that the Jews were ritually killing Christian children. Had racist anti-Semitism been defeated only for Christian anti-Semitism to renew itself? Could the two be that distinct?

In 1947, Jurek and Renée, who had been reunited in Turin the previous year, went to England, where Jurek was demobilized from the army. He then began attending Nottingham Technical College, from which he received a degree in industrial engineering in 1948.

With the war's end, Lolek completed his studies for the priesthood at the university. He was ordained on the Feast of All Saints in 1946, with now-Cardinal Sapieha presiding in the chapel at the palace. As the pope relates in *Gift and Mystery*, he was thinking a great deal on that day about the millions who had not survived the war, including one secret seminarian who, before the palace became a refuge, was caught by the Gestapo and executed. On the day after his ordination, All Souls Day, he celebrated his first mass at the Wawel Cathedral, with Father Figlewicz acting as *manuductor* (guide) through the sacred rituals.

As a priest, his loyalty to friends and his love of learning and the arts were far from abandoned. He was only entering a new phase and enfolding the past in its embrace. Later that first week, he said masses at the parish church in Debniki, at the Church of the Presentation of Our Lady in Wadowice, and another at the Wawel for his *Unia* colleagues from the cultural resistance. Ten days after his ordination, he performed his first baptism, christening Monika Kwiatkowska, the daughter born to his beloved friend Halina Krolikiewicz and her husband, the writer Tadeusz.

Today, Halina remembers the moment when Wojtyla, holding the baby tenderly in his strong arms, let the droplets fall and pronounced the words in his rich voice, "*Ego baptizo...*" It came to her then that she and his other dear friends had not lost a fellow artist to the priesthood but had gained a new Lolek who would be with them and behind them one way or another, giving them renewed spiritual energy. She thought of the many heroic Polish and other dramas in which they had played opposite each other, especially Sophocles' *Antigone*, when she played the title role opposite Lolek's Haemon. In the play, they had died together in defiance of the unjust laws of the state, which was exactly the principle for which the Rhapsodic would always stand.

Soon afterward, Wojtyla left Poland under Cardinal Sapieha's sponsorship for travel and study in France and to write his doctoral dissertation at the Dominican Angelicum University in Rome, where he lived at the Belgian College. In the spring of 1948, he was still in Rome completing his thesis, entitled *The Issue of Faith in Saint John of the Cross*. His letters home were filled with wonder at the Eternal City. When Zbigniew Silkowski wrote that he was organizing a reunion, set for a date in June, to celebrate the tenth anniversary of their high school graduation, Wojtyla asked if it could be postponed for a month so that he could attend.

On July 18, Father Wojtyla, having completed his doctoral studies, joined his classmates in sitting at their old desks in Wadowice High School. Halina's father, who had resumed his position as principal at the school, stood before them and read the roll as it had been in 1938. Perhaps half of the original forty answered "Present." It was an emotional moment, with all those empty desks. At least ten had been killed in the war—as soldiers, in the underground, or, like Selinger and Zweig, while trying to leave Russia. Others were missing. If Teofil Bojes had survived his experience as a slave laborer in Germany, his whereabouts remained unknown. Some who had fought with General Anders had stayed abroad.

One after another, they recounted their wartime experiences and contacts with other classmates. What about Jurek Kluger and his father? Lolek wanted to know, broaching a somber subject. Wadowice was such a different place now with the Jews gone, nearly all killed at Auschwitz. Perhaps twenty were known to have survived and emigrated to the United States. In the building where Wojtyla had lived with his father, there were no Jewish families left. The Kluger house on Zatorska Street had passed from the Gestapo to the new government housing bureau and was occupied by several families. The synagogue was still in ruins, and there were plans to level it, as there were no Jews to worship in it. But what about Jurek and Dr. Kluger?

Tomasz Romanski had just been released by the Communist security forces; like all returning soldiers who had fought with Anders, he was under suspicion of having so-called capitalist sympathies. He reported that Jurek and his father had been demobilized with the rest of the II Polish Corps. Other than that, no one had any information about them. They would certainly not be returning to Poland. Of the six million Poles killed during the war (17.2 percent of the entire prewar population), half were Jews. Only about fifty thousand Jews remained, and more were emigrating to Israel and America every year. The ruins of the Wadowice synagogue stood as an eloquent reminder of them.

BY THE TIME THE CLASS HELD ITS SECOND REUNION IN 1958, FATHER Wojtyla had just been nominated as a bishop. He continued to write scholarly and religious articles as well as a succession of poems, plays, and theatrical reviews. He regularly attended the productions of the Rhapsodic, which was suppressed during a period of Stalinist censorship from 1953–56. His reviews under a nom de plume enabled him to express his support without compromising the delicate position of the clergy in Poland under the Communists.

As a bishop, he would live in Krakow and commute to his classes as a professor of philosophy at the Catholic University of Lublin (the only Church-run university within the Communist world). He was an extremely popular, respected teacher and was beloved by his students, who called him Uncle. During university holidays, he regularly led male and female students on mountain expeditions for skiing, climbing, boating, and free-ranging discussions of all manner of personal as well as religious problems. Women students appreciated his treatment of them as intellectual equals and his admonitions to the young men that they must guard against the temptation to treat women only as sexual objects rather than as independent persons meriting respect. His constant theme was the dignity of the individual human person, and examples of his concern for the treatment of women in particular peppered his teachings, both as a professor and as a religious leader.

Someone had the wit to tape-record a talk he once gave to the young people from the Jagiellonian. The bishop spoke about the women who appear in the New Testament and the effect that encountering Jesus had on them.

"Women," he told the students, "must develop what I would call a spiritual instinct for self-preservation, and a certain method of defending their own personalities. The path to this is interior independence." In the Gospels, he explained, the women who meet Christ as a person achieve interior independence and are at peace with their self-knowledge. The woman at the well, for instance, has had five husbands and is living with a man who is not her husband. Christ knows this and reminds her of it, yet he does not reprove or humiliate her; in effect, he *liberates her to be herself*, relieving her by sharing the truth with her. He deals in the same way with Mary Magdalene, the prostitute; with Martha, who is too taken up with her daily work to give love; and even with his own mother. And the Blessed Mother, the bishop reminded the students, freely chose her motherhood and achieved her individuality and fulfillment alike through this choice.

Elsewhere, the bishop stated that women can never find personal fulfillment through a man and must never allow themselves to become merely objects for men. "With Christ, women are independent and, so to speak, do not need men; when they get married, this independence means that they are persons and not objects," he explained. "Who am I, and what have I done with my life?" was the Christ-like question that he said the young women should ask themselves in their pursuit of personal liberation and in the interest of giving and receiving unselfish love.

AT THE REUNION, BISHOP WOJTYLA SAID MASS FOR THE PRESENT STUDENT body at the high school, introducing his own classmates as "these strange altar boys you see in their forties, your schoolmates from twenty years ago." In the Rynek, he spotted one classmate, Tadzio Bryzek, who was now a high government official and was pointedly not attending the mass, or even the reunion, of which the new bishop was naturally the focus of attention. Wojtyla rushed across the square and, before Bryzek could escape, wrapped him in a big hug, lifting him off the ground.

"That will ruin Comrade Bryzek's career!" Teofil Bojes joked.

Bojes, who had finally made contact with his old colleagues, was working as a high official in the coal industry, but he didn't let that interfere with friendship or, for that matter, serving as one of the bishop's altar boys. "To be hugged by a bishop!" he laughed. "That's our Lolek! For Bryzek, it's Siberia!"

As the classmates took their seats in the old schoolroom, the bishop pointed to the empty desk behind him. Still no one had heard anything of Jurek Kluger.

In 1966, plans were laid for a special celebration commemorating the hundredth anniversary of the high school, which seemed a good occasion also to hold a reunion. But this time the government clamped down. Two years earlier, Wojtyla had been named Archbishop of Krakow. To permit an archbishop to enter the premises of the people's school was unthinkable. The government absolutely forbade it, especially since by then, Wojtyla was one of the two most visible rallying points for opposition to the Communist regime. He was also lending his support to the building of a new church in Krakow, a project forbidden by the state. Rather than hold a reunion without their favorite classmate, the Class of 1938 canceled it.

They did attend a mass that Archbishop Wojtyla said for them at the parish church. Afterward, chatting with his classmates on the edge of the Rynek, the archbishop agreed with them that they could no longer hold reunions in Wadowice. What would be the point, with the use of the school denied them? Then the archbishop had an excellent idea. Why not celebrate instead at the Archbishop's Palace in Krakow? He suggested the last Sunday in December, 1968, for the thirtieth anniversary.

But that was the Christmas season, his friends pointed out. Wouldn't His Excellency be too busy at that time? On the contrary, he replied. Nothing could be so important as to interfere with their good fellowship. The date was made definite, and he said that they should come early for mass in the private chapel and plan to spend the entire day at the palace. He would provide everything.

The more he talked about it, the more pleasure he displayed in contemplating the possibilities. As the classmates were getting older, the reunions took on greater significance. Why not hold them more often? They should come every year. After all, he lived in such a big house now. His friends ought to take full advantage of it and the hospitality he could offer.

Stanislaw Jura was standing off to the side with Bojes, taking all of this in and feeling special delight in Wojtyla's scheme to circumvent government restrictions. It was typical of Lolek to make a virtue of necessity. Jura himself had been harassed by the government ever since his return to Poland from England. He had found the only work he could in a sawmill owned by an uncle. When the mill was nationalized, Jura was without work altogether, all because of his service with the RAF. Finally, he found a position as an economist, which was socialist jargon for "clerk." But now he would be a guest of the Archbishop of Krakow, no matter what the bureaucrats thought.

It would be good for Lolek, too, Bojes said. It must be lonely for him every year at Christmas with no family around him. His classmates were his real family, the only one he truly had. They would do their best to make sure he knew how much they loved him and how proud they were of him.

Just then, the archbishop announced some wonderful news. He had located one of their lost classmates.

Chapter 21

Only a few weeks earlier, in late November 1965, Jurek Kluger was driving his bronze Jaguar sedan on the road home to Rome, where he had lived for a decade. He had been to Naples on a brief business trip with his partner, Kurt Rosenberg. Jurek's father had died in London in 1962 at the age of seventy-eight, so his only contact with the distant past was Rosenberg, who had survived the war by escaping from Lvov and joining up with General Anders's army in Italy. Jurek had come upon Rosenberg during the Adriatic campaign in 1944, when he discovered his old friend running a rest camp for soldiers.

Jurek and Rosenberg had just finished clearing some American tractors through customs and were on the Via Appia somewhere between the turnoff for Monte Cassino and the one for Anzio, when Rosenberg, who irritated Jurek by reading the newspaper aloud during these trips, noticed an item he had overlooked.

"Would you look at this," he said. "Some Polish bishop has made a big speech at the Vatican Council. It seems everybody is talking about it."

"Bishops are always making speeches," Jurek said. "That is what they do for a living. I should have such a job."

"This one's from Krakow. He is the archbishop."

"What's his name?" asked Jurek.

"Wojtyla," Rosenberg answered. " 'Council delegates in the last phase of the historic enclave continued to discuss this week the speech made by Archbishop Karol Wojtyla of Krakow on the 28th of last month urging the Church to prepare itself for the modern world. The Church, the archbishop said, ought not to be didactic and patronizing, as if it possessed the whole truth and expected the world to do as it said. This was the sort of attitude that had created barriers between the Church and the world. It was no good to lament the unhappy state of the world and to give the Church sole credit for everything that was good in it. A moralizing and preaching tone should be avoided.' "

Jurek let Rosenberg read on. He was half-absorbing what the archbishop had said while at the same time trying to figure out whether this could all be true, that Lolek was in Rome.

" 'Just as students were better led to the truth by discovering it for themselves, by example not by imposition, the Church should not demand that the world conform to its teachings but present the truth in a way that people can grasp it, rather than having it forced upon them. The Church has much to learn from the world, just as the world should learn from it, of people's free will through rational inquiry.' That doesn't sound like a bishop," Rosenberg commented. "It sounds like Socrates, or Spinoza. Not bad for an archbishop, certainly."

"Spell his name for me," Jurek said, speeding up.

Rosenberg did so, adding that the first name was Karol.

"It's Lolek," Jurek said calmly, although a tumult of emotions assailed him. Wojtyla was an unusual name. On first hearing it, a jumble of images of Lolek from childhood up to the last year that they had spent together filled his head. He was not quite able to believe that his friend had actually grown up to become an archbishop until Rosenberg started reading the article. But the gist of the argument, that religion should not be something imposed but freely explored and accepted—who else would say such a thing, and in the Vatican?

Jurek had spent the years since the war trying not to think about such matters. He would talk about his army experiences but about nothing else, not even the labor camp, and not even with

Renée. Now it was as if the past had suddenly caught up with him, and he did not know how to deal with it.

"Who is Lolek?" Rosenberg asked.

"From Wadowice. He was my friend. He played goalie for the Jews. You don't remember; you are from Bielsko."

"Nobody from Wadowice could become an archbishop," Rosenberg observed.

That did it. "I will prove it to you!" Jurek shouted.

"How are you going to do that?"

"I will call him on the phone!"

Jurek drove straight to the Parioli apartment. Rosenberg stayed with him, wanting to judge for himself whether this improbable association actually existed. At home, Renée was less skeptical than bemused; she knew so little about Jurek's childhood that anything was possible.

Jurek had no idea how to locate any archbishop, let alone a Polish one. His knowledge of the Vatican consisted of a visit to Saint Peter's, the museums, and the Sistine Chapel. Renée was a regular communicant but did not hobnob with the hierarchy. Then, as he looked under *Polish* in the telephone directory, he had the idea that a Polish prelate visiting the Council, which seemed to have been going on forever, might be staying at something called the Polish College, which was on the Aventina. He tried that and was referred to the Polish Institute on the Via Pietro Cavallini, which Jurek knew was near the Cavour Bridge, not far from the Vatican. Yes, Archbishop Wojtyla was staying there, he was told, but he was out. Would the gentleman care to call again later?

At this point, so near his goal, Jurek got cold feet. It had been twenty-seven years. Would Lolek want to talk to him, or would the call be a nuisance to him? Although he had never made one before, calls from out of the blue to old friends often turned out badly. What if he reached Lolek, only to find him indifferent? That would be worse than not contacting him at all. He left his name and number. If Lolek wished to see him, that would be up to him. He was supposed to return in an hour or so.

Rosenberg said he was happy to wait that long to see if His Excellency, as Renée informed them was the proper designation for a bishop, rang up. Renée made a pot of tea.

Twenty minutes later, the phone rang. Jurek grabbed it.

"*Pronto*," he said.

"Jurek? Is it really you?" That voice! It was unmistakable.

"Yes, it's me, Jurek!"

"Where are you?"

"I am at home. I live here now, in Rome."

"You must come to me *immediately*," his friend said.

He did not bother to rub it in to Rosenberg, but dropped him at his house on the way to the Polish Institute. He was there within fifteen minutes. A pleasant nun opened the door and summoned a priest, a young fellow who introduced himself as Stanislaw Dziwisz, the archbishop's personal secretary. Father Dziwisz led him to a small, plain waiting room with the usual crucifix and, on a wall opposite, an image that Jurek recognized as the Black Madonna of Czestochowa. He felt at once as if he had been dropped into a Catholic home from his past, and yet he was also conscious of being very much out of place.

He did not have long to ponder further. He heard Lolek's voice and peeked out to see him coming down the stairs. He was wearing a cassock with a red sash and was flanked by two older gentlemen who were similarly attired but with a different shade of red. Jurek stepped into the hall.

His friend rushed down to him and silently embraced him with a bear hug. Then he introduced him to Cardinal Wyszynski and John Cardinal Krol of Philadelphia, who, surprisingly, acknowledged him in Polish.

"My schoolmate and dear friend," Archbishop Wojtyla called Jurek, keeping his arm around him.

"You'll have to excuse me," Jurek said to him. "I don't know what to call you now. I'm not exactly familiar with the proper form of address.'"

"You will call me Lolek, of course, as always, Jurek."

The archbishop led him down the hall to the spare, small room where he had stayed in Rome for the past few years during the sessions of the Council. There was a narrow bed and a desk heaped with books and papers. In a corner, Jurek noticed to his amusement, stood a pair of skis.

Jurek thought that his friend looked fit and remarkably the same except for his hair, which was turning white. Lolek immediately expressed his sorrow for what had happened to Jurek's family. Jurek in turn supposed that Lieutenant Wojtyla must have passed on, as he would be nearly ninety. They talked for quite a while about their fathers, and for the first time, Jurek revealed his feelings about the war. On the bright side, he mentioned Renée and the children.

"Let's take a walk," the archbishop suggested.

The part of Rome near the Vatican and within sight of the Castel Sant' Angelo was especially beautiful. Jurek felt as if they had been apart only a short time, especially when Lolek talked about their former classmates in great detail, even down to the names of their wives and children. As curious as he was about them, Jurek also found it painful to hear all those names again. Then his friend said something that absolutely threw him: on the following Saturday, Zdzislaw Bernas's son was being confirmed. The archbishop was invited and was planning to go; Jurek should come, too. It would be a wonderful excursion.

"Bernas? But where is he? I haven't seen him practically since the battle of Monte Cassino!" Jurek exclaimed.

"You haven't? Why, he's here in Italy, at Eboli. He married an Italian, and he's a dentist there. Are you free?" the archbishop asked.

"I'll drive us," Jurek offered.

"I'm an early riser," Wojtyla said.

"Shall we leave at sunrise? You're sure it's all right for me to come?"

"Why wouldn't it be?"

"Well, a Jew at a confirmation?" Jurek wondered.

The archbishop only laughed and said not to worry, it would not turn him into a Catholic.

EBOLI LIES IN THE CAMPANIA, BELOW NAPLES AND INLAND FROM THE AMALFI Coast and Salerno. On the drive, Archbishop Wojtyla was ebullient.

When he wasn't reading from his breviary, he was asking Jurek about Monte Cassino, of which he said all Poles remained immensely proud. Of course, the destruction had been terrible, but at last the monastery had been almost completely restored. And he also spoke with enthusiasm about some of the reforms enacted at the Council, which would be concluding in December. Only a month earlier, they had finally passed a document concerning the Jews, which had taken years to work out and which, among other resolutions, condemned anti-Semitism as a sin. It would hardly solve the problem, but it was a start.

Jurek said that he had heard about it, but he could not resist commenting, "Better late than never."

At Eboli, Jurek stayed at the Bernas house and the archbishop stayed in the local rectory. Jurek had a wonderful time, reminiscing with Bernas about the II Polish Corps and entertaining everyone with stories of some of his unofficial activities during the Italian campaign, such as driving off one night for a poker game in a small town only to find his Jeep completely dismantled by thieves when he was ready to drive back to his base. That had been a narrow escape from court martial! After he threatened to call in the artillery to flatten the town, the Jeep reappeared a couple of hours later, miraculously reassembled.

At the confirmation ceremony, he did not feel out of place and enjoyed the gentle teasing he received from the archbishop about newfound piety.

That Christmas, the Klugers received a card and a letter from Archbishop Wojtyla, signed simply "Karol," with a small cross drawn beside the name, which Jurek earned was customary for a bishop. He was looking forward to his next visit to Rome, he said, and to meeting Renée and the children. Jurek carefully saved these and all the other communications that he began finding in the post from his old friend. He did not know how Lolek found the time to be so attentive.

GRADUALLY, ALMOST IMPERCEPTIBLY, THE RENEWAL OF THEIR FRIENDSHIP began to change Jurek's life. Every time the archbishop came to Rome, Father (soon Monsignor) Dziwisz would ring up and ask if

Jurek was available—which, needless to say, he always was. Lolek was not much concerned with food and drank only a single glass of wine at meals; it was the conversation and the companionship that clearly meant most to him.

Sometimes the archbishop would bring another friend or two along, almost always Polish priests or bishops such as Andrzej (later Cardinal) Deskur, of whom Jurek was especially fond. He was quite familiar with the Deskurs, although he had never actually met one before. Theirs had been one of the great names in Polish nobility; their family castle was once the seat of power in Sancygniow, where Deskur had been born in 1924. His had been a late vocation; he had started out studying law and had not entered the seminary in Krakow until after the war. With his brush-cut, still-blond hair and his rather blunt, humorous manner, he no more fit any ecclesiastical stereotype than his friend did. And like the archbishop, he was entirely unaffected in the company of a Jew, acting neither diffident nor solicitous.

Deskur seemed especially attentive when the archbishop described the musical evenings at the house on Zatorska Street. He asked Jurek the names of the regular and alternate members of Dr. Kluger's string quartet in case he knew any of them, which, as it turned out, he did. Mikolaj Kuczkowski, who was a young lawyer when Jurek knew him, was now a priest as well as a doctor of laws and was actually the Chancellor of the Krakow Curia under Archbishop Wojtyla.

FOR JUREK, COMING TO KNOW CATHOLIC CLERGY NOT JUST AS PRIESTS BUT AS human beings who treated him not only as an equal but, oddly, almost as a colleague was both gratifying and reassuring. He had no doubt that there were still plenty of anti-Semites in the Vatican, but in the archbishop's company, he wouldn't meet any. And he was certain that he was not being fooled by anyone, since he prided himself on being able to sniff out even the most dissembling of anti-Semites. He was even better at it since his marriage to Renée, who would warn him of hidden prejudices held by Christians. In her view, it was the unusual Christian who was not at heart an anti-Semite, an observation that Jurek suspected was as true as it was disheartening. His father would probably not have believed it. Did Lolek? Jurek wondered. Someday he would ask him.

It was not until some years later that Jurek learned why Bishop Deskur was such an avid supporter of Israel, which was by no means a general sentiment among the clergy in those days, even after Vatican II.

Through a cousin, Jurek learned that Bishop Deskur had visited Israel and was received there with great affection. He asked the bishop about it the next time he saw him in Rome. It was true, Bishop Deskur said, that although it had been purely a private visit, he had been welcomed effusively in Israel from the minute he stepped off the plane. He had scarcely been able to pay for a taxi or a meal. It seemed that people there knew all about how the Deskurs had helped Jews in Poland during the war.

He had been only a boy then, about eighteen or nineteen, living in the family castle, which, for some reason, the Germans had ignored. One day, his father told him and his younger brother that a family of Jews was hiding in the woods. It was too dangerous to take them into the house, but the brothers were told to take baskets of food out to the starving family. The bishop had never forgotten the sight of them. A dozen or more were living together in a hole that they had dug in the ground and covered with branches. Like hunted animals, they were frightened and emaciated; it was a terrible sight for a boy who had grown up privileged.

For weeks, Andrzej and his brother carried food, blankets, and clothing to them. In the winter, the family was allowed to hide in the basement so that they wouldn't freeze to death; they remained there for two years. Bishop Deskur kept up with them and now wrote to them in Israel, where they had settled after the war. Other families had helped Jews, too, he explained. Besides, he had only acted as his father had instructed. It was the way he had been brought up.

AFTER ARCHBISHOP WOJTYLA WAS MADE A CARDINAL ON JUNE 26, 1967, HE visited Rome frequently, often several times a year. His Eminence, as he was now properly addressed, was still the same man, only busier. Yet, as always, he found time to go to the seaside to swim or to travel to the nearest ski slopes in the Apennines. It was nothing compared to the Tatras, he and Jurek agreed, but it was a wonderful respite all the same.

Jurek had no illusions about what he provided the cardinal in the way of companionship. He could not discuss philosophy with him or even music, the way his father could have. They often talked about the history of the Jews, however. Jurek got the idea that his friend was becoming increasingly interested in the subject and must have been doing a great deal of reading about it. It pleased him to think that he was becoming a sort of unofficial consultant to the cardinal in this field. When the cardinal spoke about the death camps, he continually made the point that although many Catholic Poles had been killed, it was usually because of underground activities or outspokenness, whereas the Jews had been murdered simply for being Jews. That was of intense moral concern to him, along with the entire phenomenon of death camps.

Aside from such discussions, their friendship was what it had always been since childhood, just two fellows who enjoyed each other's company sharing an evening of relaxed conversation or a skiing trip.

As an incorrigibly competitive person, Jurek could not help reminding his friend, albeit gently, that no matter how many years had passed, he was still the better skier. Neither of them, however, could match Monsignor Dziwisz, who would take off by himself and zip down the most challenging runs like Jean-Claude Killy. It turned out that the monsignor had been a top ski instructor at Rabka, a resort in the Tatras. It was on the slopes that Wojtyla, at about the time he became a bishop, first met him.

Bit by bit, Jurek's friend was giving him back his past. Jurek also realized that the cardinal was altogether conscious of this and of how their relationship would ultimately provide Jurek with a spiritual peace that otherwise would never have been his.

Before meeting up with Wojtyla again, Jurek had done a fairly thorough job of erasing memories, or of keeping them at bay. He lived his life as if it had begun around 1944, perhaps when he'd met Renée at the Ghezirah. His father had been his last link to Poland, and when Dr. Kluger died, that link was severed.

And there was one other reminder. While in Munich on business in 1958, Jurek visited the art museum during a free hour. There he saw something that made him very angry—a canvas entitled "Morning after a Pogrom," by Wojcieck Kossak, which showed a Jew lying dead in the street and a Cossack riding away. He was sure that it was one of several canvases that he remembered hanging in his father's office in Wadowice. He felt like shouting "This belongs to me!" and ripping it off the wall, but he did not care to be arrested, and in Germany at that.

He went at once to see the director of the museum and said simply, "I want this painting. How do I claim it?" This turned out to be a long process for which he had to hire an attorney. Three months later, he succeeded in having the painting taken down and removed from its frame; on the back were the words, "Property of Wilhelm Kluger." Obviously, the Germans had looted it from Dr. Kluger's office, and it had ended up in the museum somehow.

Jurek got the painting. Now it hung on his own wall in the Parioli apartment as a reminder, but one that he was glad to have.

IN 1968, JUST AFTER JUREK RECEIVED A LETTER FROM CARDINAL WOJTYLA DEscribing their thirtieth class reunion, which he had hosted as promised at the Archbishop's Palace, another old acquaintance from Wadowice wrote to him. Her name was Danuta Zajacowa-Kurczewska, and she was now a lawyer in Wadowice. It was a very long, emotional letter. She had always loved Jurek, she said, and had even had a crush on him when they were in high school—something that was news to him.

She said that her father, who had been a friend of Dr. Kluger's, was administrator of housing in the town after the war. In visiting various buildings, he discovered that Mrs. Kaminski, the wife of one of the members of the string quartet, had saved something that Jurek's mother had given her when the family was evicted from their house and forced into the ghetto. It was a bust of his mother, and she wondered if Jurek would like to have it. The sculptor, Jozef Jura, Stanislaw Jura's uncle, had cleaned it up, refusing payment for the service.

Of course, Danuta remembered, Mrs. Kaminski's daughter had been Tesia's closest friend. And Danuta, Tesia, and the Kaminski girl had all been students of Mrs. Szczepanska, who had helped Lolek's father take care of him. Danuta told Jurek that the older woman remembered him fondly and sent her love. Everyone was so happy to know, as they had learned from Lolek, that Jurek was alive and well in Rome after all the tragedy that had befallen his family. She said that he might also like to know that she was living in a house that a Jewish family, the Korns, had deeded to her in 1943 before they were sent to Auschwitz.

Obviously, the cardinal must have given her the address. Suddenly the past was alive again, and now he did not try to resist it. Danuta managed to get permission to leave Poland, which was not an easy task then, and traveled by train to Vienna, where Jurek met her and drove her to Rome. He was astonished to find that she had with her not only the bust of his mother but also three paintings, rolled up in newspapers to disguise them from customs, that had belonged to the Klugers. The Kaminskis had squirreled them away just on the chance that Jurek and his father had survived the war. But until their beloved Lolek had seen him, no one had known his fate, or where on Earth he might be. Danuta had also collected many photographs of himself, his family, his classmates, and others from the old days. She was sorry that there were not more. Everyone had misplaced things or had them destroyed during the war.

She kept one item for last—his old Hebrew prayer book. Mrs. Kaminski had saved that, too. Danuta could not remember how Mrs. Kaminski had obtained it, but perhaps Jurek's mother had given it to her along with the bust. Rozalia certainly would not have wanted the Gestapo to get hold of it when they took over the house on Zatorska Street. Yes, there was his name, inscribed by him in childish script, and the date, 1931.

Holding it with trembling hands, practically unable to speak,

Jurek felt as if he had just come from synagogue on some Saturday long ago. He managed to muster: "Just now, I can feel Rabbi Seltenreich giving me an elbow in the ribs!"

He did not know how to thank Danuta. None of this was from her alone, she said. All of those in Wadowice who loved him and his family sent them. She hoped that he had not forgotten how loved and respected his family had been. She understood that it was difficult to remember, with all that had happened.

"DEAR LOLEK," JUREK WROTE TO CARDINAL WOJTYLA ON JANUARY 14, 1975. "You know my granddaughter, Stephania, named after my poor sister. She is now four-and-a-half years old." The decision to name Linda's child after Tesia had been a general and spontaneous one in the family. The infant had at once reminded Jurek of his sister, and when Wojtyla first saw the blond child, he also was taken aback and said, "It's Tesia." From the beginning, her grandfather babbled to her in Polish baby talk, and by the time she was two, he had begun reciting Polish nursery rhymes to her. Renée and the others teased him about it, asking how he could expect the child to understand a syllable of what he was saying, but he couldn't help it, the phrases just tumbled out. In his letter, Jurek continued:

> She speaks English and Italian, and I have been telling her a few little Polish verses, e.g., "A Cat Got on the Fence," and then some legends about the Dragon of Wawel, Pan Tvardowski, and others. [Pan Tvardowski, whom Mickiewicz wrote about, was a merry, drunken rogue who made a pact with the Devil in return for limitless drink, women, and money. He had to surrender his soul in a tavern called Rome, and the Devil strung him from the moon.] But all I have is my memory. I can't find any Polish children's books here in Rome. Recently, little Stephania got appendicitis and was recovering in a clinic here. A priest assigned to the hospital made his rounds and came to see her. Somehow Stephania figured out that the priest is a Pole and straightaway she began to sing "A Cat Got on the Fence." The priest started to cry. And after that he went to see her twice every day, and was telling her all those wonderful legends we knew. And he brought

her a Polish wall calendar, each month showing an illustration and a few verses from a legend. Now Stephania is out of hospital and sort of pestering me to tell her all the details of those legends. "What does Tvardowski look like," etc. Could you by any chance get me any bibliographical background on these legends, so that perhaps I can find them in print? I would be very thankful.

I was very saddened to hear of Stanislaw Banas's death. How I remember his beautiful carriage and horses! When you'll be in Rome, please let me know. I repeat my best wishes for the New Year.

Jurek

P.S. I am sorry that this letter is not perfect, but I never was a great "man of letters"!

About two weeks later, Jurek received this reply:

Dear Jurek,

I am deeply moved by your letter of 14 January, and I thank you with all my heart for everything that you have written in it. It is truly beautiful that your granddaughter is so interested in Polish songs and Polish legends. I am going to help enrich the resources of your memory.

I shall be in Rome from the 3rd to the 8th of March. At that time I must see, not only you, but also little Stephania. You will be in touch by phone with Rev. Dziwisz, to arrange everything. On December 30th we had a celebration of the thirty-five-year anniversary of our high school graduation, and on that occasion we drank to the health of the absent ones.

The New Year is here, and I wish you, and with special underlining for Stephania, all the best.

Karol

A few days after Jurek received the letter, a large box full of Polish children's books arrived from Krakow. He began reading them to Stephania right away, paraphrasing them into English and Italian. That March, he took Stephania to a tea at the Polish College on the Aventina to see Cardinal Wojtyla, her "Uncle Lolek," who held her in his lap and kissed her and recited verses for her. *Mala Tesia*, he kept calling her in Polish: "Little Tesia."

Chapter 22

JUREK'S RENEWED FRIENDSHIP WITH WOJTYLA WAS NOT WITHOUT ITS DISturbing consequences. While the cardinal spoke warmly about his encounters with classmates, Jurek preferred not to contemplate how disturbing such experiences would be for him, especially in Poland. In attempting to bury his past, he was no different from most Holocaust survivors who kept their nightmares to themselves and remained silent about the positive, enriching Jewish life in Central and Eastern Europe before the war. As Chicago Rabbi Byron L. Sherwin has written, during the 1950s and 1960s, "American Jews were engaged in an exercise in amnesia, trying hard to forget their largely East European roots." What was true of American Jews also described Jurek.

In 1939, more than eighty percent of all Jews in the world were either living in Poland or descended from people who had lived within historic Polish boundaries. Now Poland was a Jewish graveyard far away and, since it was under Communist rule, not easily visited. As with all the Iron Curtain countries, it was rare to hear or read about Poland, except during rebellions and other political crises. The nation had been shamefully sold out by the Allies at Yalta, as Harold Macmillan sorrowfully admitted in his 1949 introduction to General Anders's memoirs, and became something of a nonsubject in the West, like a child given away at birth. Only leftist intellectuals could defend its surrender to Stalin as anything but a betrayal of the Atlantic Charter and of the pledges the Allies made in declaring war on Hitler to begin with. All of this encouraged forgetfulness.

Even discussion of the Holocaust was rare during the first quarter-century after the war. Raul Hilberg, whose monumental, three-volume *The Destruction of the European Jews* appeared in its first version in 1962, remembers the indifference of the 1940s and 1950s: "During those days, the academic world was oblivious to the subject, and publishers found it unwelcome. In fact, I was advised much more often not to pursue this topic than to persist in it."

This avoidance or collective denial encouraged the sense of isolation that Jurek experienced. Moreover, married to a Catholic, he moved almost completely in a Gentile world, and except for his partner, Rosenberg, he had few Jewish friends. The Klugers' social life centered around mostly Gentile tennis clubs. Tennis was for him not only a passion but a means of acculturation, and an effective one, whether in Leeds, at the grander All England Croquet and Lawn Tennis Club (Wimbledon), or at the Parioli, Positano, and other enclaves of privileged sport. He could still outplay most men his age—and make useful business contacts as well.

"The riches of a soul are stored up in its memory," the Polish-American rabbi and philosopher Abraham Joshua Heschel wrote in 1951, distressed by the extent to which Jews were denying their past, as if the Holocaust had wiped out hundreds of years of precious culture and experience. "This is the test of character—not whether a person follows the daily fashion but whether the past is alive in his present. When we want to understand ourselves, to find out what is most precious in our lives, we search our memory."

Jurek did attend Rosh Hashanah and other holiday services, alone, and then his memory was rekindled in a brief flicker. But he found this a nearly unbearable burden. Services at the Great Temple in Rome, which derive from the oldest rites known in Europe, seemed almost foreign to him. And the texture and spirit of Jewish life as he had known it in Wadowice had vanished. At home, there was no one to light the candles on Friday nights. His daughters were raised as Catholics. Stephania, whose mother, like many of her generation, believed in letting children pursue their own religion, had not been baptized. In order for his grandchild to become a Jew, she would have to choose to convert. By Jewish law, since her mother was not Jewish, she was not. With his father gone, Jurek was the last of the Jewish Klugers.

In bringing the past alive for him, the cardinal *was making him feel more Jewish.* It was as if his core, which had been dormant or even moribund, were coming alive again. And as difficult as it was to deal with the avalanche of memories and sensations that his friend's presence released, the result was on the whole a positive one.

His family noticed it. He seemed more cheerful. He did not explode as often into rages ignited by some trivial irritation. Renée and his daughters assumed that his love for Stephania was the cause. It was, in part, but Jurek dimly understood that Lolek was somehow the key. To Renée, there was one singular difference in him. He had begun to talk about his past as he never had before and to take an interest, even a passionate one, in Jewish subjects. She was astonished to discover the depth of his feelings and the strength of his opinions in areas that he had barely mentioned in the nearly thirty years that they had known each other.

On May 17, 1971, for instance, Cardinal Wojtyla was in Rome to act as concelebrator—along with cardinals Wyszynski and Krol and other dignitaries—at the mass of beatification for Father Maximillian Kolbe, which was to be celebrated by Pope Paul VI. It was the first time in history that a mass of beatification was being celebrated by a pope himself. Some fifteen hundred other Poles came to Saint Peter's for the occasion, which was extensively covered by the media. Jurek, with his friend a participant, took an intense interest in proceedings that he otherwise would have ignored, and he watched the mass on television.

The man Father Kolbe had saved from execution at Auschwitz, Franciszek Gajowniczek, was in the basilica that morning. At a press conference before the ceremony, Cardinal Wojtyla observed that Father Kolbe had not only saved one man out of ten condemned that day in the death camp, he had also shown the other nine how to die.

His act of heroism "had made life more human in a place of supreme inhumanity" and was eloquent in the cause of universal justice.

All this was indisputable. But Jurek remembered something else about Father Kolbe, or Saint Maximillian, as he was soon certain to be known. Was this not the same Franciscan who had been the founder and a director of the publishing house that issued *Maly Dziennik*, the most anti-Semitic of any Church-affiliated daily newspaper in Poland before the war? Did Kolbe himself therefore not bear some responsibility for disseminating the type of propaganda that, while it played no role in the German invasion of Poland, had contributed to the atmosphere that made the Holocaust possible? This, of course, included the murders of Jurek's grandmother, mother, sister, and other relatives.

A scrupulous examination of the record showed that Father Kolbe's own writings indicated that personally he had not been an anti-Semite. He had opposed the boycotting of Jewish shops—although more on the grounds that this did nothing to improve Catholic Polish trade than because such discrimination was intrinsically immoral. Not only had he opposed the Nazis, but his outspokenness had landed him in Auschwitz.

From a Catholic point of view, the definition of Father Kolbe's saintliness was inherent in the manner of his death. Even if Father Kolbe was guilty in life of a sort of passive anti-Semitism, surely his anti-Nazism and indisputable heroism in death might outweigh that fault.

From the Jewish point of view, however, the issue was not so much Father Kolbe himself or even his personal connection to an anti-Semitic newspaper. It was that he was a priest and that by sponsoring such newspapers, the Church in Poland and throughout Europe abetted racial hatred and played into Nazi hands. This was an argument that few Catholics were willing to concede at that time.

Jurek had no question about where he stood in this matter: a man who was a founder-director of a viciously anti-Semitic newspaper ought not to become a candidate for sainthood unless the circumstances of his martyrdom had involved saving a Jew's life. In taking this position, he was in agreement with prominent Jews in

America and Israel, who expressed misgivings about the Kolbe beatification. The matter was especially sensitive because at this time the Communist Polish government itself refused to acknowledge that Jews comprised the overwhelming majority of the victims murdered at Auschwitz. To beatify Father Kolbe, it seemed, further minimized Jewish martyrdom.

It was certainly not something that Jurek chose to argue about with Cardinal Wojtyla when the two saw each other for dinner that week. Perhaps if their renewed friendship had been beyond the infancy stage, he would have felt more comfortable discussing the matter. Yet he sensed that his friend would agree that as a Jew, Jurek ought to believe as he did and be troubled by an event that brought back harsh memories.

The paradoxes of Father Kolbe, which reached deeply into centuries of Christian-Jewish relations, could hardly be resolved as part of dinner conversation. To deny sainthood to Father Kolbe because of the taint of anti-Semitism made sense to Jurek and many other Jews. But if this were accepted and acted upon, it would call into question a disturbingly large proportion of the calendar of saints compiled throughout millennia because so many of them were virulent anti-Semites. To use this as a criterion of disqualification from sainthood would throw the entire history of canonization into doubt.

In *The City of God*, Saint Augustine clearly defines the diaspora as punishment for the Jews' having killed Christ. Saint Jerome wrote that the Jews' "prayers and psalms are like the inarticulate cries of animals." And in 386, Saint John Chrysostom called Jews "unclean and savage beasts" and stigmatized Judaism as "a mockery, a parody, and a disgrace" to religion. "God has forsaken the Jews," Saint John added, "because they have denied the Father, crucified the Son.... Henceforth their synagogue is the house of demons and idolatry." The effects of such rhetoric were demonstrated in 1099 by the Crusaders who, when they captured Jerusalem, set fire to the synagogue after trapping Jews inside.

So deeply embedded has anti-Semitism been within Christian thought that even the most liberal Catholic philosophers have been blind to its presence. Jacques Maritain, who defended the civil rights of Jews against the Nazis, still denied the merit of Judaism as a living religion. He cited its value only as a prelude to Christianity.

In questioning the beatification of Father Kolbe, Jurek and others touched on issues more pervasive in Christianity than any of them knew. When saints and broad-minded philosophers denigrate Jews, how grave was Father Kolbe's sin of compliance with ideas that were promoted by the Church? Was the manner of his death redeeming? These are questions that are not easily resolved. Nor did Jurek know how deeply this history troubled Cardinal Wojtyla or how different he was from even the most progressive Catholic thinkers before him. Only after the cardinal was elected pope in 1978 did Jurek and others begin to understand that John Paul II would make the reversal of a lamentable Catholic record the major theme of his papacy. His unprecedented Catholic affirmation of the eternal validity of Judaism, an idea that was previously inconceivable, would demonstrate this theme most dramatically.

Likewise, only after John Paul assumed the papacy did his friendship with Jurek come into full flower and then evolve into a union significant beyond itself. Then the saintliness of Father Kolbe could be understood in the light of monumental changes in doctrines and attitudes. Like every human life, his cried out for redemption. His holiness lies in his example, not in every aspect of his life.

THROUGH THE FIRST DOZEN YEARS AFTER WOJTYLA'S ELECTION AS POPE JOHN Paul II, world politics obscured the spiritual motives behind his words and actions. Historians, journalists, and political commentators of all stripes were unanimous toward the end of 1978 that his election would bring change to the Communist countries of Central and Eastern Europe. They disagreed, however, on what the nature or extent of those changes would be, and the question of how this pope actually did affect the eventual collapse of Marxist totalitarianism remains a subject of debate.

Because Wojtyla had, on the surface, actually negotiated on various issues with Polish government officials as a bishop and a cardinal, some anticipated that he would have an ameliorating influence on Cold War tensions. Others, not understanding the strong Western allegiances of the Polish culture and character, imagined that the pope would focus primarily on rapprochement with Eastern Orthodox churches, effecting a Christian alliance behind the Iron Curtain. Within Poland itself, however, those who knew Wojtyla well, including his surviving high school classmates, believed at once and with complete certainty that one way or another, his papacy meant the end of Communism in Poland and probably in all the other Soviet satellites. They could not spell out exactly how this would happen; they were simply convinced of it. The most common metaphor they used in talking about it among themselves or in thinking about it was that Karol Wojtyla's election would be the final nail in the Communists' coffin.

When millions turned out to greet His Holiness during his first visit to Poland as pope (June 2–10, 1979), they sensed that the end, and a new beginning, would come sooner than anyone outside Poland imagined. As Stanislaw Jura recalls today, "As soon as I heard the news that Karol Wojtyla was pope, I knew the Communists were finished. When we learned he was coming to Poland, we felt that we were already free. That is why we rejoiced so much. Not only for him but for ourselves."

He went to Wadowice on the fifth day of his visit. In an address there, the pope paid tribute to the murdered Jews and mentioned how pleased he was to have Jurek Kluger living near him in Rome. With all of the frenzied media attention he was receiving, he took time out to meet with those of his classmates who could be notified of his visit, talking with them for a half-hour at the Parish House across the street from the Church of Our Lady. In the short time available, he let them know that he hoped that his election would not mean the end of class reunions. He invited everyone in the class to come to Rome as soon as possible. This honor that had come to him brought with it grave responsibilities, he said, and he needed their love and support as always. He doubted, he said in that pointed, humorous way he had, that the government would deny any of them permission to travel. It was not difficult to imagine what outrage a refusal to let his classmates visit their friend would cause. As for the cost, he indicated that some way would be found to assist those who could not afford the journey. For most, it would be their first trip outside Poland since World War II.

And so a small, intimately experienced instance of what were becoming astounding changes did occur. On September 18, only three months after the pope had personally invited them, ten of his classmates arrived at the Fiumicino Airport in Rome, where they were greeted by Jurek, Rosenberg, and two Polish priests. Nine others arrived from England, Canada, and elsewhere, with their wives. Among them they represented a broad range of occupations and life experiences. Most had fought in World War II, either in the army or in the underground. One was not actually a member of the same high school class but was the brother of twin classmates killed during the war, one at Auschwitz and the other in the Middle East. Many had experienced difficulties with the postwar Communist regime, including imprisonment on false or accurate charges of sedition. They had earned their livings in a variety of ways: there was a doctor and Jagiellonian professor; an economist-scholar; a clerk; an airline pilot; coal miners and mine officials; a lawyer; a trade official; a chocolate factory worker and official; a furniture maker; a road worker and beekeeper; a physical therapist; a forester; a dentist—and, of course, an importer of tractors to England and Italy. They had in common, aside from being classmates, their love and admiration for Wojtyla.

For Jurek, this reunion, which lasted day and night for a full week, was uniquely emotional. For more than thirty years, he had avoided returning to Poland. Then had come the reunions with Wojtyla, the reappearance of certain precious objects and a few people from his past, a certain partial recovery of identity—and now, en masse, as it were, so many of those still alive from his past had descended on Rome! The faces, the stories, the embraces—it was all quite overwhelming. And he, the only surviving Jew among them, became their guide to the Holy City and other sites, leading them on side trips to Assisi and Monte Cassino. It was Jurek, too, who arranged for their accommodations and meals at the Pensione Anita, which was on the Via Domingo near the Vatican and where, as Teofil Bojes said,

"We drank quite a bit of good wine which did not go to the head." (Jurek had supplied the wine from his own small vineyard.)

For Renée, the experience was intense in another way. Few of the visitors had ever been in a capitalist country, and she led exhausting, although far from extravagant, shopping expeditions and entertained the lot of them at dinner in the Kluger apartment. When she had the chance to speak to His Holiness later that week, she told him that in her next life, she hoped that he might arrange for her to be reincarnated as a man. He found the remark hilarious and promised to see what he could do.

The pilgrims saw their favorite classmate twice during general audiences in Saint Peter's Square, when he alighted from his Jeep to mingle with the crowd and greeted them individually and talked about his plans for visits to Ireland and the United States. But Sunday, September 23, was reserved for the actual reunion, which the pope himself had planned to be as much as possible like the ones they had enjoyed in Wadowice and Krakow. At five that afternoon, led by Jurek—who was happy to show them that he knew his way around the Vatican and was a familiar presence to the Swiss Guards—they ascended to the large reception room in the papal apartments.

Jurek was glad to see the results of the renovations since his last visit here. Where all had been dark and dingy, light poured through tall windows; the carpet had been pulled up to reveal the polished marble floor, white with green borders and with the papal seal showing the keys of Saint Peter at the center. The brightness and airiness was much more like Lolek, he thought. Others, Catholics who were aware of this change, understood it in the symbolic sense that this pope, with his love of physical beauty, was restoring not just a suite of rooms but a sense of joy in life to the Church. It was during this period that he also approved the cleaning of Michelangelo's Sistine Chapel frescoes, whose brilliant colors began to show through centuries of neglect.

After a few minutes' conversation, the classmates assembled in the pope's private chapel, a contemporary granite-and-marble structure that held about thirty people. It had been installed in the papal apartments under Paul VI, and John Paul had left it intact except for the addition of a large image of the Black Madonna of Czestochowa to the right of the silver crucifix behind the altar. After mass, when everyone assembled again in the reception hall, Bojes presented the pope with two gifts on behalf of the class, a miner's lamp and a statue of Jesus the Mountaineer, made by the people of the Tatras. Jurek was teased about attending the mass; but he was quick to say that it was hardly his first and would not be his last. "It does everyone some good," the pope said with a deep chuckle, then led them all in to dinner.

It was just like old times, or almost. As had long been their custom, they talked about their lives and families and discussed news of the absent ones, enjoying the Polish food and Italian wine. Plans were laid for 1983, the forty-fifth anniversary of their *Matura*, and they heard the Holy Father say that, of course, the reunion would take place again in Rome, or perhaps next time at Castel Gandolfo, the papal summer palace. At a certain point, after many toasts, they began singing the old songs, with the pope's voice deeper and more powerful than any other. From the doorway of the kitchen, the Polish nuns watched, until the pope waved them in to join the chorus.

"Jurek," His Holiness suggested to his friend at the far end of the table, "perhaps it would be a good idea if you kept quiet and listened. After all these years, you are still out of tune."

At ten o'clock, Monsignor Dziwisz came into the room and quietly suggested that the pope had a busy schedule and that perhaps it was time for everyone to retire for the evening.

"You see," the pope said, "even I have to obey someone."

Outside, the rain fell heavily on Saint Peter's Square as the classmates, arm in arm, wound in and out among Bernini's columns, some breaking into snatches of song.

"It is raining," Bojes shouted, "but ours is a heavenly mood!"

THE REUNION WAS NATURALLY THE TALK OF WADOWICE AFTERWARD, NOT SO much because another delegation of Poles had gone to Rome (there was a steady stream of pilgrims from the motherland now) but because with all of his present glory, Wojtyla remained a friend as always. He was meeting with world leaders, traveling around the globe, and writing a profusion of speeches and encyclicals. In subsequent months, the political situation in Poland became further destabilized with the growth of the Solidarity workers' movement and increasing pressure from Moscow.

On December 13, 1979, the Secretariat of the Central Committee of the Soviet Communist Party in Moscow approved a six-point "Decision to Work against the Policies of the Vatican in Relation with Socialist States" (as Tad Szulc first revealed in his 1995 biography of John Paul II), indicating how seriously the Soviets took the papal threat. The pope had neither said nor done anything specifically aimed at toppling the government in Poland or anywhere else. It was simply his presence, the kind of humanity that his classmates knew about better than anyone else, that was becoming a more powerful force in the world than any ideology or army.

During that first visit to Poland, the pope also confronted an issue that was highly sensitive in his native land, as elsewhere: the death camps. On June 7, he visited Auschwitz, where he paid tribute to the millions murdered at the various camps, including Father Kolbe and Edith Stein, a scholar of philosophy who was born Jewish but who became a nun under the name Theresa Benedicta of the Cross and was killed at Auschwitz. He was criticized for supposedly trying to *Christianize* the place where more than a million Jews had perished. The actual speech, however, which was delivered near the gas chambers and was broadcast all over the world, did quite the opposite. It included all the dead and cited the Jews as having specially suffered.

> I have come and I kneel on this Golgotha of the modern world, on these tombs, largely nameless like the great Tomb of the Unknown Soldier. I kneel before all the inscriptions that come one after another bearing the memory of the victims of Oswiecim in the languages: Polish, English, Bulgarian, Romany, Czech, Danish, French, Greek, Hebrew, Yiddish, Spanish, Flemish, Serbo-Croat, German, Norwe-

> gian, Russian, Romanian, Hungarian, and Italian. In particular, I pause with you, dear participants in this encounter, before the inscription in Hebrew.

Those present at this scene of nearly unbearable gravity heard the pope's voice quaver and saw his eyes fill as he concluded:

> This inscription awakens the memory of the people whose sons and daughters were intended for total extermination. This people draws its origin from Abraham, our father in faith, as was expressed by Paul of Tarsus. The very people who received from God the Commandment, "Thou shalt not kill," itself experienced in a special measure what is meant by killing. It is not permissible for anyone to pass by this inscription with indifference.

This statement was entirely characteristic of him in three notable ways. First, it confronted the issue that the Jews had been "intended for total extermination," unlike other victims who were killed for specific activities. Second, it linked Christianity and Judaism together through Abraham, an approach that had increasingly preoccupied Wojtyla, at least since 1940, when he wrote his play *David*. And last, there was his strong use of the phrase "not permissible," to describe the indifference of anyone toward Jewish suffering. This was John Paul II the unwavering moralist. The Jews were the people of the Ten Commandments, the moral foundation of both Judaism and Christianity; to be indifferent to them was to be indifferent to God, the sin against the Holy Spirit itself.

Four months later, while the pope was in the United States, he addressed leaders of the New York Jewish community in Battery Park and sounded similar themes. He quoted Paul VI as saying that "our two communities are connected and closely related at the very level of their respective religious identities," and he called for extensive interfaith dialogue, "inspired by our common biblical heritage."

> As one who in my homeland has shared the suffering of your brethren, I greet you with the word taken from the Hebrew language: *Shalom*! Peace be with you.

It was among the first of dozens of such statements that would mark his papacy and that foreshadowed concrete steps toward ending millennia of alienation between the religions. He was already gaining a reputation in some quarters as a conservative. Actually, what he had in mind was so radical that it had been lost, forgotten, and denied for nearly two thousand years.

JUREK HEARD AND READ ABOUT THESE SPEECHES AND WAS MOVED AND GRATified by them. Then, early in May of 1980, he received a letter from the pope's old neighbor, Mrs. Helena Szczepanska, who was then eighty-five years old. The letter further buoyed his hopes that perhaps John Paul II represented not only a goodness in himself but also one that had been too long dormant in the world, one that could now somehow emerge—or re-emerge. Wherever he went, positive things seemed to be happening. Even in his small and insignificant personal life, Jurek thought as he read Mrs. Szczepanska's remarkable words, a healing was taking place.

She began by saying how well she remembered Jurek and how the pope's visit to Wadowice had brought back many memories. The Holy Father had visited her, and they had talked about Jurek. She was glad to learn that he was happy and well and had a fine family. Then she said some things that were as welcome to Jurek as they were painful, even excruciating, to read.

> You had a fantastic mother. It was not only that [Rozalia Kluger] was so beautiful and so educated and so good, but she was so full of sincerity to everyone around her. She went to school, you know, with my younger sister, who was praising her all the time as someone exceptional. I was, you remember, the teacher of Tesia, only for one year—but at teachers' conferences I was always hearing about what a wonderful student she was. Once we were going on a rather expensive school excursion, and Tesia did not put her name down as one of the participants. So I said to Rozalia, "Why isn't Tesia going?"
>
> "You shouldn't give children everything they want, you know," your mother said. "You never know what life has in store for them."

The last sentence leapt out at Jurek. He could hear his mother saying it. She had always been careful not to let him and Tesia think that simply because they were better off than most people in Wadowice, they should feel above anyone else. Obviously, she had thought that it would be good for Tesia to understand what the poorer girls in her class felt like when they could not afford to go on the field trip. But those last phrases had been so horribly prescient! Writing them, Mrs. Szczepanska had clearly been thinking about what lay ahead for Tesia, Rozalia, and Grandmother Huppert.

> I have a photographic memory. I remember what self-control your mother had when she was taking care of your grandmother. And that she wouldn't leave her. And she said that if God put on us this kind of disaster, we should accept his will. I was so moved by her religious faith. The last time I invited her to tea, she said, "I shan't come anymore, because it will put you in danger."

And so, Jurek thought, up to the end, Mrs. Szczepanska was receiving his mother and trying to comfort her. What more eloquent statement could there be of the helplessness of all? It all boiled down to that, didn't it—the faith of some, and their kindliness, in the face of hate. It must have been painful for Mrs. Szczepanska to write, but she was thinking of him, and she wanted him to know.

> I shouldn't have written this to you and hurt you, breaking open your scars. But the last few years, since I heard from our Lolek that you were alive, I have been thinking of writing to you. I won't put in any more details of those last months I spent with your mother and Tesia. The daughter of my sister is coming to Rome, invited by the pope. Please see her, so I can know that she has met you and been with you. I was very lucky because on 7 June 1979 the Holy Father came to Wadowice and gave me the only private audience!
>
> With all my love and feelings for you,
> Auntie Helena

Jurek wrote back with an overflowing of emotion, and he shared the letters with the pope. When Auntie Helena's niece came to Rome for her own papal audience, Jurek showed her around the city and gave her photographs of himself and his family to take back to Mrs. Szczepanska. Their correspondence became regular. She filled pages with descriptions of family members whom he had been too young to remember or who had died before he was born. She remembered everyone and everything that he had forgotten. She wrote about how he would come with his book bag to visit Lolek and Lieutenant Wojtyla, how much he and Lolek had loved sports, and what joy there had been in those days. She even recalled the times when they were very young that he and Lolek used to play at Grandfather Kluger's clothing shop. They would dress themselves up in gentlemen's suits and pin old veterans' medals on themselves.

"Don't play with those!'" Jurek's paternal grandmother would tell them. "'The next thing we know, you'll be wearing those medals around town!'"

Chapter 23

FROM THE FIRST DAYS OF HIS PAPACY, JOHN PAUL II BROKE BARRIERS OF protocol that had separated most recent pontiffs from ordinary people. Even in old age, he continues to display a lack of Northern European reserve, engaging in embraces that appear more Mediterranean than Polish. What begins as an attempt to kiss the pontiff's ring may result in the pope gripping both of a visitor's hands and exchanging close-up, unblinking eye contact that can make the recipient wish to confess, as to a long-lost uncle who has emerged from obscurity bearing gifts.

At the same time, the pope's moral seriousness, which is apparent in his eyes and in the ironic set of his mouth, induces a childlike resolve to go and sin no more. Both sides of Catholicism, the moral certainty and the boundless absolution, emanate from him. John Paul II actually does believe that all people are made in the likeness of God, and while the concept is reassuring, it imposes a certain burden of conduct.

These are exactly the qualities that have inspired mistrust or even hostility among the pope's critics: if truth is found only in biology, psychology, or one kind of material determinism or another, what right does this man have to assume such a confident, if seemingly benevolent, demeanor? The massive crowds that collect wherever he visits and react to him with tremendous enthusiasm make him all the more suspect. He is a polarizing figure. The ordinary and uneducated are drawn to him, and secular intellectuals are repelled, although he is a man of learning who is superbly capable in many fields. For those with great intelligence schooled in the modern way, he is a paradox of mind and matter and must be rejected.

Such antithetical emotions have also inspired violence. On May 13, 1981, as he was riding through Saint Peter's Square in his open Jeep, someone tried to kill him.

The motives of Mehmet Ali Agca, a Turkish terrorist, have never been proved. That afternoon, one bullet from the would-be assassin's 9mm Browning Parabellum penetrated the pope's abdomen. The second shot missed. A Franciscan nun grabbed at Agca, and others from the crowd wrestled him down. In twelve minutes, an ambulance had the pope at the Agostino Gemelli Polyclinic, where a lengthy operation to remove the bullet and repair his colon and small intestine saved his life. Later, the pope thanked the Virgin and expressed the belief that he had been spared because he had important work left to do.

WHEN JUREK KLUGER HEARD THE NEWS OF THE ASSASSINATION ATTEMPT, HE reacted at first with fury, then with grief. It was the first time his daughters and granddaughter had ever seen him cry.

In the next few days, he received good news from Monsignor Dziwisz, who was present during the attack and had administered the last rites to an unconscious John Paul. The monsignor reported that the Holy Father was recovering from his wounds and would likely regain full health. Jurek visited the pope in the hospital three days after the shooting and again a week later. "It is all that skiing and mountain climbing that has saved him," Jurek said to Renée about the pope's recovery, "and we can give the Blessed Virgin some credit, too."

On June 12, Jurek again went to see his friend, who was still in the Gemelli clinic. Monsignor Dziwisz was waiting for him on the tenth floor, where the pope was residing. John Paul, fully dressed, was sitting in a chair and writing something. Jurek had little time in which to express his concern and his joy at seeing his friend alive. Instead of encountering an invalid, as he had expected, he found a vigorous man who was anxious to talk about a subject of mutual concern: relations between the Vatican and the Jews.

Earlier that week, eight F-16 Israeli fighter-bombers had dropped two thousand bombs on Iraq's nuclear reactor at Tuwaitha, near Baghdad, destroying Iraq's capacity to manufacture atomic weapons. (Iraq insisted that the installation was for peaceful purposes only, but that assertion was not widely believed.) In the Soviet Union and Western Europe, the reaction to this preemptive strike was indignation; in the United States, it prompted a milder degree of condemnation. In Israel, there was a general feeling of euphoria. Prime Minister Begin, who was in the middle of campaigning for a June 30 election, defended the action at a press conference, saying, "There won't be another Holocaust in history. Never again, never again. We shall defend our people with all the means at our disposal."

Without commenting directly on the Israeli action, the pope volunteered a brief homily on the sort of situation in which Poles and Jews alike often seemed to find themselves. American Jews were always verbally attacking Poland for its anti-Semitism, almost as if it had been the Poles and not the Germans who built and operated the death camps. Meanwhile, anti-Semitism in Poland remained strong, even as the number of Jews remaining there was approaching the vanishing point. At the same time, American Jews were increasingly critical of the Vatican for not granting recognition to Israel, which was experiencing intensified international isolation. It seemed that Poles and Jews—or Catholics and Jews, for that matter—could never be perceived fairly in each other's eyes.

Jurek and His Holiness agreed that the problem had both religious and political dimensions. The Vatican's refusal to grant diplomatic recognition to Israel and its reluctance even to mention the State of Israel by name gave the appearance of denying Jews the right of return to the Holy Land. As things stood, there were no proper diplomatic channels through which Vatican and Israeli representatives could communicate. The pope understood all of this.

"We must do something about that," he said. "Are you willing to help?"

Jurek was quite taken aback. He had come on a sick call, and now this? "Of course I am willing to help," he said, having no idea what that meant. "But what am I to do?"

"Monsignor Dziwisz will be in contact with you," the pope said. "We must proceed cautiously, officially and unofficially."

AS JOHN PAUL PROMISED, MONSIGNOR DZIWISZ TELEPHONED JUREK AT HIS office to suggest that a certain Polish monsignor, Janusz Bolonek, who was an official in the Vatican Secretariat of State, would be a good person with whom to talk.

"What am I to say to him?" Jurek asked.

"This is just to open discussions," Monsignor Dziwisz said. "Why don't you go to see him this afternoon? He's expecting you." The monsignor gave him directions to Monsignor Bolonek's office, which was located off a loggia that had been painted by Raphael and was closed to the public.

The Vatican, walled up within a mere one hundred ten acres, is the world's smallest sovereign state, with its own railway station, post office, mint, radio and television studios, publishing house, library, museums, and other entities appropriate to a country. With nearly a billion members, Roman Catholicism is (by a percentage point more than the Muslim faith) the largest religious denomination in the world. As its administrative headquarters, Vatican City exerts a political influence entirely out of proportion to its physical size, with diplomatic representatives in every important nation. From around the world, they report to the Secretariat of State, which in 1981 was headed by Cardinal Casaroli. The man Jurek was going to see, Monsignor Bolonek, was attached to the Polish desk in the department of international relations. The department head, Achille Cardinal Silvestrini, was, in effect, the foreign secretary.

The most difficult thing for an outsider to understand or even imagine about the Vatican Foreign Ministry is that its officials, all of whom are ordained priests, think of themselves as *political* administrators, not religious ones. However illogical it seems, it may be said that the Secretariat of State represents a separation of church and state within the Church. The training that Vatican diplomats receive isn't theological; it more closely resembles the instruction offered by academies of foreign service. But how can there ever be a real distinction between church and state when the Roman Catholic Church is not a state but a religion? While there can be no definitive answer to this reasonable question, it does help to remember that the pre-nineteenth-century Church was a temporal power as well as a spiritual one. Today, its political influence remains enormous, although it now exerts that influence in spiritual rather than political ways—or at least without armed troops.

This distinction between the political and the religious can result in some rather peculiar decisions and judgments, especially when one considers the question of the Vatican's relations with Israel, or the lack of them, in the 1980s. From the Jewish point of view, this lack was clearly both religious and political. From the point of view of the Vatican Foreign Ministry, however, the issue could have no religious dimension at all.

Jurek discovered this attitude when he had the first of his many meetings with Monsignor Bolonek at the Foreign Ministry. He found the monsignor, who was born in the diocese of Lodz in 1938, to be a pleasant and suave, even elegant, fellow. Very much the diplomat, the monsignor showed great awareness of and sensitivity toward Jewish suffering during the war. He had what Jurek considered an unusually thorough appreciation of the contributions of Jews to Polish life and culture before the Holocaust and quickly indicated his personal abhorrence of anti-Semitism. These were certainly among the reasons, along with his being Polish, that Monsignor Dziwisz had chosen him as the man for Jurek to see. Unfortunately, Monsignor Bolonek seemed to know very little about Israel itself. And it was difficult for him to figure the religious dimension of Vatican-Israeli relations into the political equations that he had been trained to calculate.

The Vatican gave twenty-one Arab states some sort of diplomatic recognition, Jurek observed, while it offered Israel none. Why was this? Could it be, Jurek dared to suggest, that there were anti-Semites within the Curia or the College of Cardinals who did not want to see Israel recognized or perhaps even hoped that the Jewish state would eventually disappear?

This was possible, the monsignor admitted, but he would have to study the problem.

"Discretion is everything," Jurek reminded him. "No one must know that the Holy Father has asked us to explore this matter."

Monsignor Bolonek agreed, and Jurek felt that he could trust him. He worried, however, that if the Secretariat of State refused to consider the religious dimensions, progress would be extremely difficult. Officials would consider only the negative results of recognition—offending the Arabs, risking the lives of Middle Eastern Christians, and seeming to endorse Israeli political and military policies—and ignore the positives, namely reconciliation between Catholics and Jews and the gradual defeat of anti-Semitism everywhere. Without the establishment of mutual trust between Rome and Jerusalem, these goals were impossible to achieve.

About this time, Jurek also went to see another, more powerful Polish figure, a man who was perhaps closer to John Paul II than any other high church official—Cardinal Deskur. Sadly, the cardinal, who was only in his midfifties, was partially paralyzed as the result of a serious stroke that occurred during the Papal Conclave in 1978. He was intellectually unimpaired, however, and held the important position of President of the Pontifical Commission on Social Communications.

Cardinal Deskur was extremely receptive to Jurek's ideas. He was also strongly in favor of recognition for Israel, which was unsurprising considering his help to Jews during the war. On his own, he promised to do certain sensitive research. He confided to Jurek that several strong anti-Semites were ensconced in the Secretariat of

State, but he said that he would demand that they give him access to the constitutions of several Arab states, which he suspected of countenancing slavery and other human rights violations. If he could show that the Vatican had relations with such countries, it would provide leverage to force movement on the Israeli matter.

"That is an ingenious idea, Your Eminence," Jurek told him. He was seated in the study within the cardinal's Vatican apartments; on one wall, he noticed a framed photograph of the Deskur family castle near Kielce—now, of course, in the hands of the Communist Polish government. "May I have your permission to inform Minister Nathan Ben-Horin, who has succeeded Dr. Mendes in dealing with matters relating to the Holy See?"

"If you can trust him to keep quiet," Cardinal Deskur said. "By the way, shut that door. You know what the Vatican is like—everybody spying on everybody. You can't imagine! Only Dante could describe it. I'd shut it myself but it takes me so much effort to get into that infuriating wheelchair. What a nuisance!"

"It's a tragedy. I am so sorry," Jurek said. He knew that the cardinal had just returned from a Swiss sanitarium, where even weeks of physical therapy had failed to improve his mobility. He was such a dynamic, congenial person—it was very sad to see him like this, although he seemed to be without self-pity.

"I tell you what the real tragedy is, *Ingegnere* Kluger. Do you want to know?" asked Cardinal Deskur.

"What is that, Eminence?" Jurek responded.

"The real tragedy is, I can no longer play bridge. I can't hold the cards with my one good hand and play them! It was my greatest pleasure, and now it's lost." Deskur continued that it was a shame for poor Cardinal Rubin, too, because he had lost his bridge partner. "He doesn't win so often now, without me!" he laughed.

Not long after this meeting, Jurek happened to see a televised championship bridge match and noticed that one player, a partially paralyzed woman, had her cards lined up on a specially designed holder. Kurt Rosenberg was very talented at digging up obscure items such as this, and soon he found one at a medical supply shop.

When Jurek called on Cardinal Deskur again, he presented the gadget to him, along with a fresh deck of cards. The device worked well for the cardinal, and he was so delighted and grateful that he invited Jurek to come back one evening the following week for a match and to bring anyone he liked as a fourth. "But he'd better be good," the cardinal cautioned. "Cardinal Rubin and I are no pushovers!"

So it was that Jurek began playing bridge regularly with the two cardinals. Led by his competitive instinct, he took along one of the top players in Europe, Dr. Wolf Gross, a professor of mathematics at the University of Rome, who was a Grand Master. They did not play as a team but switched sides with each game in an atmosphere of great conviviality that was aided by a glass or two of wine.

Jurek, of course, took every opportunity to bring up the matter of Israel, reporting on what were now his frequent meetings with Monsignor Bolonek, whom he often took to dinner at the Parioli Tennis Club. Cardinal Deskur provided him with thumbnail sketches of men in the Curia. "Watch out for that one," the cardinal said of a certain archbishop. "He's no good. He's a vicious anti-Semite and probably should be exiled."

Cardinal Rubin was less humorously volatile than Deskur, whose aristocratic self-confidence allowed him to blurt out anything he thought, but he was also supportive of the Jewish cause. Both provided Jurek with suggestions for further contacts, the most important of whom was Johannes Cardinal Willebrands, who since 1968 had served as president of the Pontifical Commission for the Promotion of Christian Unity and whose idea it had been to establish a special subsection of this entity to deal solely with Jewish-Christian relations.

Nothing would happen overnight, Jurek knew, but he was greatly encouraged by the amount of goodwill that he was encountering and amazed at how he was being welcomed into these Polish Vatican circles. One evening at Cardinal Deskur's, he looked up from his hand and saw Michelangelo's brilliantly illuminated dome through a window. He turned to the professor and the cardinals and said, "I don't know what's going to happen from here, but I can tell you one thing for sure. This is the first time in history that two Jews are playing bridge at the Vatican with two cardinals!"

JUREK KNEW THAT HIS ACCESS WAS POSSIBLE ONLY BECAUSE OF HIS FRIENDSHIP with the pope and the sincere commitment of the *Santo Padre* to combating anti-Semitism. Since Jurek's unofficial diplomacy had begun, the pope had repeatedly shown this commitment both privately and publicly. And from Monsignor Bolonek, Jurek learned the extent to which this concern had been a consistent feature of Wojtyla's tenure as Bishop and Archbishop of Krakow.

He already knew that Cardinal Wojtyla had openly condemned the persecutions during the anti-Semitic outbreaks of 1968–69 that were incited by the Polish government. But one night over dinner at the tennis club, where other members and the staff were becoming curious and somewhat amused about the frequency with which *Ingegnere* Kluger was inviting Monsignor Bolonek and other *monsignori* and bishops to dine with him, he learned of a less public action that Wojtyla had taken during the early 1960s.

Jurek had been reminiscing with the monsignor about his experiences with anti-Semitism in Poland and about how peaceful Wadowice had been for Jews until around 1937 or so. Even then, Christian-Jewish relations had remained rather good, thanks in part to his father. But every year at Easter, he recalled, there were incidents in the surrounding countryside after the Passion Play at Kalwaria Zebrzydowska. There was a certain painting there, he seemed to remember, that was part of the problem. He had never seen it, but supposedly it depicted Jews as rapacious animals.

"Oh, that!" Monsignor Bolonek said. "I know just the painting you mean. It was horrible and disgusting! But didn't you know? Your friend Wojtyla had it removed when he was archbishop."

"Removed to where?" Jurek asked. "A museum?"

"Oh, no," the monsignor said. "Better than that. He had it put down in the basement at the monastery, where it would be eaten by rats."

Jurek thought this was marvelous news, and he raised his glass to the rats of Kalwaria, whom he hoped had had a pleasant feast.

The pope confirmed the story the next time Jurek saw him, at what turned out to be the most significant evening he had ever spent with his friend.

ON THE MORNING OF SEPTEMBER 28, 1981, MONSIGNOR DZIWISZ CALLED to invite him to dinner at Castel Gandolfo, where His Holiness was still convalescing from his wounds.

Castel Gandolfo is about a forty-five-minute drive from the center of Rome and lies near a large lake in the village that bears its name. This region, famed for its delicious dry white wines, especially Frascati, has been celebrated since the time of Horace as a retreat from the parching summer heat. It is still a favored location for get-away cottages and estates. The pope's summer palace, originally the seat of the powerful twelfth-century Gandolfi family, sits at the end of the main village street on a bluff some twelve hundred feet above the lake. Once, while the pope was staying at Castel Gandolfo, he received a letter from his old friend Halina, who by then was revered in Krakow as the grande dame of the postwar stage. It was postmarked in Malta, where Halina had stopped while on tour with a Polish theatrical troupe. The view of the Mediterranean from her hotel window was superb, she said—a rocky beach where the waves crashed dramatically and glowed a rosy pink at sunset. It was marvelously romantic, like something out of Norwid or Byron.

"The view from here isn't bad, either," the pope could not resist commenting when he replied to her.

Jurek, who had visited Castel Gandolfo before, was as charmed by the setting as he was taken by the elegance of the *palazzo* itself. Monsignor Dziwisz led him upstairs to a sitting room, where the pope was waiting. The *Santo Padre* looked fairly well, although he moved about gingerly and was obviously still in some pain. His doctors were somewhat worried about infection, a common aftermath of the sort of highly intrusive surgery that he had endured.

Jurek brought him up to date on the work that he had been

doing with regard to Israel. Two weeks earlier, Nathan Ben-Horin, who was First Secretary at the Israeli embassy in Rome, had obtained formal authorization from the Begin government for Jurek to conduct talks with the Vatican on behalf of Israel. All of this was to be kept strictly secret, not least of all because Jurek wasn't an Israeli citizen, let alone an official representative. In his talks with Monsignor Bolonek, cardinals Deskur and Rubin, and others, certain problems were isolated and proposals were floated. As it happened, the monsignor had something in common with Kurt Rosenberg that may have heightened his awareness of how everyone should stick together: both of their fathers had been Polish officers who were murdered by the Russians at Katyn.

On the disappointing side, one of the other officials, Monsignor Monterisi, was supposed to be dealing with the Israeli issue in the Vatican, but Jurek did not find him terribly helpful and believed him to be very much pro-Arab. The monsignor had agreed, however, to interim recognition, meaning that a "mission-status" representative from the Vatican would be placed in Jerusalem and the same level of official from Israel would be sent to the Vatican. Monsignor Mejia, on the other hand, an Argentine who was actually Monterisi's superior, was both friendly and encouraging.

Meanwhile, Ben-Horin had suggested on advice from Jerusalem that it would be very helpful if the pope could send a telegram to the president of Israel, congratulating him on the Jewish New Year (Rosh Hashanah, October 1–2).

"There is no problem about that," His Holiness said at once. "This is a religious matter, not a political one, so I can do it. I'll speak to Monsignor Mejia about setting it up."

Jurek was surprised at how readily the Holy Father agreed to this. He had thought that the pope would at least put the matter off. Instead, he made an instant decision and then went on to say how much he looked forward to meeting the president and other Israeli leaders someday. The idea of sending the telegram appealed to him because it would affirm the religious bond between Catholicism and Judaism while also reassuring the Israelis about his respect and sincere good wishes. He added, however, that of course it should not be publicized, as others might misinterpret it as a partisan political gesture.

These were the most delicate of times, the Holy Father continued. The Camp David agreements were the most important steps ever made toward peace in the Middle East, but they had put Egypt and its president in a very difficult position and involved extremely complex negotiations. It was very important to discreetly encourage peace on all sides. The Holy Father could not go out on a limb by himself, at least not yet, so he had to work through the "experts" at the Secretariat of State.

"I am well-aware of what the attitudes of some of them are," His Holiness said, "and you can be sure I won't be misled by them. On your side, you have to be careful about which Israelis you speak to. Make sure they are reliable and don't leak word of what we're trying to do." The more smoothly Israel's negotiations with its neighbors proceeded, the better the chance that the Vatican could do something official without either appearing to manipulate the peace process or possibly wrecking it.

At this point, the pope said that he had been thinking more and more about the history of relations between Christians and Jews and that doing so had made him more determined than ever to normalize relations with Israel. It was one thing to have a general knowledge that the Jews had been persecuted throughout modern history; it was another to examine the matter closely, as he had done. In doing so, he had to face, regretfully, the Church's role in this persecution, both directly and indirectly. Unfortunately, the Church's attitude seemed to have a lot to do with what sort of man happened to be pope at one time or another. But the problem lay deeper than that. John Paul had come to see that it had to do with a misunderstanding of God's Chosen People and the true relation of Judaism to Christianity, which had been obscured and grossly distorted over the centuries.

Jurek sat and listened to his friend talk as the light outside began to fade. He began to feel that he was being made privy to something of great historical meaning that might have a monumental effect on Jewish-Christian relations. The pope spoke with great feeling, drawing on his vast intellectual and emotional resources. It was all Jurek could do to keep up with the story that John Paul was telling and the lessons he was drawing from it.

At one time or another, the pope continued, various Church synods and councils passed into Canonical Law restrictions against Jews that are now seen as completely unacceptable from a human point of view, not to mention a Christian one. The Synod of Elvira actually prohibited Christians and Jews from eating together. Later, Jews were forbidden to hold public office, to employ Christian servants, or to walk in the streets during Passion Week. Church-sanctioned burnings of the Talmud and other sacred books were common throughout the Middle Ages and later. Beginning with the Lateran Council in 1215, Jews were required to wear identifying signs or marks; later, Christians were forbidden to attend Jewish ceremonies. His Holiness did not make the specific parallel, but Jurek understood the implication: Church rulings over the centuries had sometimes been eerily similar to the Nuremberg Laws and other Nazi restrictions against Jews. A precedent had been established.

There had been positive moments, the pope reflected. In the fourteenth century, for instance, Clement VI defended Jews against charges that they had poisoned wells to cause the Black Death. Three hundred years later, however, Benedict XIV issued a directive to the bishops of Poland that condemned the intermingling of Christian and Jewish people in Poland; excoriated the practices of permitting Christians and Jews to live in close proximity to one another in cities and hiring Jewish managers for businesses and estates; and forbade the clergy to have any dealings whatsoever with Jews.

It saddened him to have to draw the conclusion that the Church had to bear an important degree of responsibility for creating the anti-Semitic climate that had led to slaughter. Many Jews saw this, but most Christians denied it. Catholics must somehow be educated to accept the melancholy truth so that Christians and Jews could begin a new millennium in peace, harmony, and mutual respect. It would take a great deal of work. He was appointing a special commission to look into the other errors that the Church had made over the centuries, to set the record straight. But the goal of establishing better relations with Judaism was close to his heart.

The pope also talked about his concrete plans. Perhaps next April, on the anniversary of the Warsaw Ghetto Uprising, he would make a speech commemorating the bravery of the fighters. He would wait for the appropriate opportunity. He would do everything he could to encourage the extension of the Camp David Accords. He said that only that morning, he had spoken to the Egyptian foreign minister about this, and the distinguished gentleman had complained that Israel broke its promises.

"I told him that this was not true," the pope said. "I said that many promises had been made to the Jews and broken, but that Israel would keep its word. I also explained to him that while the Vatican strives now for evenhandedness, we are as concerned as anyone about the plight of the Palestinian refugees, who somehow must be given a homeland."

Here Jurek's personal partisanship asserted itself. He had to disagree, he said, about the Palestinians: "No one chased them away. They were invited to stay. They left of their own accord. It was the Grand Mufti of Jerusalem who frightened them with a lot of anti-Semitic propaganda that he learned from the Germans. The Mufti spent the war in Berlin, you know. A fine fellow!"

The pope took a far more sympathetic view of the Palestinians. He felt that their situation would not go away. It was not so easy to suddenly become a minority where before one had lived as the majority, and to be shunted from one camp to another in Jordan and Lebanon and so on was possibly even worse. Their fate would have to become part of any settlement. The Israelis would have to realize this; some already did. But the Holy Father did not want Jurek to misunderstand: he admired the heroism of the Jews who had fought in 1948 against fantastic odds to reclaim their homeland. They had every right to return after centuries of being persecuted elsewhere. But the Palestinians had rights, too. This was a matter that had to be resolved.

Although Jurek could not quite disagree without reservation, he still found it emotionally difficult to concede Arab rights. The pope had to remind him that Muslims, too, were human beings, and that they also numbered Abraham among their forbears.

"That's what they say," Jurek grudgingly allowed. "Maybe I should try to be more *Christian* about it."

"That would be an interesting development," the pope laughed.

At that point, Monsignor Dziwisz appeared and announced that dinner was served. It was eight o'clock. The pope had meditated on the Jewish-Christian question for nearly two hours. He had been gravely serious throughout, obviously conscious of the enormity of the task he had set for himself—namely, to change the course of history after nearly two thousand years. But Jurek sensed that John Paul had no doubt that he would succeed, because it was God's will that he do so. It both thrilled and humbled Jurek to think that he, too, was playing a small role in this, and that this friendship itself was an important factor in the pope's determination. John Paul was, after all, the first pope who had grown up with Jews and knew them as friends. Whatever he could do, Jurek thought, he would. At the very least, he could help to assure Jews of the pope's honorable intentions and trustworthiness. He could become a kind of balm in Gilead.

"And now I have a surprise for you, Jurek," the pope said as they made their way into the dining room. "Another old friend of yours is here to greet you."

Another Wadowice classmate, Zbigniew Silkowski, was waiting at the table; he and Jurek embraced. Silkowski was among those whom Jurek had not seen since 1939, as Silkowski had been unable to make it to Rome for the 1979 reunion at the Vatican. He was married now, with three daughters, and had just retired from managing several state enterprises in Poland. He had come to Castel Gandolfo after the assassination attempt out of concern for his old friend and had already been there for several weeks, keeping His Holiness company and making sure that he was recovering.

"He has made me mend faster," the pope said cheerfully, and his mood brightened further as they talked of old times. It was just the four of them at dinner—the classmates and Monsignor Dziwisz.

Around ten o'clock, the pope took Jurek out into the garden alone to again discuss the question of "mission-status" for a possible Vatican representative in Israel. He said that he was looking forward to returning to Israel someday, as his only visit to the Holy Land had been years earlier as a bishop.

"I had a wonderful time," he said. "There are so many Poles there, and we could speak Polish. It was like home."

"I visited my cousins in Israel in 1963," Jurek said. "The Jews were making it fine for the Catholic Church. The shrines were very safe from harm."

"Be careful," the pope said. "I guess that's enough for tonight."

Chapter 24

WHEN JUREK INFORMED MINISTER BEN-HORIN THAT THE POPE WAS actually going to send a 1981 Jewish New Year's telegram to the president of Israel, he was met with skepticism. Jurek insisted that if his friend said he would do something, he would do it, period. Who was to stop him? He was the pope!

But after Rosh Hashanah, no official word came from Jerusalem that the telegram had been received—and it would not come, Jurek knew, because of the secrecy of the gesture. Ben-Horin voiced doubt that the message was ever sent.

"I tell you, it happened!" Jurek insisted. "He would not lie to me." Jurek conveyed his frustration to Monsignor Dziwisz, who instructed him to see a certain archbishop at the Vatican the next day for confirmation. As it happened, Jurek was playing bridge with Cardinal Deskur that evening and asked him about this archbishop, who was from an Eastern European country other than Poland. The cardinal, with characteristic vehemence, denounced the archbishop as an anti-Semite and warned Jurek to be very careful with him. "Don't turn your back," was the way His Eminence put his warning.

The archbishop in question received Jurek cordially the next afternoon. Evidently, he had been ordered to do so by the real boss, as

Jurek thought of Lolek. The archbishop not only assured Jurek that the telegram had been sent but also opened the file of private papal correspondence so that Jurek could examine it himself. There it was, an elegantly phrased message that cited historic ties between the religions and conveyed not only good wishes but a full understanding of the significance of this particular holiday to the Jews.

"So, I have seen the thing myself!" Jurek was able to say to Ben-Horin, and he paraphrased the telegram from memory. "I told you, if the *Santo Padre* says he will do something, he does it! With him, there is no pussyfooting. He is the bravest, most honest man in the world. At the same time, my friend and dear colleague, I must tell you that I understand your skepticism. You are doing your job. After two thousand years of betrayals, we should be a little wary."

Jurek could not tell whether Ben-Horin's reaction was more pleasure that the telegram had been sent or astonishment that Jurek had actually been shown the file. From that point on, Jurek's credibility was absolute.

Jurek, with his impulsiveness and his tendency to see everything in terms of winners and losers, good guys and bad guys, found playing the role of the discreet diplomat rather difficult. He also believed that had the Jews been less acquiescent at the beginning of World War II, or even before, lives would have been saved. For him, the paradigm of how to handle an enemy was Monte Cassino—or something like the Israeli strike against Iraq's nuclear reactor.

The pope, however, was a far more patient type and naturally took a longer view of things. He also had the sort of Christian faith that told him that no matter what suffering needed to be endured, those who were doing God's will would be rewarded in the long run. Great progress had been made in Catholic-Jewish relations already, but even these preliminary steps had been taken with great difficulty. The Holy Father knew that it was a process that called for gradual education, or re-education, after millennia of lies. What was needed was an entire change of consciousness, not simply fiats or rash actions. The story behind the adoption of *Nostra Aetate* was the operative lesson here. It was accomplished largely because one man, a true teacher to the world, began the process.

THIS SINGLE MOST IMPORTANT FIGURE WAS A FRENCH JEWISH HISTORIAN, JULES Isaac (1877–1963). Although his role has been unjustly neglected, he may rightly be called the father of *Nostra Aetate*. Beyond that, Isaac—as Pope John Paul II was and is acutely aware—was the progenitor of all contemporary re-examinations and re-evaluations of the nature of Judaism at the time of Christ. It was Isaac who first carefully researched and articulated the growth of anti-Semitism as a contagion within Christian doctrine itself; through his writings and personally, in audiences with two popes, he took his message to the Vatican. He wrote that Christian beliefs, that is to say Jesus' actual message, had been grossly distorted over the centuries, and this distortion led inevitably to the Holocaust. That Isaac actually succeeded in getting the Vatican to take his work seriously is one of the most remarkable conversion stories in history. Only this time, it was Catholics who had to consider conversion, not to another religion but to an entirely new way of understanding the most basic Christian doctrine.

As with any great change, of course, no one person was solely responsible. But there had to be a beginning, and Isaac's labors and eloquence provided it.

Before World War II, Jules Isaac was known to every French student as the author of the standard history textbooks—admired for their clarity, liveliness of style, and erudition—that were used in all secondary schools. During the 1930s, he was chief inspector of history teaching at the Ministry for Education, a position that in France carried great prestige and power. In essence, he was the keeper of the flame of *La Civilisation Françaises*. He was alarmed by the spread of fascism and anti-Semitism in Europe, but he later conceded that at the outbreak of war, he saw only the end of democracy. He did not foresee what would happen to the Jews or even suspect that many of his countrymen would become compliant with the Nazis and aid in the betrayal of French Jews and their deportation to Auschwitz. In the middle of the war, he began research into the origins of anti-Semitism and understood that Hitler's pogrom was the culmination of a long history of Christians hating Jews.

When the Germans occupied France, Isaac was removed from his post by the Vichy government. It was his first personal experience with anti-Semitism, and it caused him to intensify serious work on a manuscript that he entitled *Jesus and Israel*. "I viewed my work as a fight for wounded Israel," he later said, "for brotherhood against hatred. I had a task to fulfill. It was a sacred mission." In 1943, while he was away from his home working on the problem, his wife, daughter, younger son, and several other relatives were arrested. Before Madame Isaac was shipped away with the others to Auschwitz, she managed to get this message to her husband: "Save yourself for your work; the world is waiting for it."

In 1947, Isaac turned over the 600-page manuscript of *Jesus and Israel* to his publisher. The book caused a sensation and much controversy. In it, he compares the actual texts of the Gospels with widely accepted Catholic and Protestant commentaries on them. He demonstrates beyond all reasonable doubt how these commentaries have distorted the originals to give a false picture of Jesus' attitude toward the Jews, of Jesus' own identity as a Jew, and of the nature of Judaism at the time of Christ. His conclusions are startling, and it is important to summarize them because in every instance, Isaac's propositions form the basis of John Paul's beliefs about the relationship between Christianity and Judaism. Isaac's arguments are the keys to *Nostra Aetate* and Pope John Paul's passionate advocacy of it.

1. The Christian religion is the daughter of the Jewish religion. For this reason alone, Judaism is worthy of respect.

2. In his human life, Jesus was a Jew, a humble artisan. No Christian has the right to ignore this fact.

3. Jesus' mother, his entire family, and all of his friends were Jewish. "To be at once a Christian and an anti-Semite is to marry reverence with abuse," Isaac states in *Jesus and Israel*.

4. On each New Year's Day, the Church commemorates the circumcision of the infant Jesus. Only after much hesitation did early Christianity abandon circumcision, which is sanctioned by the Hebrew Bible.

5. The name Jesus is essentially Semitic, the Greek form of a Jewish name; Christ is Greek for the Jewish word *Messiah*.

6. The New Testament was written in Greek, but Jesus spoke Aramaic, which is closely related to Hebrew.

7. The characterization made in commentaries of Judaism as a merely legalistic religion without a soul is completely false.

8. Jesus' teaching took place in a Jewish setting. As a carpenter's son, he was permitted to speak in the temple by a very liberal Jewish custom.

9. As the Dead Sea Scrolls show, Jesus' preaching was closely in line with purification and reform that was widespread in the Judaism of the day.

10. The diaspora, or "dispersion," of the Jews did not take place as punishment for their rejection of Jesus but rather was already an accomplished fact. At that time, the majority of Jews no longer lived in Palestine.

11. No one has the right to say that the Jewish people "as a whole" rejected Jesus. In fact, the Gospels give us good reason to doubt that most Jews ever saw Jesus.

12. Most Jews who met Jesus did accept him, or "take him to their hearts." Did an entire people then suddenly turn against him? This is nonsense.

13. Jesus never condemned Jews as a people, only a certain pharisaism among a few of them. He would never have condemned his own people.

14. No accusation could be more pernicious or absurd than that of Deicide against the Jews.

15. Jesus named those responsible for the crucifixion, including dignitaries and doctors of the law, who can be found among all peoples.

16. Joan of Arc was similarly tried and killed. Do we condemn the entire French people for this?

17. Arbitrary interpretations have ignored the Roman trial of Jesus, the Roman death sentence, and the Roman method of execution.

18. In light of the previous fact, to use the specter of the crucifixion against the Jews is bad religion and bad history.

19. "Whatever the sins of Israel may be, [Isaac writes] she is entirely innocent of the crimes of which Christian tradition accuses

her: She did not reject Jesus and did not crucify him." And Jesus did not curse Israel. The "evangelical law of love knows no exception. May Christians come to realize this at last and redress their crying injustices. At this moment, when a curse seems to weigh upon the whole human race, it is the urgent duty to which we are called by the memory of Auschwitz."

The impact of these propositions, as explosive now as they were then, was such that Isaac was able to help form an international conclave of scholars to re-examine Christian doctrine toward the Jews. One issue that was not touched on at the time was who allowed these distortions to intrude and why they not only survived but multiplied. More recent scholarship has hinted at the answer. Elaine Pagles's *The Gnostic Gospels* (1979) depicts early Christianity as divided into many disputing sects. Currently, the most plausible explanation for the growth of anti-Semitism within Christianity is that it was a convenient, if not pernicious, means of distinguishing Christianity from Judaism in order to promote Christ among the Greeks, who for political reasons considered Jews as rivals. What may have started as a sort of public relations ploy developed into a convenient means for the dispossessed to blame an "other"—the Jews—for all actual and imagined wrongs. Benjamin Netanyahu's *The Origins of the Inquisition in Fifteenth-Century Spain* (1995) argues exhaustively that the Inquisition's persecution of the Jews had little to do with belief and much to do with the socio-political resentments of an underclass. If so, the anti-Semitic strain in Christianity would appear to have more to do with social envy than with theology.

Jules Isaac's concern was the vicious resentment that had invaded a religion based on love rather than how this lamentable infection began. He followed *Jesus and Israel* with the brilliant *The Teaching of Contempt* (*L'Enseignement du mépris*; 1962), which was completed in his eighty-fourth year. It is a scathing yet hopeful exposé of pernicious teachings about the Jews that are common in Catholic and Protestant schools and universities. Meanwhile, Isaac managed to approach the Vatican itself, in private audiences with popes Pius XII and John XXIII. That these two very different pontiffs both received him and were without doubt affected by his ideas may indicate the intellectual and moral power of the man.

Isaac was effective in his advocacy of Church reform. Shortly after his visit to Pius, the phrase "perfidious Jews"—actually a mistranslation of the Latin *perfidis*, or simply "unbelieving"—was correctly rendered. This was still offensive, however, as it could imply Jewish atheism. In 1959, Pope John XXIII ordered the entire phrase dropped and made other changes in the liturgy; in 1965, Paul VI ordered the elimination of still more phrases that were likely to encourage false stereotypes of Jews. It was slow, incremental progress, but Jules Isaac had indeed started something. His arguments to Pius XII may even have affected that pontiff's preference for a true reformer, John XXIII, as his successor. Cardinal Deskur, for one, believes this to be so.

In July 1960, John XXIII received Jules Isaac. Shortly afterward, on September 18, the Holy Father received Augustin Cardinal Bea, a German Jesuit who had been close to Pius XII, and asked him, as President of the Pontifical Council (or Secretariat) on Christian Unity, to prepare a special declaration dealing with the Jewish people. Cardinal Bea opened a special office in Rome and soon invited representatives of several American Jewish organizations to prepare memoranda offering suggestions. The first of these, composed by the American Jewish Committee, bore the stamp of Jules Isaac. It presented negative images of the Jew as found in Catholic school books. This and subsequent memoranda followed the basic outline of Jules Isaac's condemnation that he had stated in *The Teaching of Contempt.*

Isaac's ideas were in the front of ’s mind when he began his behind-the-scenes efforts to reassure the Israeli government that John Paul II endorsed the right of Jews to return to the Holy Land without having to convert to Christianity. The issue that had kept *Nostra Aetate* a limited document was that it scrupulously avoided mentioning the State of Israel or the Land. But Isaac's impeccable scholarship had demolished the entire basis for the long-held Christian belief that the Jewish diaspora was punishment. As Isaac showed, because of Greek and later Roman imperialism, most Jews had left Palestine by the time of Jesus, but some remained a thousand years after his death. If anything, it was the Christian Crusades that finally crushed the Jewish presence in Jerusalem, until the return finally began. It was Roman imperialism, not any matter of belief, that initiated the major dispersion. In other words, it was a matter of politics and militarism, not faith.

The idea of the diaspora as punishment was so ingrained in the Christian mind, however, that in January 1904, when Theodor Herzl went to see Pope Pius X to solicit support for a Jewish homeland in Palestine, the pope told him politely but firmly, "The Jews have not recognized Our Lord, therefore we cannot recognize the Jewish people."

When Herzl assured Pius (the account appears in Herzl's diaries) that the Jews were not even asking for Jerusalem but only "the secular land," His Holiness was adamant: "We cannot be in favor of it." There was only one way that the Jews could merit Church endorsement of their return, and that was by conversion. "And so, if you come to Palestine and settle your people there, we shall have churches and priests ready to baptize all of you," Pius declared. That would have been an enthralling scene!

Pope Benedict XV, who was pope from 1914 to 1922, was much more receptive to the idea of Jewish settlement in Palestine. A Zionist delegation went to see him, but Benedict couldn't give them an official Vatican endorsement. The doctrine of diaspora-as-punishment was too well entrenched to be overturned as yet. Indeed, there was great doubt during the three years of Vatican II (1962–65) that any statement on the Jews whatever would be issued by the Church, let alone one that accepted the right of return. At the end of the first session, a profusion of anti-Semitic literature was distributed to the Council Fathers; whether it was supplied by Catholic right-wingers, Arabs, or both, no one knew. It included allegations that Cardinal Bea was an Israeli agent and a secret Jew himself.

Bowing to conservative pressures, drafters of the statement on the Jews at one point included a passage praying for Jewish conversion. An exasperated Rabbi Heschel, who traveled from New York to Rome several times to lobby for a strong statement and had an audience with Paul VI, told his friend Johannes Cardinal Willebrands that a prayer for conversion would vitiate any statement. Orthodox rabbis were already so suspicious and hostile toward the idea of even talking with Catholics on these matters, Rabbi Heschel said, that it would hardly serve the interests of reconciliation to prove their cynicism about Christians correct. If a plea for conversion was in fact included, the rabbi told the cardinal, he would personally travel to Auschwitz and gas himself.

A limited good was finally accomplished during Paul VI's pontificate by men working behind the scenes. American bishops and cardinals, particularly Francis Cardinal Spellman of New York and John Cardinal Cushing of Boston, were among the leaders. Cardinal Willebrands today remembers the drama of those days vividly, and how his friendship with Rabbi Heschel played a part in his own efforts on behalf of Jews. Cardinal Willebrands, born in Haarlem, Holland, in 1909, brought to the Council and to his efforts as Cardinal Bea's successor his personal wartime experience with Jews that deeply affected him. He also was an avid student of the works of Jules Isaac and others that have reformed attitudes toward biblical Judaism.

"Only knowing the living Jewish religion can make a real difference. When you see Jews practicing their religion and when you participate in the beauty of that, you cannot possibly hate these wonderful people," Cardinal Willebrands has said. As a young priest in Amsterdam before and during the war, he lived in buildings owned by the Church and occupied by many Jewish shops. He became friends with his Jewish neighbors, accepting their invitations to holiday observances. With the coming of the German occupation in 1940, when the synagogues were closed, he attended a Jewish wedding held secretly on the second floor of a hotel. He remembers the terror and the sweetness of that occasion.

In 1941–42, when young Father Willebrands was chairman of the department of philosophy at a seminary, a young woman named Rachel came to see him. She had heard of his kindly attitude toward

Jews. She brought him flowers and asked him for an important favor. She wanted a baptismal certificate so that she could be saved from arrest by the Nazis. They had a long talk.

"But in your beliefs, your culture, your personality," Father Willebrands told her, "you are Jewish. How can I baptize you? It would be an insult to you and to my own faith. To become a Roman Catholic, you must take instruction and actually believe in Christ."

Rachel said that she was willing, so for almost a year they met at the seminary once a week. The experience was as instructive for the young Willebrands as it was for his initiate: he learned as much about Judaism in talking with Rachel as she did about the Roman Church. He baptized her and gave her the certificate against execution. He also warned her that it might not be sufficient to protect her. Alone in Europe to do so, the Dutch Episcopate had condemned Nazism and the persecution of Jews. The German response to this courageous witnessing was to target not only Jews or those with one Jewish grandparent but also converts to Christianity.

A few months later, Rachel came to him and said that she wanted to marry in the Church.

"Is the man you intend to marry a Jew?" Father Willebrands asked. As he suspected, she admitted that this was so. With the Nazi deportation of Jews from Holland under way, Father Willebrands was now not quite so fastidious about Church regulations. He performed the nuptials without worrying about the husband's faith.

Within a few weeks, Rachel came to say goodbye. As before, she brought him flowers, and she told him that she had given all her money to a man who promised to get her and her husband out of the country. They were going to Sweden. Father Willebrands wished them Godspeed, but he also warned them to be careful.

He did not hear from Rachel again until after the war, when she contacted him. The man to whom she had given her money betrayed her to the Germans, who deported her and her husband to the Theresienstadt concentration camp. From there they were sent to Auschwitz, where her husband was gassed. She survived.

Years later, during Vatican II, Willebrands often thought about Rachel and her husband and was deeply troubled. Was there something more he could have done for them? This and his memory of other murdered Dutch Jews, plus his friendship with Rabbi Heschel, strengthened his resolve to change attitudes. In 1992, Cardinal Willebrands published an important book, *The Church and the Jewish People*, which is built upon the insights of Jules Isaac but goes beyond them to envision a mutually beneficial dialogue between the religions.

When Karol Wojtyla became John Paul II, he asked Cardinal Willebrands to continue his work as head of the Council for Christian Unity and of the special section the cardinal had established on Jewish-Christian relations. The cardinal said that he would do anything His Holiness asked of him, but he was also Bishop of Utrecht, and it was very difficult to do justice to both jobs.

"Then I am relieving you of your duties in Utrecht," John Paul said. "Your work for Jewish-Christian harmony is most important. You must stay in Rome—and help me understand the Protestants also. You know, there weren't any of them in Krakow!"

Officially retired, although still active as president emeritus of the council on unity, Cardinal Willebrands lives in a high-ceilinged, book-crammed apartment across the street from the Vatican. A tall, still-vigorous man, he has a gentle and sophisticated manner, at least until matters of life, death, and faith evoke something of the Old Testament prophet in him. The subject of the history of the Church and the Jews continues to animate him. Asked how it can be possible that the Church no longer advocates conversion of the Jews after centuries of the opposite doctrine and numerous efforts during various periods at forced conversions, he draws himself up with visible exasperation and vehemently states, "To proselytize is not an attitude of love, nor is it one of knowledge!"

Christianity is a matter of choice, he explains, not brainwashing. To profess the faith is different from attempting to impose it, not only by force but by threats of damnation and the like. These practices are now understood as abhorrent and indeed anti-Christian. As for the Jews, God made a promise to them, and God does not go back on his promises. If Christians would take the trouble to understand the Jewish people and their faith, they would respect them, or should.

The cardinal explains to the curious that the silver menorah that sits atop his television set and the seven-striped prayer shawl that rests in a glass case on a bookshelf are gifts from Jewish friends. He touches them with reverence, with a caress. The nine candles held by his menorah are burnt halfway down.

THE MATTER OF CONVERSION CROPPED UP IN JUREK KLUGER'S OWN FAMILY during that year of the failed assassination of the pope, 1981, and caused much soul-searching. Jurek's grandchild, Stephania, was then eleven, four years beyond the age of reason, according to traditional Church chronology—that is, able to make up her own mind and be responsible for her choices. During the previous year, she had expressed the wish to become a Roman Catholic. Although Stephania's mother had been raised a Catholic, Linda had kept to her decision to let the child decide on matters of faith. (Linda was divorced from Stephania's father, who had left Italy, and Linda and Stephania had both assumed the Kluger family name.) Attending mass with her grandmother, having the Holy Father as an avuncular presence in her life, and living in Rome no doubt contributed to Stephania's decision.

For Jurek, the prospect of Stephania's baptism evoked mixed emotions. He could not help but imagine what Grandmother Huppert would have thought about her great-grandchild's becoming a Christian after more than five thousand years of continuity, after all that suffering and death, after Belzec and Auschwitz. The idea of her grandchild's baptism would have provoked great sorrow, lamentation, some indignation, and no doubt a fair amount of teeth-gnashing. Catholic families, of course, can be nearly as protective and are quite capable of making a pariah out of an unfaithful member. But for Jews, the loss of a family member to another religion is a calamity that, in some respects, is worse than death.

As painful as the question of baptism was for him, Jurek did remind himself that Stephania was not actually Jewish. What distress he felt at her acceptance of Catholicism was actually more sorrow and some guilt on his own account. He had married a Christian, whom he still not merely loved but was bound to, no matter what befell them, as long as he lived. Their children—what could he say? Baptized, still they went their own ways, as was the dubious fashion of the era.

Stephania, *mala Tesia*—that was where the anguish began. If Stephania was indeed the reincarnation of Tesia, the embodiment of the failure to annihilate Jews, and the resurrected spirit of Jews murdered at Auschwitz, it placed a terrible burden on the little girl. She was bright and pretty, and a Roman, as a matter of fact. Whatever else she chose to be was her free decision.

Jurek was emotionally affected enough by the prospect of Stephania's baptism, however, to write to Mrs. Szczepanska, who was then close to ninety. As Tesia's teacher and a link to everything in Wadowice, she was like a mother to him. In his letter, Jurek tried to convey no doubts to her. He merely reported that his granddaughter had decided to be baptized.

What happened after that will never exactly be determined. What is certain is that, as she later confirmed to Jurek, Mrs. Szczepanska wrote at once to the fellow she remembered so well who was now in residence at the Vatican. If Jurek's granddaughter was going to be baptized, she said, the Holy Father himself should perform the rite. So gracious a gesture from His Holiness would honor the memory of the child's beloved Aunt Tesia as well as her namesake. It was worth remembering, Mrs. Szczepanska added, that Tesia might be alive today if she and her mother had permitted her baptism during the war.

One morning in January of 1981, as they were breakfasting together at the Vatican, His Holiness asked Jurek if indeed it was true that Stephania was going to be baptized. Jurek said yes, and that it was going to happen soon, although he did not know exactly when. The pope said simply, "In that case, I would like to baptize her myself, if that's all right with you."

Jurek could only think, "If my granddaughter has to be baptized, let it be by the pope."

Later that week, Renée and Monsignor Dziwisz agreed on a date early in May at Castel Gandolfo. It was not early enough, as things turned out, for on the appointed day, John Paul was in intensive care at the Gemelli Clinic, fighting for his life from wounds inflicted by the assassin's bullet.

Nearly seven months later, on December 6, 1981, the pope was well enough to fulfill his promise. He had been so anxious to do so that he insisted that Stephania wait for him to recover and not rush to have the baptism performed by someone else. And so, early that morning, Stephania, her mother, aunt, and grandparents, along with about thirty guests, arrived at Castel Gandolfo under a cloudless sky. Everyone had been sworn to secrecy. The pope felt that this was a private matter and did not want the press hearing about it and descending on the little town. It was the only time within memory that a pope had baptized anyone. When the word did get out at last, the Vatican would no doubt be besieged with requests. What Catholic monarch or politician or movie star would not like to boast that his child or hers had been baptized by the pope? And none would be.

As Stephania entered the palace gates, the Swiss Guards saluted her as the Holy Father's honored guest. The child enjoyed this so much that she saluted back and, to double the pleasure of it, retraced her steps to be saluted again. The guards could not keep themselves from grinning.

The pope's small chapel at Castel Gandolfo barely held the guests. Stephania and her family sat in the front row and admired the profusion of white lilies that graced the altar and lined its steps, sending their perfume through the room. Stephania was wearing a white dress that, because it had been bought the previous spring, was now rather too short, but it served as baptismal gown, First Communion, and Confirmation dress for her. The Holy Father had suggested that since she was of age, he would administer all three sacraments to her that morning.

Any other child would likely have been shaking with fright in anticipation of such a rare experience and honor, but not Stephania. Other than allowing a few giggles to escape as she waited for the pope to enter, she betrayed not an ounce of nervousness but looked the picture of childish happiness. When she called this man *Santo Padre*, it was as if he weren't the actual Holy Father but a friend, uncle, and father all in one. When he entered from one side, wearing gold-and-white vestments and carrying his silver staff, he smiled at her, and she went forward eagerly for the first ritual.

The font and the golden vessel holding holy water had been brought specially from the Vatican. Stephania bowed her head as the pope began the words "*Ego baptizo...*" and held the pitcher over her head. He tipped it slightly, then more. Nothing came out. The hinged stopper was stuck shut. The pope gave the thing a slight shake and lo, the water cascaded forth, drenching her hair and running down her neck and onto her dress. She could not help smiling, and the pope smiled, too.

Chapter 25

Early in his papacy, on November 17, 1980, Pope John Paul II delivered a speech to the Jewish community of Berlin that was so explicit about his beliefs and intentions in the area of Jewish-Catholic relations and so revisionist in its argument that one can only be puzzled about how little international attention it drew—or perhaps not. The ideas he expressed were still so new or strange to most that they didn't truly register. The ten thousand or so Berlin Jews who still lived in the city may have been taken aback to hear the pope—and a Pole at that—speak to them as brothers. He greeted them with "*Shalom*!" and directly addressed the significance of the place in which they were gathered, where orders for the extermination of the Jewish people had been issued. "Grim," His Holiness termed the scene, but rejuvenation was his theme.

> The concrete brotherly relations between Jews and Catholics in Germany assume a quite particular value against the grim background of the persecution and the attempted extermination of Judaism in this country. The innocent victims in Germany and elsewhere, the families destroyed or dispersed, the cultural values or art treasures destroyed forever, are a tragic proof of where discrimination and *contempt* of human dignity can lead, especially if they are animated by perverse theories on a presumed difference in the

> value of races or on the division of men into men of "high worth," "worthy of living," and men who are "worthless," "unworthy of living." Before God, all men are of the same value and importance. (Italics added.)

The pope went on to praise such Jewish thinkers as Franz Rosenzweig and Martin Buber, "who, through their creative familiarity with the Jewish and German languages, constructed a wonderful bridge for a deeper meeting of both cultural areas." And he acknowledged how false Christian teaching had distorted perceptions of the Jews and led to calamitous acts. But humanity had to progress out of this morass. Dialogue must now take the place of falsehood and hatred.

> The first dimension of this dialogue, that is, the meeting between the people of the Old Covenant, *never revoked by God* and that of the New Covenant, is at the same time a dialogue within our Church, that is to say, between the first and second part of her Bible. Jews and Christians, as children of Abraham, are called to be a blessing for the world [cf. Genesis 12:2 ff], by committing themselves together for peace and justice among all men and peoples.... In the light of this promise and call of Abraham's, I look with you to the destiny and role of your people among the peoples. I willingly pray with you for the fullness of *Shalom* for all your brothers in *nationality* and in faith, and also for the land to which Jews look with particular veneration.... May all peoples in Jerusalem soon be reconciled and blessed in Abraham! (Italics added.)

It is impossible to say what reaction the pope expected from this speech. He has never discussed it or dwelled on such matters as reactions to his utterances. But it contained these dramatic assertions.

1. The Old Covenant, the designation by God of the Jews as the Chosen People, *has never been revoked*. This means that the goal of conversion of the Jews is abandoned and that their salvation as a people is embraced, setting aside forever the notion that their baptism is required. This, by the way, puts the Roman Catholic Church

at odds with other Christian denominations that insist on baptism as a requirement of salvation.

2. As a corollary of this assertion, the pope asserts that Catholics must embrace the Hebrew Bible, or Old Testament, as equally valid with the New. Such an assertion contradicts the traditionally held assumption in Catholic teaching that the Catholic faith is a religion of the New Testament as opposed to the Old. John Paul insists that both Old and New remain valid.

3. The pope explicitly endorses the continuing life and vitality of the Jewish faith and people and prays for Jewish continuance.

4. Most boldly of all, given the political controversies of 1980 and beyond, the pope affirms the validity not only of the faith but of the *nationality* of Judaism and its *land*, a pointed reference to Israel.

It should be added that by his reference to "all the peoples of Jerusalem," the pope meant Muslims as well as Christians and Jews. Although he did not specifically mention the Palestinians on this occasion, he continuously raised the Palestinian issue and insisted on the importance of establishing a homeland for them. He often referred to them as "dispersed," thus linking them to other dispersions, or the diaspora. As he knew well enough from his conversations with Jurek, this was the single most difficult issue in the Middle East and the one on which both sides were usually incapable of reasonableness.

It is one of the unfortunate facts of modern communications that truth still proves elusive and that a world leader must repeat a position over and over again—usually in sound bites convenient to television and newspapers—to achieve acceptance or even recognition of it. This is especially true when a leader's message contradicts past positions. The pope's message to the Jews of Berlin and by extension to all Jews contained no slogans that could be extracted from what was actually a complex argument, although it was expressed in direct language. And his message was difficult for world Jewry to accept at face value, because it was so different from the past silences, ambiguities, and hostilities of many pontiffs. It was precisely this sort of skepticism that the Holy Father hoped his friend Jurek could help overcome.

IN ADDITION TO THE VATICAN AND ISRAELI REPRESENTATIVES, JUREK WAS ALSO working closely with Dr. Joseph A. Lichten, the distinguished representative in Rome of the New York–based Anti-Defamation League (ADL). Dr. Lichten, who had been a respected attorney in Poland before the war, regularly prepared memoranda for Jurek to present to the Vatican and was delighted to hear about his lengthy and productive evening at Castel Gandolfo. He also added the endorsement of the ADL to the idea of an interim, "mission-status" recognition for Israel.

To encourage further development of trust between the parties, Jurek hosted dinners at the Parioli Club for Monsignor Bolonek, Dr. Lichten, Minister Ben-Horin—and Kurt Rosenberg. He was pleased to be able to report that, at dinner at the Vatican on December 8, 1981, the Holy Father told him that he had met with a large number of bishops, many of them from South America, and instructed them that it was part of the Church's pastoral responsibility to fight vigorously against all signs of anti-Semitism. Neo-Nazi groups in Europe and elsewhere had become active in defacing Jewish cemeteries and synagogues with swastikas and slogans. Jurek was also able to inform Dr. Lichten and Ben-Horin that Cardinal Willebrands had sent personal letters to dignitaries in Jerusalem expressing the Church's and his own regret over these incidents.

It is superfluous to say that this was a period of rising tensions in the Middle East. In October of 1981, Muslim-fundamentalist terrorists assassinated Egyptian President Anwar Sadat in retaliation for being the prime mover behind the Camp David agreements and recognizing Israel. In February 1982, Syrian government forces crushed a revolt at Hamas, killing an estimated twenty-five thousand people. Between March and May, thirteen Arab civilians were killed by Israeli fire in the West Bank area during riots and repressions. In June, Israel's ambassador in London was shot and seriously wounded by

Arab gunmen. Also in June, Israel invaded Lebanon, primarily on the grounds that Syria was protecting Palestinian guerrillas there.

Any one of these events was enough to suggest that this was not a propitious moment for the Vatican to become directly involved by recognizing Israel, yet activity toward this end quietly went forward. The most significant action occurred on January 9, 1982, when John Paul received Israeli Foreign Minister Yitzhak Shamir at the Vatican.

Foreign Minister Shamir had every reason to distrust John Paul II, as a Pole. Polish-born Shamir had acute family reasons to be wary. During World War II, Shamir's father, having escaped from the Germans in Poland, had been murdered by Polish-Ukrainian peasants. Jurek briefed the pope about the degree of suspicion that His Holiness would likely encounter.

Five days before his visit to Rome, however, on January 4, 1982, the foreign minister delivered to the Knesset, the Israeli parliament, a remarkable speech that was obviously intended as a conciliatory message to the pope. In it, Shamir, who was second only to Menachem Begin in power and would succeed him as prime minister only two years later, called Israeli attention to the political unrest in Poland, calling it "a crack in the totalitarian iceberg" and an "authentic mass movement." He was referring to Solidarity, the rebellious Polish labor movement, which he termed "marvelous." Shamir went on to praise Solidarity as a "miracle" and to ask Israelis to understand that their cause was Poland's also. He drew parallels between Poland's struggle for freedom, suppressed anew by the Soviet Union, and Israel's. He called upon the democratic nations of the world to come to Poland's aid. He asked that a conference "be convened and that its first item of business be the mobilization of the entire democratic world on behalf of Poland's struggle for freedom."

This speech wasn't widely noticed at the time, except by John Paul. It is a singular document, coming as it did from a Polish-born Jewish statesman. Shamir did address the fact that millions of Jews "were slaughtered in that country by the Germans, with the active assistance of very many members of the Polish nation. Our account with the Polish nation is long and bitter. But it is not this account," he added, "which today draws our attention to what is transpiring in Poland." It was democracy, Shamir said, that mattered now, not past grievances.

And now Shamir was in Rome to see the pope. As Jurek later learned, John Paul greeted the foreign minister by placing both hands on his head, a traditional rabbinical blessing, and wishing him *Shalom*. Naturally speaking in Polish, the pope soon made reference to the close ties he had enjoyed with Jews during his youth in Wadowice and mentioned in particular Jerzy Kluger and the deaths of his family at Auschwitz. Because of the foreign minister's speech and the connection to Jurek as well as John Paul's good intentions, a degree of trust was established between the two leaders at this meeting, which otherwise could have been a minor disaster.

Before hearing about the details, Jurek had a fair idea of how well things had gone because Foreign Minister Shamir invited him to tea at the Israeli Embassy the next day. A tough, short, gruff, plain-spoken man with a political reputation as a militant, Shamir put Jurek entirely at ease by promising to personally telephone all his cousins back in Israel. Jerzy's friendship with the pope was a wonderful thing, Shamir said, and it was a benefit for Israel.

"I thank you," the foreign minister said, "on behalf of all the Jewish people."

For Jurek, it may have been the proudest moment of his life. He left the embassy feeling elated. Having fought for Poland, he was now praised by Israel. That was about as much as he could ask.

When the pope told him how much he liked Shamir—"A real man," the Holy Father called him, direct and to the point—Jurek was happy to agree.

Eight months later, on September 15, this rather euphoric interlude in Vatican-Israeli relations abruptly dissipated when John Paul II met with Yasser Arafat at the Vatican at the height of Israeli military involvement in Lebanon. Minister Ben-Horin and other Israelis were incensed at what appeared to them to be a very damaging legitimizing of the chairman of the Palestine Liberation Organization (PLO), who at that time was generally regarded in the non-Arab world as an arch-terrorist with Jewish blood on his hands.

Jurek tried to mollify them by explaining that the papal meeting with Arafat had occurred "by accident" and was of no significance—but few, if any, believed him.

On the very day of the pope's encounter with the PLO leader, the Israelis occupied West Beirut; two days later, Maronite Christian forces entered Palestinian refugee camps at Sabra and Chatila and massacred hundreds of civilians. It was the greatest internal crisis in Israel's brief history—and the country's most serious experience of international condemnation and isolation.

Although the pope's gesture to Arafat made this hardly a harmonious period between the Vatican and Israel, John Paul II was virtually alone among Western leaders in refraining from openly condemning Israeli military actions in Lebanon. As Israeli anger over the Arafat meeting receded, the pope's restraint was noticed and quietly appreciated—in Israel if nowhere else.

JUREK'S RELATIONSHIP WITH THE POPE WAS UNAFFECTED. WHATEVER HIS OWN feelings were, Jurek understood that the pope was evenhanded in his concern for all human beings, whether Christian, Jewish, Muslim, or anything else. At that point, however, it was beyond imagining that one day an Israeli prime minister would also be talking to the PLO leader and hesitantly shaking his hand—and that John Paul II would appear in retrospect to have been prescient in this as in other matters.

As 1983 began, Cardinal Deskur, who disapproved of the pope's meeting with Arafat, had lunch with him on most Sundays and was urging him to make a concrete move toward recognition of Israel. Commenting on the photos that appeared showing the pope with Arafat, the cardinal said to Jurek, "Arafat looks like a proper cardinal," and added that something had to be done on the Israeli side as a counterweight. Another crisis concerning the Jews also had to be resolved. A banker who had allegedly been close to Adolph Hitler had inadvertently been placed on the board of overseers of the Vatican Bank. The man, Herman J. Abs, got the position on the recommendation of a German cardinal, who may have been ignorant about what he was doing. Simon Wiesenthal, the renowned Nazi-hunter who had been instrumental in the apprehension of Adolph Eichmann in 1960, had informed Dr. Lichten about Abs's alleged past. Dr. Lichten brought the matter up with Jurek, who in turn brought the controversy to the attention of His Holiness.

Jurek telephoned Wiesenthal at his office in Vienna. According to records that Wiesenthal said were in his possession, Abs, then in his eighties, had been the head of Hilter's Central Bank from 1940 to 1945. Abs, so Wiesenthal and others alleged, had also been a director of I. G. Farben, the firm notorious for its chemical and other plants at Auschwitz and its use of Jewish and other slave labor. The Israelis also remembered Abs for his role as a Deutsche Bank official and leader of the West German delegation to war-reparations talks in London in 1952, which delayed the settlement of Jewish claims. Of course, Abs denied the wartime allegations against him, insisting that he had been only a minor functionary under Hitler. Within a few weeks of Jurek's involvement, although not as a direct result of it, Abs was eased off the Vatican Bank board.

To pursue the idea of establishing Vatican and Israeli diplomatic missions, Cardinal Deskur came up with an idea. If Israeli officials could be persuaded to formally endorse the concept, it would be easier to overcome resistance within the Secretariat of State. Why not take advantage of Jurek Kluger's good relationship with Yitzhak Shamir? If he could obtain a letter from Shamir stating the Israeli government's favorable disposition to such a plan, it might give Cardinal Deskur and his allies the leverage they needed to make real progress. It was decided to send Jurek on a mission to Jerusalem.

On January 19, 1983, Jurek flew to Israel, which he had not visited in twenty years. He checked into the King David Hotel in Jerusalem and began meetings with several foreign office officials. They welcomed him graciously and showed little doubt of John Paul's sincerity. They all expressed worry, however, that if Israel supplied the requested letter and the pope proved, for one reason or another, to be unable to deliver on the promise of a diplomatic mission shortly thereafter, the Israelis would end up losing face internationally. Jurek's assurances that the letter would be kept secret did not assuage their fears. If the letter was used to put pressure on recalcitrant officials in the Vatican Secretariat of State, such men would have every motive to leak it to the press.

Jurek met with Foreign Minister Shamir in his modest office in a building next door to the Knesset on January 23 and 25. Equally as cordial as he had been in Rome, Shamir nonetheless wanted assurances that if Israel requested such a mission, the request would be quickly granted. In the interval between the first and second meetings with the foreign minister, Jurek visited with his cousins and attempted to gain further assurances from Rome over the telephone.

At their final meeting, Shamir was at the same time conciliatory and firm: "I believe in you and in what you are saying," the foreign minister told Jurek when they were alone. "I am not asking for a promise in writing from the Vatican, even though we are willing to make our request in the form of a letter. I will take your word. When and if you *personally* can tell me, and give me your word, that this won't be a flop and leave egg on our faces here in Jerusalem, you will get the letter from me requesting the mission."

Unfortunately, Jurek, who was by now all too familiar with Vatican delays and the evasions of some in the Curia, was not in a position to make such a promise. He also knew that, although the Holy Father was an absolute monarch and was far from hesitant to make definitive statements on matters of faith and morals, when it came to questions of a sensitive international nature, the pope had to try to act on the basis of consensus within the Curia.

"Okay, Your Excellency," he said. "I'll do the best I can."

Back in Rome, he went at once to see Cardinal Deskur. The cardinal's immediate reaction was that Shamir had been absolutely correct in his refusal to commit Israel in writing at this time. Persistent resistance within the Secretariat of State boiled down to three issues: a demand for the city of Jerusalem to have international status in order to protect the holy places there for Catholics, Muslims, and Jews alike; a resolution of the problem of the "occupied territories," or those annexed in the Six-Day War of 1967; and agreement on a homeland for the Palestinians.

Jurek had heard these arguments often and did not need to reiterate his position on them to Cardinal Deskur. Jerusalem will always be the capital of Israel, he had told less sympathetic Vatican figures than Cardinal Deskur again and again. As for the so-called occupied territories, Jurek's position was the same as that of Begin, Shamir, and other Israeli hard-liners—these places had not been seized or occupied but reacquired. They were the ancient regions of Judea and Samaria and belonged by right to Israel. And as for the question of a Palestinian homeland or state, why did the Arabs need another country when they already had so many?

On the last issue, Jurek knew that his attitude was different from the pope's. He also knew, however, that the pope affirmed Israel's right to exist and prosper. Personally, he wondered how much these territorial matters had to do with the old, underlying religious issue, that unconverted Jews had no right to live in the Holy Land. No one could tell how many cardinals still believed this way. It was not something that was openly discussed within the Church any longer, except by extremists such as French Archbishop Marcel Lefebvre, who was still calling the Jews reprobate and accursed and insisting on their conversion. (Pope John Paul excommunicated Lefebvre in 1988 for these and other reactionary opinions.) But Jurek could only assume that denial of the Jews' right to live in Israel remained a factor somewhere in the recesses of many Christian souls.

The truth was that the diaspora-as-punishment idea was far from dead within Christianity, whatever the pope said about it. One of the principal reasons that the Vatican clung to the idea, until Pope John Paul II began to steadily banish it, was that if the Jews could be kept out of the Holy Land, the Church might be able to gain control of holy places.

Protestants were another matter. By definition, they were of several minds, and many of them had pro-Zionist positions. Some denominations or sects argued that since the Bible predicted the Jews' return, it should be encouraged. Some Evangelical sects under the umbrella of so-called end-time thinking, which welcomed the end of the world as a boon for those accepting Christ, thought that the sooner the Jews returned, the better. This literalism concerning the Hebrew Bible, with its inference that the return of the Jews would hasten Gloryland, was pronounced among nonconformist Christians in Britain and influenced British political policy toward the Jews. Pro-Zionists could also be found among the British ruling or upper class—apart from the many who were enthusiasts for Hitler—and was based less on theological grounds than on the affinities that were natural throughout Europe between landed aristocracy and Jews. In addition to a shared aversion to the lower orders, landed aristocrats and Jews could mutually understand attachment to the Land as a sacred thing.

Internationally, Protestant opinion was mixed. The World Council of Churches, which represented mainline Protestant denominations, had since the 1950s issued a series of doubtful but increasingly sympathetic statements about Israel after it achieved statehood. In 1983, however, in the teeth of the Lebanon fiasco, the council released a memorandum charging that some Christians were permitting guilt about the Holocaust "to corrupt their views of the conflict in the Middle East," leading to "uncritical support" of Israeli policies. Attempts by the council to engage in Christian-Muslim dialogue, which was an uphill battle given the resurgence of Muslim fundamentalism, had the principal effect of influencing a more anti-Israel line among these Protestants. The World Muslim Congress, for instance, stated officially that the "Zionist scourge aims at controlling the world and, if that is not possible, at annihilating the entire human race." "The Talmud," the president of the congress insisted to a United Nations seminar, "says that if a Jew does not drink every year the blood of a non-Jewish man, he will be damned for eternity," and argued that "the whole world is the property of Israel and the wealth, blood, and souls of non-Israelis belong to them." The acceptance of such assertions as "dialogue," which was done perhaps in the spirit of multiculturalism, would appear to make defense of Israeli arguments difficult. If they were entertained as even debatable, they must have rendered World Council of Churches' discussions unproductive.

As many theologians have concluded, Christian ambivalence about Israel reflects the story of the Jewish-Christian experience throughout history. Pope John Paul II, in embracing the Hebrew

Bible, has brought Roman Catholic teaching more closely in line with that of many Evangelical Christians. The significant difference between these two unlikely allies, however, is that while the pope has rejected the goal of converting the Jews and affirms the permanence of their covenant, American Southern Baptists and various types of Protestant Evangelicals advocate conversion, and some assume that with the Second Coming of Christ, most Jews will "see the light" and accept Jesus. In this, these Protestants seem more of a mind with Pope Pius X and his vision of mass conversions in the Holy Land than with John Paul II.

Courtesy of Jurek Kluger

John Paul II greets Renée and Jurek at a reception during the first year of his papacy.

Courtesy of Jurek Kluger

Jurek at the gravesite of his paternal grandmother during a visit to Wadowice in the 1990s.

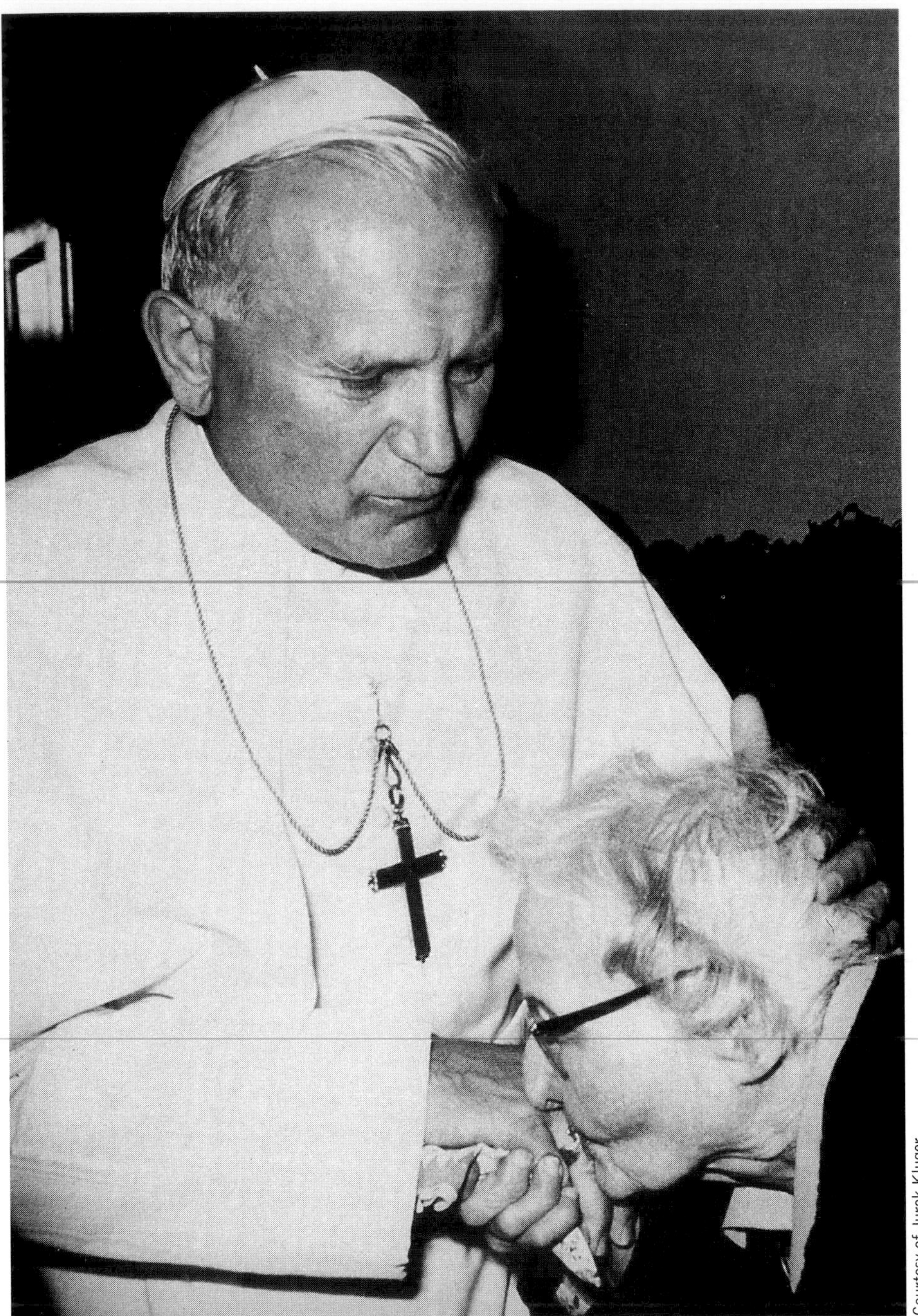

Courtesy of Jurek Kluger

John Paul II receives a greeting from Mrs. Helena Szczepanska in June 1979. During his first official visit to Poland, the pope granted his only private audience to the eighty-five-year-old neighbor from Wadowice, who had helped take care of him as a boy and also taught Jurek's sister, Tesia. Although the pope did not want Mrs. Szczepanska to kneel, she did anyway.

Suzanne O'Brien

The nursery school that was built on the site of the Wadowice synagogue. In 1989, Jurek traveled to Poland for the first time since the war to attend the dedication ceremony and read a letter from the pope.

Suzanne O'Brien

The commemorative plaque on the nursery school. The inscription, in Hebrew and Polish, begins, "Here stood the Wadowice synagogue..."

Courtesy of Jurek Kluger

Key figures in the behind-the-scenes efforts toward Vatican recognition of Israel. From left are Jurek, Johannes Cardinal Willebrands, Israeli Ambassador Avi Pazner, and Roger Cardinal Etchegaray after an informal meeting at the pope's summer residence, Castel Gandolfo, in April 1994.

L'Osservatore Romano

Stephania, who had recently broken her leg, with the pope at a Vatican reception in 1980.

Grzegorz Galazka

The baptismal ceremony for Stephania in 1981 at Castel Gandolfo.

Grzegorz Galazka

After overcoming a slight problem with the stopper in the holy-water ewer, the pope completes the baptism.

L'Osservatore Romano

At a meeting with the pope in the 1990s, Jurek points out photos of family members in a book on the history of the Jews of Wadowice.

L'Osservatore Romano

The pope says early mass in his private chapel in the papal apartments at the Vatican, April 1996. Jurek is seated in the doorway at the rear; author Darcy O'Brien is at right.

L'Osservatore Romano

The pope presents a rosary to the author's wife, Suzanne O'Brien, after a private mass in April 1996. The author is at center.

Suzanne O'Brien

The author interviews two Wadowice classmates, Stanislaw Jura (left) and Teofil Bojes (center) in 1996.

A special moment for special friends, April 1996.

L'Osservatore Romano

Suzanne O'Brien

Halina Krolikiewicz, Wojtyla's co-star in many early productions, in her Krakow apartment in 1996. The poster announces a play from 1938 and lists the future pope in a leading role.

Grzegorz Galazka

Stephania's marriage to Edward Walsh, performed by the pope at Castel Gandolfo in September 1997.

Grzegorz Galazka

Stephania and Edward recite their vows.

Grzegorz Galazka

The pope bestows a personal blessing at the end of the ceremony.

Grzegorz Galazka

From left, Stephania, John Paul II, Edward, and Jurek greet guests after the ceremony.

Grzegorz Galazka

The pope uses a solitary moment to record his thoughts during a flight from Angola in June 1992.

Grzegorz Galazka

Always at home in the mountains, John Paul II takes in the winter view at Val d'Aosta, Italy, in 1995.

Grzegorz Galazka

A springtime stroll in Val d'Aosta, 1995.

Chapter 26

Pope John Paul II has had other places besides Israel on his mind. In 1983, he visited Portugal, Costa Rica, Nicaragua, Panama, El Salvador, Guatemala, Honduras, Belize, and Haiti, all during the month of March. In June, he went to Poland; in August, France; and in September, Austria. Later he was to spend more time in Africa than on any other continent but Europe.

In Central America, particularly in Nicaragua, the pope made clear his opposition to the mixture of Marxism and the Gospels that is called liberation theology, which he considers not a theology but a political ideology. His argument was that the Church betrayed its purpose by neglecting spiritual goals for political ones and that there was as much error in supporting Communist-oriented guerrillas as there was in shoring up corrupt right-wing regimes. His message provoked criticism from the left and from those who misunderstood his condemnation of capitalist social policy, or the lack of it, as an endorsement of socialism. That John Paul had experienced life under both the Nazis and the Communists and thus could hardly be inclined to endorse tendencies to either the extreme right or the left was either ignored or not known.

Much debate has also focused on what role John Paul II played in the fall of Communism in Eastern Europe. Many months before his 1982 trip to Poland, a Soviet invasion seemed possible. According to journalists Marco Politi and Carl Bernstein in their 1996 biography, *His Holiness*, a U.S. diplomat showed the pontiff satellite photographs depicting Soviet troop movements toward the Polish border. The biography assumes that the pope appreciated being let in on a great power's state secrets. Given John Paul's self-confidence and his own sources of information, however, this is highly unlikely. He needed no one's intelligence service to inform him about the Soviet threat. In any case, his actual role in helping topple Communist rule did not come from any specific acts or statements, and certainly not because of any secret collaboration with the Reagan Administration. He affected change simply by being there, whether in the Vatican or in his motherland. John Paul knew that he represented a far greater power than America or any other temporal authority.

In fact, at one point, he said to Jurek, referring to the Soviets' possible incursion, "I don't know about you, Jurek, but if the Russians do invade Poland again, I think I should go to the front lines. How about you?"

"I'll go with you!" former lieutenant Kluger said. That would have been quite a sight. Jurek liked nothing better than to be reminded of his service to Poland, and John Paul was always happy to oblige him, even in fun.

That 1982 trip to Poland, his second visit to his homeland, couldn't have been more dramatic. The country was in a virtual state of siege and was well on its way to rejecting Communism and extricating itself from the Soviet sphere. For the Kremlin, Poland had long been the most troublesome of satellites. Solidarity leader Lech Walesa was again shaping the labor revolt that, with the Church, formed the left and right arms of resistance to the regime. To most Poles, the pope's arrival in this atmosphere seemed a certain harbinger of imminent change. His presence was so powerful, and he inspired so much affection and respect, that Polish Prime Minister General Wojciech Jaruzelzki later admitted that, on first meeting the pontiff, "I was aware that my legs were trembling and my knees were knocking together."

On his return to Rome from his travels to Poland and elsewhere, John Paul always invited Jurek for a meal. Then, in a relaxed and intimate setting, the pope could convey his impressions and tell his friend about meetings with Jewish communities around the world. Everywhere he went, the pontiff said, the Jews asked him not to forget about Israel.

"I am in no danger of forgetting," the pope told Jurek that he would assure the Jews, "because I have a Jewish friend back in Rome who is constantly reminding me of it."

The pope was constantly reminding Jurek about the homeland as well and continued to involve him one way or another in the life of the place that he had once thought he had left behind forever. The most surprising of these involvements placed the pope's friend in the position of helping to build a church, of all things.

As a priest, bishop, and archbishop in Krakow, Wojtyla followed much the same approach to undermining Communism as he had taken toward Nazism during the war. He worked to keep alive the cultural and spiritual activities that weakened the foundations of authoritarian political rule. He also delivered public sermons and speeches that in their eloquence and precise reasoning acted like charges of spiritual dynamite against the regime. On the Feast of the Epiphany in 1976, for instance, Cardinal Wojtyla delivered a memorable address at Wawel Cathedral that attacked increasing government pressures against the Church and the subjection of workers to reprisals for practicing their religion.

> We cannot remain silent, these anxieties weigh upon our hearts; the problem is fundamentally one of social ethics.... And so it cannot happen that one group of men, one social group—however well-deserving—should impose on the whole people an ideology, an opinion, contrary to the will of the majority. We are all Poland, all of us, believers and unbelievers. But it cannot be that Poland's destiny should be decided by the nonbelievers against the will of the believers. For Poland is not a chance reality. Poland is a thousand years of history, Poland is this Wawel Castle, this cathedral, these tombs of our Kings. Poland stands for innumerable victories and

> innumerable sufferings! That is all my wish, and the wish is for every man, for every man who believes, for every man who is seeking, that he may seek without the fear that someone may say to him, it is forbidden....

This address, which must have created unease among the bureaucrats, was disseminated through means other than government-controlled newspapers or broadcasts. Why the cardinal was not instantly shot or jailed for it may indicate the degree to which Soviet-style totalitarianism had its limits in Poland. Cardinal Wojtyla's impunity presumably also had to do with the degree of his personal strength. To dare to arrest him would have provoked an insurrection. It is instructive to reflect that these words actually defend the right to seek the truth, not to impose it.

This struggle to reassert the ancient Polish identity once again came to a head under Communist rule in a suburb of Krakow that was imposed on the people by industrial planners. Shortly before Stalin's death in 1953, the Soviets ordered a gigantic steel mill built on the city's outskirts. By the time Wojtyla was appointed archbishop in 1964, the workers' apartments adjacent to this industrial monstrosity formed a city in themselves.

Far beyond the Rynek lies Nova Huta, or New Mill, a geometrically laid-out complex of dull buildings designed by dreary collectivist architects to house steelworkers and their families. Each five- or six-story building is uniformly gray. The rectangular high-rise condominiums that line the beaches of South Florida or the wretched public-housing cubes that sprawl outside Rome by comparison look warm and alive. Although there are thousands of people living in them, the buildings of Nova Huta look dead, all with communal yards and kitchens without windows.

It is not a coincidence that much of Moscow looks like this. What steel-brain dreamed it up? Who could have conceived of a workers' paradise to kill the spirits of workers? What person in his right mind would actually choose to live here? No one, is the answer, and no one ever lived here by choice. The workers were trucked in from the countryside, where at least there were pigs and cabbage crops. They were told that this was the City of the Future, but could any of them have believed it? Krakovians believe that the Communists put the steel plant there and built Nova Huta to punish Poland's cultural capital and kill it. Noxious fumes and smoke from the mill, only recently controlled, blew into Krakow on the prevailing winds, giving people coughing fits and irritated eyes as well as shortening their lives.

The Polish people, who after the war were worn out from hunger and tired of shooting Germans and Russians and burying the dead, accepted it. What they could not accept was that there would be no churches in the City of the Future. God was bourgeois and no longer welcome. It took the people a certain amount of time to realize how much they missed going to church, or at least having the freedom to do so. Eventually, they began listening to what Archbishop Wojtyla had to say.

Complaints led to protests. Anger increased when people realized that the mill was not only poisoning the air, it was polluting the soil for miles and miles around. Nothing would grow. Birds disappeared. Even worms for fishing grew scarce, but the fish that had survived were diseased. Five years after Nova Huta was built, people noticed that the rivers weren't freezing anymore. And of course, the people of Nova Huta couldn't return to their farms, which had been taken over by the state.

They wanted a church. Protest meetings turned nasty. The people put up a cross where they wished their church to stand; the authorities took it down. The people put it up again. Over the years, from the mid-1950s into the 1960s, the protests became riots, with stones thrown at soldiers and bullets fired back. Wojtyla, as bishop, archbishop, and then cardinal, was with them, preaching patience but speaking out again and again against the enforcement of atheism and the attempt to erase Poland's history. He knew and felt what ordinary people did. He had not become a Church bureaucrat. He was not merely their cardinal but their priest, always available. He said mass in the open air in Nova Huta and worked behind the scenes to try to make the authorities budge.

In that part of Poland, Nova Huta became the predominant symbol of resistance to Communism, with Archbishop Wojtyla the chief advocate of building a church. Had the struggle been publicized at all in Western Europe or America, it would have looked eccentric. Whoever heard, in this day and age, of people putting their lives on the line to build a Catholic church? Protests were staged over unjust wars or too many trees cut down or racial or sexual discrimination. Sophisticates cared about nuclear power, whales, blood sports, furs, and how tuna were netted, perhaps, but a church?

That was not the way it was in Poland. After ten years' agitation, a permit was granted. Construction began in 1967, but by 1972, the church was only half finished. The bureaucrats were skillful at obstructionism. Pope Paul VI did notice, and he sent the foundation stone, taken from Saint Peter's tomb in Rome. Cardinal Wojtyla had the pontiff's ear. Once a year, the cardinal celebrated mass on the construction site. Slowly, the structure went up.

It was of a stark design symbolic of Nova Huta itself, but shaped to resemble a looming Noah's Ark afloat in a dangerous sea. In 1977, Cardinal Wojtyla consecrated the church and dedicated it to the Queen of Poland. It is now known as the Ark of God's Majesty and is the most dramatic architectural statement in Europe of anti-Communist resistance. It is all the more remarkable for having been completed during the Cold War. A second church serving the Nova Huta district was begun during Cardinal Wojtyla's tenure and remained unfinished by the date of his election as pope.

Shortly after John Paul's election, Jurek encountered a priest at the Vatican who knew all about both churches and who also recalled vividly the music of Dr. Kluger's string quartet at the house on Zatorska Street. A young lawyer and reserve player with the ensemble then, he was now Monsignor Dr. Mikolaj Kuczkowski, formerly the chancellor and legal counsel to the Krakow diocese under Cardinal Wojtyla. Two days after John Paul's installation, Monsignor Kuczkowski and Jurek met for the first time in forty years and had dinner at a restaurant in the Borgo Pio that night. They had a great deal to catch up on.

The monsignor told Jurek about the various problems that he had handled in Krakow for the cardinal, especially the nearly endless negotiations to secure building permits for the Nova Huta churches. The second one remained unfinished because marble for the interior and granite for the floor could not be found at a price the Poles could afford.

"I can help with that," Jurek blurted, although he had no idea how. "There is no problem." This was Jurek's standard response no matter what was asked of him. He also volunteered his partner.

Reliable Rosenberg immediately thought of the most famous and revered marble quarries in the world, located at Carrara, in the north above Viareggio. The marble there had been good enough for Michelangelo, why not for a Polish church? As for the price, surely any Italian chiseler, or whatever they were called, would give a supplicant monsignor an even break.

By the summer of 1980, after much preliminary haggling over the phone, Jurek made the first of nineteen automobile trips back and forth to Carrara, in the company of Monsignor Kuczkowski and his architect, Jozef Dutkiewicz, to examine the materials and negotiate for them. On one of these excursions, Jurek was refueling his car at Orvieto and realized that they had left all the blueprints and specifications behind at Massa Carrara. He had to drive the two hundred miles back to fetch them and returned to Rome at four A.M. At nine, he was still asleep when Monsignor Dziwisz phoned, inviting him to lunch.

As Jurek walked into the papal dining room, His Holiness quoted the old Polish proverb: "If you do not have it in your head, you must have it in your legs!"

By chance, one quarry happened to have on hand a large supply of Brazilian granite slabs that had been polished for an American company that canceled the order because the dimensions were too short. Monsignor Kuczkowski appealed to the quarry manager's piety, anti-Communism, desire for a good place in heaven, respect for the *Santo Padre*, and so on, and snapped up the goods at a steep discount. The architect reworked his plans to arrange the stone into a stunning, four-thousand-square-foot floor.

Over the next few months, this Polish trio, racing up and down the coast, managed to obtain for the walls a much greater quantity of first-quality travertino marble than the budget allowed, with a further discount on shipping.

When he returned from Poland, the Holy Father told Jurek that he had seen Mrs. Szczepanska again and told her about how well the baptism of Stephania had gone and how Jurek had helped with the materials for the new church. The Polish organizations that had raised funds were delighted with the result and amazed at how little the marble and granite had cost.

"I hope the Communists are very jealous," Jurek said.

The church was completed, and a statue of John Paul II now stands outside the sanctuary. The church is dedicated to Saint Maximillian Maria Kolbe. Jurek chose to ignore any misgivings he might have had about that and took great pleasure and pride in having helped. He also was moved by the sad irony that a Jew had contributed time and effort to the construction of a church in a city whose synagogues stood in ruin or were being used for secular purposes. Only a few hundred Jews were left in Krakow to attend the one that was still functioning as a place of worship. He had acted more out of old friendships than from any other motive; he felt that his father would have done the same. With what the pope was doing to help Jewish-Catholic relations, it seemed only natural.

A DIFFERENT CATHOLIC SANCTUARY IN POLAND, AT AUSCHWITZ, DID NOT turn out so well. It provoked the most acrimonious dissension between Catholics and Jews since World War II and threatened to unravel the tapestry of Catholic-Jewish relations that had been so painstakingly woven since Jules Isaac visited the popes and inspired *Nostra Aetate.*

On the twentieth anniversary of *Nostra Aetate* in 1985, the Catholic Church published *Notes on the Correct Way to Present Jews and Judaism in Catholic Preaching and Teaching*, a handbook meant to clarify vagaries and rectify omissions in the Vatican II document. Although some matters were still in contention, the *Notes* were on the whole embraced by both sides. They came under scrutiny at numerous interfaith discussions, particularly in America, where Rabbi Leon Klenicki, director of interfaith affairs for the Anti-Defamation League, and Dr. Eugene J. Fisher, associate director of the Secretariat for Ecumenical and Interreligious Affairs of the National Conference of Catholic Bishops, took the lead in sponsoring dialogue and scholarship.

Some progress toward enlightenment, including getting across John Paul II's views on Judaism, was being made. Many priests, however, continued to refer to Jews as "killers of Christ," as if there had been no *Nostra Aetate*. Some Catholics were too often content in the anti-Semitism that they had absorbed in their religious education. A new Catechism was being prepared, but it was years from completion, and a depressingly large segment of the population in Europe and America, encouraged by pseudo-scholarship, now professed disbelief that any mass slaughter of the Jews had actually occurred in World War II. Denial of the Holocaust has also surfaced as an aspect of reverse racism in ethnic studies at supposedly respectable universities, where truth takes a back seat to politics. The word *Holocaust* itself has become debased as various ethnic groups claim equal rights with Jews to "victimhood." This anti-Judaism sentiment is part of neo-Nazi and extreme nationalist sentiments in Europe and America.

In 1984, a series of incidents began that, along with the situation in the Middle East, totally derailed all of John Paul II's intentions toward the formal diplomatic recognition of Israel—and with them Jurek's efforts to bring Vatican and Jewish representatives together toward that end. In that year, a group of Polish Carmelite nuns moved into a building standing at the edge of the Auschwitz death camp. They intended to remodel the building, which had been a theater before the war, into a convent and a shrine dedicated to silent meditation and prayers for expiation of the sins committed against humanity at the camp. From all evidence subsequently accumulated, the nuns did not know at the time that the building had been used by the Germans to house various supplies, including the Zyklon-B gas that was used to kill inmates, about 90 percent of whom were Jews.

The move was not much remarked upon at the time. There was already a similar shrine at Dachau in those days. Under the Communists, there was little tourism to Poland, but later, Auschwitz would become the most popular attraction, as it were. The building's former use to store a roach killer that was also lethal to humans was not internationally remarked upon either, as yet. But all this changed in May 1985, when the pope was visiting Belgium and the Netherlands. A month earlier, addressing an interfaith colloquium at the Angelicum in Rome to commemorate the twentieth anniversary of *Nostra Aetate*, John Paul spoke of the theological links between Judaism and Christianity, the need for closer relations, and "the catastrophe which so cruelly decimated the Jewish people, before and during the war, especially in the death camps." He prayed for increased spirituality in the modern world, citing Deuteronomy: "Hear, O Israel, the Lord our God is one God." But in the Netherlands that May, the old animosities resurfaced, and in the mouth of a Catholic priest.

Using the pope's visit to attract greater publicity, Father Wernerfried van Straaten, founder of a conservative organization called Aid to the Church in Need, launched an appeal for donations to the Carmelite convent at Auschwitz. In doing so, he employed language that was highly offensive, referring to the nuns' project as "The Triumph of the Cross over Auschwitz."

At this point, an international furor erupted. The Belgian Jewish community was among the first to react, stating that "Auschwitz is a world of ashes which no one can appropriate," objecting to the presence of a convent there, and referring to "an elementary lack of ecumenical perspective" and "an offense to the memory of millions of Jewish martyrs." Many members of the Roman Catholic hierarchy expressed sympathy for Jewish concerns. Albert Cardinal Decourtray, Archbishop of Lyons, objected to the creation of the convent, saying that it was "like putting a synagogue in a Christian cemetery." The cardinal called the fund appeal disconcerting and said that for world opinion, Auschwitz would always remain a reminder of the *Shoah*, the attempt to exterminate Jews because they are Jews.

Other Catholic reactions were less sympathetic. The controversy heightened when a Belgian journalist quoted a Polish priest as saying that the convent was a "gift to Pope John Paul II." Asked whether the pope had personally approved the project, Dr. Joaquin Navarro-Valls, head of the press office of the Holy See and the Vatican's chief public spokesman, told the *New York Times*: "It is my impression that he was unaware of the controversy. The pope was probably informed of the move, but he neither encouraged nor discouraged the initiative. The matter doesn't concern the Vatican one way or another. The personal line of the pope is that local bishops have responsibility for the local affairs of the church."

It was an earnest attempt by Dr. Navarro-Valls to try to distance the pope from what was becoming a damaging issue for the Church, but in fact the pope was concerned. He could not have removed himself from involvement, even if he had wanted to, after the remark about the convent's being a "gift" to him had been publicized. The idea lodged in many minds, especially of those who were hostile to him in the liberal wing of the Church, that since John Paul was Polish, the convent must have been his idea, or at least he must have approved of it.

In Rome, Jerzy Kluger was able to assure Dr. Lichten of the ADL, who was quite calm about the matter, that something would be done about the convent. Soon it was announced, as Jurek knew it would be, that early the next year (1986), Catholic and Jewish representatives would meet in Geneva to resolve the problem. The Jewish delegation would be led by Theo Klein, president of the Council of Jewish Organizations in France and chairman of the European Congress. Cardinal Decourtray would lead the Catholic delegation, which also would include cardinals Daneels of Brussels, Macharski of Krakow, and Lustiger of Paris.

Jean-Marie Cardinal Lustiger, Archbishop of Paris, happened also to be Jewish. He had converted to Catholicism as a boy in April 1940, just before the German invasion. His mother and most of his other close relatives were killed at Auschwitz. He still considers himself a Jew and was eager to be involved in the resolution of the Carmelite matter because he was coming under personal attack about it. Certain Jewish scholars were accusing him of being in league with John Paul II to "Christianize" the Holocaust, arguing that the convent at Auschwitz was proof of this intent. The cardinal instead regarded himself as the embodiment of continuity between Judaism and Christianity, not as someone who had rejected Judaism—a position that was difficult for many Jews to accept. He was anxious to demonstrate his sensitivity to Jewish concerns. He told a reporter for the *Jerusalem Post* that the attacks on him were "a despicable polemic" done "on the lines of the most abject anti-Semitism."

The controversy was already having a chilling effect on Jewish-Catholic relations in general, causing a kind of polarization that had not existed since the early days of Vatican II. An example of this plunge in temperature was a 1985 Op-Ed page article that appeared in the *New York Times*. Rabbi Arthur Hertzberg, who was vice-president of the World Jewish Congress, had been an active participant in Jewish-Christian dialogues for fifteen years. Now, however, he sounded an impatient note, even a frustrated one. His essay, headed "Rome Must Recognize Israel," accused the Vatican of hedging, procrastinating, and double-talking: "There is something very wrong with the dialogue between Catholics and Jews. For twenty years now, even as the relationship was formalized and deepened, the Roman Catholic Church has used every tactic to avoid the issue that matters most to world Jewry—recognition of Israel."

Rabbi Hertzberg strongly suggested that the reason behind this Catholic refusal was theological, despite what Church authorities may have said: "They [Catholics] want to treat us as a purely spiritual entity so they can avoid dealing with the issue that matters most to us—explicit recognition of Israel." The rabbi wished to show that his suspicions were not his alone: "That is why Edgar Bronfman, president of the World Jewish Congress, has asked Archbishop John O'Connor of New York to help push the Vatican to recognize Israel." (Archbishop, later Cardinal, O'Connor was in fact doing just that.) The rabbi insisted that the temporal concerns of Jews must form the basis of dialogue with Catholics. After all, the Holocaust had been a decidedly temporal phenomenon, not a matter of theological debate. Rome was making gestures to enhance the status of the PLO while asking for more time on the question of Israel. This was no longer acceptable: "Israel has to be a central issue on the agenda, not something for whispered conversation in the corridors of the consultations."

Although only a handful of *New York Times* readers would have made the connection, the reference to whispering in corridors was an obvious allusion to what Jerzy Kluger had been up to in Rome during the past four years, with no concrete result in sight. When the ADL sent him the clipping, however, he certainly got the inference, and he passed the word on to the Holy Father.

Chapter 27

EVEN AS IT EXACERBATED JEWISH IMPATIENCE AND AROUSED SUSPICIONS about the Vatican, the Carmelite controversy made it more difficult for the Church to recognize Israel without appearing to react to Jewish pressure. The pope felt that acting before the matter was resolved would boomerang against the Jews. Jurek had to agree, although while His Holiness was concerned about possible reprisals by Arabs against Christians, neither Jurek nor Cardinal Deskur was as worried about that possibility. What would really make a difference was a breakthrough of some kind between Israel and at least some of her Arab neighbors. Otherwise, the Vatican would appear to be trying to tip the scales in Israel's favor, an argument that was naturally not much appreciated in Jewish circles.

To try to allay Jewish suspicions and stop the deterioration in relations, John Paul was anxious to make a concrete gesture, something truly dramatic. The idea of visiting a synagogue first came up at a breakfast meeting between the pope and Jurek on January 5, 1984. From what Jurek gathered then, His Holiness had also mentioned the idea to another Jewish friend of his, the philosopher Emanual Levinas. At another breakfast with Jurek almost a year later, His Holiness mentioned the idea again, saying that visiting a synagogue might quiet some of the political criticism while being understood as strictly a religious gesture. No specific synagogue was mentioned, and no plans were made. It was not until late in 1985, with feelings over the Carmelite convent running high, that the pope decided to make a dramatic appearance in a synagogue. By then, it had been ascertained that no pope had ever set foot in one.

His Excellency Clemente Riva, Auxiliary Bishop of Rome, lived in the rectory attached to the Church of San Carlo al Corso, which was located only a few blocks from the area of the old ghetto and the Great Temple of the Roman Jews. On daily walks through his neighborhood, he enjoyed calling in at Jewish-owned shops to chat with the proprietors. For several years, Bishop Riva had harbored the idea that the pope ought to visit a synagogue. And so, in the course of a meeting on matters of religious freedom with John Paul that December, and with the Church under heavy criticism concerning the Polish Carmelites, Bishop Riva made his suggestion. He dropped the idea casually and lightly, but he made his point: "Why don't you do it, Your Holiness? The synagogue, the Great Temple, is just across the Tiber, ten minutes by car. You could be back before lunch."

Bishop Riva was surprised at how readily His Holiness welcomed the idea. John Paul did not confide that he had been thinking along similar lines for more than a year and talking about it with Jurek. The notion of making the gesture in Rome had the special appeal of showing the world how the two communities could live side by side in harmony. The Holy Father said that Bishop Riva should present his idea to several people in the Vatican and, if there was no objection, broach it to the Jews. John Paul had already met the Chief Rabbi of Rome, Professor Elio Toaff, who, as everyone knew, had come to Saint Peter's Square to pray on the night of John XXIII's death. It didn't seem likely that this man would be against the visit.

Bishop Riva found general enthusiasm for the idea within the Vatican, which was an indication of how much things had changed. And at the pope's suggestion, Jurek offered to help in any way he could. He was not particularly close to Rabbi Toaff, but he admired a second rabbi who was attached to the Great Temple, and he went to see him.

This was Dr. Alberto Piattelli, whose family had the distinction of being one of the four in Rome that could trace their residence in the city back to more than a hundred years before Christ. Their origins were by way of Ostia, originally the Roman seaport, where they had arrived somewhere between the first and second centuries B.C. Rabbi Piattelli was living proof of one of Jules Isaac's principal arguments, that the diaspora could not have been a punishment for the Jews' so-called rejection of Christ since it was already well under way long before Christ was born.

Rabbi Piattelli was well-aware of John Paul II's views on Judaism and the pontiff's efforts to change Christian attitudes. He believed that the pope would have an even more telling effect on the Church in this area than John XXIII had, for two reasons. The first was that Karol Wojtyla was not Italian. As the Hebrew Bible tells us, the prophet is usually not accepted in his own country and must come from somewhere else to have the greatest effect. The rabbi had known and observed John XXIII when that great man was Archbishop of Venice. He was a brave and magnificent person, but he came from within the restricted inner circle of the Italian Church and could not have gone further than he did in the matter of reform. John Paul II was operating under no such inhibitions or restraints. He did not have a lifetime of obligations and debts within the Italian hierarchy to worry about. Jurek, who was talking to Dr. Piattelli in the rabbi's office at the Great Temple, was astonished by the degree to which this Jewish scholar had studied the Vatican. But come to think of it, why not? Saint Peter's was only just down the street. And yet, it was so far away from this Great Temple, for so long!

"And the second reason this pope will go further in reform than any other, as far as Jews are concerned, is you, *Ingegnere* Kluger," Rabbi Piattelli said.

"Me?" Jurek asked.

"Because you are his friend. Because Pope John Paul grew up knowing Jews. That has not been true of any other pope, ever, not in the entire history of the Church. Or not since Saint Peter, at any rate. Do you think Pius XII knew what a Jew was as a person? Of course not."

Meanwhile, Bishop Riva had met with Rabbi Toaff and, more important, with members of the Jewish community of Rome, including its president, Dr. Giacomo Saban, who was professor of mathematics at the University of Rome. Every Roman Jew concerned was highly enthusiastic about the prospect of a papal visit, although they also made a strong request. They hoped that His Holiness would take this opportunity to mention the State of Israel and to endorse the centrality of the Land to all Jews. Bishop Riva said he could not promise that, but he would convey the message.

A date for the historic visit was agreed upon and set—April 13, 1986, in the season of Easter and Passover. When the news went out, it attracted even more international attention than anyone except the pope had anticipated. Five days before the event, Bishop Riva, Cardinal Willebrands, and French Archbishop Pierre Duprey, who was a member of Cardinal Willebrands' council on unity, held a press conference at the Vatican at which the prelates faced aggressive questioning. The issue of the Polish Carmelites was raised, along with the matter of Vatican recognition of Israel. Archbishop Duprey, a shy man, was made so nervous by the journalists' tone that he abruptly left the room and did not return. Cardinal Willebrands was self-conscious about his less-than-perfect Italian and said nothing. That left Bishop Riva to field all the questions.

The bishop is a man of almost ghostly delicacy and asceticism. An experienced teacher, he is used to fielding questions and was well-prepared for all the ones that touched on sensitive areas. Having informed His Holiness of the Roman Jews' concerns about Israel, the bishop would not presume to speak for the pope on this matter and had the strong impression that the Holy Father wanted his visit to be perceived and received as a religious gesture, whatever its likely political repercussions. Bishop Riva, therefore, had an answer carefully prepared, and he delivered it forcefully when an Italian reporter asked about recognition for Israel: "This is not a proper question," he replied in his most fastidious manner. "People go to the synagogue to pray, not to get involved in political questions."

And that was that, for the moment.

SECURITY AT THE GREAT TEMPLE BY THE TIBER IS ALWAYS TIGHT. IN 1982, PLO terrorists exploded a bomb in the doorway of the synagogue and sprayed a crowd of Jews with machine-gun fire. A two-year-old child was killed and others injured; one man was saved by his Hebrew prayer book, which stopped a bullet that was headed for his heart. The morning of the pope's visit, it was pouring rain, the first rainfall after a very long drought. Attendance was by screened invitation only, with very few invitations going to members of the Church hierarchy. Bishop Riva, cardinals Willebrands, Silvestrini, and Deskur, and a half-dozen others who had long supported reconciliation with the Jews were invited.

The hall of worship in the Great Temple has seats for about two thousand worshipers arranged in four rows beneath a great dome topped with amber glass. A women's gallery rises on columns to the left of the *bimah*, a wooden lectern that is inserted into the gallery surrounding the *aron*, or altar, as Christians would understand it.

Jurek, who was sitting with Rosenberg about halfway back, watched as John Paul II entered, flanked by Rabbi Toaff and Professor Saban, and the three took chairs before the *aron*. Jurek thought to himself that at least Lolek did not have to borrow a yarmulke because he was always wearing one anyway. Like everyone else, Jurek was in awe at the uniqueness of this moment, something that had been inconceivable until this pope. To think, he and Lolek had been discussing this for more than a year, and now it was happening! There was the pope, in white, and Rabbi Toaf, also in white robes but wrapped in the familiar blue-and-white prayer shawl and wearing the distinctive five-cornered white hat that was favored in Roman Jewish worship.

Jurek's mind was also circling back through time to another synagogue in Wadowice some fifty years ago. On that day, Jurek had sat with Lolek and Lieutenant Wojtyla to hear the great young tenor sing Hebrew hymns. He felt the spirits of the old lieutenant and of his own father and mother and Tesia and...it was almost too much to bear. He took some deep breaths.

Professor Saban spoke first, delivering a very strong speech. Jurek's eyes shifted back and forth from the professor to the pope during the oration. He could see that the pope was tense, leaning slightly forward with his hands gripping the gilded arms of his chair.

"Your Holiness," Professor Saban began. The professor and his wife and family had arrived in Rome only a few years before from Turkey, where they had been born Sephardic Jews, but he spoke elegant Italian. "I have the honor of being the first to welcome you to this major temple on the banks of the Tiber. I greet you on behalf of the most ancient Jewish community of the Diaspora.... In expressing our satisfaction at seeing a Roman pontiff for the first time cross the threshold of a synagogue, I feel it my duty to recount briefly the history of the Jewish community of this city, a history which goes back several thousand years."

Professor Saban then told the story of the Roman Jews from the second century "prior to the destruction of the Second Temple." He described the freedom that Jews knew under most of the Roman emperors, especially Augustus, and touched on ensuing sufferings from about the year 1000 onward. He alluded to the liberality of Pope Alexander VI, who welcomed Jews who were expelled from Spain after 1492. But the professor did not fail to mention the oppression of Jews under other popes, the burning of the Talmud, and the removal of the Jews into the ghetto, on the site of which this Great Temple now stood. A lack of freedom and intermittent persecution had been the lot of Roman Jews for the next three centuries. An interval of freedom after 1880 had ended with the horrors of fascism and World War II.

After a rather delicately phrased reference to the silence of the Vatican during those times, together with praise for Italian Christians, including priests and nuns who sheltered Jews from the Nazis, Professor Saban closed with a direct plea for Vatican recognition of the State of Israel. The great Pope John XXIII had taken the first steps. *Nostra Aetate* was his legacy. Now it was time for a further step. "I do not hesitate to believe that this step will be taken," the professor said. The pope's visit to the temple was "lively testimony to the spirit of the council. It fills us all with joy, inasmuch as it is a sign which foreshadows better days."

Rabbi Toaff, who followed Professor Saban to the *bimah*, also referred to the State of Israel in his speech, although with a less direct call for diplomatic recognition, and stressed the return of universal brotherhood as ordained by the Hebrew Bible. Neither the rabbi nor the professor referred to the several occasions on which the pope had already explicitly affirmed the right of Jews to live in Israel "in desired security and the due tranquillity that is the prerogative of every *nation* and condition of life and of progress for every society." (April 20, 1984; italics added.) Formal ties remained the sticking point. As Jurek had reminded the Holy Father, it was a bit strange that the Vatican had formal links to the Solomon Islands but not to the land of King Solomon himself, a remark that the pope found as appropriate as it was witty. The time will come soon, was all he could promise for now.

But Rabbi Toaff's emphasis was not on differences but on the wonder of this occasion, about which he expressed his "intense satisfaction. This gesture is destined to be remembered throughout history." And he linked it appropriately to John XXIII, "your illustrious predecessor."

The rabbi, in praising this "turning point in Church policy," evoked Jules Isaac and "the teaching of contempt" that he had brought to the attention of Pope John. Rabbi Toaff put greatest stress on the combined efforts that Judaism and Catholicism could make to fight for "inalienable human rights: like the right to life, to freedom of thought, conscience, and religion." He also defined the concept of freedom as being free from such evils as attacks on one's honor, good name, and self-respect. The rabbi closed with a lyrical passage from Isaiah, ending, "For as the earth brings forth its shoots, and as a garden causes what is sown in it to spring up, so the Lord God will cause righteousness and praise to spring forth before all the nations."

The pope certainly recognized and understood that this wasn't a randomly chosen expression of optimism. It was the definition of the Messianic Age as understood in Judaism, a time of peace among nations and between religions. By citing it, the rabbi was according John Paul II the greatest honor, implying that by this historic mission, the pope was acting in accordance with Divine Providence. It was in this sense that the rabbi's colleague, Rabbi Piattelli, affirmed to Jerzy and to others his own belief that John Paul II was a prophet, come from a far country to set his people on the true path toward days of righteousness. Within Judaism, there can be no greater esteem expressed for any human being.

Then it was the pope's turn to speak. Whatever tenseness Jurek had noticed in his friend was gone by the time he rose to deliver his address. He did so in dignified but entirely colloquial, concrete language, as if he were addressing an audience of friends on the issues of greatest importance among them. He sprinkled in a liberal number of quotations from and allusions to the Hebrew Bible, which were in keeping with his principal theme, that Judaism and Christianity were not separate faiths, whatever their important differences, but were continuous from Abraham. In making this point in various ways, he also came up with one especially memorable phrase.

> The Jewish religion is not "extrinsic" to us, but in a certain way is "intrinsic" to our own religion. With Judaism, therefore, we have a relationship which we do not have with any other religion. You are our dearly beloved brothers and, in a certain way, it could be said that you are our *elder brothers*. (Italics added.)

The implications of those last two words, which have the literary virtue of penetrating consciousness, are profound in that they restore the proper relationship between the religions. Jurek recognized that in referring to the Jews as "our elder brothers," John Paul was adapting a phrase from Mickiewicz. It was not an allusion that was likely to be caught by many in the audience. The pope closed with a passage from Psalm 118, quoting seven lines in Hebrew and then in Italian, concluding, "Let those who fear the Lord say, 'His steadfast love endures for ever.' Amen." It was one of John Paul's favorite themes, that whatever the nightmare of history, we should "be not afraid."

After the service, as the pope and Rabbi Toaff embraced and other Church and Jewish dignitaries congratulated one another before the *aron*, Rabbi Piattelli heard the pope remark, "You know, it's true that this is the first time a pope has ever been inside a synagogue, but I have been in one before, a long time ago." And he recalled that Sabbath in Wadowice.

The Chief Rabbi began to walk His Holiness to his waiting car, which would whisk him back to the Vatican, a ten-minute journey that had taken two thousand years to complete. But John Paul did not feel like leaving quite yet. He turned and walked a few steps along the Lungotevere Cenci to gaze at the plaques inscribed in Hebrew on the temple wall and asked Rabbi Toaff to explain them to him. One was in memory of Jewish soldiers who fell in World War I; another commemorated the two thousand Roman Jews who were deported to Auschwitz; a third honored those killed in caves near Rome. The pope recognized lines from Psalm 44 inscribed in stone. They were taken from verses 23 and 24 and evoked King David's search for the hidden God.

After His Holiness pulled away in the rain, Rabbi Toaff said to Bishop Riva, "This has been such a wonderful thing. I can't quite begin to understand it. Why have I been the one so honored? Why did it happen to me?"

"It is a sign from Divine Providence," the bishop said.

Chapter 28

It was remarkable how much trouble ten nuns could cause. Or, to be fair to them, it was deplorable how the Carmelite sisters, through no real fault of their own, were made into a political-religious issue because of the ill will of some men and the mistakes of others.

Meeting in Geneva on July 2, 1986, and February 26, 1987, the Catholic and Jewish representatives reached an agreement stating that within two years, the nuns would move to a new convent constructed well outside the boundaries of the death camp. Unfortunately, the concord, achieved without rancor and in good faith, did not take into account the extent to which the Polish government would take advantage of the situation to delay the issuing of permits to construct the convent. Two years later, the Carmelites were still at Auschwitz. Two months after the deadline for the nuns' removal, Cardinal Lustiger of Paris told the *Jerusalem Post*:

> We have probably taken a very unwise step by setting such a close deadline for the removal of the convent. We did it, on both sides, because we felt the pressure of our public opinions. It was totally unrealistic to have thought that we, Westerners, could materially get the Polish nuns to move so quickly. We all didn't realize what the real situation is in Poland.

At an interfaith meeting that he attended in Krakow, and later at Auschwitz itself, Rabbi Klenicki of the ADL discovered that the nuns had never been consulted by anyone from the West about their original plans or the Geneva directive for them to move. Moreover, there was some question about the Church's authority to actually order the nuns to do anything. After Geneva, the Superior General of the Carmelites wrote to Council of Jewish Organizations president Theo Klein that the agreement must be obeyed. He said that the Carmelites at Auschwitz must accept the planned transfer to another location, and that the Father Provincial of the Carmelites in Poland, while not in favor of the move himself, had agreed to carry it out.

In 1988, the Archdiocese of Krakow was given a piece of land for the new convent. A year later, the deed transferring ownership was finally signed, but no construction had begun. As the delays continued, various European Jewish groups began demonstrating at the camp to demand the nuns' departure. These protests attracted much worldwide publicity.

The only thing that was being built in Poland was increasing resentment. Poles felt that they were being ordered around by outside entities. A factor in this attitude not recognized in the West was that while the Jewish martyrdom during the Holocaust was honored and appreciated through a profusion of books, articles, documentary films, and even a television miniseries, the non-Jewish Polish sacrifice during World War II had been forgotten. It was not only the tens of thousands of Polish Catholic victims at Auschwitz that were at issue but also the three million non-Jewish Polish deaths that the war had inflicted, together with the valor of General Anders's army-in-exile. "Why are the Jews receiving all the sympathy and attention when no one speaks of us?" was a common attitude. It was a view that was not confined to intensely anti-Semitic Poles but was also shared by some who had helped Jews during the war.

Rabbi Klenicki, who succeeded Dr. Joseph Lichten at the ADL after the doctor's death in 1987, was one of the few Jewish leaders to express sympathy for the Polish Catholic sensibility. At the interfaith meeting in Krakow, the rabbi pointed out that when it came to Jewish martyrdom, the French were much worse than the Poles. French collaborators had betrayed Jews to the Germans during the war, while Poles had not. "Why," he asked, "are we in sympathy with the French and not in sympathy with the non-Jewish Poles who suffered more?"

On the Jewish side, still another factor was causing heated reaction to the Carmelites. A similar convent at Dachau had been established without controversy. The difference between that and Auschwitz was that Dachau is in the West. In Communist Poland, no reference to specifically Jewish suffering was allowed because to acknowledge the attempt to exterminate a certain religious and ethnic group would have been contrary to Marxist dogma, which permitted reference only to anti-fascist victims. Given the absence of any shrine or even a plaque in tribute to Jews at Auschwitz, it is not surprising that they reacted as they did at the prospect of a Catholic center. It did indeed appear to indicate the "triumph" of the cross at Auschwitz.

IN ROME AT THE BEGINNING OF 1989, JUREK KLUGER WAS DOING HIS BEST TO assure various Jewish leaders that the Carmelites would be removed. He enjoyed an excellent relationship with the new First Secretary at the Israeli Embassy, Miron Gordon, who understood that this and other matters would have to be resolved before the Vatican could finally formally recognize Israel.

Jurek had his own Polish dilemma, and he was not sure how to deal with it. He received an invitation to attend the unveiling of a plaque on May 9 at the site of the old synagogue in Wadowice. He was grateful to be asked and pleased that at least the synagogue would not be completely forgotten, but he didn't want to go. He had seen twenty of his classmates, along with four 1938 graduates of the girls' school, late the previous year at a reunion with the pope at the Vatican. There had been an emotional dinner with the pope, Halina Krolikiewicz Kwiatkowska, and the others. Halina had recited a long passage from Norwid's *Chopin's Piano*, an epic poem about threats to Polish culture, that had reduced everyone to tears. For Jurek, that was enough for now. The piece of Poland that he loved most was only a few minutes across town in the Vatican or at Castel Gandolfo, and he saw him all the time.

When he told His Holiness about the invitation, however, the pope urged him to go. He thought it would do Jurek good to see all the old places. Jurek said no, it would be too painful, especially now with all the fuss going on about the Carmelites. He had no wish to go to Auschwitz, either. The past was past. The pope disagreed.

"Fortunately, you cannot excommunicate me for disagreeing with Your Holiness," Jurek said.

"You should go anyway," the Holy Father said. "This ceremony is to commemorate all the Jews of Wadowice, including your family. Think about it."

"I'll think about it," Jurek said to end the matter.

His friend was too clever for him. One day as he was coming in from work, Renée told him that he had a letter from the pope. That wasn't so unusual, but the letter was. The papal stationery was embossed with John Paul II's personal seal, which had never appeared before on personal letters from His Holiness. The letter began "*Drogi Jurku*" ("Dear Jurek"), but otherwise it was obviously intended for more eyes than his. In translation from Polish, it read:

> On the 9th of May this year, 1989, on the site of the synagogue which was destroyed during the last World War, a plaque will be unveiled commemorating the Jews from Wadowice and nearby, who were victims of persecution and were exterminated by the Nazis.
>
> I thank you very much for the letter in which you advise me of this event. Many of those who perished, your co-religionists and our fellow countrymen, were our colleagues in our elementary school and, later, in the high school where we graduated together, fifty years ago. All were citizens of Wadowice, the town to which you and I are bound together by our memories of childhood and youth. I remember very clearly the Wadowice Synagogue, which was near to our high school. I have before my eyes the numerous worshipers, who during their Holidays passed on their way to pray there.
>
> If you are able to be there, in Wadowice, on the 9th of May, tell all who are gathered there how, together with them, I venerate the

memory of their so cruelly killed co-religionists and compatriots and also this place of worship, which the invaders destroyed.

I embrace with deep reverence all those whom you are remembering this day—the 9th of May, 1989, in Wadowice.

Allow me to quote the words, which I have delivered to the representatives of the Jewish community of Warsaw, during my third pilgrimage to the Fatherland:

"The Church and all people and all nations within this Church are united with you.... Indeed, when they speak with warning to people, to nations, and even to the whole of humanity, they place at the forefront your nation, its suffering, its persecutions, its extermination. The pope also raises his voice of warning in your name. To the pope from Poland, this has a special significance, because together with you, he survived what happened in this land." (14th June 1987).

Should you consider it appropriate, you may read this letter in public.

I greet you from my heart,
John Paul II
Vatican, 30th day of March, 1989

There was no refusing now, not with such a letter. Jurek made arrangements to return to Wadowice. He would carry this letter next to his heart like a prayer book, to protect him.

Renée offered to travel with him, but he thought that he should go alone. It would not be difficult to get into Poland, not with all the changes that had already taken place there. The Church and the Polish government were talking. On April 6, a date in June was set for democratic, parliamentary elections, and on April 20, Lech Walesa and other Solidarity leaders flew to Rome to thank John Paul II for the great help he had given to the re-establishment of democracy after fifty years. In Poland, Communism was over.

No, entering Poland would be no problem for Jurek. Actually being there was another matter.

At the Krakow airport, Jurek rented a car and drove into the city to meet his classmate Dr. Jan Kus. Kus then accompanied him on the forty-minute drive to Wadowice. On the whole, everything looked a good deal shabbier than he remembered it, although the orchards were in bloom. He had so steeled himself for this moment that in the Rynek he felt almost nothing. There was no longing or bitterness as he looked briefly at the house on Zatorska Street, his father's office building, or the church. He did not go around to Lolek's or Ginka's old houses. Mrs. Szczepanska had died by then.

They went straight to the site of the synagogue. There was no trace of it, of course. In its place stood a nondescript stucco building described as a children's center. Most of his surviving classmates were waiting for him and Kus: Jura, Silkowski, the irrepressible Bojes, of course, and others. Jurek told them that he had a letter from His Holiness, and he removed it from his jacket pocket. "It has the papal seal on it," he said, and everyone examined it with approval.

Perhaps two hundred people were gathered around. The mayor gave a brief speech, then Jurek was invited to speak. Someone removed the cloth from the bronze plaque affixed to the building that gave a brief account of the synagogue's existence. There were only four to five thousand Jews left in all of Poland. On this afternoon, about forty were present, including a group from Israel led by Dr. Cesia Berkowicz, who had been a schoolmate of Tesia's, and a rabbi from Warsaw.

Rather than speaking his own words, Jurek said that he would read a letter from His Holiness John Paul II, which was meant for everyone. The passage about remembering the Jews at the synagogue on the Holidays almost got to him, but he made it through. There was respectful applause. He thought he could see a few people crying, but he tried not to look at them.

Afterward, he walked over to the high school with his classmates and even ventured inside. Again, he didn't react much, although his friends were anxious for him to look at everything. It was only up the street in the park that his grandfather had given to the town that his emotions broke through. He was dismayed to see the condition of the tennis courts where he had played with Tesia; they were in such disrepair that they weren't even playable. Everything was unkempt. The overgrown grass was all weeds, and the trees were either untrimmed or nothing more than dead stumps. He felt a knot of anger in his stomach. After all that his grandparents and parents had done for this town, now this! One had to blame Communism, he supposed. It drained pride and initiative from everyone. He said nothing and went to lunch with his classmates.

BACK IN ROME, HE REPORTED TO THE POPE ABOUT HIS TRIP. THINGS WOULD begin to improve in Wadowice and throughout Poland now, the Holy Father said. Jurek would notice the next time he went back.

"What do you mean—I'm going back? Your Holiness has another mission for me?" Jurek asked. The Holy Father just stared at him benignly and knowingly.

Later that summer, the Carmelite situation entered a new phase of hostility. The new Polish government said that it didn't wish to become involved in what had become such a delicate matter, but it supported the fulfillment of the Geneva agreement: "Further fanning of tensions has negative international implications, especially on the eve of the fiftieth anniversary of World War II. It weakens the significance of the martyrdom of Jews and Poles."

Early in August, a group of seven American Jews, dressed in prison stripes and led by a rabbi, jumped over the fence in front of the convent. Shouting damnations, they attempted to enter the building, terrifying the nuns. The intruders were quickly arrested and deported, but the incident made headlines everywhere. Reactions ranged from outrage against the trespassers to sympathy with their frustrations and renewed calls for the Church to do something.

On August 10, Cardinal Macharski announced that any removal had to be postponed for the time being because of the "lack of respect for the nuns and for the human and Christian dignity. The peace to which they are entitled was disturbed. Christian conventions, the symbols of faith and piety, were not respected. Our wishes and our aims were misrepresented in a unilateral way and judged in bad faith."

The next day, Cardinal Decourtray responded by saying that "the decisions made at Geneva regarding the convent of Auschwitz are not negotiable. An agreement is binding on those who sign it. Regrettable demonstrations and reactions can in no way bear weight....We are in need of mutual respect so that the memory of Auschwitz will not be endangered."

In Rome, Jurek tried to reassure Israeli and other Jewish leaders that this apparent disagreement between cardinals was not really as it appeared. Cardinal Macharski, who had been attacked himself by anti-Semites, was only defending the dignity of the nuns, who were under his protection, after all. The cardinal was actually very anxious to have the Carmelites move. As for the Holy Father, it would be much better if he could stay personally above the fray and let the cardinals work matters out. For the Holy Father to dictate a move now would only exacerbate problems and give the anti-Semites in Poland and elsewhere every excuse to challenge his authority.

Jurek believed that he was successful in these pleas for patience. But then, on August 27, the Primate of Poland, Jozef Cardinal Glemp, delivered a homily at that sacred Polish place, Czestochowa, that can only be described as a bombshell. Echoing what many right-wing Polish nationalists had been saying, Cardinal Glemp called the four cardinals who had reached the Geneva agreement incompetents and said that Poland was under attack by an international conspiracy of Jewish-controlled media. To Jurek, as to most Jews and many non-Jewish observers, the cardinal's outburst was proof that anti-Semitism within the Church remained a threat. What had begun as a problem involving a few well-intentioned but misguided nuns was now an international scandal, with intemperate behavior on all sides.

Jurek believed that his own credibility with the Jews had been badly damaged. How could this pope whom he revered so much allow such language from the Primate of Poland to go unchallenged? Knowing that Jurek would have his hands full trying to explain Glemp's speech, a highly placed official in the Secretariat of State had given him a copy of it before it reached the newspapers.

He appreciated a phone call from Monsignor Dziwisz, who urged him not to "doubt our goodwill." The monsignor telephoned three times that day. Cardinal Deskur also phoned to say that something had to be done. The cardinal did not specify "about Glemp," but Jurek assumed that what he meant was that a situation that had been allowed to fester was getting out of control.

"What do you really think?" Monsignor Dziwisz asked him. "You must tell us."

"I am deeply hurt," Jurek said. "After all these letters and telegrams I've sent to everyone, the ADL, the Israelis. After all these meetings."

"What has hurt you the most? Tell me," the monsignor persisted.

"I am too depressed to discuss it," Jurek said.

The truth was that Jurek was unable to express exactly what he felt, even to himself. He had allowed himself to be placed in an excruciating position. Obviously, he was a Jew, yet his belief in his friend the pope was greater than that of any devout Catholic because it was based on personal knowledge and friendship, not abstract theology. Yet in this uncompromising faith, he had tied himself to an institution whose behavior toward his own people had often been deeply hostile. Jurek was angry not so much at Cardinal Glemp as at himself for having put himself out on a limb. Had he become a fool for love of his friend?

He felt somewhat better when four American cardinals immediately criticized Cardinal Glemp's homily for its anti-Semitic emanations. As a result of the controversy, Cardinal Glemp canceled a planned visit to the United States. The Archbishop of Milwaukee, a city situated among the heaviest concentration of Polish-Americans, was pointed in his reaction. "We all regret very much Cardinal Glemp's uncalled-for comments," His Excellency Rembert G. Weakland, who was to have been Cardinal Glemp's host, stated. "I hope the Jewish community in Milwaukee realizes that [Cardinal Glemp's remarks] do not represent the feelings of most Roman Catholics."

On September 5, Jurek went to dinner at Castel Gandolfo, where the pope assured him that the matter would be taken care of. He left that evening with the vague impression that he had a better understanding of how the pope wished to govern the Church. For the most part, the Holy Father saw his role as one of establishing clear principles, not as dictating day-to-day behavior. It was up to the hierarchy to enforce those principles. Gross violations, such as those by Bishop Lefebvre, could result in the drastic action of excommunication. Certain theologians (there were about five of them) who were teaching in contradiction to those principles could be removed from their posts at Catholic universities. But in general, it was better and more politic for the pope to remain publicly aloof from specific controversies and allow the hierarchy to resolve them. Behind the scenes, of course, the pope placed men he trusted in key positions. Jurek knew that the four cardinals involved in the Geneva accords over the Auschwitz matter were held in the highest esteem by John Paul.

Jurek soon faced some consequences of this method of governance directly and personally. The Carmelite controversy was arousing more indignation among dispersed Jews than within Israel, possibly because Israelis had more immediate threats to their existence on their minds. When representatives of a certain American-Jewish organization appeared in Rome and asked for an audience with His Holiness, the request was granted, but only on the condition that they not bring up the matter of the Carmelites directly with the pope. On this issue, they had to go through official channels and/or the unofficial one, meaning Jerzy Kluger.

One of the representatives insisted on presenting a statement on the Carmelites directly to His Holiness. The audience was canceled with the understanding that this incident would not be leaked to the press because it could further heighten tensions. It was Jurek who worked out the agreement for discreet silence.

Unfortunately, only two hours after he had been given the promise of discretion, a second American representative, apparently unable to resist giving the media a scoop, held a press conference and revealed all. The impression the representative gave was that the pope refused to consider the Jewish point of view on the Carmelite situation. In the space of a few weeks, Jurek's credibility had been undercut first by a cardinal and then by a Jewish official.

AFTER THE NEW YEAR, 1990, JUREK FELT HIMSELF DRAWN BACK TO POLAND. He did not have a specific reason to go there this time, only a vague sensation that something was unresolved. When he'd been there the previous May, he had barely looked around. The experience had been painful, but he wanted to repeat it. Was this what the pope already understood?

Jurek did not make definite plans until he learned that the new Polish government was returning some property to Jewish heirs and others whose houses and other real estate had been confiscated by the Germans or the Communists. Over the next few years, he returned several times, noticing on each trip how rapidly the economy was picking up. He was able to negotiate with the authorities for the return of his father's office building. He sold it quickly but for too little, everyone told him. "You should never have been a businessman," Stanislaw Jura told him. "You should have been an artist. You should have hung on. Prices are rising." But Jurek did not want it on his mind, as the memories were too painful.

As for the house on Zatorska Street and the other buildings that Grandmother Huppert had owned, he did not bother about them. Many families were living in them now, and the deeds would have been difficult to sort out. He neither wished to throw the residents out nor to become a Polish landlord. Some things were beyond recovery.

But he kept going back to visit classmates and for other reasons beyond his comprehension. He toyed with the idea of investing in a business in Poland. It would be like regaining something and proving a point, perhaps, but nothing much came of that. In 1992, Renée finally accompanied him on a trip. She much preferred Krakow to Wadowice, which, in mutually unflattering terms, she compared to provincial towns in Ireland. But Jurek was mildly pleased that his grandfather's park was being restored. A little sign at the entrance stated that town fathers had "acquired" the land more than a hundred years ago, but neglected to mention who had donated it. The only visible evidence that Jews had lived in Wadowice, other than the graveyard, was the plaque on the synagogue site.

Krakow was a different story. The city was truly alive again. Its Rynek thronged with Jagiellonian students, and cafés, new shops, and restaurants were flourishing. With two synagogues now open for worship, there were at least a few diamonds in the ashes.

Throughout Poland, a growing number of Catholics were discovering that they had been born Jewish and had been baptized and sheltered by Christians during the war. The reaction of many was to reassert their Jewishness. Abraham H. Foxman, national director of the ADL in New York, had himself been such a "hidden" Polish Jew and was now urging the Church to open sealed baptismal records so that the actual numbers of such people could be known. After all, Foxman argued, it would be of benefit to both sides to know that in Poland, where the worst of crimes against humanity were committed, the most altruistic acts also were more frequent than was previously known.

After their trip, Jurek and Renée dined with the pope at Castel Gandolfo. The pope asked Renée if she had noticed any signs of anti-Semitism in Poland. There were many Jewish tourists in Poland now, His Holiness knew, including some on pilgrimages to cemeteries. Renée recalled observing American Hassidim in Krakow. "You could hardly miss them, in those dark suits and hats and the curls they have," she said. "I'm afraid I may have stared at them. No one else did. The Poles just accepted them as normal, it seemed to me."

Jurek and the pope chimed in, almost as a chorus, about how that was the way it had been long ago in Poland, with the two communities living together for hundreds of years more peacefully than anywhere else in Europe. Anti-Semitism was there, but more in the east, until it spread like a virus.

"Listen, the two of you," Renée broke in, as she liked to do. "Your Holiness, with all due respect and honor and so on, you and Jurek are always going on and on about anti-Semitism this and anti-Semitism that. If anyone deserves to be an anti-Semite, I should be, as you can imagine, living with *Jurek* all these years! Talk about Purgatory!" The pope got a terrific laugh out of that remark and never let Jurek forget it.

GOING BACK TO POLAND BECAME ODDLY RESTORATIVE FOR JUREK. SEEING HIS classmates and then reporting back to the pope about them did him good in ways he could not explain. It was the Germans, after all, who had turned their country into a Jewish graveyard, and a Catholic one, too. Perhaps he felt that he was reclaiming a birthright. His conversations with his friend dwelled more and more on the tangled history of Jews and Catholics in Poland. And as they talked, and Jurek continued to visit Poland, the Holocaust shifted into a somewhat different perspective. It became an aberration, not the definition of Jewish history. There was happiness to recover, too, and the spiritual life of centuries.

On one trip back, Jurek was showing an American couple around Krakow. They were Catholic. On their own (Jurek would never go), they visited Auschwitz and were suitably shaken. That night, they asked Jurek to take them to a café that their guidebook said offered Jewish music on Saturday nights—supposedly a bit of prewar atmosphere.

It was called Ariel and was on Szeroka Street in the heart of the Kazimierz district, which Jurek hardly ever had occasion to visit. Normally he called on Jura, Kus, other old classmates, and Halina, none of whom lived near Krakow's old Jewish neighborhoods. On the way, Jurek drove past Engineer Zilz's former house and an apartment that had belonged to an aunt.

The restaurant, with a silver menorah in the window, was candlelit, warm, and packed. The Ashkenazic food was good, Jurek thought, although he noticed that his American guests balked at stuffed goose necks. The vodka flowed. Soon they were talking in a hodgepodge of languages to the people at the next table. They were Jews about Jurek's age who had fled Poland just before the war, two of them to Argentina and two to England. This was their first trip back. They found it difficult to be in Krakow because they couldn't help thinking of what had happened.

"Better not to think!" Jurek said, typically for him. A troupe from Kiev—two young men and a pretty, dark woman of perhaps twenty with a gorgeous, full voice—began to entertain. Jurek noted that she reminded him of someone from a long time ago, but he couldn't remember who. Maybe someone in Russia.

The trio engaged in much energetic clowning and sang hearty Russian songs with a satirical edge. Then they began to sing in Yiddish, comically at first, with slapstick asides that must have been what vaudeville was like, or perhaps where it had come from. The music and songs then became melancholy, and the girl's voice had tears in it.

"I don't know Yiddish," Jurek said, "but I know these words." When they finished "Yiddische Mama," he shouted at them to sing it again.

This time he sang along, with his eyes closed and in perfect tune. The musicians approached the table, encouraging him. He sang beautifully until his voice broke, he coughed, and he had to take out his handkerchief. The people at the next table finished the verse for him and then embraced him.

Chapter 29

THE CARMELITE AUSCHWITZ CONTROVERSY SIMMERED AND FROM TIME to time boiled over for nearly eleven years. During that remarkable period, the Berlin Wall was torn down, Communist police states vanished from Eastern Europe, the Soviet Union dismantled itself—and Israeli and Palestinian leaders began working out the terms of a peace agreement. In the end, Pope John Paul II did have to intervene personally. On April 9, 1993, he addressed a letter to the nuns at Auschwitz, giving them the option to either move to a new, interfaith center established about a mile away from the boundaries of the death camp or return to "the mother convent."

The letter, which carries at its head a quotation from the autobiographical manuscripts of Saint Therese of Lisieux that has to do with finding one's place in the heart of the Church—rather, presumably, than out of it—is a model of kindly advice more than a summary order. But it is also quite firm.

> Now, according to the will of the Church, you should move to another place in this same Oswiecim. It remains a matter for the free will of each of you whether you wish to continue leading the Carmelite life within the existing community or whether you wish to return to the mother convent. May it please the crucified and resur-

> rected Christ to enable you to recognize his will and the particular calling to the Carmelite way of life.

The order also shows sympathy and respect for the nuns by saying that they have an important role to play at Oswiecim. Their "task" may be understood through what is linked with Auschwitz-Birkenau "in the memory of the sons and daughters of Israel, and also through what is linked with the history of the Poles, the history of our homeland." The pope reminds the sisters of "how much our contemporary world—fifty years after the terrible war, which produced among other things Auschwitz—is still threatened by hatred!" The letter closes with an Easter blessing.

In composing this letter, John Paul made a diplomatically useful distinction between the Polish *Oswiecim* and the German *Auschwitz*, using the former to refer to the town or the place in general and the latter to designate the death camp. In other words, the nuns would still be in the same place, although away from the camp's boundaries. They would be linked to it in their spiritual mission, which was defined as embracing both Jews and Catholics.

Why didn't the pontiff send this letter sooner, even years before? It took that long to provide the nuns with an alternative rather than humiliating them by simply ordering them out. That summer, the nuns did move to a new convent built for them, which sits next door to the interfaith Center for Information, Dialogue, and Prayer. The move came just in time for Jewish groups to call off a planned boycott of official ceremonies to mark the fiftieth anniversary of the Warsaw Ghetto Uprising. On April 6, Pope John Paul sent a message to Warsaw that read in part:

> I wish to remember those terrible days of World War II, days of contempt for the human person, manifested in the horror of the sufferings endured at that time by so many of our Jewish brothers and sisters....
>
> As Christians and Jews, following the example of the faith of Abraham, we are called to be a blessing for the world. This is the common task awaiting us. It is therefore necessary for us, Christians and Jews, to be first a blessing to one another. This will effectively

> occur if we are united in the face of the evils which are still threatening: indifference and prejudice as well as displays of anti-Semitism.

The message was sent to Archbishop Jozef Kowalczyk, the papal nuncio in Poland, for transmission to the Coordinating Commission of the Hebrew Organizations in Poland. Before assuming his post as nuncio late in 1989, the bishop had been one of Jerzy Kluger's principal contacts within the Secretariat of State and a frequent guest at the Parioli Club and other places where Jurek encouraged Catholics and Jews to get to know one another. It was the archbishop who first alerted Jurek to Cardinal Glemp's controversial speech. Like most of Jurek's Vatican contacts, Archbishop Kowalczyk was a Pole. It may be said that during the long years that Jurek worked quietly—his temperamental eruptions aside—toward the goal of full relations between the Vatican and Israel, he was the focal point of a distinctly Polish initiative.

THEIR EFFORTS SHOWED THE FIRST CLEAR SIGNS OF BEARING FRUIT ON JULY 29, 1992, when the State of Israel and the Holy See agreed to establish a working commission to discuss "bilateral affairs of common interest." This was the language of diplomacy for a goal of establishing full relations. Although the Carmelite matter had not yet been formally resolved, its outcome was by then widely assumed in both Catholic and Jewish circles. What remained at issue between the two sides by that date were longstanding questions that were beginning to look as irrelevant to the Vatican as they always had to the Jews.

John Paul II had effectively demolished the theological objections in speech after speech, letter after letter, and most dramatically by his visit to the Great Temple in Rome. Israel had by then established full relations with some one hundred forty other states, and the Vatican had full relations with several of Israel's neighbors, including Syria but not Saudi Arabia or Jordan. Jerusalem was firmly in Israeli hands. If the Vatican was truly still concerned about the safety and openness of the holy sites, it no longer made sense to have these shrines in Israel without having complete diplomatic access to the nation that controlled them. How could the Church adequately protect its interests with no proper means of negotiating about them? And finally, the question of a homeland for the Palestinians, which was the last sticking point from the point of view of those who still resisted recognition for Israel, was being discussed between Israeli and Palestinian representatives. Discussions took place first in Oslo and later at open conferences in Madrid. If the Palestinians and the Jews were talking, what possible objection could there be to the Vatican and Israel doing the same?

The international political scene had changed so markedly that the negotiators achieved in a year and a half what had not been possible since the establishment of Israel almost fifty years earlier. On September 13, 1993, in a ceremony on the lawn of the White House, Israeli Prime Minister Yitzhak Rabin and PLO Chairman Arafat signed what was termed a "declaration of principles" on Israeli-Palestinian cooperation, which established a Palestinian territory separate from Israel. Less than four months later, on December 29, 1993, the bilateral Vatican-Israel commission reached agreement on full diplomatic ties, which were formally established on June 15, 1994. Israel's Deputy Foreign Minister Yossi Beilin, who, with Monsignor Claudio Celli, Vatican Undersecretary for Relations with the States, was one of the two signators to the agreement, called it "a historic breakthrough" and linked it with the Palestinian accord.

> This is the second historical breakthrough this year.... Both were difficult psychologically. The signing of the agreement with the Holy See today in Jerusalem is a victory of sanity, a victory for the Jewish People and for the State of Israel. The first breakthrough [with the Arabs] came on the eve of the Jewish New Year. The second breakthrough today is happening on the eve of the Christian New Year. Let us pray together that the coming year will be the year of comprehensive peace, in the Middle East and throughout the world.

The peace did not turn out to be comprehensive. Among other tragedies, the agreement with Arafat cost Yitzhak Rabin his life at the hands of a Jewish fundamentalist who believed that he was doing God's will. No doubt there are Christian fanatics who are prepared to shoot John Paul for his efforts in reconciling the Church with the Jews. But the agreement between the Vatican and Israel has all the marks of a permanent alliance.

A profusion of comments worldwide greeted the event. In America, the ADL published a commemorative booklet with an attractive yellow, blue, and white cover that showed—doubtless for the first time in print—the papal flag and that of the State of Israel side by side. It contained a prologue by His Eminence John Cardinal O'Connor, who had been a powerful force in the achievement. The roster of other contributors consisted of two rabbis; a Catholic priest and professor; a Catholic scholar; the ADL's chairman, its director, and its representative in Italy; and one diplomat, the Honorable Shmuel Hadas, who was the first Ambassador of the State of Israel to the Holy See. This mixed assembly of Catholics and Jews was emblematic of what the agreement meant. Rabbi David Rosen of Israel stated soon after the agreement was signed:

> This is the end of the beginning. The implications of *Nostra Aetate* and subsequent documents called out for full relations between the Holy See and the State of Israel. Their absence had suggested that the reconciliation between the Church and the Jewish people was not a complete one. Accordingly, for the last three decades, Jewish representatives have called on the Vatican to take this step. The agreement that was signed last week, therefore, has historical and philosophical importance as well as diplomatic significance. Now we can address the meaning of our relationship and get on to many other matters of common interest.

YET ANOTHER REMARKABLE JEWISH-CATHOLIC COMMUNION TOOK PLACE ON the evening of April 7, 1994, at the Vatican. In the spring of 1991, maestro Gilbert Levine, the American-born conductor of the London Royal Philharmonic, who had also been director of the Krakow Symphony, conceived an idea for a concert under Vatican auspices to commemorate the Holocaust. His inspiration came from his own Jewish background and musical passion as well as from his knowledge of the pope's interest in promoting better Catholic-Jewish relations. He spoke first with Monsignor Dziwisz, who sent back word of the pope's approval. Levine, however, hadn't thought through where the concert should be held. He suggested various locales in Rome, but Monsignor Dziwisz said that the Vatican's concert hall was a big and beautiful place, named after Paul VI. Why not use that?

Maestro Levine organized the event with the help of the monsignor as well as Cardinal Lustiger and Edward Idris Cardinal Cassidy, an Australian who had succeeded Cardinal Willebrands as president of the council on unity. As the maestro later commented, he felt complete understanding between Church officials and himself about what the concert should be. He also came to understand how John Paul's passion to promote better Christian-Jewish relations and combat anti-Semitism was derived from his personal experiences under the Nazis and the loss of friends under Nazi and Communist rule.

The concert was attended by twenty-two cardinals, four rabbis, Italian President Luigi Scalfaro, ambassadors and other dignitaries from around the world, and a delegation of more than two hundred Holocaust survivors, including maestro Levine's mother-in-law and survivors of the Warsaw Ghetto Uprising. Pope John Paul's personal honored guest was Chief Rabbi Elio Toaff. And, of course, Jerzy and Renée attended.

Maestro Levine conducted the London Royal Philharmonic and a Vatican choir that for the first time sang in Hebrew. The program consisted of Max Bruch's *Kol Nidre*; Beethoven's Symphony No. 9, Movement 3; Franz Schubert's *Psalm 92*; an excerpt from Leonard Bernstein's *Kaddish*, narrated in Hebrew by American actor Richard Dreyfuss; and Bernstein's *Chichester Psalms*, Movements 2 and 3.

For anyone who was there or has heard the recording of it, the concert was an ineffably moving experience. Levine's idea was to express through music what is beyond words: to celebrate what only years before had been the unimaginable reconciliation between Catholics and Jews and to honor the dead by paying tribute to the survivors while some were still alive to hear it. At the conclusion of the concert, John Paul, who still looked vigorous, although he moved rather slowly, and whose voice remained beautifully musical, found words to express what everyone felt. He spoke in English.

> The melodies and songs that re-echoed in this auditorium were the expression of a common meditation and a shared prayer. Different voices blended in a unison of sounds and harmonies which moved and involved us intimately. We prayed in the knowledge that the Lord, if invoked, responds, cheering those who despair, breaking the chains of the oppressed, dispelling the shadows that linger in life's dark valleys.

Because of recent events, the concert was also dedicated to celebrate the Vatican's recognition of the State of Israel—politics, religion, and art blending into one in a manner that is unusual in a secular age. The pope also opened the concert with brief remarks, quoting what he was pleased to call David's song of ascents:

> "How good and how pleasant it is when brothers live in unity!"[Psalm 133:1] This is the hope I express for Jews and Christians everywhere. This hope enlivens my hope for peace in the Holy Land, which is so close to all our hearts.

For once in this century, beauty became truth, and truth beauty.

Jurek had reason to believe that he had played an important role in the reconciliation of Catholics and Jews that culminated in the recognition of Israel. The proudest moment of his life had been ten years before, when Foreign Minister Shamir thanked him on behalf of all the Jewish people. He did not quite believe Renée when she told him that it could never have happened without him; that was going a bit far. But when Achille Cardinal Silvestrini, who was already being mentioned as among the few who might possibly succeed John Paul II as pope, told him the same thing in the same words, he was almost prepared to accept it.

Jurek was again overjoyed for Catholics and Jews and for his friend on Thursday, September 29, 1994, when he gathered with the pope and distinguished guests at Castel Gandolfo to observe Ambassador Hadas present his credentials to His Holiness. Shmuel Hadas, a soft-spoken gentleman, had previously been Israel's Ambassador to Spain, and he delivered his address to the Holy Father in Spanish. He spoke of the uniqueness of the occasion, of how it hardly fit any conventional diplomatic category or language because the Catholic and Jewish peoples are uniquely alike, beyond national boundaries.

In his response, the pope expressed the wish that this new achievement would open the way for the Holy See to be of assistance in advancing the Middle East peace process. Calling attention to the shared, monotheistic heritage of Jews and Christians, John Paul prayed that the "Most High" would grant Ambassador Hadas, his loved ones, and all his compatriots "an abundance of gifts." John Paul himself chose to speak in French, the traditional language of diplomacy. The words he chose, however, subtly blended traditions in phrases that were palpably Middle Eastern. He was still the poet he had been in youth.

Jurek found that nearly all the faces of the diplomats, cardinals, monsignors, rabbis, and others present—Catholic and Jewish alike—were familiar to him. It was almost like being at a reunion of old friends. Jurek's father would have been very proud, the pope reminded him.

THE NEXT FEW YEARS WERE CALMER FOR JUREK, SINCE HE NO LONGER HAD A part to play on the world's stage. But he enjoyed them no less, especially the breakfasts and lunches and dinners with his friend, which went on as before. John Paul's health was not robust after 1995, when a deteriorating hip joint that was not improved by an operation put him in constant pain. It was difficult for him to stand or walk, and he developed a visible tremor in his left hand. He continued at his usual pace, however: up at five, saying mass every morning at seven, working late, and continuing his travels. As always on his return, he gave Jurek an account of this or that experience, usually of his meetings with a Jewish community somewhere in the world.

Jurek particularly enjoyed one anecdote from the pope's seventh trip as pontiff to Poland. More than a million of those who love him as their own turned out to greet him in a meadow in Krakow in

1996. He took a day off during that excursion to rest at his beloved Zakopane. He could no longer ski, but he could breathe the mountain air and visit with a couple of the eight high school classmates who were still alive. Bojes and Jura came to see him and brought Halina with them. They all sat before a fire.

"How long are you going to stay with us in Poland this time, Your Holiness?" Jura asked. "A month, I hope?"

"Oh, no," John Paul replied. "I have to go back to Rome the day after tomorrow. I am the pope, you know. There's a great deal of work at the Vatican."

"Why run off so quickly?" Jura said. "Haven't you left Jurek Kluger in charge there?"

Chapter 30

RENÉE WAS DISAPPOINTED, FRUSTRATED, AND BECOMING SLIGHTLY cross.

"Why didn't you just leave us at the cemetery?" she said to the bus driver. "That would have saved you all this time and effort. God knows, at my age, I'm ready to give it up!"

The driver insisted that there was no way that he would even try to force his bus up the narrow, cobbled street that ended at the gates to Castel Gandolfo. His passengers, Renée's guests, would have to walk. Renée bestowed on him a fecund Italian curse that, since it came from a woman his grandmother's age, he accepted with a shrug. There they were, all thirty-six of them in their finery, parked at the base of the little town's walls at a little past seven on the morning of Thursday, September 11, 1997.

"Thank God it's not raining," Renée said as she led the charge of wedding guests the five hundred yards or so along the street, past shops and little restaurants where proprietors were just beginning to arrange tables outside. The air smelled of coffee and bread. "Of course, Jurek didn't have to struggle this way. The limousine dropped him at the gates, naturally," she complained. "Isn't that the way of it? Jurek leads a charmed life."

Shutters opened above the shops and faces poked out of windows as the parade of guests scurried up the street. The women wore hats and were dressed in light colors; most of the men wore dark suits and were bareheaded, except for the best man, who dragged on a cigarette beneath his topper. Well in the lead, Renée, in blue-gray silk, was bareheaded. She wasn't the hat or mantilla type, she had said. Not any more. The pope wouldn't give a fig one way or another, she knew. "It's these damned heels," she said so that everyone could hear. "The next time, I'm coming back as a man! I truly am. The pope promised me!"

The occasion was Stephania's wedding to Edward Walsh, a fellow student she had met at university in England. The couple would live in Paris, where Stephania was a whiz with currency fluctuations at a bank and Edward was on the way up at IBM. Ever since the pope had baptized her, he had monitored Stephania's boyfriends rather closely, considering that he had had other things on his mind during the past sixteen years. She had been serious about only one other boy, a rower from Oxford of whom His Holiness had approved. But everyone, including the pope and certainly the bride, loved Edward more. "When are you going to marry Edward?" the Holy Father would ask every time she brought the young man to Rome. "He is a good fellow. When you decide, remember that I will perform the rites."

To accommodate everyone, Monsignor Dziwisz had moved the ceremony from the chapel to the Swiss Hall (presumably named after the guards), where chairs were arranged and an altar was set up on a long table. Everything had to be improvised. If there had ever been a wedding at Castel Gandolfo before, no one could remember it. Someone suggested that this was to be the first time that a pope had performed nuptials for anyone since Napoleon and Josephine, which was unlikely, but no one was about to challenge the claim. Whatever the case, everyone prayed that this marriage would be more successful than poor Josephine's had been, with her first husband guillotined and her second, well.... Fortunately, Edward Walsh did not seem the type to lose his head or run off to conquer Europe.

During the rehearsal the day before, Renée had failed to persuade Monsignor Dziwisz to move the ceremony back an hour. "Absolutely not," the monsignor said. The pope had a busy day, meeting with the French ambassador and dealing with other matters. His Holiness would begin the ceremony promptly at seven-thirty whether Stephania and Edward were there or not.

Jurek had not attended the rehearsal. He would march down the aisle with his grandchild and give her away. "Do I need to practice such a thing?" he said. "After that, they don't need me. In case you have forgotten, it's not my religion." In fact, he was so excited about the event that he was sleeping even less than usual. Stephania being married as a Catholic was not as stinging to him as it might have been. She was still a poignant reminder of Tesia, but no one could undo past sufferings and tragedy or ask Stephania to bear the weight of them. If she was getting married in a church, he joked to himself, at least Castel Gandolfo was a rather impressive one.

That morning, the continuity he felt with the pope overwhelmed the sadness that was never absent from his heart. Tanned, fit, and beaming in a cutaway coat and striped trousers, he waited in a hallway of the palace for the ceremony to begin. He thought only of the joy of the occasion and his gratitude for having been spared to participate in it. Stephania told him that she had never seen him so happy. "It is for you I am happy," he told her. "If I am not happy today, I don't deserve to live on this Earth." And he was thinking to himself that he believed he had been a good Jew, too, in his way.

Pope John Paul haltingly entered the Swiss Hall through a door to the right and behind the altar. Bent and gripping his silver staff, he was obviously in great pain, yet he was as determined as ever. He wore vestments of reddish yellow-gold and a matching miter; its peaked shape was derived from the headdress of ancient Jewish high priests and was symbolic of his office. A priest in a red cassock attended His Holiness and six others in gold robes followed, arranging themselves at either side of him before the altar.

Jurek brought his radiant granddaughter down the aisle. He glanced over to smile and nod at Stanislaw Jura and Halina Krolikiewicz Kwiatkowska, who were sitting together. Halina, wearing her hat at a stylish angle and sitting as straight as a ballerina, looked ready to perform and gave no hint of having spent the previous twenty-four hours on a bus. And so there were four in that room who had loved one another through most of this century and its difficulties. Jurek gave Stephania's arm over to the waiting bridegroom and sat down with Renée and their daughters. He had done his part. The rest was for Lolek to complete.

THE MARRIAGE CEREMONY ENCOMPASSED ALL THAT THE POPE HOLDS DEAR: affirmation of life, reverence for the family, respect for the human person, and the unity of mankind through the mystery of Christ's love and sacrifice.

Within Roman Catholicism, a man and a woman freely choose to confer upon themselves the sacrament of matrimony. In so doing, they become a living symbol of the community of believers, in which Christ is bridegroom to the Church and the faithful are their children. Those who marry not only make a contract between themselves, they also celebrate a far greater unity.

Marriage is a cornerstone of John Paul's thinking, but he knows as well as anyone that in this century, it has become a fragile one. Aside from lamenting the frequency of divorce and the proliferation of children whom he calls orphans with parents, he has taken practical steps to strengthen marriage. As early as 1960, in Poland, he was thinking along these lines when he established The Family Institute, which was eventually incorporated into the theology department at the Jagiellonian. And in 1981, he established the Pontifical Institute of John Paul II for Studies in Matrimony and the Family, a graduate program attached to the Lateran University in Rome. It has affiliated programs in the United States, Spain, and Mexico.

The institute is not merely a platform to oppose condoms, the pill, contraceptive implants, sterilization, or other birth control devices and procedures. Nor does it focus exclusively on one of the most divisive concepts of our time, abortion as murder. Rather, its purpose is to educate clergy in the true meaning of marriage and the problems that families face in a world that has grown oblivious to the spiritual dimensions of marriage. As always, John Paul's approach is not simply to preach but to study and teach—to inquire and discuss what can be done to nurture married love. Without family unity, he counsels, society disintegrates.

As Karol Wojtyla learned as a young priest hearing confessions, married life can be a nightmare, especially for women who endure abuse. It can be characterized by brutal sex, alcoholism, and depression. At the same time, most priests are ignorant of even the most basic aspects of married life, not to mention the female reproductive system. To address this appalling lack, M.A. and doctoral students at the institute (priests and nuns who are preparing for teaching and pastoral occupations) take required courses that include studies in reproductive anatomy and biology, the history of the family in the development of civilization, spousal love, sensuality, and the political philosophy of the family.

Behind the entire curriculum lies the pope's belief that only through a combination of absolutely uninhibited inquiry—scientific or philosophical—and ethical conviction can the modern person make correct moral choices. The old ways of rote learning and scientific ignorance will no longer do for Catholics. At the same time, however, he insists that knowledge alone, without faith, is an empty and dangerous thing that can lead society into a purposeless void. This is the rationale behind John Paul's certainties. His opposition to "artificial" means of contraception, for example, is not based on a wish to breed more Catholics. He has often expressed his concern about world overpopulation. He has also written that for men to use women as sexual objects, for women to permit themselves to be used in this way, or for couples to use sex only to gratify spontaneous psycho-biological urges leads to the death of love and marriage.

In his book *Love and Responsibility*, first published in Poland in 1960, he argues that the artificial inhibition of the sexual act's natural possibility of conception makes a woman into a mere receptacle for a man's urges or a man into a dehumanized provider of services. He suggests that sexual pleasure can be enhanced and communication encouraged by periodic mutual restraint, the exercise of choice and will over impulse.

Many Catholics and others may disagree with this analysis, but those who do should realize that the pope's view of the possibilities inherent in marital sexual relations derives not from hostility to sex or to women but from respect for both. His purpose is to preserve marriage by ennobling it, by fostering the dignity of the human person. His argument is a response to the agony and the sense of alienation felt by married people whose love has run dry because of the absence of a spiritual purpose.

The respect for the human person that marriage affirms is also a large part of John Paul's belief in the sanctity of life itself. In what is probably his most widely read and discussed encyclical, *Evangelium Vitae* (*The Gospel of Life*; 1995), he inveighs against what he terms the culture of death as opposed to a culture of life. He explains that laws permitting euthanasia and abortion are by definition unjust, since no law favoring death over life can be anything but "incompatible with the love of God and the dignity of the person created in his image." Although he does not phrase the matter in precisely this way, in effect he argues that when human sacrifice is not only permitted but encouraged, contemporary society lurches backward into a pre-civilized state. In this analogy, lives are not sacrificed to primitive deities, as was the practice of the Mayans, early European barbarian tribes, and Native American tribes such as the Mohawks (whose name means "man-eater"). Rather, people are murdered for the god of personal convenience and "self-fulfillment." A more contemporary analogy would be the death camps and *gulags* of World War II, in which human beings were sacrificed to the gods of racial superiority or the state.

It goes without saying that John Paul's teachings with regard to the possibility of rational and moral behavior in marriage and in society are highly idealistic. He is the pope. He is the titular head of a religion whose premise, derived from Judaism, is not that human beings are intrinsically good if left alone or that they naturally make the right choices unless they suffer from a mental disorder. Nor is it that people can trust that the laws of a democratic state are just simply because they have been endorsed by a majority. No, his belief is that in order to know right from wrong and make moral choices, a person must look to a higher law. The question is not the law, but who made it.

Behind John Paul's fear and condemnation of the culture of death lies Auschwitz. The growth of his personal moral philosophy began after the joys and sorrows of youth in Wadowice. It began with the defining moral question of the age: Is it possible to speak of God after Auschwitz? How did the town of Oswiecim, a place known as a market center, where the railway hauled away coal and a certain Jewish family made vodka flecked with gold, become Auschwitz? It is not only that the Germans, those people of high culture who proved high culture morally bankrupt, made it so. Certainly the Poles, whatever their degree of anti-Semitism, did not make it so. It happened because the culture of death is perversely powerful. Neither democracy nor individual conscience nor even civil laws could resist it.

It happened also because, sadly, the Church herself strayed from the Christian doctrine of love into quarrels about who was saved and who was not. Meanwhile, the world descended toward catastrophe. The Church neglected or paid only lip service to the doctrine that admits no exception, including God's Chosen People. It forgot that Jesus was no orphan but the child of Abraham and Moses, to whom God gave the commandment "Thou shalt not kill."

After Jules Isaac whispered some uncomfortable truths about Christianity into the papal ear, after John XXIII and *Nostra Aetate*, it remained for John Paul II to remind us that *only at its Judaic root can Christianity rediscover the authentic basis of correct moral choice.* Christ gave us the keys to the kingdom of love in the Beatitudes, but he could not have done so if God had not already given to Moses and other Jewish prophets the Ten Commandments and other eternal wisdom of the Hebrew Bible.

This is the greatest marriage that John Paul has performed—or reaffirmed—after millennia of separation that amounted to divorce and ended in many deaths, both spiritual and physical. The marriage of love and law, of justice and mercy, and of ethics and forgiveness is the Judeo-Christian tradition, and we almost lost it forever. The revitalization of these truths was symbolized in the pope's visit to the Great Temple in Rome. The brotherly affection of that visit is the most powerful answer to the decline of religion in the West since

Friedrich Nietzsche derided Christianity as the weak child of Judaism and proclaimed that God is dead.

Like any marriage, this one will take great effort to sustain, especially after John Paul dies. By establishing educational programs and other resources, the pope is trying to ensure that the legacy of the Judeo-Christian reunion is not squandered. He has called on Christians to recognize and repent the role that religious anti-Semitism played in preparing the way for the atheistic anti-Semitism of Nazi Germany and Soviet Russia. For this reason, in 1997, the French Catholic bishops, led by Cardinal Lustiger, publicly acknowledged the culpability of the Church in failing to condemn collaborators who betrayed tens of thousands of Jews to the Nazis. In September 1997, the pope issued guidelines for the teaching of the new Catechism, instructing bishops worldwide that combating anti-Semitism and inculcating an appreciation and understanding of Judaism as a living religion should be central to Catholic education. He is making these efforts not only to prevent renewed persecutions but also for the sake of Christianity and the world. Whether Judaism needs Christianity is for the Jews, our "elder brothers," to decide.

Although most Catholics may not yet understand it, the Church today is becoming a radically different institution. To be a "good Catholic" now is to be fully engaged in the moral and ethical questions of the times. It means having what John Paul has called a contemplative spirit, or having a disposition toward serious moral thought, not blind obedience. At its fullest, it means appreciation of the essential value of Mosaic law, which the pope extols in *Evangelium Vitae* as the "negative moral precepts" of the Torah that define the "absolute limit beneath which free individuals cannot lower themselves." Thus the commandment "Thou shalt not kill" also leads us to "promote life actively and to develop ways of thinking and acting which serve life." It follows, then, that the "No" of the Hebrew Bible is inherently a "Yes," a negation that carries with it a joyous affirmation of creation. In this way, the pope has shifted the balance of Christian faith and works in favor of life on Earth. Theologically, he has given renewed meaning to the Mother of Christ, in whose living womb the Incarnation took place.

In an era drugged by therapy and self-involved New Age philosophy, John Paul's exhortations to love humanity and life are invigorating. As we near the end of this century, we are coming to suspect that Marx and Freud are of limited utility, that Darwin described only physical evolution, and that Einstein's discovery that time, space, and motion are relative doesn't apply to ethics. A century of blood, John Paul tells us, shows that just laws depend on a supreme, sovereign lawgiver. Auschwitz proves not the existence of God but the necessity of believing in Him.

Someone—a prophet, as Rabbi Piattelli calls him—had to resurrect the song of an almost-exterminated wisdom and make it resound in a clear voice with great range. We know now that John Paul first heard its melody created by Jewish and Christian players together in a building that faced the Rynek—the house on Zatorska Street.

AS RENÉE HAD REQUESTED, THE POPE PERFORMED THE RITES IN ENGLISH, which was the only common language among the guests, who included Irish, French, Dutch, Italians, English, Americans, and, of course, Poles. Renée read aloud a passage from Corinthians. In his homily, the Holy Father meditated on the sacrament of marriage. There was none of the airy badinage typical of clerics at contemporary weddings, where the minister of God tries to be cool. At moments, the pope's voice grew faint, but then it rang out, filling the hall like a cello. He was still dramatic, still the Karol of the Rhapsodic.

The pope spoke of the inviolability of the bonds, although he must have known that within that congregation, there were more divorced people than not—or at least that the odds were so. Statistics mean nothing to him. He is only after the truth. He spoke about divorce as a sadness, an affront to God's love that is born of indifference—a sin that has always distressed him. When he resumed the mass and reached the consecration, he lingered lovingly over every syllable that recalled the Last Supper as if the words were new to him. Holding the sacred Host aloft, he broke it and placed a particle deliberately into his mouth, with his eyes closed and his strong Slavic face compressed in concentration.

After the exchange of rings and the kiss, Stephania and Edward circled around behind the makeshift altar to greet the pope as wife and husband. John Paul put his arms around Stephania and planted a kiss on the top of her head.

Later, off to the side of the hall, the Vicar of Christ and his Jewish friend embraced. Jura and Halina came up to hug Lolek and Jurek and chat with them. It was like old times, there at Castel Gandolfo, and it was very much John Paul's sort of Catholicism. A bomber pilot, an actress, a businessman, and the Holy Father were as one in love.

Sources and Acknowledgments

At seven o'clock on Wednesday morning, May 22, 1996, Jerzy Kluger escorted my wife and me to mass in Pope John Paul II's private chapel at the Vatican. The experience was all the more moving for the absence of pomp. The pope was already kneeling at a *prie-dieu* when we entered the small sanctuary, following a group of about twenty Franciscans wearing white surplices over their coarse brown robes. The Holy Father said mass in Italian, speaking deliberately in his deep, distinctive voice, as the monks raised their voices in song. The room filled with simple faith, as natural as the scent of flowers. Once or twice I glanced over at our Jewish host. He was smiling with fraternal affection.

Afterward, in another room, I watched the two old friends greet one another with hugs and banter in Polish. The pope, laughing softly, seemed different from the moral scourge that I had read about. It was at that moment that I settled on the title of this book.

Jerzy introduced me, saying, "This is the writer I have been telling you about. Mr. O'Brien writes about the conflict between good and evil and the hope for the triumph of good."

"That is a very important theme," His Holiness said. As Jerzy had advised me to do, I then presented copies of some of my books, which the pope held and examined with a degree of attention and courtesy that I hoped they deserved.

"Oh!" he exclaimed of one, "*The Hillside Stranglers*."

We discussed my ideas for a book about the implications for Christians and Jews of his lifelong friendship with Jerzy and its relevance to changes in the Church. I could scarcely believe that it had been only a few weeks since I had first proposed the project, although my interest in Christian-Jewish relations has persisted for decades and is a theme in a novel that I published twenty years ago. John Paul placed his hand on my head and said, "I bless you, and I give my blessing to the literature which you are about to create."

I hardly need to explain that this was the most significant moment in the preparation of this book. There were immediate practical results, including what I believe to be the unprecedented access that I was given to Vatican and other sources. At that instant, however, I was nearly overwhelmed by a sense of the responsibility that I had assumed—or been given.

Later, I asked Jerzy what the Holy Father had said to him that morning before the conversation switched into English. The pope, it turned out, had been teasing him about going to church. "Good morning, Jurek," he said. "Nice to see you at mass. I didn't know you were becoming so devout."

I WISH TO THANK ROBERT GOTTLIEB, EXECUTIVE VICE-PRESIDENT OF THE William Morris Agency, for understanding me and my writing so well that he anticipates what I wish to do even before the idea has taken root in my mind and then creates a way to make it possible. For his loyalty, imagination, and tireless efforts—not least of all finding the ideal publisher for this book—I am most grateful.

Karen Kelly, editorial director of Daybreak Books, has offered complete understanding and encouragement and has been as sympathetic as she has been a careful and wise editor. To have a publisher with aesthetic and spiritual commitment as well as intelligence and learning exceeds my fondest hopes.

My wife, Suzanne O'Brien, who is my research associate, partner, and confidant, joins me in expressing these appreciations and others that follow. Her aesthetic judgment and emotional and intellectual companionship are gifts beyond price.

I also wish to thank Cindy Ratzlaff and Jane Sherman of Daybreak Books and Claudia Cross and Marcy Posner of the Morris Agency for their energies and commitments.

In the fall of 1996, we returned to Rome for seven weeks of intensive interviews with Jerzy Kluger, members of his family, and others who are acknowledged below. Later that year, Jerzy joined us in Krakow after we had visited Wadowice, Kalwaria, Auschwitz-Birkenau, and other locales and met other classmates of his and the pope's. On our return to the United States, we met with Jewish leaders in New York and studied videotapes and other documents at the United States Holocaust Museum in Washington, D.C. I carried out further research at the McFarlin Library at the University of Tulsa and in my own library.

Obviously, Jerzy was the principal source. I am grateful to him for his oral and written responses to nearly endless questions and his willingness to recall certain matters that he would sooner have left unexamined. His 1979–94 diaries detailing every meeting he had with John Paul II and other dignitaries proved invaluable regarding Vatican-Israel diplomacy; to my knowledge, they are unique in the annals of Vatican diplomatic history. Jerzy also was able to relay my questions to His Holiness during their frequent meetings and to report back on his responses.

In September 1997, we returned to Rome for further interviews and to attend the wedding of Stephania Kluger and Edward Walsh at Castel Gandolfo. At that time, I was able to inform the Holy Father about the progress of the manuscript and to discuss plans to have him read it before publication.

I thank Renée Kluger for her kind indulgence of our questions, her hospitality, and, not least of all, her wit. I am quite aware of how much she did behind the scenes to assure our access to certain people and institutions. I also wish to thank Stephania Kluger Walsh, Linda Kluger, and Lesley Kluger Lestini for providing their unique perspectives.

For their courtesy, time, and insightful contributions, I wish to express respectful thanks to the following people for granting personal interviews in Rome: His Eminence Andrzej Maria Cardinal Deskur, President Emeritus of the Pontifical Council for Social Communications; Professor Stanislaw Grygiel of the John Paul II Institute at Lateran University in Rome; The Honorable Nathan Ben-Horin, First Secretary of the Embassy of the State of Israel (ret.); His Excellency Shmuel Hadas, Ambassador of Israel to the Holy See; Professor Giacomo Saban of the University of Rome, President of the Jewish Community of Rome, and Mrs. Saban; Dr. Joaquin Navarro-Valls, Director of the Sala Stampa della Santa Sede (chief Vatican press spokesman); His Excellency Archbishop Clemente Riva, Auxiliary Bishop of Rome; Dr. Alberto A. Piattelli, Rabbi to the Jewish Community of Rome at the Great Temple; His Eminence Achille Cardinal Silvestrini, Prefect of the Congregation of the Eastern Churches and Grand Chancellor of the Pontifical Institute for Eastern Studies; His Excellency Archbishop Jean-Louis Tauran, Vatican Secretary of State for Relations with the States (Foreign Minister); The Reverend Monsignor Luigi Gatti, *Consigliere di Nunziatura di 1a classe* in the Vatican Secretariat of State and aide to Archbishop Tauran; His Eminence Johannes Cardinal Willebrands, President Emeritus of the Pontifical Commission for the Promotion of Christian Unity (and Relations with the Jews); Dr. Dominick Morawski, correspondent for various Polish newspapers and periodicals; The Reverend Professor Tadeusz Styczen of the faculty of philosophy at the University of Lublin; His Excellency Archbishop Crescenzio Sepe, Secretary of the Congregation of the Clergy; The Reverend Dr. Leonard E. Boyle, Director of *Biblioteca Apostolica Vaticana* (ret.).

For many kindnesses, I also wish to thank the staff of the Residence Aldrovandi and Mr. Camillo Pavia of the Aldrovandi Palace.

In Krakow, I wish to thank Mrs. Halina Krolikiewicz Kwiatkowska, whom we also had the privilege of meeting again in Rome. Mr. Stanislaw Jura gave us invaluable help, showing us Krakow, Kalwaria, and Wadowice, lending helpful documents, and sharing his insights and memories of schooldays, the war, and

Poland under Communism during several wonderful days in Poland and again in Rome. Mr. Piotr Kropiwnicki was most helpful, especially in guiding us through Auschwitz-Birkenau, Nova Huta, and along the road from Krakow toward the Ukrainian border.

In Wadowice, I was privileged to interview Mr. Teofil Bojes, who kindly provided a copy of his book (see bibliography) about Karol Wojtyla's high school class.

At the United States Holocaust Museum Archives in Washington, D.C., I wish to thank Joan Ringleheim, Amy Rubin, Aaron T. Kornblum, and research director Radu Ioanid for their help.

In Toronto, Mrs. Danuta Zajacowa-Kurczewska was kind enough to share her memories of the Kluger family and the story of the rescue of some of their possessions.

In New York, I am especially grateful to Rabbi Leon Klenicki, Director of the Interfaith Affairs Department for the Anti-Defamation League, National ADL Director Abraham H. Foxman, and Myrna Shinbaum, Director of Media Relations.

I am also grateful to Mr. Bennett Feinsilber of San Antonio; Molly O'Brien of Los Angeles; Mr. Charles B. Clement Jr. of Chicago; and Gerard Campbell and George Singer of Tulsa.

Mrs. Sandy Vice of Tulsa deserves thanks for her long hours putting the manuscript into legible form.

THE FOLLOWING BIBLIOGRAPHY IS NOT INCLUSIVE BUT LISTS WORKS OTHER than papal encyclicals cited in the text that were especially useful in writing this book.

Anders, Wladyslaw. *An Army in Exile.* (London, 1949).

Blumberg, Abraham, "The Last Jews in Warsaw," *Granta* no. 55 (1996).

Bojes, Teofil. *Ostatni Mohikanin Czyli: Klasa gimnazjalna Karola Wojtyly 1930–1938* (Myslowice, Poland: privately printed, 1994). Translated as *The Last Mohikans: Karol Wojtyla's High School Class*, by Rafal Klopotowski. (Typescript, 1997).

Bullock, Alan. *Hitler and Stalin.* (New York, 1991).

Craig, Mary. *Man from a Far Country: A Portrait of Pope John Paul II.* (London, 1979).

Deák, István. "Memories of Hell," *New York Review of Books* vol. XLIV, no. 11 (June 26, 1997), pp. 38–43.

Encyclopaedia Judaica. (Jerusalem, 1972–1994).

Fisher, Eugene J., and Leon Klenicki, eds. *A Challenge Long Delayed: The Diplomatic Exchange between the Holy See and the State of Israel.* (New York, 1996).

_________. *Celebrating the 30th Anniversary of the Vatican II Declaration of* Nostra Aetate (no. 4). (New York, 1995).

_________. *From Desolation to Hope, an Interreligious Holocaust Service.* (New York, 1990).

_________. *Understanding the Jewish Experience.* (New York, N.D.).

_________, et al. *Interfaith Focus: Catechism of the Catholic Church, Catholic and Jewish Readings.* (New York, 1994).

Flannery, Austin, ed. *Vatican Council II.* (Collegeville, Ind., 1992).

Fortis, Umberto. *Jews and Synagogues.* (Venice, 1973).

Foxman, Abraham H. "A Polish Jew Meets a Polish Catholic" (Mimeograph, N.D.).

Gilbert, Arthur. *The Vatican Council and the Jews.* (New York, 1968).

Gutman, Yisrael, and Michael Berenbaum, eds. *Anatomy of the Auschwitz Death Camp.* (Bloomington, Ind., and Washington, D.C., 1994).

Hadas, Shmuel (Samuel). "Diplomatic Relations between the Holy See and the State of Israel." (Typescript, 1996).

Heaney, Seamus. *Jesus and the Sparrows.* (Deerfield, Mass., 1996).

_________. *Station Island.* (New York, 1985).

Heschel, Abraham Joshua. *The Earth Is the Lord's.* (New York, 1950).

Hilberg, Raul. *The Destruction of the European Jews*, 3 vols. (New York, 1985).

Isaac, Jules. *Jésus et Israël.* (Paris, 1947).

_________. *The Teaching of Contempt.* (New York, 1964).

Johnson, Paul. *John XXIII.* (Boston, 1974).

Klenicki, Leon. *The Carmelite Convent at Auschwitz: Past and Future,* in *Studium Papers* (vol. XIV, no. 1–2, Winter-Spring, 1990), pp. 53–61.

_________. *Catholic Education and Preaching on Jews and Judaism.* (New York, 1992).

_________. "Jacques Maritain's Vision of Judaism and Anti-Semitism," in Robert Royal, ed., *Jacques Maritain and the Jews.* (Notre Dame, Ind., 1994) pp. 72–78.

Klenicki, Leon, and Eugene J. Fisher, *Root and Branches: Biblical Judaism,*

Rabbinic Judaism, and Early Christianity. (Winona, Minn., 1987).

__________, eds. *Passion Plays and Judaism.* (New York, 1996).

Klenicki, Leon, and Richard John Neuhaus. *Believing Today.* (Grand Rapids, Mich., 1989).

Kluger, Jerzy. *Diaries, 1979–1994.* (Unpublished holograph in Polish).

Lukas, Richard C. *The Forgotten Holocaust: The Poles under German Occupation, 1939–1944.* (Lexington, Ky., 1986).

Malinski, Mieczyslaw. *Pope John Paul II.* (New York, 1979).

Ministry of Foreign Affairs, Polish Government-in-Exile, eds. *German Occupation of Poland, Polish White Book.* (New York, 1942).

Netanyahu, B. *Origins of the Inquisition.* (New York, 1995).

Neuhaus, Richard John. "The Very Liberal John Paul II," *National Review* vol. XLIX, no. 15 (August 11, 1997), pp. 32–35.

O'Brien, Conor Cruise. *The Siege: The Saga of Israel and Zionism.* (New York, 1986).

Pagles, Elaine. *The Gnostic Gospels.* (New York, 1989).

Sherwin, Byron L. *Sparks amid the Ashes: The Spiritual Legacy of Polish Jewry.* (New York, 1995).

Shirer, William L. *The Rise and Fall of the Third Reich.* (New York, 1959).

Stravinskas, Peter, and Leon Klenicki. *A Catholic-Jewish Encounter.* (Huntington, Ind., 1994).

Styczen, Tadeusz. "Freedom and Law." (Typescript, 1996).

Szulc, Tad. *Pope John Paul II: The Biography.* (New York, 1995).

Tec, Nechama. *When Light Pierced the Darkness: Christian Rescue of Jews in Nazi-Occupied Poland.* (New York, 1986).

Warner, Marina. *Alone of All Her Sex: The Myth and the Cult of the Virgin Mary.* (New York, 1983).

Wigoder, Geoffrey. *Jewish-Christian Relations since the Second World War.* (Manchester, 1988).

__________. *The Vatican-Israel Agreement: A Watershed in Christian-Jewish Relations.* (Jerusalem, 1994).

Willebrands, Johannes Cardinal. *The Church and the Jewish People.* (New York, 1992).

Willey, David. *God's Politician: John Paul II at the Vatican.* (London, 1992).

Wojtyla, Karol (Pope John Paul II). *Crossing the Threshold of Hope.* (New York, 1995).

__________. *Gift and Mystery.* (New York, 1996).

__________. *The Jeweler's Shop.* (San Francisco, 1992).

_________. *Love and Responsibility*. (New York, 1994).
_________. *The Place Within: The Poetry of John Paul II*. (New York, 1982).
_________. *Spiritual Pilgrimage: Texts on Jews and Judaism, 1979–1995*. Eugene J. Fisher and Leon Klenicki, eds. (New York, 1995).
_________. *The Way to Christ*. (San Francisco, 1994).
Wood, E. Thomas and Stanislaw M. Jankowski. *Karski: How One Man Tried to Stop the Holocaust*. (New York, 1994).

BIBLICAL QUOTATIONS IN MY TEXT ARE FROM THE KING JAMES AUTHORIZED Version (an aesthetic choice) except within John Paul II's own works, which are translated by the Vatican and use the Revised Standard Version. Other than quotations from John Paul II's poetry and prose and from other works cited in the bibliography, all translations from the Polish are by Jerzy Kluger, as revised by me under his supervision. A slightly different translation of the March 30, 1989, letter from John Paul to Jerzy Kluger appears in Gian Franco Svidercoschi, *Letter to a Jewish Friend* (New York, 1994). All other correspondence is published here for the first time.